THE
SILVER PALATE

COOKBOOK

in Large Print

G·K
Hall
&Cº.

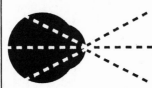

This Large Print Book carries the
Seal of Approval of N.A.V.H.

THE
SILVER PALATE
COOKBOOK

in Large Print

BY JULEE ROSSO & SHEILA LUKINS
WITH MICHAEL McLAUGHLIN

ILLUSTRATED BY SHEILA LUKINS

G.K. Hall & Co.
Thorndike, Maine

Published in Large Print by arrangement with Workman Publishing Company, Inc.

G.K. Hall Large Print Book Series.

Set by Lynn Hathaway and Barbara Ingerson in 16 pt. News Plantin.

Printed on acid free paper in the United States of America.

Library of Congress Cataloging-in-Publication Data

Rosso, Julee.
    The Silver Palate cookbook / Julee Rosso & Sheila Lukins with Michael McLaughlin ;
    illustrated by Sheila Lukins.
       p. cm.
    ISBN 0-8161-5764-2 (hc : lg. print)
    ISBN 0-8161-5765-0 (pb : lg. print)
    1. Cookery. 2. Large type books. I. Lukins, Sheila. II. McLaughlin, Michael.
III. Silver Palate (Shop) IV. Title.
[TX715.R8414   1993]
641.5—dc20   93-9108
                                                        CIP

Molly, Annabel, Richard, June and Frank

Who have always been there for us
We love you very much —

Beth
Barb

Bobbie
Bert

CONTENTS

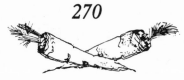

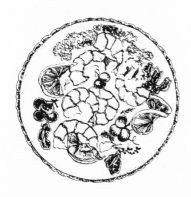

PREFACE

"The discovery of a new dish does more for the happiness of mankind than the discovery of a star."
— Brillat-Savarin, 1838

We agree — food has long been our passion. And we are fortunate to be involved professionally with what we call the miracle of food, at the outset of what is certain to be one of the most exhilarating culinary eras that America has ever enjoyed.

There is a growing appreciation of fine foods today, thanks to an unprecedented availability of fresh and canned domestic and imported ingredients, advanced equipment, mastered techniques, and a new adventurous, confident spirit in Americans' search for culinary excellence. Day by day, we see unusual, rare, exotic, previously unobtainable, fragile, complicated or newly created foods become less mysterious and more familiar to people. These foods become personal joys — recognized, understood, and delicious daily habits. What this signifies to us, very simply, is that most of the people who work professionally in food must be accomplishing their goals.

Some of the recipes in this book have been gathered from personal and professional travels; some are treasured "receipts" from old friends, our families, our chefs, or are versions of classic dishes that we have adapted and refined to make our very own; most are yesterday's new idea in the kitchen. They are all the result of experience gained from cooking almost every day for five years.

Our professional preparation of food is essentially the same as that in our own homes. It is cooking with simple ingredients, always the best available. When combined, they retain a clear, fresh, but intriguing flavor. "Homemade" or traditional dishes are often thought of as peasant food — we like this kind of cooking, and distinguish it with an added touch of style in color, taste and presentation. Like our country, our food is truly a blending of ethnic traditions, reflecting a mixture of heritages that we call our own.

Our style of preparing and presenting food will be found throughout this book: in suggested menus, in our serving and garnishing tips, and in entertaining ideas from our Silver Palate Notebook. We hope our approach will encourage you to entertain more often and show you how it can be done beautifully as well as simply. Breaking bread with friends is one of the most enjoyable social encounters there is.

When we discover something magical, we've found that the real joy is in sharing it. We now know that there is no limit to food horizons and we hope you discover that too with this book. Enjoy it, and let your culinary imagination soar.

Do come and visit us when you are in New York.

Sheila Lukins and
Julee Rosso
New York City,
December, 1981

THE STORY OF
THE SILVER PALATE

The Silver Palate was born of two women's personal desperation. Our lives had become increasingly active and it was getting more and more difficult to juggle it all. There were school schedules, business appointments, political activities, art projects, sculpting classes, movie going, exercising, theater, chamber music concerts, tennis, squash, weekends in the country or at the beach, friends, family, fund raisers, books to read, shopping that couldn't be avoided, and, last but not least, trying to prepare creative, well-balanced meals daily and an occasional dinner party at home. It was much too much. The wonder women we thought and were being told we were, had to acknowledge we might not be. If we were having trouble — and we were both well-regarded as cooks, and could usually do six things at once — there must be others who were in the same boat who needed help. That's when we got the idea for The Silver Palate.

The concept was simple: a tiny gem of a shop where the best foodstuffs could be available — no pretense, just good simple food prepared in a special way, making it easy for the working woman to entertain, the bachelor to have relief from restaurants every night of the week, and a family to have a special picnic in the park spontaneously. We wanted it to offer one-stop provisions: cheeses, pâtés, sausages, cocktail fare, salads, soups, main courses, vegetables, breads, cookies, cakes and mousses. And, most of all, we wanted it to have a pleasant ambiance, to be an enjoyable place for people to discover the joy and excitement of food.

Julee, who grew up in Kalamazoo where steak and potatoes were the norm, had ventured to New York after college to see what there was in the world beyond academia. Twelve years later, after working in the world of American and European fashion design, supervising print and commercial advertising, and developing on the side a love for cookbooks, good food, and the specialized food shops of Europe, she was ready to embark on her dream of leaving corporate life to begin her own business.

Sheila, married and the mother of two very young and active daughters, had long enjoyed cooking and entertaining. It was an integral part of the Lukins' life-style. Sheila had graduated from the Cordon Bleu School in London, and as her involvement with cooking grew, the more naturally her imagination flowed. Back in New York, she created The Other Woman Catering Company, with the motto "So discreet, so delicious and I deliver" directed primarily to New York bachelors who were in trouble with entertaining graciously and deliciously at home without a "little woman" in the kitchen.

The two women finally met several years later when Julee, then advertising director for a major textile firm, needed a caterer for a press party. That morning the menu included red and black raspberry mousse on croissants — and the beginning of a fantasy food partnership was born.

"Nothing good was ever achieved without enthusiasm."
— Ralph Waldo Emerson

Once the recipes were retrieved from each of our files, tested, tasted, and tested again, the store selected and on its way to renovation, the staff interviewed, and the chocolate chip cookie and brownie contests judged, we were still in a quandary as to what it should be named.

Then one day, several months before opening, Florence Fabricant, who was writing an article on the Renaissance of Columbus Avenue, made it all easy for us. She had tasted our food, she liked what we had planned, and came up with "The Silver Palate." It was perfect. When we said "print it, we'll go national" we had no idea where we were headed.

We opened our 165-square-foot shop during one of New York's summer of 1977 heat waves. It was 103°F., the Philharmonic was playing for picnickers in Central Park, and our air conditioner broke — but we were swamped with customers. The array of food, which had been cooked in Sheila's kitchen and carried down the block to the store, was sold out by the time we closed the door and collapsed for the evening.

We cooked fresh every day, using the best ingredients available, and tried to create clear, full flavors. We aimed for food that was beautiful as well as delicious. We tasted while we cooked and, if we were in doubt, we revised and improvised. Sheila cooked, sometimes not seeing the sky for several days on end. Julee cared for customers, and slowly but surely everyone became more confident about trying our then-unfamiliar dishes: escabeche, pâté, vegetable purées. Some days were a delight. Others seemed like nightmares. But we survived. All of it can be laughed about and treasured at this point; we knew we were doing exactly as we wanted to do, and people liked it.

The neighborhood supported us, watching us grow while we worked out the kinks. We extended our horizons and catered picnics, brunches, cocktail parties, dinners, buffets, weddings. If we were asked, we produced. When neighbors wanted to convince their mothers in California that they were eating properly, or someone from Michigan wanted to take a taste from their New York corner store to their family for the holidays, we were the ones they came to.

This led us to think that perhaps some of our recipes should be preserved for easier transport. Then people who lived in other parts of the country could take home a taste of The Silver Palate. The summer of 1978 found us up to our elbows in yet another project — our Canning Kitchen. As we had learned to do with the fresh food in the store, the objective was to make good things taste and look beautiful — but this time in a jar. Every day saw a new batch of something: Damson Plums in Brandy, Blueberry Vinegar, Winter Fruit Compote, Cranberry Conserve, Italian Plums in Port, Lady Apples in Wine, Vegetable Mosaics, Seckle Pears in Wine, and Strawberry Jam. We tied bows to bottles, put doilies everywhere and delivered our boxes to Saks Fifth Avenue, our first customer, in a taxi.

And so it went — one minute the store, one minute the catering, the next preserving natural and wonderful foods, trying not to lose sight of packaging, quality, sales, or staff. It was always a challenge. We wanted to take the mystery out of good food and allow people to have an honest appreciation for it, and we've watched a new quest for excellence take place in Americans' attitudes toward foodstuffs. There is a sense of adventure, the redefinition of personal preferences. The curious become the passionate seekers of the new, the better, the best. Taste is an acquired art and quality cannot be measured but certainly mastered. It is a process of tasting, questioning, understanding, personalizing, and then individually creating.

The two of us have in the meantime become a part of an industry long in existence and now in a period of growth and change. We've met and cooked with some of the greatest chefs in the world, discussed and enjoyed food with international food historians and writers, done business with some of the best retailers in the world, even judged a potato chip contest. We're still wishing for a day of "beauty," we take more vitamins than we thought possible, and we laugh at one another when our wardrobes seem to consist of whatever is clean. But the business we began is still thriving, we're happier, most days, than we've ever been, and we've been lucky enough to watch a business and staff develop beyond all our wildest aspirations. It's been wonderful.

We're not certain where any of this will end, but along the way we hope to stay true to our objectives and ourselves, and hope that people continue to enjoy what we do.

TO BEGIN A
GREAT EVENING

The opening of the evening is ideal for mingling your favorite interesting friends. The transition period between day and night is also a good time for mixing a tennis partner, the chairman of the board, your favorite aunt, your college roommate who just opened to rave reviews on Broadway, a princess or two, an industrial giant, the bass player in the string quartet and your next-door neighbor. For all of them, you'll want your menu to be very special.

Herewith a collection of our favorite hors d'oeuvres. Many are "finger food," easily eaten while standing — perfect at a cocktail party. Others are more elaborate, requiring a small plate and a fork. These are the sturdier foods we serve as part of a cocktail buffet. Finally, we've also presented more elegant and involved appetizers, best suited as sit-down openers to a dinner party.

FROM THE SILVER PALATE NOTEBOOK

❖ ❖ ❖ ❖ ❖ ❖ ❖ ❖ ❖ ❖

• Grand and unusual flowers, soft lighting and music — all can set the scene for a shining memory. If the mood is lovely, no one will notice the crack in the hallway mirror.

• The most successful hosts are those who welcome their guests by making them feel special; be sure that everyone is properly introduced.

• A small informal group becomes a party more quickly when there is no official bartender. A serve-yourself bar makes people comfortable and promotes friendly interaction.

• Arrange each hors d'oeuvre on a separate plate or tray. Your guests will be better able to identify the offering without interrupting a lively discussion.

• Trays should be beautifully but naturally garnished with fruits, vegetables, or flowers.

• Finger food should, obviously, be just that. Awkward, soggy or drippy food has no place at a stand-up party.

• Beautiful glasses are like candlelight — they make the drink and the person holding it look much better. Invest in a dozen or so; it's a small price to pay for a very special effect.

• Schedule just enough time to relax with a quiet drink before the party begins; this way you may catch your breath. Welcome the first players to your scene with a confident smile and enjoy your own party!

FANCY FINGER FOOD

Finger food complements easy conversation during cocktail time. It is the most difficult kind of food to create: interesting and attractive but not messy. We find that a little bit of pastry wrapped around or filled with something is one solution. Others include such edible 'containers' as mushrooms, figs or grape leaves.

SESAME, HAM AND CHEESE BITES

Accompany these tiny sandwiches with an assortment of your favorite mustards.

8 slices of boiled ham, about 7" x 5", ⅛ inch thick
4 thin slices of prosciutto cut in half crosswise
8 slices of Gruyère cheese, about ⅛ inch thick,
   to fit across ham slices
5 teaspoons corn oil
5 eggs
freshly ground black pepper to taste
dash of cayenne pepper
1½ cups sesame seeds
2 cups bread crumbs
½ cup chopped Italian parsley
1 cup unbleached, all-purpose flour
¾ cup melted sweet butter

1. Lay out 8 slices of boiled ham. Cover each with a slice of prosciutto and a slice of Gruyère, and top with a second slice of boiled ham. Cut each into 6 squares.
2. Beat the oil, eggs, pepper to taste, and the cayenne together in a shallow bowl. In another bowl toss sesame seeds, bread crumbs and parsley together.
3. Preheat oven to 400°F.

4

4. Dip each square first into flour, next into the egg mixture, last into sesame-seed mixture.

5. Put squares on a buttered baking sheet and drizzle melted butter on top. Bake for 10 to 13 minutes, until sandwiches are golden and cheese is melted.

6. Drain on a paper towel for 1 minute; serve immediately.
48 sandwiches

PROSCIUTTO

Prosciutto is ham aged and air-dried after having been cured in a spiced brine. It should be firm but chewy, rosy-colored with a slight gloss. The flavor should be both peppery and salty, with a subtle nuttiness. It should not be greasy.

Most prosciutto produced in this country has been aged only 5 to 8 months, while to create the best taste a longer aging process is required. If you are truly a lover of prosciutto, it is best to buy it, remove the paper wrappings, wrap it with clean toweling, and allow it to hang in a cool dry area for about 3 months. Then it is wise to scrape off the mold flecks. Serve thinly sliced with an edge of fat and sprinkled with pepper.

FRESH FIGS

Ripe fresh purple figs with rosy centers and luscious fresh green figs can make perfect cocktail fare. Allow 1 fig, quartered, for each guest. For each fig, cut 2 thin slices of prosciutto lengthwise into halves. Wrap a half slice around each fig quarter so that it looks like a rose. To serve, sprinkle with fresh lime juice and freshly ground black pepper. Garnish with fresh mint sprigs.

Another of our favorites: Slice each fig lengthwise into halves, 1 fig per person. Into each half, spoon 1 teaspoon of Pecan Cream Cheese (see page 595). Sprinkle with finely chopped pecans.

5

MINIATURE QUICHES

Buttery miniature quiche shells filled with custardy surprises are always a cocktail favorite. Use our *pâté brisée* recipe for the crust and bake the tiny quiches in 2- or 3-inch tart molds (available at better houseware stores).

1. One recipe of Pâté Brisée (see page 573) will produce about 16 two-inch tarts. One recipe of Basic Quiche Custard (recipe follows) will fill a similar number of tarts. Yield will vary slightly depending on size of tart molds used.

2. Prebake the shells at 375°F. for 10 minutes. Cool slightly, unmold, set on baking sheets and place a spoonful of your chosen filling in each shell (see our list of favorites). Spoon in basic quiche custard to cover filling and come just below the edge of the tart shell.

3. Bake at 375°F. for 10 to 15 minutes, or until filling is puffed and lightly browned. Serve immediately.

BASIC QUICHE CUSTARD

1½ cups heavy cream
3 large eggs
salt, pepper, grated nutmeg to taste

Whisk cream and eggs together thoroughly. Add seasoning to taste. Reserve until baking time.

1½ cups custard, enough for one 10-inch quiche or sixteen 2-inch tarts

SOME FAVORITE QUICHE FILLINGS:
(About 1 tablespoon per 2-inch tart)

♥ Crumbled imported Roquefort cheese and diced unpeeled apple in equal amounts
♥ Finely minced smoked salmon with chopped fresh dill to taste
♥ Equal parts of chopped ham and grated Gruyère. Whisk Dijon-style mustard to taste into the basic custard
♥ Equal parts of flaked crabmeat and butter-sautéed scallions
♥ Mushrooms sautéed in sweet butter
♥ Equal parts of red and green pepper, sautéed in sweet butter until tender

MINIATURE CHEVRE TARTS

double recipe of Pâté Brisée (see page 573)
1½ pounds Montrachet or other soft mild chèvre cheese
4 tablespoons sweet butter, softened
⅓ cup whipping cream
4 eggs
salt, white pepper, cayenne to taste
⅓ cup chopped scallions (green onions)

1. Working with one fourth of the dough at a time, roll it out to ⅛ inch thick. Use it to line 2-inch tarts. Line dough in tart pan with aluminum foil and fill with either uncooked rice or beans. Bake at 375°F. for 15 minutes or until lightly browned. Cool tart shells and remove foil and weights. Slip shells carefully from pans and cool completely.

2. Combine Montrachet, butter, cream and eggs in the bowl of a food processor fitted with a steel blade, and process until completely smooth. Shut off motor. Season filling to taste; chèvre can be quite salty and peppery and may not need additional seasoning. Stir in the scallions.

3. Arrange the cooled shells on a baking sheet and spoon in the filling. Slide the sheet onto the center rack of a preheated 375°F. oven and bake for 15 to 20 minutes, or until tarts are puffed and brown. Serve immediately.
Approximately 24 two-inch tarts

PEPPERS PROVENCAL

These peppers add a vibrant accent of color when served on little toasts as an hors d'oeuvre.

¼ cup best-quality imported olive oil
2 tablespoons sweet butter
2 cups yellow onions, thinly sliced
2 sweet red peppers, sliced into very thin strips
½ teaspoon herbes de Provence
salt and freshly ground black pepper, to taste
2 garlic cloves, finely minced
½ cup finely shredded fresh basil leaves

1. Heat oil and butter together in a heavy skillet or saucepan until butter is melted. Add the onion and peppers; season with *herbes de Provence* and salt and pepper to taste. Simmer, stirring frequently, for about 45 minutes, or until vegetables are limp, tender and lightly browned. Peppers Provençal should have a marmaladelike appearance.

2. Add garlic and basil and cook for another 5 minutes. Remove from the skillet and let cool to room temperature. Drain excess oil.

3. Fill a quiche shell with this mixture, or fill your own little tarts. We also love it as a vegetable side dish, served warm or at room temperature.

2 cups

OLIVES

We love to suggest bowls of olives as part of a "to begin" table. Their saltiness is perfect with drinks, and their earthy colors complement a variety of other foods. Olives have been a dietary staple around the Mediterranean for over 4000 years; they are still prepared today as they have been for centuries.

The ripeness of olives when picked and the curing process they undergo before packing contribute to the taste of the finished product. Traditionally, imported olives have more flavor, while the domestically produced olive has been fairly bland. Tastes are changing, we're glad to see, and the domestic product is acquiring more flavor. In either case, offer your guests a choice between at least two kinds of olives.

Some of our favorite choices are these:

♥ **Alfonso:** Black, huge and delicious; a great American and Italian specialty.

♥ **Calabrese:** A dull bronze-green olive, more mellow.

♥ **Kalamata:** This large, almond-shaped Greek olive is purple-black, powerful in flavor; often considered to be the best of all olives.

♥ **Gaeta:** Small, black, smooth Italian olives, packed in brine or in oil and herbs.

♥ **Greek black olives:** Round, meaty, pungent and brine-cured; this is the one most familiarly sold in bulk; it is also the style on which the California brine-cured olives are based.

♥ **Nyons:** Small round, reddish brown, oil-cured and pleasantly bitter.

♥ **Niçoise:** This tiny, tender, black French olive is cured in brine and packed in oil, frequently with Provençal herbs; often used in making olive oil.

♥ **Picholine:** These French green olives are crisp, tender, delicate and mild.

♥ **Royal or Victoria:** Very large, black Greek olives that are cured in olive oil; wonderful.

♥ **Sicilian:** Small, oval, cracked green Italian olives cured in salt brine; traditionally spiced with red pepper and oregano.

CHEESE STRAWS

These crisp and mildly spicy twists of puff pastry have been our most popular "nosh" for years. Arrange a basketful on the bar and watch them disappear!

1 pound Puff Pastry (see page 575)
¾ cup grated imported Parmesan cheese

1. Roll out puff pastry dough into a rectangle 20 by 24 inches. Sprinkle half of the Parmesan evenly over the dough and gently press cheese into the dough with the rolling pin.
2. Fold the dough in half crosswise, roll it out again to 20 by 24 inches, and sprinkle on remaining cheese.
3. Using a sharp thin knife, cut the dough into ⅓-inch strips. Take each strip by its ends and twist until evenly corkscrewed. Lay the twists of dough on an ungreased baking sheet, arranged so they are just touching each other; this will prevent untwisting.
4. Set the baking sheet in the middle of a preheated 350°F. oven and bake until the straws are crisp, puffed and brown, 15 to 20 minutes.
5. Remove from the oven, cool for 5 minutes, then cut apart with a sharp knife. Finish cooling the straws on a rack, then store them in an airtight tin or plastic bag until serving time. They will stay fresh for about 1 week.

About 20 straws

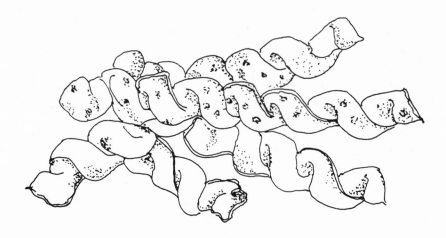

WORKING WITH PHYLLO (FILO)

One of the most versatile, delicious and widely available aids to the party-giver is phyllo, the tissue-paper-thin dough commonly used in Greece and other Middle Eastern countries. While those of us in large cities can usually visit an ethnic pastry shop that makes its own fresh phyllo daily, the frozen variety is available in nearly all large supermarkets or specialty food shops. Best of all, this ready-when-you-are frozen phyllo is virtually interchangeable with the fresh variety. The dough usually comes in 1-pound packages, each of which contains 24 or more sheets.

Bring it home and let it defrost in its original wrapper in your refrigerator for at least 2 days. (When well wrapped and still sealed in its original package, defrosted phyllo will keep in the refrigerator for up to a month. This is preferable to refreezing, which can make the dough crumbly.)

Be sure the phyllo is completely defrosted before beginning to work with it. Have a damp (not wet) towel handy. Unwrap the dough, unroll it, and cover it immediately with the towel. Let stand for 15 minutes; moisture makes phyllo easier to handle.

PHYLLO TRIANGLES

One of the traditional shapes for phyllo pastries, and one of the easiest to make.

1. Uncover the dough and remove a sheet. Brush well with melted butter. Sixty triangles will use about one-half pound of butter. Stack a second sheet on top and butter again. Be sure to cover the unused phyllo with the damp towel each time.
2. Cut the buttered phyllo sheets into fifths the short way with a sharp knife.
3. Place a teaspoon of filling in the center of the first strip, about 1 inch from the top. Fold a corner across the filling and then continue to fold, as if you were folding a flag, until the strip is all folded; filling will expand as it cooks so do not wrap the triangle too tight. Tuck any excess under.
4. Place the triangle on a buttered baking sheet. Brush the top with butter. Continue until you have the desired number of triangles. Filled, unbaked triangles can be refrigerated for up to 24 hours before baking.
5. Bake in the upper third of a 350°F. oven for about 25 minutes, or until triangles are well browned and filling is bubbling and hot. Serve immediately.
6. Completed triangles freeze beautifully and are ready in minutes when you need a quick appetizer. Prepare as above, but place the triangles on an unbuttered baking sheet and omit the final brushing with butter. Freeze them overnight on the baking sheet and then wrap them tightly in clear plastic wrap or in a plastic bag until needed. *Do not defrost;* they get soggy. Put frozen triangles on a buttered baking sheet, brush with butter, and bake at 350°F. for about 45 minutes, or until well browned and hot (test one to be sure). Serve immediately.

One pound of phyllo, containing 24 sheets, will make about 60 triangles.

THREE FILLINGS FOR
PHYLLO TRIANGLES

ROQUEFORT AND PISTACHIO FILLING

¼ pound imported Roquefort cheese
¼ pound cream cheese
1 egg
½ cup coarsely chopped shelled pistachios (or substitute walnuts or pecans)
nutmeg and freshly ground black pepper, to taste

1. Bring Roquefort and cream cheese to room temperature and mash them together thoroughly in a small bowl.

2. Stir in the egg, combine well, and stir in the pistachios.

3. Season to taste with nutmeg and pepper. The Roquefort is usually so salty that no additional salt is needed. Use as a filling for phyllo triangles.

Enough filling for approximately 60 triangles

SPINACH-FETA FILLING

10 ounces frozen chopped spinach
½ cup finely chopped yellow onion
3 tablespoons olive oil
nutmeg, to taste
salt and freshly ground black pepper, to taste
½ cup finely chopped fresh dill or fresh mint
⅓ cup ricotta cheese
¼ cup feta cheese

1. Defrost the frozen spinach. Drain it, then squeeze out as much remaining moisture as possible with your hands.

2. Sauté the onion in the olive oil until tender and golden, about 20 minutes. Add the spinach and cook over low heat, stirring constantly, for 10 to 15 minutes, or until mixture is dry. Season to taste with nutmeg, salt and pepper, and scrape out into a bowl. Cool to room temperature.

3. Stir in the dill or mint, the ricotta, and finally the feta, crumbled into small pieces. Taste and correct seasoning. Use as a filling for phyllo triangles.

Enough filling for approximately 60 triangles

ROSEMARY AND PROSCIUTTO FILLING

2 egg yolks
1 cup ricotta cheese
¼ pound prosciutto, finely chopped
¼ cup grated imported Parmesan cheese
1½ teaspoons crumbled dried rosemary
salt and freshly ground black pepper, to taste

Beat egg yolks into ricotta. Stir in prosciutto, Parmesan and rosemary. Season to taste with salt and pepper. Use as a filling for phyllo triangles.

Enough filling for approximately 60 triangles

✚ FROM THE SILVER PALATE NOTEBOOK

You can never plan and organize too much; the larger the party, the more you must prepare.

Planning ahead will leave extra time for you to enjoy the marketing, the preparation and the presentation of the meal to your guests.

Working from checklists can be an invaluable aid. You may prefer index cards or some other system. Don't try to plan a large gathering in your head.

GOUGERE

Gougère, the splendid hot cheese pastry from the Burgundy region of France, makes a spectacularly easy cocktail snack. Of course it is delicious with a glass of red wine, but we also love to serve it with the best vintage Port we can muster. Traditionally it is baked into a large, wreathlike ring, but it is easier to handle at cocktail time if formed into tiny individual puffs.

1 cup milk
8 tablespoons (1 stick) sweet butter
1 teaspoon salt
1 cup sifted unbleached, all-purpose flour
5 eggs
1½ cups grated imported Parmesan cheese (or half Parmesan, half Gruyère), plus an additional ½ cup grated Parmesan to top puffs (optional)

1. Combine milk, butter and salt in a small saucepan and bring to a boil. Remove pan from heat and add the flour all at once. Whisk vigorously for a few moments, then return the pan to medium heat and cook, stirring constantly, until the batter has thickened and is pulling away from the sides and bottom of the pan — 5 minutes or less.

2. Again remove pan from the heat and stir in 4 eggs, one at a time, making certain the first egg is completely incorporated before adding the second. Then stir in the cheese or cheeses.

3. Preheat oven to 375°F. Lightly butter a baking sheet.

4. Drop the batter by tablespoons onto baking sheet, spacing the puffs at least 1 inch apart.

5. Beat remaining egg in a small bowl. Brush the tops of the puffs with the beaten egg, and sprinkle with additional Parmesan if you use it.

6. Set baking sheet on the center rack of the oven, reduce heat to 350°F., and bake for 15 to 20 minutes, or until *gougères* are puffed and well browned. Serve immediately.

About 20 puffs

STUFFED GRAPE LEAVES

50 medium-size preserved grape leaves (1 or 2 jars)
1 pound very lean lamb, ground
16 ounces canned Italian plum tomatoes, crushed
1 cup raw long-grain rice
1 cup best-quality olive oil
2 bunches of scallions (green onions), chopped
3 cups loosely packed fresh mint leaves, chopped juice of 2 lemons

1. Drain the grape leaves, separate them and rinse them under running water, being careful not to tear them. Reserve.

2. Combine lamb, crushed tomatoes and their liquid, rice, olive oil, scallions and mint.

3. Lay a grape leaf, vein side up, stem toward you, on your work surface. Place 1 tablespoon of filling at the base of the leaf and roll up, tucking in excess leaf at the sides to made a tiny bundle. Repeat with remaining filling and leaves, packing each bundle seam side down into a small kettle.

4. Squeeze lemon juice over the leaf bundles, and add water nearly to cover. Weight with 1 or 2 small plates or saucers. Cover, bring to a boil, reduce heat, and simmer for 1 hour, or until rice in stuffing is completely cooked.

5. Serve hot, or cool and refrigerate the leaves in their cooking liquid. Offer plain yogurt seasoned to taste with lemon juice and coarse salt as a dip or sauce.

Approximately 50 grape leaves

COCKTAIL PUFFS

Any number of soft, savory mixtures can be used to fill a tiny cocktail puff. For the puffs, use Pâté à Choux (see page 574). Elsewhere in this book you will find recipes for Tapenade, Pâté Maison, Taramosalata, Salmon Mousse and Peasant Caviar. We have tried them all in puffs at one time or another with great success.

SAUSAGE-STUFFED MUSHROOMS

2 Italian sweet sausages, about ⅓ pound
¼ teaspoon fennel seeds
pinch of red pepper flakes (optional)
¼ cup finely minced yellow onion
1 garlic clove, peeled and minced olive oil, as necessary
¼ cup chopped parsley
¼ cup chopped black olives, preferably imported
⅓ cup thick Béchamel Sauce (see page 585)
salt and freshly ground black pepper, to taste
12 large white mushrooms
imported Parmesan cheese to taste

1. Remove sausage meat from casings and crumble into a small skillet. Sauté gently, stirring often, until meat is thoroughly done. Season with fennel and, if desired, red pepper flakes. With a slotted spoon, remove sausage to a bowl, leaving the rendered fat in the skillet.

2. Sauté onion and garlic in the rendered fat, adding a little olive oil if necessary, until tender and golden, about 25 minutes. Stir in chopped parsley and add to reserved sausage meat.

3. Stir olives and béchamel into the sausage mixture; combine thoroughly. Taste the mixture, and season with salt and pepper if necessary.

4. Pull the stems off the mushrooms and save for another use. Wipe mushroom caps with a damp cloth and season lightly with salt and pepper.

5. Fill each cap generously with the stuffing. Arrange caps in a lightly oiled baking dish. Sprinkle the tops of the stuffing with Parmesan cheese to taste.

6. Bake at 450°F. for about 15 minutes, or until bubbling and well browned. Let settle for 5 minutes before serving.

3 or 4 portions

MUSHROOMS STUFFED WITH WALNUTS AND CHEESE

12 medium-size mushroom caps
1 tablespoon olive oil
1 tablespoon sweet butter
½ cup finely chopped yellow onion
2 tablespoons coarsely chopped walnuts
1 garlic clove, peeled and minced
5 ounces frozen chopped spinach, thoroughly
  defrosted and squeezed dry
1 ounce feta cheese, crumbled
1 ounce Gruyère cheese, crumbled
2 tablespoons minced fresh dill
salt and freshly ground black pepper to taste

1. Remove stems from mushrooms and save for another use. Wipe the mushroom caps with a damp cloth or paper towel and set aside.
2. Heat the olive oil and butter together in a small skillet. Add the onion and cook over medium heat, covered, until tender and lightly colored, about 25 minutes.
3. Preheat oven to 400°F.
4. Add walnuts and garlic to onion and cook for another minute. Add spinach and cook for another 5 minutes, stirring constantly. Remove from heat and cool slightly. Stir in cheeses, dill, and salt and pepper to taste.
5. Arrange the mushrooms, cavity side up, in a baking dish. Divide the spinach and walnut mixture evenly among the mushroom caps.
6. Set baking dish in the upper third of the oven. Bake for 8 to 10 minutes, or until filling is browned and the mushrooms are thoroughly heated through. Serve immediately.

12 mushrooms, 3 or 4 portions

STUFFED MUSHROOMS

Easterners like them whiter than white, while Westerners prefer them a bit beige, but in any case the widely cultivated American button mushroom must always be at its freshest for the cocktail hour. It is terrific raw, marinated or cooked. When stuffed, it becomes a perfect finger food. It is quiet, attractive and completely self-contained.

MINIATURE LAMB KEBABS

cubed lamb (¼ pound per person)
cherry tomatoes
green pepper, cut into 1-inch squares
small white onions, peeled
Marinade for Lamb (recipe follows)

1. Cut lamb into ½-inch cubes and marinate overnight, refrigerated.
2. Remove lamb from marinade and drain on paper towels. Slide cubes onto metal skewers, alternating with 2 cherry tomatoes, a square of green pepper, and a small white onion.
3. Broil for about 10 minutes, basting with reserved marinade, or until done. Serve immediately.

MARINADE FOR LAMB

¼ cup red wine vinegar
1 teaspoon mixed dried herbs (for example, half rosemary, half thyme)
2 garlic cloves, peeled and slightly crushed
¼ cup olive oil
1 tablespoon Oriental soy sauce
1 tablespoon dry sherry

In a large bowl, combine all ingredients. Stir briskly.
About ¾ cup marinade, enough for 1½ pounds lamb cubes (to serve 6)

STICKING WITH SKEWERS

A simple bamboo skewer about 6 inches long, available at Oriental food stores, can make a dazzling cocktail display. Spear an assortment of complementary bites onto a single skewer, or stand them like a forest at the edge of a bowl of marinated shrimp, dilled meatballs, or other foods too messy for fingers. Smaller skewers can also be useful for single-bite hors d'oeuvres, and nearly anything edible is a little easier to handle when speared in this fashion.

FAVORITE SKEWER COMBINATIONS:

♥ Shrimp and green grapes
♥ Melon and prosciutto with smoked turkey
♥ Apple chunks and ham
♥ Lime-marinated sea scallops and avocado chunks
♥ Cherry tomatoes and vinaigrette-marinated cubes of roast beef
♥ Swiss cheese cubes, ham cubes and watermelon pickle

THE BARBECUED BITS

We love to serve tiny, tiny spareribs and chicken wings at cocktail time. They're messy finger food, but no one seems to care. If yours is a black-tie affair, then these really aren't quite appropriate, but on other occasions they tend to get nibbled up very quickly. The leftover bones somehow manage to disappear as well, though it's a good idea to think ahead and arrange for their disposal with a few strategically placed bowls.

COCKTAIL RIBLETS

Our butcher supplies us with what he calls "cocktail ribs," regular spareribs that are cut apart and then chopped crosswise into 2-inch lengths, perfect for eating with fingers. If your butcher won't, you can accomplish this task yourself with a sharp knife and a cleaver. Alternatively, just cut the ribs apart and serve them full-size. Depending on your menu, allow ¼ to ½ pound of ribs per person. Spread them in one layer in a shallow baking pan or on a broiler pan with a slotted insert, if you have one. Salt and pepper to taste. Bake at 400°F. for about 40 minutes. Turn ribs once at the halfway point.

Drain accumulated fat and brush riblets generously with Mustard Glaze (recipe follows). Bake for another 10 minutes, then repeat the glazing and baking process one more time. Serve hot or at room temperature. One cup of Mustard Glaze will glaze about 2 pounds of riblets.

COCKTAIL CHICKEN WINGS

Depending on your menu, allow 2 to 4 chicken wings per person. Remove tips and place chicken wings in a dish just large enough to hold them; pour in Barbecue Sauce (recipe follows on page 22), and marinate for 2 hours. Preheat oven to 400°F. Lift wings from marinade and arrange in a single layer in a broilerproof baking dish. Season to taste with salt and pepper and bake for 20 minutes. Baste the wings at the halfway point with more sauce.

When wings have baked for 20 minutes and are nearly done, slide the dish under the broiler for another 5 to 7 minutes, or until browned and bubbly. Serve immediately or at room temperature. One cup of Barbecue Sauce is sufficient for 6 or more chicken wings.

MUSTARD GLAZE

½ cup prepared Dijon-style mustard
1 teaspoon dry mustard
⅓ cup cider vinegar
⅓ cup packed light-brown sugar
½ cup honey
1 tablespoon dark Oriental sesame oil
1 tablespoon Oriental soy sauce

1. Whisk together prepared and dry mustards in a small saucepan. Whisk in remaining ingredients.
2. Simmer over moderate heat, stirring occasionally, for 5 minutes.
3. Let cool, cover, and refrigerate until ready to use. This glaze will keep, refrigerated, for 3 weeks.
   1 cup

BARBECUE SAUCE

⅓ *cup finely chopped yellow onion*
4 garlic cloves, minced
2 tablespoons olive oil
¾ *cup tomato paste*
1⅓ *cups water*
½ *teaspoon celery seeds*
1 teaspoon thyme
3 tablespoons red wine vinegar
2 tablespoons prepared Dijon-style mustard
¼ *teaspoon ground cinnamon*
2 tablespoons granulated sugar
1 teaspoon each salt and freshly ground black pepper, or to taste
pinch of cayenne pepper (optional)

   1. Sauté chopped onion and minced garlic in olive oil in a small saucepan until tender and golden, about 15 minutes.

   2. Add tomato paste and water and blend well. Add celery seeds, thyme, vinegar, mustard, cinnamon and sugar. Season with salt and pepper to taste and cayenne if you use it.

   3. Simmer, partially covered, for 20 minutes, stirring occasionally. Taste, correct seasoning if necessary, cover, and refrigerate until ready to use.

2 cups

✜ FROM THE SILVER
PALATE NOTEBOOK

Time cocktails to last no more than an hour before dinner is served; an endless cocktail hour can result in bored guests or guests who have drunk so much they ignore the food or cause other problems.

   After your one good drink before the guests arrive, confine yourself to sipping.

   Always remember to have sparkling water, fruit juices and unsweetened soft drinks on hand for non-drinkers.

FRESH FROM THE SEA

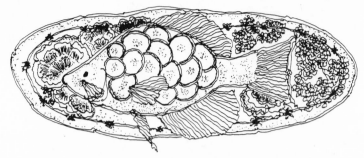

Americans are eating more seafood and loving it. Today as never before, calorie-consciousness and the urge to eat lighter food have made the seafood offerings of our catered buffets the most popular by far. Don't stint on heartier fare, but remember, if you're planning a fish or other seafood dish, make plenty!

SPICY SHRIMP

1¾ pounds large raw shrimp
2 tablespoons sweet butter
1 tablespoon olive oil
1 tablespoon finely minced garlic
2 tablespoons finely minced shallots
salt and freshly ground black pepper, to taste
2 tablespoons lemon juice, or more to taste
2 tablespoons finely chopped fresh dill

1. Peel and devein shrimp.
2. In a large skillet over low heat, melt butter with olive oil. Add garlic and shallots and sauté for 2 minutes without browning.
3. Add shrimp, increase heat slightly, and cook shrimp for 3 minutes, or until just done to taste. Add salt and pepper to taste and toss well. Remove to a bowl, scraping in all the sauce.
4. Add lemon juice and dill; toss together well. Cover and refrigerate 3 to 4 hours before serving. Adjust seasonings to taste.
5. Serve as a first course or on the ends of long bamboo skewers as an appetizer.

10 portions as an hors d'oeuvre; 4 to 6 as an appetizer

SHRIMP AND SNOW PEAS

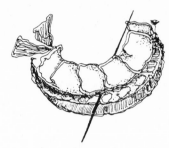

2 tablespoons peanut oil
1 pound raw shrimp, about 18, peeled and deveined
1 cup Sherry Vinaigrette (see page 394)
18 snow peas, about ½ pound
salt, to taste

1. Heat half the peanut oil in a small skillet. Sauté half of the shrimp, stirring and tossing frequently, until done, about 4 minutes; shrimp will turn pink and become firm. Do not overcook.

2. Lift cooked shrimp from skillet with a slotted spoon and transfer them to a small deep bowl just large enough to hold them. Repeat with remaining shrimp.

3. Pour ¼ cup sherry vinaigrette over warm shrimp and let stand for 1 hour.

4. Meanwhile, trim snow peas and drop them into a kettle of salted boiling water. Let them cook for about 2 minutes; the water need not even return to the boil. Drain immediately and plunge them into a bowl of ice water; this will stop the cooking process and set the brilliant green color.

5. When snow peas are completely cool, drain them and pat dry. Split them along their seams, leaving the halves joined at one end.

6. Remove shrimp, one at a time, from the vinaigrette and wrap a snow pea around each shrimp. Skewer into place with a cocktail pick and arrange on a platter. Cover the platter and refrigerate until serving time.

7. Drizzle some of the remaining vinaigrette over shrimp just before serving, if desired.

6 portions

TARAMOSALATA

We've seen this wonderful appetizer increase in popularity over the years. No longer just a Greek taste, but one that brings a tart fish flavor to a buffet without the expense of caviar.

1 pound smoked whole cod roe, casing removed
1 pound cream cheese, softened
1 garlic clove, peeled and pounded
juice of ½ lemon
¼ teaspoon freshly ground black pepper
¼ cup olive oil
¼ cup heavy cream

1. In a food processor fitted with a steel blade, combine cod roe, cream cheese, garlic, lemon juice and black pepper. Process just until smooth.

2. With motor running, pour olive oil and heavy cream through the tube until just blended. Refrigerate.

3. Serve with pita bread triangles, little toasts, or as a dip with fresh vegetables.

4 cups

"To invite a person into your house is to take charge of his happiness for as long as he is under your roof."
— Brillat-Savarin

GRAVLAX

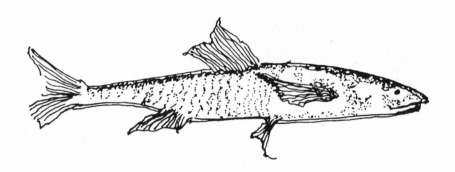

Gravlax is a Scandinavian preparation of raw salmon cured with salt, sugar and spices. The marinating action "cooks" and tenderizes the fish. The result, sliced paper-thin, is one of the best appetizers we know. Serve with ice-cold vodka, aquavit or dry white wine.

3 pounds fresh salmon, center-cut, halved lengthwise and
*   thoroughly boned*
2 large bunches of fresh dill
¼ cup coarse salt
¼ cup granulated sugar
2 tablespoons crushed white peppercorns
lemon wedges and black pepper (garnish)

1. Place half of the fish, skin side down, in a deep glass dish. Spread dill over fish. Sprinkle dry ingredients over dill. Top with the other half of fish, skin side up.

2. Cover with foil and weight with a board and a 5-pound weight. Refrigerate for 48 to 72 hours, turning the salmon and basting every 12 hours with accumulated juices.

3. To serve, remove fish from marinade, scrape away dill and spices, and pat dry. Slice salmon thinly on the diagonal and serve on small plates or squares of black bread. Garnish with lemon wedges and black pepper and accompany with Dill Mustard Sauce (recipe follows on page 28).

8 to 10 portions

SMOKED SALMON

Smoked salmon was a treasure to the American Indians long before the settlers arrived. It remains an admired and expensive food today, although the best is now imported. The quality of North Atlantic salmon and the superior smoking techniques they have developed make Ireland and Scotland the most respected producers of smoked salmon in the world. The type and size of salmon, the method used for catching it, processing, storage temperature and age all contribute to the final product. These fish are firmer and have a paler color, more delicate flavor and firmer satiny texture than those from other waters.

Smoked salmon should be sliced paper-thin, on the diagonal, as close to serving time as possible. We like to serve it as simply as we can.

• Be sure the salmon is cold.

• A squirt of fresh lemon juice is delicious; offer generous lemon wedges.

• Pass a peppermill; fresh black pepper is a must.

• Danish pumpernickel is a natural accompaniment.

• Other embellishments include a dab of caviar, a dollop of sour cream or a sprinkling of chopped fresh dill.

• Champagne or chilled vodka, neat, are the approved libations.

DILL MUSTARD SAUCE

Use this sweetly pungent dill sauce on *gravlax,* or as a dip for shrimp and other shellfish.

1 cup Sweet Mustard (see page 392)
1 cup dairy sour cream
½ cup chopped fresh dill

Mix all ingredients together. Cover and refrigerate until ready to use. The sauce will keep for up to 3 days if refrigerated.

2 cups

WHITE WINE

Extra-dry, extra-cold white wine can provide the basis for a dazzling array of "cocktails" that are lighter and more interesting than the usual party fare.

♥ Add a spoonful of Framboise, Mirabelle or Poire William to a glass of chilled white wine and garnish with the appropriate fruit.

♥ Fresh fruit makes a glass of white wine prettier and adds flavor of its own as well. Try dropping a few green grapes in the glass, or balls of fresh melon, or a slice of mango.

♥ A sprig of mint is beautiful and tasty too. Crush lightly in the bottom of the glass and pour in the chilled white wine — cool.

♥ Peel and slice a kiwi and freeze slices into ice cubes. Float 1 or 2 cubes in a glass of chilled white wine. Strawberries and black cherries are nice, too.

♥ Stir a spoonful of fresh orange juice and a splash of soda or seltzer into the white wine. Serve iced or "up."

♥ Don't forget the trusty lemon. Something as simple as a freshly cut lemon section or a twist of lemon peel dropped into a glass of white wine, iced or not, is a refreshing touch.

SALMON MOUSSE

This has become a Silver Palate classic. It was with us the first day we opened and the only time that it is not in the refrigerator on any given day of the year is when we've sold out. It is light, pretty, refreshing and one of those foods that you enjoy time after time.

1 envelope unflavored gelatin
¼ cup cold water
½ cup boiling water
½ cup Hellmann's mayonnaise
1 tablespoon lemon juice
1 tablespoon finely grated onion
dash of Tabasco
¼ teaspoon sweet paprika
1 teaspoon salt
2 tablespoons finely chopped dill
2 cups finely flaked poached fresh salmon or canned salmon, skin and
  bones removed
1 cup heavy cream

1. Soften the gelatin in the cold water in a large mixing bowl. Stir in the boiling water and whisk the mixture slowly until gelatin dissolves. Cool to room temperature.

2. Whisk in the mayonnaise, lemon juice, grated onion, Tabasco, paprika, salt and dill. Stir to blend completely and refrigerate for about 20 minutes, or until the mixture begins to thicken slightly.

3. Fold in the finely flaked salmon. In a separate bowl, whip the cream until it is thickened to peaks and fluffy. Fold gently into the salmon mixture.

4. Transfer the mixture to a 6- to 8-cup bowl or decorative mold. Cover and chill for at least 4 hours.

5. Serve on toasts, black bread or crackers. Or serve as a first course, garnished with watercress.

At least 12 portions

SPICY CRAB CLAWS

3 pounds cooked crab claws
1 cup minced scallions (green onions)
½ cup chopped parsley
2 celery ribs, chopped
3 garlic cloves, crushed
1 cup olive oil
½ cup tarragon vinegar
3 tablespoons lemon juice
1 tablespoon Worcestershire sauce
dash of Tabasco
salt and freshly ground black pepper, to taste

1. Buy baby crab fingers from fish market. If they are frozen, let them defrost and wash and drain well before using.

2. Heat remaining ingredients in a saucepan; add seasoning to taste. Pour over the crab. Cover and refrigerate overnight.

3. Remove from refrigerator 1 hour before serving. Drain off sauce. Serve crab claws with buttered black bread. Super as cocktail fare.

6 portions as a first course or 24 portions for cocktail buffet

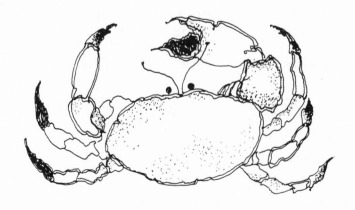

SEVICHE

Our version of a South American favorite is another of the world's great marinated raw seafood dishes. With the growing awareness that much seafood is sadly overcooked, this method of preserving the texture and flavor of fresh fish without subjecting it to heat seems beautifully simple and logical.

2 pounds bay scallops
1 fresh hot red pepper, cut into julienne
1 small sweet red pepper, cut into julienne
½ small purple onion, cut into julienne
2 ripe tomatoes, seeded, chopped, cut into ¼-inch cubes
1 garlic clove, finely minced
2 teaspoons brown sugar
2 tablespoons chopped fresh coriander
2 tablespoons chopped fresh parsley
salt and freshly ground black pepper, to taste
2 cups fresh lime juice
½ cup lemon juice
2 avocados, peeled and cut into 16 slices, brushed
  with lemon juice (garnish)
chopped parsley (garnish)

1. In a large glass bowl combine all ingredients except avocados and parsley for garnish. Toss gently but thoroughly, being certain the scallops are well coated with citrus juice.
2. Cover and refrigerate for at least 5 hours, or until scallops lose their translucent appearance. Stir them occasionally during the marination.
3. Serve in individual bowls garnished with avocado slices and additional chopped parsley.
8 portions as a first course

We love to serve a wide variety of interesting foods because it looks lush. Today people like to eat lightly, but really taste and appreciate different flavors.

Large serving trays with a small amount of a single hors d'oeuvre centered on them make a dramatic presentation. Replenish and refresh trays so that they always look full as food disappears. The food looks fresh, fine and very special, and you can control and stretch the quantity as necessary.

THE CRUDITES CONNECTION

We find the crunch of fresh vegetables is welcome at parties year round. They're light and healthful, and can be munched with guilt-free ease.

We like *crudités* to look bright and abundant. Use only the crispest and freshest vegetables possible and arrange them to resemble whole vegetables. Mass a single vegetable in a basket and carefully coordinate a design. Use a sketch to help you plan your effect by varying colors, textures, shapes and sizes; it will increase the impact of your display.

Recipes for our favorite *crudités* dips follow.

AVOCADO DIP

1 garlic clove, peeled and chopped
2 tablespoons chopped parsley
1 tablespoon tarragon vinegar
½ teaspoon tarragon
6 anchovy fillets
¼ cup tarragon shallot mustard
1 cup Homemade Mayonnaise (see page 582)
1 very ripe avocado, peeled, seeded and roughly mashed
3 tablespoons light cream
salt and white pepper to taste

1. Combine all ingredients in the bowl of a food processor fitted with the steel blade and blend, scraping down the sides of processor bowl with a rubber spatula as necessary. Add seasoning to taste, and blend again.

2. Scrape dip into a bowl, cover, and refrigerate until needed.
About 2 cups

ROQUEFORT DIP

¾ cup heavy cream
¼ cup Crème Fraîche (see page 582)
1 teaspoon Worcestershire sauce
¼ teaspoon salt
½ teaspoon white pepper
1 cup imported Roquefort cheese★

1. Combine cream, *crème fraîche*, Worcestershire sauce, salt and pepper in the bowl of a food processor fitted with a steel blade. Process briefly.

2. Add Roquefort and process again to blend. Do not overprocess; dip should remain chunky.

3. Scrape dip into a bowl, cover, and refrigerate until ready to use.
About 2 cups

★or substitute an equal amount of Stilton or Gorgonzola

THE PRESENTATION

We like to offer our sauces in hollowed-out vegetables, particularly in a purple cabbage. Use the outer leaves to line the basket and then scoop out the core to hold the dip. Add a flower or two or a bunch of fresh herbs as a garnish.

FAVORITE CRUDITES COMBINATIONS

♥ ALL-GREEN:
   artichokes
   asparagus
   broccoli
   endive
   green beans
   scallions (green onions)
   snow peas
   sugar snap peas
   zucchini

♥ GREEN AND PURPLE:
   beets
   baby eggplants
   eggplant spears
   purple cabbage
   purple string beans

♥ RED/WHITE/GREEN:
   cauliflower
   mushrooms
   red radishes
   white radishes
   cherry or plum tomatoes
   raw turnip spears
   zucchini

GREEN PEPPERCORN MUSTARD DIP

1 cup Homemade Mayonnaise (see page 582)
¼ cup prepared Dijon-style mustard
1 small garlic clove, peeled and chopped
1 teaspoon water-packed green peppercorns, drained, plus additional peppercorns.

1. Combine all ingredients in food processor and purée until smooth.
2. Taste, and correct seasoning, and stir in additional whole green peppercorns to taste. Do not process further.
3. Scrape into a bowl, cover and refrigerate until serving.
About 1 cup

THE ENDIVE SCOOP

Individual leaves of Belgian endive make natural edible scoops for some of the thicker mixtures we serve as finger food. Past successful combinations include Salmon Mousse, Taramosalata and Green Herb Dipping Sauce (see Index for recipes). We prefer the milder, more tender inner leaves, and love to surround a small bowl of our chosen dip with a pale green sunburst of endive.

TAPENADE DIP

This dark and lusty sauce speaks to us with all the accents of Provence. It seems barely tamed by civilization and still full of secrets. Do we make too much of it? Try it for yourself and see. Stuff it into sun-ripened tomatoes, hard-cooked eggs, or grilled baby eggplants. Thin it slightly and offer it as a dip for *crudités,* or toss it with cold pasta. In the heat of summer its flavor seems only logical; in winter it stirs memories of summer warmth.

½ *cup imported black olives (Alfonso or Kalamata), pitted*
¼ *cup imported green olives (Sicilian), pitted*
4 anchovy fillets
1 garlic clove
2 tablespoons capers, thoroughly drained
2 tablespoons oil-packed tuna, drained
1 tablespoon lemon juice
*1 cup fresh basil leaves, rinsed and patted dry, or more to taste**
¼ *cup best-quality olive oil*
¼ *cup Homemade Mayonnaise (see page 582; optional)*

1. Combine black and green olives, anchovy fillets, garlic, capers, tuna, lemon juice and basil in the bowl of a food processor fitted with a steel blade. Process until smooth.

2. With the motor still running, dribble in the oil to make a thick, fluffy sauce. For a lighter sauce, ideal for raw vegetables, blend in the mayonnaise.

3. Taste, and correct seasoning. Scrape dip into a bowl and cover. Refrigerate until ready to serve. Tapenade will keep, refrigerated, for 1 week.

About 1½ cups

*If fresh basil is not available, substitute 1 cup fresh parsley leaves and 2 teaspoons dried basil.

THE CHARCUTERIE BOARD

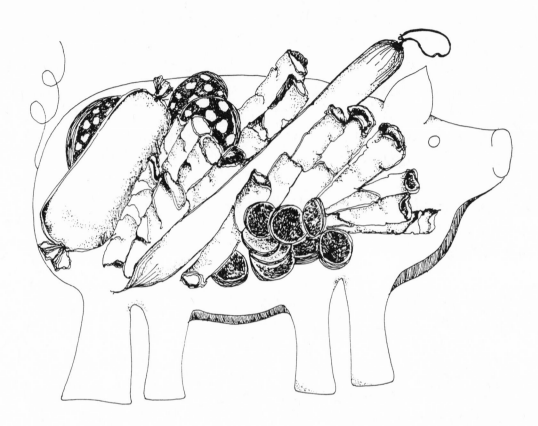

Originally the *charcuterie* in France was the only store licensed to sell pork products. Although these restrictions have been relaxed, the *charcuterie* is still a great French tradition, dispensing pâtés and sausages made on the premises, and often supplying quiches, bread, cheese, wine and other picnic food and drink.

The charcuterie board is becoming an American favorite as well, and we think it makes a fine gastronomic accompaniment to a wine tasting. Really taste the wines while your palate is clear before starting in with the spicier food.

The traditional charcuterie accompaniments are mustards, the tiny pickles called *cornichons,* cherries in tart brine, breads, cheeses, and an assortment of hearty salads.

Group the wines at one end of the table, spread with a checked cloth if you like, and arrange the bread in baskets. Display the pâtés, sausages and cheeses on heavy cutting boards, and arrange the salads, mustards and pickles in simple bowls and crocks. Your finished table should look like a rustic picnic — the image of a rural cornucopia.

STEAK TARTARE

Steak Tartare is wonderful fare for a cocktail buffet or early before-theater supper. Since the meat is served uncooked, it is most important that it be prepared as late as possible on the same day you will serve it and that you have your butcher prepare his freshest top-quality meat for you.

STEAK

2 pounds top sirloin or top round, finely ground
1 medium-size yellow onion, finely minced
¼ cup chopped fresh Italian parsley
3 tablespoons prepared Dijon-style mustard
2 uncooked egg yolks
2 teaspoons salt
freshly ground black pepper, to taste
1 teaspoon caraway seeds

Combine all ingredients in a large bowl and blend thoroughly but gently. The egg yolks will help to bind the meat with the seasonings. Refrigerate.

GARNISH

1 head of Ruby Red lettuce or Bibb lettuce
¾ cup fine-snipped fresh chives (reserve a few whole)
2 cups black Niçoise olives
2 hard-cooked eggs, chopped fine
1 sweet red onion, cut into fine dice
1 cup tiny capers, drained
2 pints cherry tomatoes, cut into ⅛-inch slices
80 thin slices of cocktail rye and black bread
2 to 3 crocks of sweet butter

TO ARRANGE

1. Choose a large round decorative tray or platter. Arrange lettuce leaves in the center.

2. Place meat in a ring form on top of lettuce. Sprinkle fresh chives over the steak and place Niçoise olives in the center of the ring.

3. Arrange the different garnishes in an attractive pattern around the meat so that everyone can choose what he or she wants.

4. If your platter is large enough, place bread slices in alternating colors in a ring around the garnish. Stick the whole chives out from different places.

5. Have crocks of butter nearby to spread on bread.

Enough for 75 to 80 pieces of bread
38 portions, 2 pieces per person

SAUSAGES

Sausage has been a part of our culinary heritage as long as there has been pork. Within every country, every region seems to have its own technique for the preparation. When serving a sausage board, let people carve for themselves. Provide good boards and sharp knives, and offer a selection of breads, mustards, horseradish and pickles.

ABRUZZI: Dry Italian sausage, made from fresh pork and spices, cured and air-dried. Spicy and nice for antipasto plates, hors d'oeuvres, or just munching.

ALLESANDRI: Italian-style; hard, dry and spicy.

ALPINO: Made from an old Alpine recipe; hard and spicy.

ARLES: French-style; lots of garlic and red pepper.

BEEF LOG: Dry, smoked beef salami.

BLUTWURST or BLOOD SAUSAGE: German delicacy; highly seasoned, very salty and totally cooked.

BOCKWURST: Mildly seasoned; usually made with veal, pork, milk, chives, eggs, and parsley.

BRATWURST: A German classic. Pork and veal seasoned with sage and lemon juice.

FRESH BRAUNSCHWEIGER: Pork and beef liver mixture, cooked but not smoked.

BRAUNSCHWEIGER: The smoked version.

BÜNDNERFLEISCH: Swiss, one of our favorites; this is salty and spicy air-dried beef.

CACCIATORE: Italian-style sausage in midget sizes.

CALABRESE: Coarse salami with hot peppers.

CAPOCOLLO: Pork butt seasoned with red peppers, cured, and air-dried. Spicy and hot.

CERVELAT: Dried German sausages that are thick, peppery and smoked.

COPPA VENEZIANA: An Italian sausage with Italian ham in the middle.

DANISH SALAMI: Smoked, small little sticks, like cervelat.

FILSETTE: Mild, Italian Genoa-style salami.

FINOCCHIONA: Tuscany soppressata.

GELBWURST: Looks like liverwurst, but actually bland, spongy pork and veal sausage.

GENOA PICCOLO: Pork and beef plus beef hearts, garlic and pepper. Dried up to 5 months, which makes it very hard.

ITALIAN SALAMI: Chopped pork and beef, mixed with red wine or grape juice, and flavored with garlic and spices.

LACHSSCHINKEN: Lightly smoked pork loin, no seasonings. Dry. Eat it with a squeeze of lemon and a grind of black pepper.

LIVERWURST: Pork liver and meat trimmings, ground with onions and spices, cooked and/or smoked. Smooth, creamy texture; mild, livery taste; is available fresh. Either you love it or you don't.

MILANO: Finely ground mixed meats.

MORTADELLA: The true bologna, to some the finest sausage in Italy. It's a smooth, subtly flavored sausage made from finely chopped pork and beef, larded with backfat. The meat is then both smoked and dried.

PEPPERONI: A dry sausage made of beef and pork with lots of red pepper, black pepper and garlic.

SALAMI: Mixed meats with varying degrees of garlic and other spices. May be cured and smoked, cured and dried, or cooked.

SETTECENTO GENOA: Another type of hard Genoa salami.

SICILIAN: Finely ground pork trimmings with white and black pepper. Smoked and dried, spicy and flavorful.

SOPPRESSATA: Coarsely ground pork, almost chunky, studded with peppercorns. No garlic, but pungent in smell and taste.

TIROLER: Cooked sausage, like salami.

CHICKEN LIVER PATE WITH GREEN PEPPERCORNS

6 tablespoons sweet butter
½ cup finely minced yellow onion
2 garlic cloves, peeled and chopped
1 teaspoon dried thyme
½ cup celery tops
10 black peppercorns
2 bay leaves
6 cups water
1 pound chicken livers
2 tablespoons Cognac
½ teaspoon salt
½ teaspoon ground allspice
5 teaspoons water-packed green peppercorns, drained
¼ cup heavy cream

1. Melt the butter in a skillet. Add the onion, garlic and thyme and cook, covered, over medium heat for about 25 minutes, or until onion is tender and lightly colored.

2. Meanwhile add celery tops, peppercorns and bay leaves to 6 cups water in a saucepan. Bring to a boil, reduce heat, and simmer for 10 minutes.

3. Add chicken livers to water and simmer gently for about 10 minutes; livers should still be slightly pink inside.

4. Drain the livers, discard celery tops, bay leaves and peppercorns, and place livers, butter, onion and garlic in the bowl of a food processor fitted with a steel blade. Add Cognac, salt, pepper, allspice and 4 teaspoons of the green peppercorns. Process until smooth.

5. Pour in the cream and process again to blend. Transfer to a bowl and stir in remaining teaspoon of green peppercorns.

6. Scrape mixture into a 2-cup terrine, cover, and refrigerate for at least 4 hours before serving. Let pâté stand at room temperature for 30 minutes before serving.

2 cups, at least 8 portions

PATE DE CAMPAGNE WITH WALNUTS

This pâté gains special character from the walnuts. We love to feature it as a first course for holiday time, or on a picnic.

1 pound lean veal, ground
1 pound lean pork shoulder, ground
2 pounds fresh pork fat, ground
1¾ tablespoons coarse salt
1 teaspoon freshly ground black pepper
1 teaspoon dried thyme
¾ to 1 teaspoon ground allspice
1 teaspoon dried tarragon
½ to 1 teaspoon dried oregano
4 garlic cloves, peeled and chopped fine
3 juniper berries, crushed
½ cup Cognac
¼ cup Madeira wine
4 eggs, lightly beaten
¾ cup finely chopped yellow onions, sautéed in
  pork fat or butter until soft, then drained
½ pound beef liver, cut into ½-inch dice
1 cup shelled walnuts
1 pound thinly sliced fresh pork fat (to line loaf pan)
2 bay leaves
3 whole juniper berries

1. Combine the ground veal, ground pork, pork fat, coarse salt, pepper, thyme, allspice, tarragon, oregano, garlic, crushed juniper berries, Cognac, Madeira, eggs and onions. Blend thoroughly without overworking the mixture. (Do not add the liver yet.) To test for seasoning, sauté, cool, and taste a small patty of the mixture. Correct all seasonings.

2. Fold in the diced beef liver and walnuts.

3. Preheat oven to 350°F. Bring a kettle of water to a boil.

4. Line the bottom and sides of a loaf pan 9½ x 5 x 3 inches with the sheets of pork fat, letting some hang over the sides. Pack the meat mixture into the pan, pressing so that no air pockets remain. The top should mound up slightly. Top with 2 bay leaves and 3 whole juniper berries. Cover with the overhanging edges of the lining fat, then with a sheet of pork fat cut to fit, then with aluminum foil. Press the foil snugly onto the edges of the pan to be sure that the pâté is completely enclosed.

5. Set the loaf pan in a larger pan and place in the lower third of the oven. Pour enough boiling water into the outer pan (the *bain-marie*) to come halfway up the sides of the inner pan. Bake for 2½ to 3 hours. The pâté is done when it shrinks from the sides of the pan and the juices run a clear yellow; you can check this by uncovering the pâté and pressing a spoon on top.

6. When pâté is done, remove the loaf pan from the boiling water bath, or pour the water from the outer pan. The loaf must now be weighted for several hours; this is done to force out the interior fat and compress the meat so it will slice evenly. To weight the pâté, place another loaf pan or a board of suitable size on top of the pâté. Put 2 bricks or an equivalent weight of heavy canned goods in the pan or on the board. Let cool, then refrigerate without the weights.

7. When the pâté has been chilled thoroughly, remove it from the loaf pan. Remove the fat around it, wrap the loaf, and return it to the refrigerator; or let it warm slightly at room temperature, then serve. The flavor is enhanced after 1 or 2 days of refrigeration. Let the pâté come to near-room temperature before serving.

1 loaf: at least 10 first-course portions, or 20 cocktail portions

CHARCUTERIE MENU
Assorted Peasant Breads
Sweet Butter

Cornichons
Pickled Pearl Onions
Pickled Wild Cherries

Dijon, Herb and Coarse
Mustards

Country and Spiced Pâtés

Black and White Radishes
Céleri Remoulade
Carottes Râpées

Smoked Dried Sausages

Brie, Chèvre and Triple
Crème Cheeses

Fresh Fruits
Butter Cookies

PERFECT PATES

French pâtés are quickly becoming as familiar in America as the meat loaf, and they are usually not much more difficult to make, once you've got the knack.

These rich and spicy meat mixtures vary greatly from cook to cook and are at home at the cocktail party, as a sit-down first course, as the main course at a picnic, or as an ingredient in a more complicated dish.

The recipes here illustrate some of the differences between types of pâtés. In the shop, each has a following and, in its own way, each is a very special pâté. Try them all to find the one that best satisfies your personal taste.

PATE MAISON

Our version of the classic smooth chicken liver pâté must surely be a winner; over the past four years we've made more than two tons of it. For those who aren't certain whether they love liver, the spices, Calvados and currants provide such interesting flavor that this is a cocktail buffet favorite. Spread on French bread or buttered toast.

2 small celery ribs with leaves
4 whole peppercorns
6 cups water
1 teaspoon salt
1 pound chicken livers
tiny pinch of cayenne pepper
½ pound (2 sticks) sweet butter
2 teaspoons dry mustard
½ teaspoon grated nutmeg
¼ teaspoon ground cloves
¼ cup roughly chopped yellow onion
1 small garlic clove
¼ cup Calvados
½ cup dried currants

1. Add celery and peppercorns to 6 cups water in a saucepan. Add the salt. Bring to a boil, reduce heat, and simmer for 10 minutes.

2. Add chicken livers and simmer very gently for about 10 minutes; livers should still be slightly pink inside.

3. Drain livers, discard celery and peppercorns, and place livers in the bowl of a food processor fitted with a steel blade. Add remaining ingredients except currants and process until well blended and very smooth.

4. Scrape into a bowl, stir in currants, and transfer the pâté to a 3- to 4-cup crock or terrine. Smooth the top of the pâté, cover, and refrigerate for at least 4 hours. Allow the pâté to stand at room temperature for 30 minutes before serving.

About 3 cups pâté, 8 or more portions

THE BAIN-MARIE

Use of the *bain-marie* (or Mary's bath) is an age-old cooking technique, reportedly developed in Italy. The item being cooked (often a pâté, mousse, custard, or other fragile concoction) is set in a larger pan of hot water and transferred to the oven or stove. The water stabilizes the oven's temperature fluctuations and distributes the cooking heat more efficiently. The most familiar everyday application is the double boiler.

SEAFOOD PATE

An elegant first course, accompanied by Tomato Coulis or a flavored mayonnaise or vinaigrette, such as Creamy Tarragon Dressing or Green Herb Dipping Sauce (see Index for recipes).

1½ pounds sea scallops, chilled
1 cup thinly sliced well-cleaned leeks
1 teaspoon salt
pinches of grated nutmeg
dashes of Tabasco
3 cups heavy cream, chilled
1 pound fresh salmon, chilled
2 very cold egg whites
1 tablespoon tomato paste
½ cup frozen peas, thawed
1 tablespoon lemon zest
3 tablespoons finely minced Italian parsley
1 tablespoon orange zest

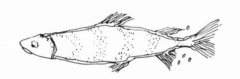

1. Remove tiny hinge muscles from scallops. Rinse scallops thoroughly and pat dry. Reserve 6 of the largest and most perfect. Combine remaining scallops with ½ cup of the sliced leeks in the bowl of a food processor fitted with a steel blade. Process until smooth.

2. Add ½ teaspoon salt, pinch of nutmeg and 2 or 3 dashes of Tabasco, and process again.

3. With the motor running, dribble in 1 cup of the chilled heavy

cream in a slow steady stream. When all the cream is in, shut off processor. Immediately taste mixture and correct seasoning. Remove half of mixture to a bowl; cover and refrigerate. Add peas to processor; process until smooth. Transfer to a bowl; stir in lemon zest and parsley. Cover and refrigerate.

4. Clean processor bowl. Skin the salmon and cut it into small dice. Remove all bones. Place salmon and remaining leeks in the bowl of the processor, fitted with a steel blade, and process until nearly smooth.

5. Add egg whites and tomato paste when mixture becomes too heavy for motor. Season with additional ½ teaspoon salt, pinch of nutmeg, dashes of Tabasco, orange zest, and process until smooth.

6. With the motor running, dribble in remaining 2 cups heavy cream in a slow steady stream. As soon as all the cream is in, shut off processor. Taste mixture, correct seasoning, and refrigerate immediately.

7. Lightly butter a loaf pan 9 x 5 x 3 inches. Spoon the plain scallop mixture into the pan. Arrange the reserved scallops in a line down the center of the pan. Press them lightly into the scallop mixture. Spoon the chilled salmon mixture over the scallop layer and smooth with a spatula. Finally, spread the pea and scallop mixture over the salmon layer and smooth it. Rap the pan firmly on your work surface several times to eliminate any air bubbles.

8. Wrap the loaf pan in aluminum foil and set it in a larger baking pan. Pour boiling water into the baking pan so that it comes about halfway up the sides of the loaf pan. Set bain-marie in the center of a preheated 350°F. oven and bake for 45 minutes, or until an instant-read thermometer gives an internal temperature of 130°F.

9. Remove the loaf pan from the hot water and cool to room temperature. Refrigerate overnight.

10. To unmold: Remove the aluminum foil and dip the loaf pan into hot water for 30 seconds or so. Run a thin knife carefully around the edge of the pâté, set a large plate on top, and invert. The pâté will drop out onto the plate.

11. To serve cold, slice and arrange on plates with a dollop of chosen sauce. To serve hot, slice pâté when cold, arrange slices on a buttered baking sheet, and cover with foil. Warm gently in a 300°F. oven for about 15 minutes. Spoon warmed Tomato Coulis onto plates and center a slice of warmed pâté on the coulis. Serve immediately.

10 to 12 portions as a first course

Originally the terms "pâté" and "terrine" were used to distinguish meat dishes baked in crusts *(pâtés)* from those cooked in a crockery or metal dish (terrines). The terms are now used more or less interchangeably.

The adventurous spirit of *nouvelle cuisine* now applies the terms *pâté* and terrine to combinations of ingredients far removed from the traditional meaty preparations. Often layered and baked in traditional loaf shapes and served as a substantial first course, they can consist of seafood or vegetables, or even a combination of both.

✜ FROM THE SILVER PALATE NOTEBOOK

It is worth the extra money to be properly staffed. Even if your affair is not to be catered, consider calling a lend-a-hand agency to provide personnel. Make certain they arrive in time to be briefed on logistics, timing, garnishes and any last-minute food preparation. Let them know your personal style (casual, organized, elegant, etc.), and be sure they recognize you as hostess in case of emergencies.

Make it a rule to clean up the night of the party, whether you have staff to help or not.

INSTANT-READ THERMOMETERS

An instant-read thermometer, unlike conventional cooking thermometers, does not remain in the food as it cooks. It is merely inserted, gives an "instant" reading, and then is removed. Although they cost more than other thermometers, they last longer and are more accurate.

LAYERED VEGETABLE TERRINE

Three layers — tomato, leek and white bean — combine in a rich, spicy and satisfying pâté.

WHITE BEAN LAYER

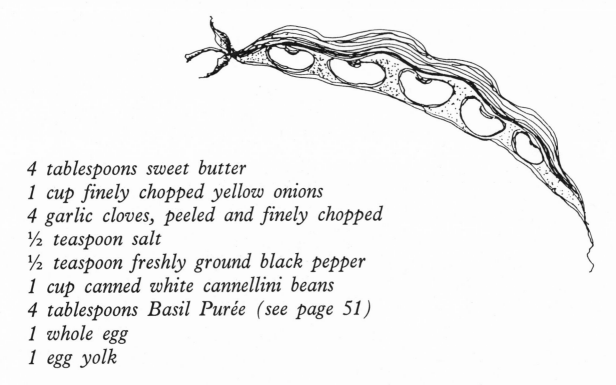

4 tablespoons sweet butter
1 cup finely chopped yellow onions
4 garlic cloves, peeled and finely chopped
½ teaspoon salt
½ teaspoon freshly ground black pepper
1 cup canned white cannellini beans
4 tablespoons Basil Purée (see page 51)
1 whole egg
1 egg yolk

1. Melt butter in a small heavy saucepan or skillet. Add onions, cover, and cook slowly until tender and lightly colored, about 20 minutes.

2. Add garlic, salt and pepper, and cook, uncovered, for another 5 minutes. Remove from heat.

3. Rinse canned beans and drain them well. Combine beans, onion-and-butter mixture and Basil Purée in the bowl of a food processor fitted with a steel blade, and process until smooth.

4. Add whole egg and egg yolk and process again until eggs are completely incorporated. Taste, correct seasoning if necessary, scrape out into a bowl, cover and refrigerate until chilled.

TOMATO LAYER

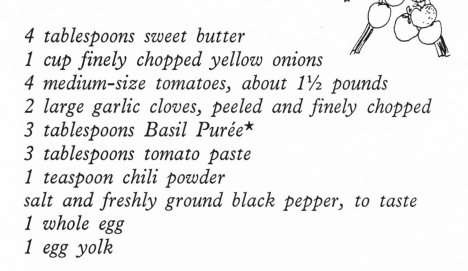

4 tablespoons sweet butter
1 cup finely chopped yellow onions
4 medium-size tomatoes, about 1½ pounds
2 large garlic cloves, peeled and finely chopped
3 tablespoons Basil Purée*
3 tablespoons tomato paste
1 teaspoon chili powder
salt and freshly ground black pepper, to taste
1 whole egg
1 egg yolk

1. Melt butter in a small heavy saucepan or skillet. Add onions, cover, and cook slowly until tender and lightly colored, about 20 minutes.

2. Meanwhile, cut a small cross in the bottom of each tomato and drop them into boiling salted water for 10 seconds. Remove with a slotted spoon, drop into a bowl of ice water, and let cool. Skins will peel off easily when tomatoes are cool. Cut tomatoes into halves crosswise, scrape out seeds, and squeeze out juice. Chop the tomatoes and add them to the onions. Cook uncovered over moderate heat, stirring often, for 20 minutes.

3. Add the garlic, basil purée, tomato paste, chili powder, and salt and pepper to taste, and cook for 15 minutes longer, or until mixture is very thick.

4. Taste and correct seasoning. Scrape into a bowl and cool to room temperature.

5. Beat whole egg and egg yolk together into tomato mixture. Cover and refrigerate until chilled.

*Basil Purée: Process or blend 7 cups washed and dried fresh basil leaves, or 7 cups fresh parsley leaves and 1 tablespoon dried basil, with 3 to 4 tablespoons olive oil. Cover and refrigerate or freeze.

51

LEEK LAYER

6 tablespoons sweet butter
4 cups thinly sliced well-cleaned leeks, white part
  only; about 8 medium-size leeks
2 teaspoons curry powder
2 garlic cloves, peeled and finely chopped
½ cup chopped parsley
salt to taste
¾ teaspoon freshly ground black pepper
1 whole egg
1 egg yolk

1. Melt butter in a small heavy saucepan or skillet. Add leeks, cover, and cook slowly until very tender, about 30 minutes.

2. Add curry powder, garlic, parsley, salt to taste and pepper, and cook uncovered, stirring occasionally, for another 10 minutes. Cool to room temperature.

3. Beat whole egg and egg yolk together in a small bowl, stir into cooled leek mixture, cover and refrigerate.

TO COMPLETE THE TERRINE

2 carrots
6 thin asparagus spears
12 large leaves of white cabbage
sweet butter

1. Bring a large kettle of heavily salted water to a boil. Have ready a large bowl of ice water.

2. Scrape the carrots and cut them lengthwise into quarters. Drop them into the boiling water and cook until very tender but not mushy. Lift from the boiling water with a slotted spoon and drop into the ice water.

3. Trim the woody ends from the asparagus spears and drop them into the boiling water. Cook until tender, remove from the boiling water with a slotted spoon and drop into ice water.

4. Drop the cabbage leaves into the boiling water and press with a spoon to be certain they are submerged and cooking. Blanch them for about 5 minutes, or until they begin to become translucent. Remove

from boiling water with a slotted spoon and drop them also into the ice water.

5. When all vegetables are cool, drain them and pat dry. Lightly butter a loaf or bread pan 9 x 5 x 3 inches. Trim the heavy ribs from the cabbage leaves. Line the loaf pan with the leaves, covering sides, ends and bottom, and overlapping leaves slightly. Be sure you have 2 or 3 leaves left for the top of the terrine.

6. Remove the leek, tomato and bean mixtures from the refrigerator. Stir leek mixture to be sure ingredients are well combined and spoon into the bottom of the loaf pan. Smooth with a spatula and arrange lengths of carrot on top in a decorative design.

7. Stir up tomato mixture and spoon on top of leek mixture, being careful not to disturb the carrots. Smooth the tomato mixture and arrange the asparagus spears in a similar fashion on top.

8. Finally pour in the bean layer and smooth it. Rap the loaf pan several times on your work surface to expel any air bubbles. Cover the terrine with remaining cabbage leaves, tucking excess down the sides of the pan.

9. Wrap the loaf pan in aluminum foil and set it in a larger baking pan. Pour boiling water into the baking pan so that it comes about halfway up the sides of the loaf pan. Set bain-marie in the center of a preheated 350°F. oven and bake for 2 hours or until center of terrine feels firm to the touch.

10. Remove the loaf pan from its hot-water bath and unwrap it. Let it cool for 15 minutes, and weight it (for example, set another similar loaf pan on top and put a weight inside — 2 cans of soup, or coffee mugs) until completely cool. Remove weight, cover, and chill thoroughly.

11. To unmold, dip the pan briefly into hot water and run a thin knife carefully around the sides of the pan. Set a platter upside down over the terrine and invert; the terrine will drop out onto the plate.

12. Serve cold, sliced and garnished with Aïoli Sauce, Tomato-Basil Mayonnaise, or chilled Tomato Coulis (see Index for recipes).

8 to 10 portions as a first course

APERITIFS

Apéritifs have a bit more kick than table wines, but are less alcoholic than distilled spirits. Often they are infused with herbs and other flavorings in combinations kept secret by their manufacturers. *Vermouths* (we like Lillet) can be garnished with a strip of orange or lemon peel. *Dry Sherry* is delicious just slightly cooled, although many now drink it on the rocks. *Campari* is a brilliantly red, slightly bitter Italian apéritif that is gaining popularity on the cocktail circuit, especially in summer. Try it with a splash of tonic or soda and a squeeze of fresh lime. (And while you're at it, remember that a splash of soda — or seltzer as we say in Manhattan — will lighten your vermouth, sherry, or even a glass of white wine.) *Pineau des Charentes* is an apéritif made in France for over 400 years and only just being exported to America. It's a slightly sweet blend of white wine and Cognac that we adore. *Pastis* is the working Frenchman's favorite apéritif — morning, noon or night. The anise-flavored liqueur pastis is mixed with water or soda in a one-to-five ratio. Or shake an egg white, 2 ounces of pastis and 1 teaspoon of extra-fine sugar together with ice until foamy. Strain into a chilled tall glass, add a splash of soda, and garnish with a mint leaf.

54

DAZZLERS

For those times when the movers and shakers must be dazzled, when laurels have been bestowed, when transitions must be acknowledged and anniversaries celebrated, something very special indeed is demanded of the hostess. The casual and easygoing gathering gives way to the event; important people and important events call for important food. This is the time to pull out all the stops and turn your entertaining eye to some of the more elegant and extravagant possibilities the world has to offer.

Caviar, oysters, *foie gras,* aïoli — even the names excite. We deal with these fabulous treats on a daily basis, and while for us the mystery is gone, the magic remains. We hope this section will encourage you to experiment with the unusual. You and your guests will love the results.

CAVIAR

If you have shopped for imported caviar recently and compared prices, you will appreciate the irony that, in the nineteenth century, large quantities of American caviar were exported to Europe! While we are as willing as the next gourmet to pay for our imported delicacies, we're pleased and excited to know that American sturgeon caviar is making a comeback, and at domestic prices. Once-polluted waters are becoming clean enough to support the big fish, and now that politics as well as price have made Iranian and Caspian caviar less than palatable, the American caviar industry is booming.

As a new elegance in entertaining replaces the laid-back casualness of the 60s and 70s, caviar is taking a new position as a classy, tasty, affordable American appetizer. Welcome home!

THE CAVIAR CODE

Caviar should always be shiny, translucent and firm, with not too much salt. (Caviar labeled *malossol* has been lightly salted.) The eggs may be jet black, golden yellow, gray, or dark brown, but should always be perfectly whole and distinct, so that you can feel the pearls with your tongue. It should not be oily or have a fishy taste or smell. Never serve your caviar in silver — it will have a metallic taste. Once you've experienced the best caviar, you will forever be on the lookout for the occasion to serve it again.

BELUGA: Delicately flavored roe from the Caspian Sea's giant Beluga sturgeon; it is considered by all to be the best.

AMERICAN BLACK: Black sturgeon roe, can vary dramatically in grade but is generally very nice; be observant.

PRESSED: Crushed and paste-like, it is a favorite especially in the Russian cuisine.

AMERICAN GOLDEN: Whitefish roe that is gold, crisp, relatively mild and clean tasting.

SALMON CAVIAR: Large-grained, light orange, milder and sweeter.

SMOKED SALMON CAVIAR: The newest caviar version, lightly smoked; it's a delicate treat.

OYSTERS

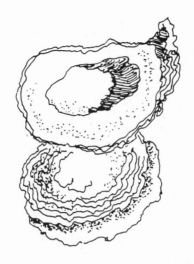

Oysters once flourished in American waters. The Indians harvested them extravagantly, and they were an inexpensive staple for years. Polluted waters endangered the oyster for a while, but each year they are increasingly available, and cultivated beds will soon ensure that if we wish to eat 100 oysters at one sitting as Diamond Jim Brady once did, we can.

Oyster lovers have their favorites and will debate the various merits of the flat versus the hollow, the pale silver and expensive Belon, the green French Marenne, the pungent ivory Limfjord as well as the popular Blue Point, Chatham, Papillion, Cotuit, Box, Kent Island, Claire, Chincoteague, Malpeque, Apalachicola, and Canadian Golden Mantle. There are differences in size, flavor, texture and saltiness. If you get a chance to taste several varieties side by side, you will learn to distinguish your favorites.

Oysters must be served freshly opened, kept cold on a bed of ice. We like them served simply with just lemon juice and freshly ground black pepper. Cocktail sauce (the kind made with ketchup and horse-radish) is taboo (you can't taste the oysters), but a shallot sauce is occasionally welcome.

FOIE GRAS

In the midst of all these other luxuries, a few words about *foie gras* seem in order. *Foie gras* is the enlarged liver of a goose (and sometimes a duck) that has been force-fed by hand. The sentiments of American animal lovers have prevented the development of a *foie gras* industry in this country. Imported foie gras in tins or jars (fully or partially cooked, since the U.S. government prohibits the importation of raw *foie gras*) is available, but will give you only the faintest clue as to what the fuss is all about. To enjoy the glory at its fullest, you must savor it in France.

At its best and purest, *foie gras* is served barely cooked and thinly sliced, accompanied by buttered toast and dry Chablis, Champagne, or the rich sweet wine, Sauternes. The liver will be silky, smooth, and rich as butter.

A visit to the *foie gras* market in Gascony or Périgord is something we wish everyone could experience; it is as if you have stepped back centuries.

First you will notice a landscape in sepia tones. Rolling hills and dirt roads lead to tiny villages. The magnificence suddenly startles as you reach the top of a hill and see a huge field of sunflowers and a flock of geese. There is garlic drying in the sun. An old man is riding his bicycle while trying unsuccessfully to balance a long *baguette*. Around the corner is a field of cornflowers, blue as the sky.

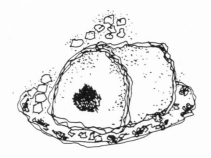

The market itself is a large wooden building, bustling with people and contrasts. Peasants and *foie gras* buyers collide on the floor, each trying to attract the other. The plucked and cleaned ducks and geese, which have been force-fed with corn to fatten their livers, are arranged on long tables covered with crisp white cloths. Their heads and necks hang over the edges of the tables and the birds, save for their livers, are whole — which is, after all, the reason for the buyers' excitement. Both birds and livers are for sale, and competition is keen. Baskets of fresh livers are offered for judgment: was the bird healthy? Was it fed only the best meal and at the proper intervals? Is the resulting liver the right color of pink or ochre? Does it have the proper texture?

To a visitor, the system and the food it produces may seem strangely harsh, but a Frenchman recognizes the making of *foie gras* as an art steeped in the antiquity of France itself.

Should you be lucky enough to be invited to a private home in this region or to dine in one of the fine restaurants of France, you will taste the treat of your life — the freshest possible *foie gras,* prepared and served by those to whom it symbolizes a way of life.

HERBED CAVIAR ROULADE

CREPE

2 teaspoons corn oil
2 eggs
½ cup unbleached all-purpose flour
1 cup milk
pinch of salt
2 teaspoons fresh chives, chopped
1 tablespoon finely chopped fresh parsley
2 teaspoons finely chopped fresh dill

1. Preheat oven to 425°F. Brush an 11 x 17 inch jelly roll pan lightly with corn oil.

2. In the bowl of an electric mixer, beat eggs, for 15 seconds until pale yellow.

3. With mixer on, add milk in a slow stream, flour and mix until smooth, carefully scraping down sides. Turn mixer off.

4. Add salt, chives, parsley and dill and mix to blend for a few seconds. Let mixture rest in bowl at room temperature for 30 minutes.

5. With a rubber spatula, spread batter evenly on jelly roll pan. Bake for 12 minutes. Remove from oven and let cool in pan. When cool, loosen bottom with metal spatula.

CREPE FILLING

1 cup dairy sour cream
½ cup finely chopped purple onion
1 cup finely chopped hard-cooked eggs (3 eggs)
¼ teaspoon freshly ground black pepper
2 ounces black caviar
2 ounces golden caviar
10 sprigs fresh dill (garnish)
10 lemon wedges (garnish)

1. In medium-size bowl, combine sour cream, onion, eggs and black pepper.

2. With small rubber spatula, gently fold caviar into sour cream mixture.

3. Spread mixture evenly over crêpe leaving a 1 inch border around edges. Beginning at short end, carefully roll crêpe.

4. To serve: With a serrated knife, cut crêpe into 1¼ inch slices and garnish with a sprig of dill and a wedge of lemon. Arrange in the center of individual plates.

8 to 10 portions as an appetizer

"There is more simplicity in the man who eats caviar on impulse than in the man who eats Grape-Nuts on principle."
— G. K. Chesterton

Purists take their caviar straight, on a spoon. Other serving options (which, incidentally, can stretch your valued stash of the precious eggs) include toast or sliced black bread, a dab of sour cream, minced hard-cooked egg, finely chopped red onion and chopped parsley. We love a squeeze of fresh lemon juice on it too.

Iced vodka (store your bottle in the freezer overnight before serving) or Champagne are the recommended accompanying beverages.

NEW POTATOES WITH BLACK CAVIAR

12 very small new potatoes (1 pound or less)
4 to 5 cups rock salt
oil for deep-frying
½ cup dairy sour cream
3½ to 4 ounces black or golden caviar

1. Preheat oven to 450°F.
2. Wash and dry potatoes. Arrange potatoes on a bed of rock salt in a shallow baking pan and bake for 30 to 35 minutes, until done.
3. Remove potatoes from oven and cut into halves. Scoop out pulp with a melon-ball cutter or small spoon, being careful to keep shells intact. Mash pulp slightly in a small bowl and keep warm.
4. Heat oil to 375°F. in a large saucepan. Drop potato shells into oil and fry till golden brown and crisp. Drain well on paper towels.
5. Fill potato shells with mashed potatoes, top with a spoonful of sour cream, and add a teaspoon or more of caviar. Serve as a first course on thick salad plates atop hot rock salt.

6 portions as a first course

COOKING WITH CAVIAR

Cooking with caviar and combining it with other ingredients is tricky because the eggs are delicate; unnecessary handling or heat can turn them into mush. There are possibilities, however: fold the caviar into sour cream and serve as a dip; fold into a warm, buttery omelet; roll into a crêpe; spoon into a 2-inch shell of *pâté brisée*; toss gently with angel's-hair pasta and *crème fraîche*; stuff into hollowed cherry tomatoes, hard-cooked eggs or tiny pastry puffs.

CAVIAR ECLAIRS

1 recipe Pâté à Choux (see page 574)
5 slices of smoked salmon
8 ounces whipped cream cheese
½ cup dairy sour cream
4 ounces black caviar
finely chopped fresh dill
freshly ground black pepper, to taste

1. Fill a pastry bag lined with a small plain tip with warm *pâté à choux*. Butter a baking sheet. Pipe out 2-inch lengths of the *pâté à choux*. They should look rather like stripes of yellow toothpaste. Top with a second strip of pastry dough. Form 20 such miniature éclairs. Brush tops of éclairs with beaten egg. Bake according to *pâté à choux* directions, and cool completely.

2. Cut each piece of salmon into quarters and reserve.

3. Slice éclairs horizontally into halves. Spread a thin layer of cream cheese in the bottom of each éclair and lay a piece of salmon on top. Spread a thin layer of sour cream on the salmon and top with a dab of caviar. Sprinkle with dill and freshly ground black pepper. Return the tops to the éclairs and serve immediately.

20 éclairs

✤ FROM THE SILVER PALATE NOTEBOOK

Hired entertainment is a lovely touch and need not cost a fortune. A string quartet might feature the son or daughter of a friend. The piano bar player at your favorite hangout might perform as a favor. A piano player, cellist or harpist might be hired from a nearby music school for a nominal fee and a good reference.

CAVIAR DIP

6 ounces whipped cream cheese
3 ounces dairy sour cream
1 tablespoon lemon juice
1 teaspoon grated onion
1½ tablespoons finely chopped fresh dill
pinch of freshly ground black pepper
2 ounces fresh black caviar or natural red salmon caviar

1. Bring cream cheese to room temperature and mix with sour cream.
2. Gently fold in lemon juice, onion, dill and pepper until well blended.
3. Fold in the caviar carefully. Refrigerate until needed.

About 1 cup

OYSTERS AND CAVIAR

fresh seaweed*
18 fresh oysters on the half shell**
2 scallions (green onions), thinly sliced into rings
2 ounces fresh black caviar
2 lemons, cut into thin wedges

1. Spread the seaweed in a flat basket. Arrange the oysters, in their shells, on the seaweed.
2. Sprinkle each oyster with 2 or 3 pieces of scallion. Top each one with a dab of caviar. Serve very cold, accompanied by fresh lemon wedges.

4 to 6 portions

*Seaweed can be ordered from your fishmonger and is usually free.
**Shuck them yourself or have the fishmonger do it.

OYSTERS, SPINACH AND CAVIAR

Inspired by Jean-Marie Amat, chef at the restaurant Saint James in Bordeaux, France.

2 large shallots, very finely chopped
½ cup sherry vinegar
32 shucked oysters, including their liquor
32 fresh small tender spinach leaves
6 ounces fresh black American caviar
1 lemon, cut into 8 wedges

1. Marinate shallots in sherry vinegar overnight.
2. In a small saucepan over medium heat gently warm oysters in their liquor until their edges curl, about 30 seconds. Remove from heat and cool. Drain.
3. Dip the spinach leaves in a strainer into boiling water and immediately drop into ice water. Drain and pat dry.
4. Wrap 1 spinach leaf around each oyster. Arrange 4 wrapped oysters on each of 8 chilled plates.
5. Remove shallots from vinegar and sprinkle equally over oyster bundles. Top each bundle with ½ teaspoon of caviar. Place a lemon wedge on each plate and serve immediately.
8 portions as a first course

"Why, then the world's mine oyster, Which I with sword will open."

— *The Merry Wives of Windsor,*
William Shakespeare

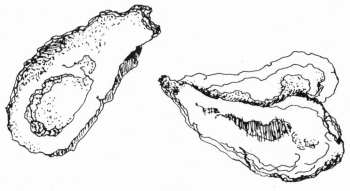

SHALLOT SAUCE

Excellent with oysters.

½ *cup white wine*
½ *cup white wine vinegar**
3 tablespoons chopped shallots
1 teaspoon freshly ground black pepper

Whisk all ingredients together in a bowl. Let sit at room temperature for 15 to 30 minutes before serving.
1 cup

*or substitute sherry vinegar or raspberry vinegar

AN AIOLI PLATTER

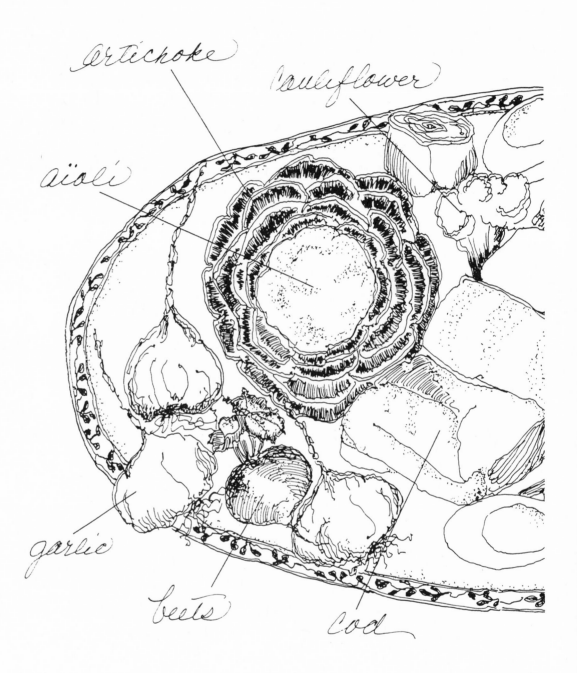

artichoke

cauliflower

aïoli

garlic

beets

cod

In Provence, feast days are often celebrated by a lusty community meal in which poached fish, cooked vegetables and a garlicky Aioli sauce are the main components. This same feast, arranged in smaller

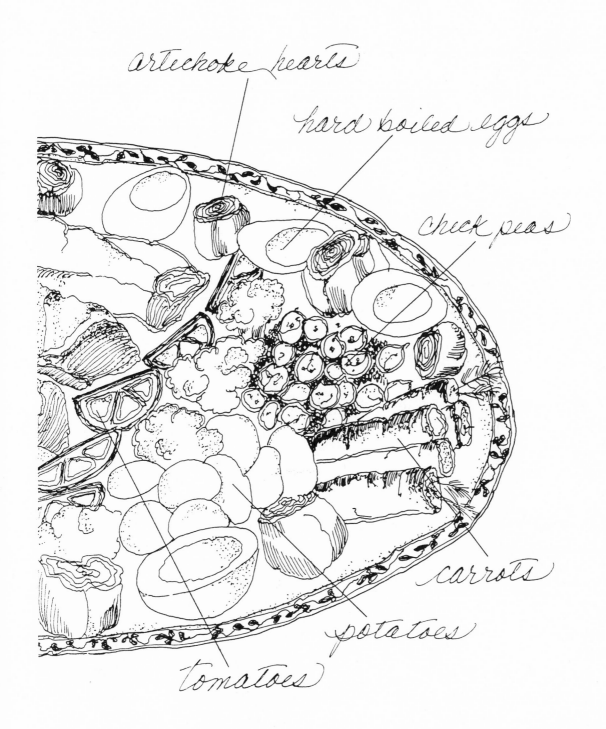

artechoke hearts

hard boiled eggs

cheek peas

carrots

potatoes

tomatoes

quantities, can become a perfect supper for guests who linger after drinks. The colors are intense, the flavors powerful. Aioli brings Provence to your buffet. (Recipe follows.)

VEGETABLES, FISH AND BEEF FOR AIOLI PLATTERS

1 double batch Aïoli Sauce (recipe follows), made
  1 batch at a time
6 small artichokes, trimmed, boiled, chokes removed
7 pounds cod, poached
1 pound carpaccio (thinly sliced and pounded
  raw beef tenderloin)
½ pound snow peas, trimmed, blanched, refreshed in cold water
½ pound green beans, trimmed, blanched,
  refreshed in cold water
1 pound carrots, pared, cut into 2-inch pieces,
  blanched, refreshed in cold water
3 pounds cauliflower, cut into florets, blanched,
  refreshed in cold water
1 pound chick-peas, cooked
3 large red or green peppers, sliced
1 pint basket cherry tomatoes, washed, stems intact
1 pound zucchini, sliced
1 pound small potatoes, boiled until tender, peeled
6 eggs, hard-cooked, peeled and sliced in half
4 tablespoons capers
½ cup chopped parsley

1. Spoon some of the aïoli sauce into the center of each artichoke.
2. Place an aïoli-filled artichoke in the middle of each plate and arrange the cod, carpaccio, prepared vegetables, and eggs around it in a spokelike fashion, making sure that each plate has some of everything. Sprinkle with capers and parsley.

12 portions

CARPACCIO

Carpaccio is lean and tender raw beef, pounded to transparency, or sliced paper-thin. If you sweet talk your butcher he may prepare it for you; if not, partially freeze the meat and slice it with your sharpest knife. Put the slices between 2 pieces of wax paper and pound out any irregularities with the bottom of a heavy saucepan.

AIOLI SAUCE

8 to 10 garlic cloves, peeled
2 egg yolks, at room temperature
salt and freshly ground white pepper to taste
juice of 1 lemon
1 teaspoon prepared Dijon-style mustard
1½ cups oil (half peanut oil, half olive oil), at
  room temperature

1. Purée garlic in a food processor or blender. Whisk the egg yolks in a small bowl until light and smooth, and add to the garlic. Add salt and pepper to taste, lemon juice and mustard, and process to a smooth paste.

2. With the machine running, pour the oil very slowly into the mixture in a steady stream, blending constantly. Continue blending until you obtain a thick, shiny, firm sauce. Transfer to storage container, cover with plastic wrap and refrigerate until ready to use.

OF GARLIC AND SAINTS

Once a year, at the height of summer, the small towns of Provence celebrate the garlic of the season in a dramatic way. Each town has its own patron saint, who is honored by a three-day festivity — culminating, on the third day, with a Grand Aïoli for all the town's inhabitants.

SOUP'S ON

One can stir up memories from childhood of watching Mother or Grandmother preparing kettles of soup. There is nothing like soup to make you feel warm and secure and to recall the love and care that went into those years of nourishing, instinctive cooking.

Soup-making has been elevated to the level of *haute cuisine,* capturing the essences and colors of the freshest vegetables and fruits. All soups can be prepared ahead of time, to be chilled or reheated for serving. Take advantage of a free afternoon or a quiet evening to prepare basic stocks. Freeze them in ice-cube trays or different-size plastic containers for instant use at a later time.

Soups are very logical. All you need is a pot large enough to make the amount of soup you want. Simply blend soup liquids with your favorite meats, beans, vegetables and fruits. The magic comes when you understand what goes with what; there is no better guide than your own good taste. Originally soup was basic sustenance, a meal in itself. Today, while soup is often served in a small quantity as a first course, it may continue to represent the entrée for a meal as we become more interested in light eating.

BASIC ADVICE TO
SOUP MAKERS

• Cook onion long and slowly in butter. Spanish onions and leeks add the best flavor. Use them as your pocketbook allows.

• A rich, homemade stock is one of the most generous contributions you can make to a soup.

• Remove soup from the stove and allow it to cool slightly before any puréeing.

• Any soup that has a particular herb seasoning should receive a generous dash of that herb just before you are ready to purée. This provides a fresher soup flavor (e.g., tomato with dill, sweet pea with mint, potato with arugula).

• The image of a long-simmering stock or soup as a catchall for kitchen leftovers is passé, if indeed it ever existed at all. Only the best and freshest of ingredients will become the finest of soups.
• Attention to the shape of ingredients and the garnishes used can make a world of difference when serving soup.
• Take care to balance the flavor of the soup with the rest of the meal. As an elegant first course, anticipatory of the meal to come, soups can provide an easy point of departure for your entertaining imagination.

SOUPS TO START

We love a light and cordial beginning to a meal, a real first course above and beyond cocktail fare; one of the best is soup. Chilled or warm, it is an elegant and cosy way to begin a dinner party. Hot soup will banish the cold of a winter evening; chilled, it will refresh the palate on a summer afternoon.

CARROT AND ORANGE SOUP

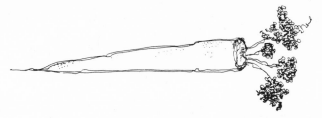

One of our most popular soups. Although particularly appropriate for the holidays, it's good, and easy, to prepare year-round.

4 tablespoons sweet butter
2 cups finely chopped yellow onions
12 large carrots, 1½ to 2 pounds, peeled and chopped
4 cups Chicken Stock (see page 587)
1 cup fresh orange juice
salt and freshly ground black pepper, to taste
grated fresh orange zest to taste

1. Melt the butter in a pot. Add the onions, cover, and cook over low heat until tender and lightly colored, about 25 minutes.
2. Add carrots and stock and bring to a boil. Reduce heat, cover, and simmer until carrots are very tender, about 30 minutes.
3. Pour the soup through a strainer and transfer the solids to the bowl of a food processor fitted with a steel blade, or use a food mill fitted with a medium disc. Add 1 cup of the cooking stock and process until smooth.
4. Return purée to the pot and add the orange juice and additional stock, 2 to 3 cups, until soup is of desired consistency.
5. Season to taste with salt and pepper; add orange zest. Simmer until heated through. Serve immediately.
   4 to 6 portions

"Soup is cuisine's kindest course."

— Kitchen Graffitti

CREAM OF WATERCRESS SOUP

This soup is rich but light, one of the few versions we know that tastes as fresh as watercress itself.

4 tablespoons sweet butter
2 cups finely chopped yellow onions
½ cup minced shallots
3 cups Chicken Stock (see page 587)
1 medium-size potato, peeled and diced
4 bunches of watercress
1 cup heavy cream
salt and freshly ground black pepper, to taste
nutmeg and cayenne pepper, to taste

1. Melt the butter in a heavy pot. Add the onions and shallots and cook, covered, over low heat until tender and lightly colored, about 25 minutes.

2. Add chicken stock and the potato, bring to a boil, reduce heat and simmer, partially covered, until potato is very tender, about 20 minutes.

3. Meanwhile, remove the leaves and tender stems from the watercress and rinse thoroughly. When potato is tender, add watercress to the pot, cover, remove from heat, and let stand for 5 minutes.

4. Pour soup through a strainer, reserving liquid, and transfer the solids to the bowl of a food processor fitted with a steel blade, or use a food mill fitted with the medium disc. Add 1 cup of the cooking stock and process until smooth.

5. Return purée to the pot, stir in the heavy cream, and add additional stock, ½ to 1 cup, until soup is of the desired consistency.

6. Set over medium heat, season to taste with salt, pepper, nutmeg and cayenne, and simmer just until heated through. Serve immediately.

4 portions

The first restaurant was opened by a Parisian soup maker in Boulanger in 1765, where he served soup exclusively. Above the entrance was the Latin motto "Come to me all of you whose stomachs cry out and I will restore you."

ZUCCHINI-WATERCRESS SOUP

This soup is light, fresh and versatile; it can begin any number of menus.

4 tablespoons sweet butter
2 cups finely chopped yellow onions
3 cups Chicken Stock (see page 587)
2 pounds zucchini (about 4 medium-size)
1 bunch of watercress
salt and freshly ground black pepper, to taste
fresh lemon juice to taste

1. Melt the butter in a pot, add the onions, cover, and cook over low heat, stirring occasionally, until onions are tender and lightly colored, about 25 minutes.

2. Add the stock and bring to a boil.

3. Scrub zucchini well with a kitchen brush, trim the ends, and chop coarsely. Drop zucchini into the stock and return it to the boil. Reduce heat, cover, and simmer until zucchini are very tender, about 20 minutes.

4. Meanwhile pull the leaves and smaller stems off the watercress; you should have at least 4 loosely packed cups; rinse well.

5. Remove soup from heat, add watercress, cover, and let stand for 5 minutes.

6. Pour soup through a strainer, reserving liquid, and transfer the solids to the bowl of a food processor fitted with a steel blade, or use a food mill fitted with a medium disc. Add 1 cup of the cooking stock and process until smooth.

7. Return puréed soup to the pot and add additional cooking liquid, about 2 more cups, until the soup is of the desired consistency.

8. Season to taste with salt, pepper and lemon juice. Simmer briefly to heat through. Serve immediately.
   4 to 6 portions

Note: For a richer soup, substitute 1 cup heavy cream for 1 cup of the liquid added after processing.

MINTED SWEET PEA AND
SPINACH SOUP

This rich, elegant soup is a perfect beginning for an important dinner. Although we use frozen peas and spinach with excellent results, the mint really must be fresh.

4 tablespoons sweet butter
2 cups finely chopped yellow onions
10 ounces frozen chopped spinach, defrosted
3 cups Chicken Stock (see page 587)
10 ounces frozen peas, defrosted
½ bunch of fresh mint
1 cup heavy cream
salt and freshly ground black pepper, to taste

1. Melt the butter in a pot. Add the chopped onions, cover, and cook over low heat until tender and lightly colored, about 25 minutes.

2. Meanwhile, drain the spinach and squeeze out excess liquid. Pour the stock into the pot, stir in the peas and spinach, and bring to a boil. Reduce heat and simmer, partially covered, until peas are tender, about 20 minutes.

3. Pull the mint leaves from their stems; there should be 2 cups loosely packed leaves. Rinse thoroughly and pat dry. When peas are tender, add mint to the pot, cover, and simmer for another 5 minutes.

4. Pour the soup through a strainer, reserving liquid, and transfer the solids to the bowl of a food processor fitted with a steel blade, or use a food mill fitted with the medium disc. Add 1 cup of the cooking stock and process until smooth.

5. Return puréed soup to the pot. Add the heavy cream and additional cooking liquid, about 1 cup, until the soup is of the desired consistency.

6. Season to taste with salt and pepper, simmer briefly to heat through, and serve immediately.

1½ quarts, 4 to 6 portions

"Beautiful soup! Who cares for fish, game, or any other dish? Who would not give all else for two pennyworth only of beautiful soup?"

— *Alice in Wonderland*, Lewis Carroll

CURRIED BUTTERNUT SQUASH SOUP

Squash and apples complement each other naturally; curry adds an exotic note. Feel free to experiment with other types of winter or summer squash.

4 tablespoons sweet butter
2 cups finely chopped yellow onions
4 to 5 teaspoons curry powder
2 medium-size butternut squash (about 3 pounds altogether)
2 apples, peeled, cored and chopped
3 cups Chicken Stock (see page 587)
1 cup apple juice
salt and freshly ground black pepper, to taste
1 shredded unpeeled Granny Smith apple (garnish)

1. Melt the butter in a pot. Add chopped onions and curry powder and cook, covered, over low heat until onions are tender, about 25 minutes.

2. Meanwhile peel the squash (a regular vegetable peeler works best), scrape out the seeds, and chop the flesh.

3. When onions are tender, pour in the stock, add squash and apples, and bring to a boil. Reduce heat and simmer, partially covered, until squash and apples are very tender, about 25 minutes.

4. Pour the soup through a strainer, reserving liquid, and transfer the solids to the bowl of a food processor fitted with a steel blade, or use a food mill fitted with a medium disc. Add 1 cup of the cooking stock and process until smooth.

5. Return puréed soup to the pot and add apple juice and additional cooking liquid, about 2 cups, until the soup is of the desired consistency.

6. Season to taste with salt and pepper, simmer briefly to heat through, and serve immediately, garnished with shredded apple.

4 to 6 portions

Eliminate or streamline the first course. Try offering borscht in a mug. Pass a tray of sliced black bread spread with a triple crème cheese. A graceful segue will lead everyone comfortably into dinner. Move to another room for coffee and after-dinner drinks or even dessert.

SOUPS OF THE SEA

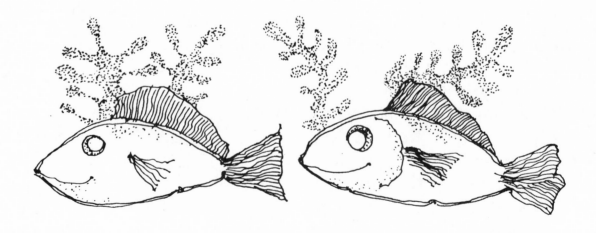

Enjoy the bounty of the sea in these subtle bisques and stalwart chowders. The freshest catch of the day, transformed into a soup of the sea, will warm the cockles of your heart.

BOUILLABAISSE

Crusty bread, a green salad and fresh fruit are all you need to complete this meal. Drink a rough red wine; Chianti, Zinfandel or a Côtes du Rhône would be our choice.

½ cup fruity, dark green olive oil
1½ cups leeks, well cleaned and coarsely chopped
1 cup finely chopped yellow onions
2 cups canned concentrated tomato purée
3 cups chopped fresh tomatoes
2 teaspoons dried thyme
½ cup chopped Italian parsley
2 bay leaves
2 cups dry white wine
4 cups Fish Stock (see page 588)
salt and freshly ground black pepper, to taste
6 tablespoons sweet butter, at room temperature
2 teaspoons flour
2 quarts fresh mussels, scrubbed and debearded
48 Cherrystone clams, scrubbed
1½ teaspoons whole saffron
3 pounds skinless firm white fish steaks (bass, snapper,
   cod), cut into large cubes
36 raw shrimp, shelled and deveined
4 lobster tails, fresh or defrosted, 1 pound each,
   shelled and halved crosswise

1. Heat the olive oil in a large soup pot. Add the leeks and onions and cook over medium heat, covered, until the vegetables are tender and lightly colored, about 25 minutes, stirring occasionally.

2. Add tomato purée, tomatoes, thyme, parsley, bay leaves, wine, fish stock, and salt and pepper to taste. Simmer for 20 minutes. (Soup can be prepared several hours ahead to this point. Return to the simmer before proceeding.)

3. Blend butter and flour together in a bowl and then whisk into the tomato mixture.

4. Add the mussels and clams in their shells and the saffron and

simmer for 5 minutes. Add the fish, shrimp and lobster tails and simmer for another 5 minutes, or until all shellfish are opened and fish is done. Do not overcook.

5. Ladle into hot soup plates, garnish with fried garlic croutons, and serve immediately.

8 to 10 portions

MAKING AUTHENTIC BOUILLABAISSE

Despite the fuss among purists regarding the making of this great fish soup, the truth is that along the Riviera it is the most common and casually assembled of meals, incorporating whatever the fishing fleet may have brought in. There are as many bad bouillabaisses as there are bad cooks; inversely, the good ones are very good indeed.

You will hear that it is impossible to make bouillabaisse in this country since many of the authentic fish are unavailable. This has frightened away many a cook who might otherwise have tried the dish, and it is a false claim. With the exception of the rascasse (or rockfish), which seems to be the main point of contention, all commonly used bouillabaisse fish are available here. Often they are called by another name, but if the fishermen feel free to improvise, so can we, and authenticity at the expense of good taste is to be avoided.

A good variety of seafood is also important, and you must really make bouillabaisse for a crowd for it to be worthwhile. Shellfish are not always included in France, but we like them and think they make the dish look more colorful. Prepare the fish stock a day ahead and shop for and dress your fish the morning of the day you plan to serve the bouillabaisse. The actual cooking time is quite short, and you can easily complete the stew after your guests arrive. In fact, this is the kind of dish you can make while guests watch or even assist. Remember, this is a working man's dish, earthy and messy to eat; don't elevate it into something so exalted you never enjoy its simple pleasure.

TURBOT EN BOURRIDE

Serve this rich fish soup as the first course of a Provençal-style meal followed by roast leg of lamb, Sautéed Cherry Tomatoes (see page 323), and new potatoes roasted with oil and salt.

4 tablespoons sweet butter
2 leeks, white part only, well cleaned and thinly sliced
1 cup finely chopped yellow onions
3 carrots, peeled and finely chopped
1 cup chopped Italian parsley, plus additional parsley for garnish
4 cups Fish Stock (see page 588)
salt and freshly ground black pepper, to taste
2 pounds turbot, trimmed of skin and bone, cut into 1-inch dice
2 cups Aïoli Sauce (see page 69), at room temperature

1. Melt the butter in a pot, add the leeks, onions, and carrots and cook, covered, over low heat until vegetables are tender, about 25 minutes.

2. Add 1 cup chopped parsley and fish stock, season to taste with salt and pepper, bring to a boil, reduce heat and simmer, partially covered, for 25 minutes, or until vegetables are very tender.

3. Pour the soup through a strainer set over a bowl, and transfer the solids and ½ cup of the liquid to the bowl of a food processor fitted with a steel blade, or use a food mill fitted with a medium disc. Purée until smooth. Return the liquid and the puréed solids to the pot and set over medium heat.

4. Add the diced fish and let it poach over low heat in the hot soup liquid for 5 minutes. Do not boil. Remove soup from heat.

5. Slowly whisk 1 cup of the hot soup into the *aïoli* in a small bowl. Whisk this mixture into the remaining soup and stir constantly over medium heat until lightly thickened, about 3 minutes. Do not let the soup boil or it will curdle.

6. Ladle into heated soup bowls, garnish with additional chopped parsley, and serve immediately.

6 portions

CALIFORNIA SHELLFISH STEW

This zesty main-dish soup is a cousin of the Mediterranean fisherman's cioppino and an even more distant relative of the great French bouillabaisse. You can vary the shellfish used — lobster, Dungeness crab, squid and octopus will all work nicely — but do not try to find a substitute for the Zinfandel.

Start with a slice of pâté, follow with a good green salad, and serve plenty of crusty bread for mopping up the juices.

4 tablespoons best-quality olive oil
2 cups finely chopped yellow onions
2 red peppers and 1 green pepper, stemmed,
  seeded and coarsely diced
6 to 8 garlic cloves, peeled and finely chopped
2 cups Fish Stock (see page 588)
2 cups Zinfandel wine
1 can (2 pounds, 3 ounces) peeled plum tomatoes, drained
1½ tablespoons dried basil
1 teaspoon dried thyme
1 bay leaf
salt and freshly ground black pepper, to taste
red pepper flakes, to taste
8 mussels
8 small clams, Little Necks or Cherrystones
8 large shrimps, peeled and deveined
¾ pound bay scallops
1 cup chopped Italian parsley

1. Heat the oil in a large soup kettle. Add the onions, peppers and garlic and cook over low heat, covered, until vegetables are tender, about 25 minutes.

2. Add fish stock, Zinfandel and tomatoes and raise the heat.

3. Stir in the basil, thyme and bay leaf, and season to taste with salt, pepper and red pepper flakes.

4. Bring the soup to a boil, reduce heat and simmer, partially covered, for 30 minutes. Stir occasionally, crushing the tomatoes with the stirring spoon. Taste and correct seasoning. (If you wish to complete the soup

through this step the day before serving, it will keep and improve upon refrigeration.)

5. Scrub the mussels and clams well and debeard the mussels. Place them in the bottom of a heavy kettle, add an inch of water, cover, and set over high heat. As they steam open, remove them one by one with a slotted spoon and reserve. Rinse the shrimps and scallops and pat dry. Freeze the shellfish juices for your next batch of fish stock.

6. At 5 minutes before serving the stew, bring the tomato and wine mixture to a boil. Drop in shrimps and scallops, then clams and mussels in their shells. Add the parsley, stir well, and remove from heat. Let stand, covered, for 1 minute.

7. Ladle the stew into heated bowls, dividing the seafood equally, and serve immediately.

4 to 6 portions

"It breathes reassurance, it offers consolation; after a weary day it promotes sociability . . . There is nothing like a bowl of hot soup, its wisp of aromatic steam teasing the nostrils into quivering anticipation."

— *The Soup Book,*
Louis P. DeGouy, 1949

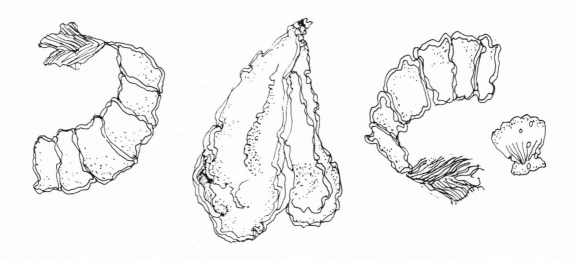

MANHATTAN CLAM CHOWDER

This saloon and steakhouse favorite is scorned by chowder enthusiasts of the New England school, and in truth it often seems to be no more than a dreary vegetable soup into which some tired clams have accidentally fallen.

We hope this recipe will rescue a tarnished reputation. Made with an abundance of fresh clams, a minimum of vegetables and — in true saloon fashion — a hearty chicken stock, it is a chowder to please the palate and fortify the spirit of even the most discerning New Englander.

4 tablespoons sweet butter
2 cups finely chopped yellow onions
1 cup chopped celery
5 cups Chicken Stock (see page 587)
1½ teaspoons thyme
1 bay leaf
salt and freshly ground black pepper, to taste
1 can (2 pounds, 3 ounces) peeled Italian plum tomatoes, drained and finely chopped
1 cup chopped Italian parsley
2 medium-size boiling potatoes, peeled and diced
3 dozen small clams, Cherrystones or Little Necks
grated orange zest (optional garnish)

1. Melt the butter in a large pot. Add onions and celery and cook over low heat, covered, until vegetables are tender and lightly colored, about 25 minutes.

2. Add remaining ingredients except clams and orange zest and simmer, partially covered, for 30 minutes, or until potatoes are very tender.

3. Meanwhile, scrub the clams well, place them in a pot with an inch of water, cover, and steam them until they open. Remove clams with a slotted spoon and reserve. When all the clams are opened, remove them from their shells. Reserve the clam juices and freeze them for your next batch of fish stock.

4. Taste the soup and correct seasoning. Just before serving, add the clams, simmer for 1 minute to heat through, and ladle into warmed soup bowls. Garnish with orange zest, if desired, and serve immediately.

6 to 8 portions

SCALLOP BISQUE

This soup is thickened in the classic French manner with flour, eggs and cream. Serve it as a first course of an elegant dinner, accompanied by a good white Burgundy or Chardonnay.

7 tablespoons sweet butter
1 cup leeks, white part only, well cleaned and thinly sliced
½ pound mushroom caps, wiped with a damp cloth and thinly sliced
⅓ cup chopped Italian parsley
salt and freshly ground black pepper, to taste
4 cups Fish Stock (see page 588)
1 pound bay scallops, rinsed and patted dry
¼ cup flour
2 eggs
1 cup heavy cream
¾ cup canned crushed tomatoes
⅓ cup dry sherry wine
fresh chives (garnish)

1. Melt 3 tablespoons of the butter in a 4-quart soup pot. Add the leeks and cook over low heat, covered, for 20 minutes.

2. Add mushrooms and cook gently for 5 minutes, or until they begin to render their juices. Add parsley, season with salt and pepper, and raise heat. Cook, stirring constantly, until mushroom juices have evaporated.

3. Add fish stock to the soup pot, bring to a boil, reduce heat and simmer, partially covered, for 15 minutes.

4. Remove from heat, add scallops and let stand, covered, for 1 minute. Pour the soup through a strainer set over a bowl, reserving both solids.

5. Transfer cooking stock to a small saucepan and bring to a boil.

6. Melt the remaining 4 tablespoons butter in the soup pot. Add the flour and cook over low heat for 5 minutes, stirring constantly. Do not allow the four mixture to brown.

7. Remove from heat and pour in the boiling soup stock all at once, beating constantly with a wire whisk. The mixture will bubble furiously and then subside.

8. Set the pot over medium heat and cook, stirring with the whisk, until the mixture has simmered for 5 minutes.

9. Thoroughly whisk the eggs and the cream together in a small bowl. Remove soup from the heat and slowly whisk 1 cup into the egg and cream mixture. Now whisk this mixture into the remainder of the soup.

10. Set the soup pot over low heat; stir in the crushed tomatoes and sherry. Cook, stirring constantly, until soup has thickened slightly, about 5 minutes. Do not allow the mixture to boil.

11. Add reserved scallop and leek-mushroom mixture and heat for another minute. Taste, correct seasoning, and ladle into warmed soup bowls. Garnish with fresh chives and serve immediately.

4 to 6 portions

"Of soup and love, the first is best."

— Spanish proverb

THE SAGA OF SOUP

French peasants living in the Middle Ages provided the first inspiration for soup as we enjoy it today. Without eating utensils, the peasants were inclined to sop up stewed meat juices with bread. For hundreds of years the evening meal in France was known as *la soupe*. The discovery of soup by the aristocracy was slow, and it wasn't until Louis XIV that soup began to take a more elegant turn. As Louis mistrusted everyone, all of his food had to be tasted. By the time the soup course got to the King, it was inevitably lukewarm or cold. In his inimitable fashion, Louis then deemed that only cold soups be served and thus the wonderful idea of cold soup was born.

CHILLED SHRIMP AND CUCUMBER SOUP

This cool, beautiful soup requires almost no cooking, is ready in minutes, and is light but filling — a perfect summer soup. Other fresh herbs such as parsley and mint can be substituted for the dill.

*2 large cucumbers (about 2 pounds), peeled and
  coarsely chopped
¼ cup red wine vinegar
1 tablespoon granulated sugar
1 teaspoon salt
1 pound raw shrimp, the smallest you can find,
  peeled and deveined
2 tablespoons sweet butter
¼ cup dry white vermouth
salt and freshly ground black pepper, to taste
1½ cups buttermilk, chilled
¾ cup chopped fresh dill (or more to taste),
  plus additional dill for garnish*

1. Toss chopped cucumbers with the vinegar, sugar and 1 teaspoon salt and let stand for 30 minutes.

2. Rinse the shrimp and pat them dry. Melt the butter in a small skillet. Add shrimp, raise the heat, and toss until they turn pink, 2 to 3 minutes. Remove them with a slotted spoon and reserve.

3. Add vermouth to the skillet and boil until it is reduced to a few spoonfuls. Pour over the shrimp and season them with the salt and pepper.

4. Drain the cucumbers and transfer them to the bowl of a food processor fitted with a steel blade. Process briefly, then add the buttermilk and continue to process until smooth. Add fresh dill to taste and process briefly, about 1 second.

5. Pour the soup into a bowl, add the shrimp and their liquid, and refrigerate, covered, until very cold. Garnish with additional chopped dill and serve in chilled bowls.

4 to 6 portions

SUMMER SOUPS

Soups provide welcome refreshment on hot summer nights. Cool soups are among the many joys of summertime entertaining. Fruits and vegetables are at their best, fragrant and tender with colors that dazzle. Pretty, elegant and light soups brighten menus, whether served indoors or out. We love them creatively garnished with fruits, vegetables or flowers, or maybe just a dollop of cream.

BORSCHT

This classic cold soup can begin a many-course European family meal or serve as a cooling luncheon main course year-round.

6 medium-size beets, peeled
10 cups cold water
juice of 3 medium-size lemons
3 tablespoons granulated sugar
2 teaspoons salt
3 eggs
1 cup milk
1 cup dairy sour cream (garnish)
1 cucumber, peeled, seeded and diced (garnish)

1. Cut beets into halves. Place them in a soup pot with the 10 cups cold water and bring to a boil. Reduce heat and simmer partially covered until beets are tender, 30 to 40 minutes. Skim foam from cooking liquid as necessary.

2. Remove beets from cooking liquid with a slotted spoon and cool to room temperature. Grate the beets and return them to their cooking liquid, along with the lemon juice, sugar and salt.

3. Return to the stove and simmer for 15 minutes. Remove from heat and let soup cool for 15 minutes.

4. Beat eggs and milk together in a bowl. Gradually whisk 3 cups of the warm borscht into the eggs and milk. Pour this mixture slowly back into the remaining borscht.

5. Cover the soup and refrigerate until very cold. Taste and correct seasoning; the soup should be nicely balanced between sweet and sour.

6. Ladle into chilled soup bowls. Garnish with sour cream and diced cucumber and serve immediately.

8 or more portions

GAZPACHO

We like to ladle gazpacho into chilled heavy mugs as a sippable summer first course while the steaks are grilling. Garnish each portion with a crisp fresh scallion.

6 large ripe tomatoes
2 sweet red peppers
2 medium-size yellow onions
2 large shallots
2 large cucumbers
½ cup red wine vinegar
½ cup olive oil
1½ cups canned tomato juice
3 eggs, lightly beaten
pinch of cayenne pepper
salt and freshly ground black pepper, to taste
½ cup chopped fresh dill

1. Wash and prepare the vegetables. Core and coarsely chop tomatoes; save the juice. Core, seed and coarsely chop peppers. Peel and coarsely chop onions and shallots. Peel, seed, and coarsely chop cucumbers.

2. In a bowl whisk together vinegar, olive oil, reserved tomato juice, canned tomato juice and eggs.

3. In a blender or a food processor fitted with a steel blade, purée the vegetables in small batches, adding tomato-juice mixture as necessary to keep blades from clogging. Do not purée completely; the gazpacho should retain some of its crunch.

4. Stir in cayenne, salt and pepper to taste, and dill. Cover and chill for at least 4 hours.

5. To serve, stir, taste and correct seasoning, and ladle into chilled soup bowls or mugs.

8 to 10 portions

GAZPACHO COOLER

Pour 4 ounces (½ cup) of Gazpacho and 6 ounces of Perrier (or other sparkling) water into a chilled glass and stir. Add ice cubes and garnish with a slice of cucumber.

GREEK LEMON SOUP

This soup is proof that less is more. A pot of *avgolemono* can be ready in about 30 minutes, and for only pennies. While it's delicious hot, it's even better cold, so plan to make it the day before you need it. Serve it in well-chilled bowls and float a paper-thin slice of lemon on top. Hot spinach-filled Phyllo Triangles (see pages 12-13) are a perfect accompaniment.

6 cups canned chicken broth
½ cup long-grain rice (not converted or instant)
3 egg yolks
¼ cup lemon juice
salt and freshly ground black pepper, to taste
sliced fresh lemon (garnish)
chopped fresh parsley (garnish)

1. Pour the broth into a pot and bring it gradually to a full boil. Pour in the rice, reduce to a simmer, and cover. Cook for about 25 minutes, or until rice is just tender. Do not overcook.

2. Meanwhile whisk the egg yolks and lemon juice together in a small bowl until well combined.

3. When rice is done, remove soup from the heat and ladle 2 cups of hot broth into the egg and lemon mixture. Whisk this mixture back into the remaining soup.

4. Return the soup to medium heat and cook, stirring constantly, until soup is just steaming. Do not let it reach a boil.

5. Season to taste and serve immediately, or remove from heat, cool to room temperature, cover and refrigerate. Correct seasoning just before serving. Garnish hot or cold with lemon slices and chopped parsley.

4 to 6 portions

SORREL SOUP

Sorrel grows in our garden; we love its sour taste and can never get enough. This summery soup is a snap to throw together in the spare minutes of a busy weekend; it makes a perfect lunch or snack when cold, and a dressy first course when hot.

½ pound (2 sticks) sweet butter
2 large yellow onions, peeled and thinly sliced
4 garlic cloves, peeled and chopped
10 cups tightly packed fresh sorrel leaves, washed and
    stems removed
4 cups Chicken Stock (see page 587)
¾ cup chopped Italian parsley
1 teaspoon salt
1 teaspoon freshly ground black pepper
2 teaspoons ground nutmeg
pinch of cayenne pepper
1 cup dairy sour cream (garnish)
snipped fresh chives (garnish)

1. Melt the butter in a soup pot. Add onions and garlic and cook, covered, over medium heat until tender and lightly colored, about 15 minutes.

2. Add the sorrel, cover, and cook until it is completely wilted, about 5 minutes.

3. Add stock, parsley, salt, pepper, nutmeg and cayenne, and bring to a boil. Reduce heat, cover, and simmer for 50 minutes.

4. Transfer soup to a blender or to the bowl of a food processor fitted with a steel blade. Purée until smooth.

5. If serving soup hot, return to soup pot, taste and correct seasoning, and heat and stir over low heat until steaming.

6. If serving cold, transfer to a bowl, cool, cover, and refrigerate for at least 4 hours. Taste and correct seasoning before serving.

7. In either case, ladle into bowls and garnish with sour cream and chives before serving.

6 portions

SORREL

There are many varieties of sorrel; all are tart and lemony. Sorrel can be added to soup wherever you want a touch of sourness and a hint of tender green color.

Sourness of sorrel varies, making exact quantities difficult to give. The taste can become overwhelming, so we recommend adding sorrel slowly and tasting as you go.

If your produce man doesn't stock sorrel, beg him to do so, or plant your own (seeds are available from many catalogs). Some cookbooks recommend that you substitute spinach if you cannot get sorrel, but there is really no similarity, and the substitution does disservice to them both.

Avoiding salt? A bit of chopped sorrel will disguise the fact that you've omitted it.

Other possibilities:

♥ Toss a few chopped leaves into coleslaw or other salads.
♥ Use in place of lettuce in a sandwich.
♥ Add a handful of chopped sorrel to any potato or cream soup.
♥ Drop leaves into boiling salted water for 1 minute; plunge into ice water, pat dry and purée. Freeze the purée for a taste of summer in the heart of winter. Or stir the purée into cream cheese and spread on a bagel; scramble into buttery eggs; stir into mayonnaise as a sauce for cold fish.

SOUP GARNISHES

The challenge is to provide a garnish that offers a clear but complementary contrast in taste, texture and color without overwhelming the soup itself. In general the more complex the soup, the simpler the garnish and vice versa. Fresh herbs, pasta, a sprinkling of vegetables or grated cheese, fruits, cream, liquor, floating flowers, or fish or meat — all should complement, not complicate, the balanced flavors already developed in the soup.

94

SWEET BLACK CHERRY SOUP

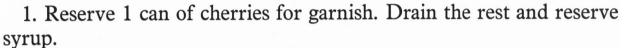

7 cans, about 9 ounces each, pitted sweet dark cherries
grated zest of 1 medium-size orange
4 teaspoons fresh lemon juice
3 tablespoons Grand Marnier
1 teaspoon salt
1 cup Crème Fraîche (see page 582)

1. Reserve 1 can of cherries for garnish. Drain the rest and reserve syrup.

2. In a food processor fitted with a steel blade, purée cherries until fine, about 30 seconds. Remove to a bowl.

3. Add 1½ cups of the reserved cherry syrup, the orange zest, lemon juice, Grand Marnier and salt. Whisk in ½ cup *crème fraîche*; save remaining *crème fraîche* for garnish. Chill until serving time.

4. Drain remaining can of cherries and divide cherries equally among 6 decorative bowls. Cherries may be cut into halves. Ladle soup into bowls and garnish with some *crème fraîche* on each serving. The whole or halved cherries will float to the top.

6 portions

SUMMER TOMATO AND MELON SOUP

3 cups peeled and seeded ripe tomatoes
2 medium-size ripe cantaloupes, seeds and rind removed
2 large cucumbers, peeled and seeded (reserve ½ cucumber and chop for garnish)
grated zest of 1 small orange
¼ cup finely chopped fresh mint, plus additional fresh mint as garnish
1 cup dairy sour cream or Crème Fraîche (see page 582)

1. Combine tomatoes, melons and cucumbers in a blender or food processor fitted with a steel blade. Process until smooth. Transfer to a bowl.

2. Stir in orange zest and ¼ cup mint. Whisk in sour cream or *crème fraîche* and chill.

3. To serve, ladle into bowls and garnish with a bit of chopped cucumber and a sprig of mint.

6 to 8 portions

CREAM OF MANGO SOUP

2 eggs, well beaten
¼ cup granulated sugar
1 tablespoon vanilla extract
juice and grated rind of 1 lemon
1 ripe mango, peeled, pitted, coarsely chopped
2 cups heavy cream
3 cups milk
blueberries and coarsely chopped strawberries (garnish)

1. Combine eggs, sugar, vanilla, lemon juice and rind, and coarsely chopped mango in a food processor fitted with a steel blade, and process until smooth.

2. Whisk cream and milk together in a large bowl until frothy. Slowly add mango mixture, whisking constantly.

3. Cover and chill well.

4. To serve, stir, ladle into chilled bowls and garnish each serving with fresh blueberries and coarsely chopped strawberries.

6 portions

**FOURTH OF
JULY PICNIC**

Blueberry Soup

---

*Shrimp and Grape Salad
with Dill*

*Raspberry-Marinated
Carrots*

Pumpernickel Bread

Lime Mousse

Brownies

BLUEBERRY SOUP

Serve this chilled fruit soup as a summertime first course, dessert, or by itself for lunch. Blissfully cool and light.

5 cups fresh blueberries, plus additional berries for garnish
4 cups water
4 whole cloves
2-inch piece of cinnamon stick
⅔ cup honey
juice of 1 lemon
3 tablespoons Crème de Cassis (black currant liqueur)
1 tablespoon blueberry vinegar
plain yogurt (garnish)
grated fresh orange rind (garnish)

1. Rinse the blueberries and remove any stems, leaves or green berries.
2. Put berries in a kettle and add the water, cloves and cinnamon stick. Set over moderate heat and bring to a boil. Stir in honey, reduce heat and simmer, partially covered, until berries are very tender, about 15 minutes.
3. Remove from heat and cool to room temperature. Force the soup through a strainer or through the medium blade of a food mill. Stir in lemon juice, Crème de Cassis and vinegar. Cover and refrigerate for at least 6 hours.
4. Serve in chilled bowls, garnished with a few whole blueberries, a dollop of plain yogurt and a sprinkle of grated orange rind.
6 portions

SUNDAY NIGHT SOUPS

There's something about those final moments of preparing for the week ahead that calls for the comfort of a Sunday night soup supper. A soup meal — crusty warm bread, a cheese board, green salad, dessert mousse and, of course, your own *soupe du jour* — can be enjoyed in front of a roaring fire or a candlelit table, and will make the transition from the weekend to the work week a little easier to swallow.

"Only the pure of heart can make a good soup."
— Ludwig van Beethoven

WINTER BORSCHT

Make this the day before, if you can, and let it improve in the refrigerator overnight.

2 pounds fresh beets, peeled and grated
1 meaty beef shin, cut into 5 pieces
1 tablespoon salt
3 cups chopped tomatoes
2 cups coarsely chopped yellow onions
1 medium-size cabbage, shredded
1 carrot, peeled and cut into small dice
1 bunch of fresh dill, chopped (reserve a bit for garnish)
salt and freshly ground black pepper, to taste
2 cups dairy sour cream (garnish)

1. Put beets in a soup pot and add cold water to cover. Set over medium heat, bring to a boil, reduce heat and simmer, partially covered, until beets are tender, about 20 minutes. Skim off any scum that may form. When beets are done, reserve them and their cooking liquid.

2. Put beef shin in another large pot. Cover with cold water, add 1 tablespoon salt, and set over medium heat. Bring to a boil, reduce heat and simmer, uncovered, for 1½ hours, until tender. Skim off any scum that may form, and add additional water as the cooking liquid evaporates.

3. Add the tomatoes, onion, cabbage, carrot and dill to the beef; simmer, partially covered, for 30 minutes.

4. Add reserved beets and their cooking liquid and simmer, partially covered, for another 20 minutes. Remove from heat and cool slightly.

5. Lift the pieces of shin from the soup pot. Remove meaty bits clinging to the bone and return meat to pot. Season soup to taste with salt and pepper.

6. Return to medium heat and simmer for 5 minutes. Serve immediately, garnished with sour cream and fresh dill.

10 to 12 portions

POTATO-CHEESE SOUP

A hearty soup with year-round potential. Serve it for lunch or as a light supper, garnished with pumpernickel croutons.

4 tablespoons sweet butter
2 cups finely chopped yellow onions
2 cups peeled and chopped carrots
6 parsley sprigs
5 cups Chicken Stock (see page 587)
2 large potatoes, about 1½ pounds, peeled and cubed (3 to 4 cups)
¼ cup chopped fresh dill
salt and freshly ground black pepper, to taste
2 to 3 cups grated good-quality Cheddar cheese

1. Melt the butter in a soup pot. Add onions and carrots and cook over low heat, covered, until vegetables are tender and lightly colored, about 25 minutes.

2. Add parsley, stock and potatoes, and bring to a boil. Reduce heat, cover, and simmer until potatoes are very tender, about 30 minutes.

3. Add dill, remove soup from the heat, and let it stand, covered, for 5 minutes.

4. Pour soup through a strainer and transfer the solids to the bowl of a food processor fitted with a steel blade, or use a food mill fitted with a medium blade. Add 1 cup of the cooking stock and process until smooth.

5. Return puréed soup to the pot and add additional cooking liquid, about 3 to 4 cups, until the soup reaches the desired consistency.

6. Set over low heat, add salt and pepper to taste, and gradually stir in the grated cheese. When all the cheese is incorporated and the soup is hot (not boiling), serve immediately.

About 6 portions

CROUTONS

Sometimes the simplest garnish is the best. A crisp crouton, made of good-quality bread and well toasted or sautéed, can make or break a soup (or salad).

Cut the bread into ½-inch cubes and spread on a baking sheet. Toast in a 400°F. oven, stirring occasionally, until crisp and brown, 10 to 15 minutes.

Or, melt butter in a large skillet. Sauté a bit of garlic in the butter first if appropriate, add the bread cubes, and sauté over medium heat, stirring and tossing the cubes until golden brown. Transfer croutons to paper towels and drain before using.

BRIDGE AND POKER SANDWICHES

The dramatic decisions that make up any good card game will sooner or later result in giant appetites, whoever is holding the aces. No one wants to spend too much time away from a winning streak, but everyone wants to eat. We suggest you make it hearty, a bit gooey, and delicious, so no one loses. (Recipes for italicized ingredients can be found in Index.)

♥ Put *Ratatouille* and Italian hot sausage on French bread.

♥ Layer freshly sliced mushrooms, meat loaf and *Tomato-Basil Mayonnaise* on pumpernickel.

♥ Combine roast turkey with guacamole on black bread.

♥ Try roast *Filet of Beef*, tomato, cucumber with chives, prepared horseradish and sour cream on white bread.

♥ Layer prosciutto and Provolone cheese on Italian bread sliced lengthwise. Spread with *Pesto Mayonnaise* and broil open faced until hot and bubbly.

♥ Spread crunchy celery rémoulade on rye bread; top with thin-sliced corned beef and even thinner slices of Swiss cheese. Run under the broiler until hot and bubbly.

♥ Combine Black Forest ham, ripe Brie cheese and your favorite mustard on *Raisin Pumpernickel Bread*.

Butter outside and grill in hot skillet.

♥ Mix crunchy-cooked broccoli, scallions and toasted cashews with *Sesame Mayonnaise*. Spread on English muffins, sprinkle with grated Parmesan cheese, and broil until hot and bubbly.

♥ Layer turkey breast, avocado and jalapeño-Jack cheese between slices of sourdough bread. Butter outside and grill sandwich in hot skillet.

♥ Spread rye bread with mayonnaise, make layers of sliced onion, avocado, tomato, mild green chilies, and 2 strips of bacon. Top with Cheddar cheese and broil until cheese is hot and bubbly.

BEEF AND RED WINE BROTH

Perfect in a thermos at a football game or on a winter hike.

4 tablespoons sweet butter
1½ cups chopped yellow onions
2 carrots, peeled and chopped
1 parsnip, peeled and chopped
8 to 10 garlic cloves (about half of a small head), peeled and chopped
¾ cup chopped fresh Italian parsley
5 cups Beef Stock (see page 586), or a combination of beef and chicken stocks
1 cup dry red wine
salt and freshly ground black pepper, to taste
1 cup small pasta (shells, orzo, etc.)
grated imported Parmesan cheese (optional)

1. Melt the butter in a soup pot. Add onions, carrots, parsnip and chopped garlic and cook, covered, over low heat until vegetables are tender and lightly colored, about 25 minutes.

2. Add chopped parsley, beef stock and wine and season with salt and pepper. Set over moderate heat, bring to a boil, reduce heat and simmer, partially covered, for 20 minutes.

3. Meanwhile, bring a quart of salted water to a boil, drop in the pasta, and cook until tender. Drain and reserve.

4. Pour the soup through a strainer and discard the solids. Return the broth to the pot, add the cooked pasta and simmer, partially covered, for 10 minutes. Serve immediately, sprinkled with grated Parmesan if you like.

4 to 6 portions

BLUE CHEESE SOUP WITH BACON

A hearty first course or luncheon main dish.

6 tablespoons sweet butter
2 cups chopped yellow onions
1 leek, white part only, well cleaned and finely sliced
3 celery ribs, chopped
3 carrots, peeled and chopped
1 medium-size potato, peeled and diced
1 cup dry white wine or dry vermouth
3 cups Chicken Stock (see page 587)
½ to ¾ pound imported Roquefort or other blue cheese
salt and freshly ground black pepper, to taste
6 to 8 bacon strips, sautéed crisp and crumbled (garnish)

1. Melt the butter in a kettle. Add the onions, leek, celery, and carrots and cook, covered, over low heat until vegetables are tender and lightly colored, about 25 minutes.

2. Add the potato, white wine, and stock, bring to a boil, reduce heat, and simmer, partially covered, until very tender, another 20 minutes or so.

3. Remove soup from heat and crumble in ½ pound of the cheese. Stir until cheese has melted into the soup, then pour the soup through a strainer, reserving the liquid. Transfer the solids to the bowl of a food processor fitted with a steel blade, or use a food mill fitted with a medium disc. Add 1 cup of the cooking stock and process until smooth.

4. Return the soup to the kettle, pour in the rest of the liquid, and set over medium heat. When soup is simmering, taste and correct seasoning; you may want to add a little more cheese, and the soup may need salt and pepper.

5. Ladle into bowls, garnish with bacon crumbles, and serve immediately.

4 to 6 portions

" 'It's a comforting sort of thing to have,' said Christopher Robin."
— *House at Pooh Corner*, A.A. Milne

BASQUE RICE AND PEPPER SOUP

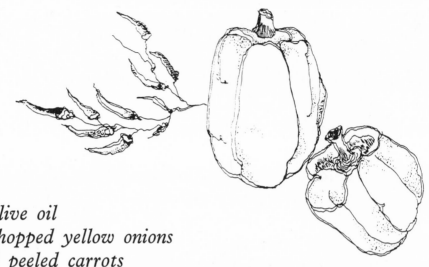

6 tablespoons olive oil
3 cups finely chopped yellow onions
2 cups chopped peeled carrots
6 garlic cloves, peeled and chopped
7 cups Beef Stock (see page 586)
½ cup uncooked rice (not converted or instant)
½ cup medium-dry sherry wine
2 red and 2 green peppers, stemmed, cored and cut into julienne
salt and freshly ground black pepper, to taste

1. Heat the olive oil in a soup pot. Add onions, carrots and garlic and cook, covered, over low heat until vegetables are tender and lightly colored, about 25 minutes; stir occasionally.

2. Uncover, add beef stock, raise the heat, and bring to a boil. Reduce heat, cover, and simmer for about 20 minutes.

3. Pour the soup through a strainer, pressing hard with the back of a spoon to extract as much flavor as possible. Discard the solids and return the broth to the pot. Add rice, sherry, peppers and salt and pepper to taste. Simmer, partially covered, for about 25 minutes, or until rice is tender.

4. Taste, correct seasoning, and serve immediately.

4 to 6 portions

CURRIED CREAM OF CHICKEN SOUP

6 tablespoons sweet butter
2 cups finely chopped yellow onions
2 carrots, peeled and chopped
2 tablespoons curry powder, or more to taste
5 cups Chicken Stock (see page 587)
6 parsley sprigs
1 chicken, 2½ to 3 pounds, quartered
½ cup long-grain rice (not converted or instant)
salt and freshly ground black pepper, to taste
1 cup half-and-half
10 ounces frozen peas, defrosted

1. Melt the butter in a pot. Add onions, carrots and curry powder and cook over low heat, covered, until vegetables are tender, about 25 minutes; stir occasionally.

2. Add the stock, parsley, chicken and rice. Bring soup to a boil, reduce heat, and cover. Cook at a simmer until chicken is done, 25 to 30 minutes.

3. Cool chicken in the stock. Remove the meat from the bones and dice it; reserve the meat.

4. Pour the soup through a strainer and transfer the solids to the bowl of a food processor fitted with a steel blade, or use a food mill fitted with a medium disc. Add 1 cup of the cooking liquid and process until smooth. Reserve the rest of the liquid.

5. Return puréed soup to the pot and add the half-and-half. Stir in additional cooking stock, about 4 cups, until soup reaches the desired consistency.

6. Add reserved diced chicken and defrosted peas and simmer the soup for 15 minutes, or until peas are done. Season to taste with salt and pepper, and serve immediately.

4 to 6 portions

To take the chill out of an afternoon of cross-country or downhill skiing, it's best to plan ahead and take a thermos of soup along with you. A picnic in the snow will give you a second burst of energy to make the most of a winter afternoon.

"*Bouquet Garni:* a small bundle of herbs, as thyme, parsley, bay leaf and the like, often tied in a cheesecloth bag and used for flavoring soups, stews, etc."
— *The Random House Dictionary of the English Language*

PEASANT VEGETABLE SOUP

Serve this as a fall or winter supper, accompanied by hearty bread, and follow with a green salad and a fruit dessert. Accompany with a glass of Beaujolais or another uncomplicated wine, or a mug of cold dark beer. It tastes even better if made the day before you plan to serve it.

1½ cups dried white beans (Great Northern, etc.)
4 tablespoons bacon fat or lightly salted butter
1 cup finely chopped yellow onions
3 leeks, white part only, thoroughly cleaned and thinly sliced
2 celery ribs, cleaned and coarsely chopped
3 carrots, peeled and chopped
1 teaspoon dried thyme
1 bay leaf
8 cups Chicken Stock or Beef Stock (see Index for recipes),
* or a combination of the two*
3 parsnips, peeled and chopped
1 ham hock
½ small white cabbage, shredded (about 2 cups)
4 garlic cloves, peeled and chopped
½ cup chopped Italian parsley
salt and freshly ground black pepper, to taste

1. Sort through the beans and discard any pebbles you may find. Soak the beans overnight in water that covers them by 3 inches.

2. Melt the bacon fat or butter in a heavy soup pot. Add onions, leeks, celery and carrots and cook, covered, over low heat until vegetables are tender and lightly colored, about 25 minutes, stirring occasionally.

3. Stir in the thyme, bay leaf and a grinding of black pepper, and pour in the stock. Add parsnips, ham hock and soaked beans, and bring the soup to a boil. Reduce heat and simmer, partially covered, until beans are tender, about 40 minutes. Remove ham hock and allow it to cool slightly. Cut the meat off the bone, cut it into chunks, and return meat to the pot.

4. Add cabbage, garlic and parsley, and simmer for another 5 to 10 minutes. Taste, correct seasoning (add salt at this point if soup needs it), and serve immediately.

8 to 10 portions

PASTA PERFECT

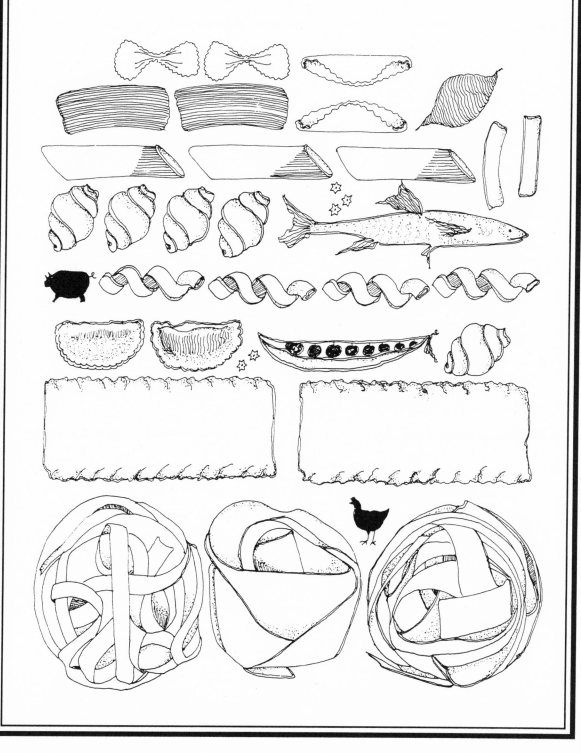

PIPING HOT PASTA

Not even the Italians know how many shapes pasta comes in. They have long considered it among their works of art, and the celebration of color and shape that seems to dominate Italian life is found in their pasta as well.

Thomas Jefferson first imported the pasta machine to America, just at the time that Yankee Doodle was calling the feather in his cap "Macaroni." Even then pasta was an Italian staple, although well-traveled Englishmen had long since made it a favorite "exotic" food back in London.

PASTA GLOSSARY

AGNOLOTTI: "Priests' caps"; these are crescent-shaped, meat-filled ravioli.
ANELLINI: The tiniest pasta rings.
BAVETTINE: Narrow linguine.
BUCATINI: Short, straight macaroni.
CANNELLONI: Large, round tubes for stuffing.
CAPELLI D'ANGELO: "Angel's hair," the finest of all pasta.
CAPELVENERE: Fine noodles.
CAPPELLETTI: Stuffed "hats."
CAPPELLI DI PAGLIACCIO: "Clowns' hats."
CAVATELLI: Short, crinkle-edged shells.
CONCHIGLIE: "Conch shells."
CORALLI: Small tubes for soup.
CRESTE DI GALLI: "Cockscombs."
DITALI: "Thimbles"; short macaroni.
FARFALLE: "Butterflies"; bows.
FARFALLONI: "Big butterflies" or bows.
FEDELINI: "Little faithful ones"; very fine rods of spaghetti.
FETTUCCE: "Ribbons"; widest of the fettuccine family.
FETTUCCINE: "Narrow ribbons" of egg noodle.

FUSILLI: "Little springs"; spindles or spirals.

LANCETTE: "Little spears."

LASAGNE: Extra broad noodles, about 2 inches wide; smooth or ripple-edged.

LINGUE DI PASSERI: "Sparrows' tongues."

LINGUINE: "Little tongues"; thick, narrow ribbons.

LUMACHE: "Snails"; shell-shaped.

MACCHERONI: Macaroni of all types; hollow or pierced.

MACCHERONI ALLA CHITARRA: Also called *tonnarelli;* noodles cut with the steel wires of a special guitarlike tool.

MAFALDA: Broad noodle, rippled on both sides; wider than fettuccine.

MAGLIETTE: "Links"; slightly curved, short lengths of hollow pasta.

MALTAGLIATI: Irregularly cut shapes.

MANICOTTI: "Muffs"; giant tubes for stuffing.

MARGHERITA: "Daisies"; narrow noodles, rippled on one side.

MARUZZE: "Seashells."

MEZZANI: Short, cut, curved macaroni.

MOSTACCIOLI: "Little moustaches."

OCCHI DI LUPO: "Wolf's eyes"; large tubes.

OCCHI DI PASSERI: "Sparrows' eyes"; tiny circles.

ORECCHIETTE: "Little ears."

ORZO: Rice-shaped or barley-shaped pasta.

PAPPARDELLE: Broad noodles, traditionally served with game sauces.

PASTA FRESCA: Fresh egg pasta.

PASTA VERDE: Green pasta, usually incorporating spinach in the dough.

PASTINA: "Tiny dough"; minute pasta shapes used in soup, many with charming names: *acini de pepe* ("peppercorns"); *alfabeto* ("alphabet"); *amorini* ("little cupids"); *arancini* ("little oranges"); *astri* ("little stars"); *avena* ("oats"); *crocette* ("little crosses"); *elefanti* ("elephants"); *funghini* ("little mushrooms"); *pulcini* ("little chickens"); *rosa marina* ("rose of the sea"); *rotini* ("little wheels"); *semi de mela* or *melone* ("apple or melon seeds"); *stellini* ("little stars"); *stivaletti* ("little boots").

PENNE: "Pens" or quills; tubes cut diagonally at both ends.

PERCIATELLI: Long thin hollow macaroni; looks like thick spaghetti.

PEZZOCCHERI: Thick, dark buckwheat noodles.

QUADRETTINI: Small flat squares.

RAVIOLI: Pasta squares filled with meat, cheese and/or vegetables.

RICCIOLINI: "Little curls."

RIGATONI: Large grooved macaroni.

ROTELLE: "Small wheels."

RUOTE: Spiked wheels with hubs.
SPAGHETTI: Variety of long thin rods, including *capellini* (very, very thin), *spaghettini* (thin), and *spaghettoni* (the thickest).
TAGLIATELLE: Family of egg noodles similar to *fettuccine*.
TORTELLINI: Small, stuffed pasta similar to *cappelletti*.
TRENETTE: A narrower, thicker version of *tagliatelle*.
TUBETTI: "Small tubes"; hollow.
VERMICELLI: Very fine spaghetti.
ZITI: "Bridegrooms"; slightly curved, large tubes.

SPAGHETTI WITH OIL AND GARLIC

Our favorite version of this pasta dish.

12 garlic cloves
¼ cup best-quality olive oil
4 quarts water
1½ tablespoons salt
1 pound spaghetti
1½ cups Chicken Stock (see page 587) or canned chicken broth
1 cup finely chopped Italian parsley
freshly ground black pepper (garnish)
grated imported Parmesan cheese (garnish)

1. Peel garlic cloves. Mince six of them and set aside. Slice remaining garlic.

2. Heat the oil in a small skillet. Add sliced garlic and cook over medium heat, stirring occasionally, until golden brown.

3. Bring 4 quarts water to a boil in a large pot. Stir in salt, add the spaghetti, and cook until tender but still firm; do not overcook. Drain pasta well and transfer to a pot.

4. Add the chicken broth to the pasta and simmer until most of the broth has been absorbed, 5 minutes or so.

5. Stir in the heated olive oil and sliced garlic, then the minced garlic and the chopped parsley. Toss thoroughly.

6. Divide pasta evenly among heated plates or shallow soup bowls. Pour any remaining broth over pasta, and serve immediately, accompanied by lots of freshly ground black pepper and grated Parmesan cheese.

6 first-course portions

TO COOK PASTA

Bring 4 quarts of water to a full boil. Add 2 table-spoons salt, stir, then drop in 1 pound pasta. Fresh pasta will be done in the time it takes the water to return to a full boil. Dried pasta will take longer, depending on the shape and size.

Pasta should not be over- or undercooked. The Italian expression *al dente* means the pasta is cooked just to the point that it is completely tender, yet still firm. Test by biting a strand.

Drain the pasta in a colander, sauce it, and serve immediately.

**FIREWORKS
PICNIC**

*Golden American caviar and
pumpernickel rolls*

*Crisp crudités with
Sesame Mayonnaise*

Sliced Filet of Beef

Minty Cucumber Salad

Pasta Primavera Gregory

Assorted cheeses

---

*Miniature loaves of French
or black bread*

Dessert mousses

Assorted cookies

PASTA PRIMAVERA GREGORY

A light and lovely tangle of pasta and fresh vegetables. Serve pasta primavera as the first course or light main course of a spring dinner on the terrace. Feel free to substitute your favorite fresh vegetables and herbs in the appropriate quantities.

4 tablespoons salt, plus additional to taste
½ pound green fettuccine
½ pound regular egg fettuccine
⅓ cup best-quality olive oil
½ cup finely chopped purple onion
¾ pound snow peas
⅓ pound sugar snap peas
¾ pound sliced prosciutto, cut into coarse julienne
2 ripe plum tomatoes, quartered
2 sweet red peppers, stemmed, cored, cut into fine julienne
8 scallions (green onions), cleaned, trimmed, cut diagonally
   into ½-inch pieces
½ cup snipped chives, basil or other fresh herbs
freshly ground black pepper, to taste
4 tablespoons raspberry vinegar
¼ cup grated imported Parmesan cheese
1 cup imported black olives (any kind)
grated zest of 1 orange, 1 lemon or 1 lime

1. Bring 4 quarts water to a boil in a large pot. Add 2 tablespoons salt and stir in the fettuccine. Cook until tender but still firm, and drain immediately. Transfer the pasta to a large mixing bowl, add the olive oil and chopped onion, and toss gently to combine. Set aside to cool to room temperature.

2. Bring another 4 quarts water to a boil. Add 2 tablespoons salt, the snow peas and sugar snap peas. Cook for 1 minute, drain, and plunge peas immediately into a large bowl of ice water. Let stand for 10 minutes. Drain peas and pat thoroughly dry.

3. Add peas to the pasta in the mixing bowl along with the prosciutto, tomatoes, red pepper, scallions and chives or herbs to taste. Season with salt and pepper, sprinkle on raspberry vinegar to taste, and toss gently.

4. Toss the pasta primavera with the Parmesan, taste, and correct seasoning. Arrange pasta on a serving platter. Scatter olives and citrus zest over the pasta and serve at room temperature.

6 portions

THE SPICE OF LIFE

Pepper, once available only to the rich, is now so widely used that it is impossible to imagine cooking without it. Paradoxically, the lively flavor that made it indispensable in peasant cooking has prompted its discovery by the chefs of the *nouvelle cuisine* as a special seasoning on its own.

This renewed interest has led to the emergence of several "new" peppers that enlarge the seasoning possibilities available to us. Black peppercorns are of course easily located at the supermarket. The others, a bit more exotic, can be found in specialty food stores and spice shops. White pepper will be found dried, while pink and green will come packed in water or vinegar as well. We prefer dried or water-packed peppers; if a recipe calls for vinegar in conjunction with the peppercorns, you can always marinate your own peppers in the vinegar of your choice.

Pepper loses its vitality soon after it is ground. Invest in a good peppermill (it will last a lifetime) and grind your own.

PASTA SAUCE RAPHAEL

Serve this spicy tomato-and-artichoke sauce over tortellini. We like it cold as well as hot, and often recommend it for picnics.

4 pounds ripe meaty tomatoes
2 jars (6 ounces each) marinated artichoke hearts
½ cup best-quality olive oil
2 cups coarsely chopped yellow onions
4 garlic cloves, peeled and finely chopped
¼ cup dried basil
½ tablespoon dried oregano
½ cup finely chopped Italian parsley
1 small dried red pepper, finely crushed
3 tablespoons whole black peppercorns
1 teaspoon salt
¼ cup grated imported Romano cheese

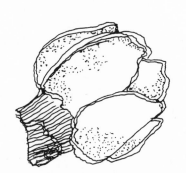

1. Bring a large pot of salted water to a boil. Drop tomatoes, a few at a time, into the boiling water. Scald for 10 seconds, then with a slotted spoon transfer to a bowl of ice water. Scald all tomatoes in this fashion, then drain and slip off skins. Cut crosswise into halves, squeeze out seeds and juice, and chop coarsely. Reserve.

2. Drain artichokes and reserve marinade.

3. Heat olive oil in a large saucepan and sauté onions, garlic, basil, oregano, parsley and dried red pepper over medium heat for 5 minutes.

4. Crush the black peppercorns and add them to the onion mixture.

5. Add tomatoes to the sauce, season with about 1 teaspoon salt, and simmer uncovered over medium heat for 1 hour.

6. Add reserved artichoke marinade and simmer, stirring often, for another 30 minutes.

7. Stir in artichokes and continue to simmer until sauce is rich and thick, another 20 minutes or so. Stir in Romano cheese, taste and adjust seasoning, and serve over your favorite pasta. (If serving pasta Raphael cold, toss with sauce and cool to room temperature.)

Enough sauce for at least 4 pounds pasta

PASTA WITH SAUSAGE AND PEPPERS

Everyone should have a hearty pasta sauce like this one in his repertoire. A printed recipe for a dish this casual may seem superfluous to those who throw such simmered sauce improvisations together on the spur of the moment. We think balance and harmony are as important here as anywhere else; however, you must feel free to change the herbs, omit the hot peppers, or increase the garlic as you see fit, in order to make the dish your own.

We like to serve this over short tubular pasta such as ziti or rigatoni. While it's perfectly delicous with the traditional sprinkling of grated Parmesan cheese, we suggest you try topping it with a dollop of fresh ricotta and a grinding of black pepper for a change of pace.

2 pounds sweet Italian sausage
3 tablespoons best-quality olive oil
1 cup finely chopped yellow onions
3 sweet red peppers, stemmed, ribs and seeds removed, cut into
   medium-size julienne
1 cup dry red wine
1 can (2 pounds, 3 ounces) Italian plum tomatoes, including the liquid
1 cup water
1 tablespoon dried oregano
1 teaspoon dried thyme
salt and freshly ground black pepper, to taste
dried red pepper flakes
1 teaspoon fennel seeds
½ cup chopped Italian parsley
6 (or more) garlic cloves, peeled and finely chopped

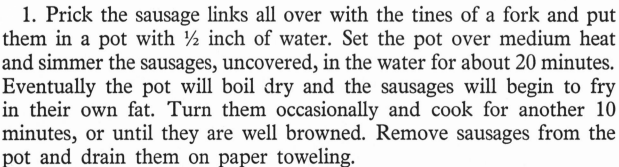

1. Prick the sausage links all over with the tines of a fork and put them in a pot with ½ inch of water. Set the pot over medium heat and simmer the sausages, uncovered, in the water for about 20 minutes. Eventually the pot will boil dry and the sausages will begin to fry in their own fat. Turn them occasionally and cook for another 10 minutes, or until they are well browned. Remove sausages from the pot and drain them on paper toweling.

2. Pour sausage fat out of the pot but do not wash pot. Set it over

low heat, add the olive oil and onions, and cook them, covered, until tender, about 25 minutes.

3. Add the peppers, raise the heat, and cook uncovered for another 5 minutes, stirring often.

4. Add the wine, tomatoes, water, oregano and thyme, and season to taste with salt, black pepper and red pepper flakes. Bring to a boil, reduce heat and simmer, partially covered, for 30 minutes.

5. Meanwhile, slice the sausages into ½-inch-thick rounds. When the sauce has simmered for 30 minutes, add sausages and fennel seeds and simmer, uncovered, for another 20 minutes.

6. Add parsley and chopped garlic and simmer for another 5 minutes.

2 quarts sauce, enough for about 2 pounds pasta

PASTA PUTTANESCA

It is not known whether the Italian ladies of the night (the *puttane*) who gave their name to this racy pasta sauce did so because they were short of time or cash or both. In any case, *puttanesca* is quick and cheap and we hope it offends no one's memory to say so.

This dish, with its zesty nuggets of garlic, capers, olives and anchovies, is not for the faint-hearted. Serve it to food-loving friends and pour an earthy red wine. With practice you can have this sauce ready to eat in 20 minutes.

1 pound spaghetti, linguine or other thin dried pasta
2 cans (2 pounds, 3 ounces each) peeled Italian plum tomatoes
¼ cup best-quality olive oil
1 teaspoon oregano
⅛ teaspoon dried red pepper flakes, or to taste
½ cup tiny black Niçoise olives
¼ cup drained capers
4 garlic cloves, peeled and chopped
8 anchovy fillets, coarsely chopped
½ cup chopped Italian parsley, plus additional for garnish
2 teaspoons salt

1. Bring 4 quarts water to a boil in a large pot. Add salt and stir in the spaghetti. Cook until tender but still firm. Drain immediately when done and transfer to 4 heated plates.

2. While spaghetti is cooking, drain the tomatoes, cut them crosswise into halves, and squeeze out as much liquid as possible.

3. Combine tomatoes and olive oil in a skillet and bring to a boil. Keep the sauce at a full boil and add remaining ingredients except pasta, one at a time, stirring frequently.

4. Reduce heat slightly and continue to cook for a few minutes, or until sauce has thickened to your liking. Serve immediately over hot pasta and garnish with additional chopped parsley.

4 main-course portions

"I'd rather have roses on my table than diamonds on my neck."

— **Emma Goldman**

✤ FROM THE SILVER PALATE NOTEBOOK

If fresh herbs are plentiful, use them in bouquets around the house; their dark green or gray leaves are beautiful with flowers.

Make an edible centerpiece of such herbs as basil, dill, and mint: wash fresh herbs, shake dry, and arrange with salad greens in a bowl of crushed ice.

CREAMY PASTA SAUCE
WITH FRESH HERBS

This delicate sauce is perfect over angel's-hair pasta.

1½ cups heavy cream
4 tablespoons sweet butter
½ teaspoon salt
⅛ teaspoon grated nutmeg
pinch of cayenne
¼ cup grated imported Parmesan cheese
1 cup finely chopped mixed fresh herbs (our favorite
   combination — basil, mint, watercress, Italian parsley
   and chives)

1. Combine cream, butter, salt, nutmeg and cayenne in a heavy saucepan and simmer for 15 minutes, or until sauce is slightly reduced and thickened.

2. Whisk in Parmesan and fresh herbs and simmer for another 5 minutes. Taste and correct seasoning. Serve immediately.

2 cups sauce, enough for 1 pound of angel's-hair pasta, 6 or more portions as a first course

PASTA CARBONARA

An authentic version of this classic dish would use Italian bacon *(pancetta)* or perhaps prosciutto. With a glass of rough red wine, it is one of the best late-night suppers we know. The use of American bacon can, however, transform *pasta carbonara* into something else altogether — a wonderful breakfast dish. However and whenever you serve this dish, it is hearty and satisfying.

1 pound thick-sliced bacon, diced
2 tablespoons salt
1 pound spaghetti or linguine
3 eggs
⅓ cup chopped Italian parsley
grated imported Parmesan cheese (optional)
freshly ground black pepper, to taste

1. Sauté the diced bacon in a small skillet until crisp. Remove with a slotted spoon and drain well on paper towels.
2. Bring 4 quarts water to a boil in a large kettle. Add 2 tablespoons salt and then drop in the spaghetti. Stir with a wooden spoon to separate strands and let water return to the boil. Cook until tender but not mushy, about 8 minutes, although cooking time will vary.
3. Meanwhile, beat the eggs thoroughly in a large bowl suitable for serving. Have the cooked bacon and the chopped parsley ready at hand.
4. When the pasta is done, drain it immediately in a colander, shaking briefly to eliminate excess water.
5. Pour drained hot spaghetti into the bowl of eggs and immediately begin tossing it. As the strands of pasta become coated with the beaten eggs, their heat will cook the eggs.
6. Sprinkle on bacon dice and chopped parsley, toss again, and serve immediately. Grated Parmesan is delicious (but optional at breakfast); freshly ground black pepper is essential.

4 to 6 portions

TORTELLINI WITH GORGONZOLA CREAM SAUCE

Here pungent Gorgonzola is mellowed by heavy cream in a sauce for tortellini. No additional grated cheese is required at the table, but provide your guests with a pepper mill.

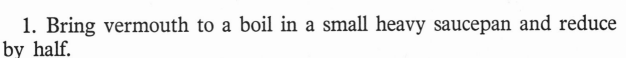

1½ cups dry white vermouth
2¼ cups heavy cream
freshly ground black pepper, to taste
big pinch of freshly grated nutmeg
2 tablespoons salt
1½ pounds fresh tortellini
¾ pound sweet Gorgonzola cheese, crumbled
1½ tablespoons grated imported Parmesan cheese

1. Bring vermouth to a boil in a small heavy saucepan and reduce by half.
2. Add heavy cream, bring to a boil, and lower heat to a simmer. Season to taste with freshly ground black pepper, add the nutmeg, and simmer uncovered for about 15 minutes or until reduced by one third.
3. Bring 6 quarts water to a boil in a large pot, add salt, and cook the tortellini until tender. Drain and return to the hot pot.
4. Remove cream sauce from the heat, stir in half of the Gorgonzola and all the Parmesan, and pour over the tortellini. Set over medium heat and cook gently, stirring constantly, for 5 to 8 minutes, or until cream has thickened slightly and the tortellini have absorbed some of the sauce.
5. Divide the tortellini among 6 heated plates, sprinkle each with the reserved half of the Gorgonzola, and serve immediately.

6 portions as a first course or light main course

```
┌─────────────────────────────────────┐
│                                       │
│        AN ITALIAN FLAG                │
│            MENU                       │
│                                       │
│        *Tomato Dill Soup*             │
│                                       │
│     *Tortellini with Gorgonzola*      │
│            ──────────                 │
│                                       │
│     *Roast Shoulder of Veal*          │
│                                       │
│    *Watercress and Endive*            │
│            *Salad*                    │
│            ──────────                 │
│                                       │
│      *Strawberries with*              │
│      *Champagne Sabayon*              │
│                                       │
└─────────────────────────────────────┘
```

AMERICANS LOVE PASTA

Americans eat more pasta than Italians do — at least at one sitting. The frugal Italians, for whom a light first course of pasta blunts the edge of hunger, are often appalled at the enormous platefuls of spaghetti we serve here as a main course.

Try it their way one time, and you may become a convert. Serve a sixth of a pound of pasta or less per person, and follow with a light entrée teamed with a seasonally perfect vegetable. A simple salad, then cheese and fruit, conclude a classic meal.

LINGUINE WITH WHITE CLAM SAUCE

Use only fresh clams, please.

¾ cup best-quality olive oil
6 garlic cloves, peeled and minced
4 dozen raw clams, Little Necks or Cherrystones,
　shucked and chopped coarsely, all liquor reserved
bottled clam juice (about 2 cups)
½ cup finely chopped Italian parsley
1½ teaspoons dried oregano
1½ tablespoons salt, plus additional to taste
freshly ground black pepper, to taste
24 fresh clams, in their shells (optional garnish)
1 pound linguine

1. Heat the olive oil in a deep heavy kettle. Add the garlic and cook over low heat until golden, about 5 minutes.

2. Combine the reserved clam liquor and enough bottled clam juice to make 3 cups. Add this to the kettle along with the parsley, oregano, and salt and pepper to taste. Simmer, partially covered, for 10 minutes. (Sauce may be prepared ahead to this point.)

3. Meanwhile, scrub the garnishing clams if you are using them and put them in another pan. Add 1 inch of water, cover, and set pan over high heat. Shake the pan or stir the clams and remove as they open. Reserve them in their shells.

4. In a large pot, bring 4 quarts water to a boil. Add 1½ tablespoons salt, stir, and drop in the linguine. Cook until tender but still firm.

5. Meanwhile, reheat sauce if you have allowed it to cool. Add chopped clams and heat gently; clams should not overcook or they will become tough.

6. Drain linguine and toss it in the kettle together with the sauce. Serve in the kettle, topped by the clam garnish, or transfer to individual wide soup bowls and garnish each serving with clams in their shells.

6 portions

GREEN LASAGNA

This beautiful dish of pasta is an intriguing departure from the usual lasagna, and yet respects the traditions of freshness and lightness that permeate the best Italian cooking. The combination of soft, fresh goat cheese and fresh basil is one we find especially exciting, and the contrast of flavor and color is wonderful. This is not a main-course pasta; serve it as a first course, followed by a light entrée of fish, veal or chicken.

3 tablespoons salt, plus additional to taste
¾ pound fresh spinach pasta, uncut, about 3 sheets
2 10-ounce packages frozen chopped spinach, defrosted
1 cup ricotta cheese
⅓ cup grated imported Parmesan cheese
freshly ground black pepper, to taste
½ cup Basil Purée (see page 51)
1 Montrachet cheese or other soft chèvre, about 11 ounces
3 tablespoons heavy cream
1½ cups medium Béchamel Sauce (see page 585)

1. Bring 4 quarts water to a boil in a large pot. Stir in 2 tablespoons salt and cook the sheets of spinach pasta, one at a time; each will be done in 3 minutes or so. It is particularly important, when the pasta is to be cooked further in the oven, that you not overcook it now. As each sheet is done, transfer it immediately to a large bowl or sink full of cold water.

2. Bring 2 quarts water to a boil in another pan. Add 1 tablespoon salt and stir in the defrosted spinach. Cook for 1 minute, drain immediately, and transfer spinach to another bowl of cold water.

3. Mix ricotta and 2 tablespoons of the Parmesan together in a small bowl. Season with salt and pepper and set aside.

4. In another bowl, cream together the basil purée, three-quarters of the goat cheese, and the heavy cream. Set aside.

5. Drain spinach and squeeze as much water as possible out of it with your hands. Stir spinach into the ricotta mixture and correct seasoning; you may need more pepper or Parmesan; you will probably not need more salt.

6. Drain the sheets of pasta, cut them lengthwise into 2-inch-wide strips, and pat thoroughly dry on paper towels.

7. Preheat oven to 375°F.

8. Smear one third of the béchamel evenly over the bottom of a baking dish 9 x 13 inches. Arrange about one third of the pasta strips over the béchamel, trimming them as necessary to make an exact fit. Spread all of the spinach and ricotta mixture evenly over the pasta strips, being sure to cover the pasta completely to the edges. Cut a second layer of pasta strips and arrange them over the spinach. Spread half of remaining béchamel over the second layer of pasta and spread all of the basil and goat cheese mixture over the béchamel. Top this with the final layer, again trimming and fitting the strips. Spread the remaining béchamel evenly over the top layer of pasta and crumble remaining goat cheese over the béchamel. Sprinkle with the remaining Parmesan cheese.

9. Set baking dish in upper third of oven. Bake the lasagna for 10 to 15 minutes, or until it is bubbling and top is lightly browned. (The short baking time is perfectly adequate for this light, fresh lasagna; do not overcook it.) Serve immediately.

6 portions

✤ FROM THE SILVER
PALATE NOTEBOOK

Throw a theme party, but avoid cliché. Originality is what counts. Don't be afraid to pull out all the stops — serve a Middle Eastern dinner on the living room floor.

Base your menu on seasonally fresh foods; they'll look and taste better, cost less, and coordinate more easily with the party theme.

We like to use fresh tomato spaghetti with this dish, making it a symphony of reds and pinks. Ordinary spaghetti is fine, however, and tastes just as good. This is another of those pasta dishes requiring no grated cheese; just pass the peppermill.

PASTA WITH LOBSTER AND TARRAGON

A beautiful and sophisticated pasta dish, perfect as the first course of an important dinner. Begin with caviar or oysters, follow the pasta with Roast Veal or Filet of Beef (see Index for recipes), and fresh raspberries and cream.

2 tablespoons best-quality olive oil
½ cup finely chopped yellow onion
1 can (2 pounds, 3 ounces) Italian plum tomatoes
2 teaspoons dried tarragon
salt and freshly ground black pepper, to taste
1 cup heavy cream
2 tablespoons salt
1 pound spaghetti
pinch of cayenne pepper
½ pound lobster meat or more, about 1½ cups,
*   the equivalent of a 3- to 4-pound lobster*
parsley, fresh basil or fresh tarragon sprigs (garnish)

1. Heat the oil in a saucepan. Add the onion, reduce the heat and cook, covered, until tender, about 25 minutes.

2. Chop and drain the tomatoes and add them to the onions. Add the tarragon, season to taste with salt and pepper, and bring to a boil. Reduce heat, cover and simmer, stirring occasionally, for 30 minutes.

3. Remove the mixture from the heat and let it cool slightly. Purée it in the bowl of a food processor fitted with a steel blade, or use a food mill fitted with a medium disc.

4. Return purée to the saucepan, stir in heavy cream, and set over medium heat. Simmer the mixture, stirring often, for 15 minutes, or until slightly reduced. Taste the sauce, correct seasoning, and stir in cayenne and lobster meat. Simmer further, 3 to 5 minutes, or just until lobster is heated through.

5. Meanwhile, in a large pot, bring 4 quarts water to a boil. Add the salt, stir in the pasta, and cook until tender but still firm. Drain immediately and arrange on warmed serving plates. Spoon sauce evenly over pasta and garnish with a sprig of parsley, basil or tarragon. Serve immediately.

6 portions as a first course, or 4 as a main course

SUMMER PASTA

Happily pasta is no longer just a heavy dish that you can only indulge in once or twice a season. New light sauces and increasing use of vegetables and fish have opened up a whole new world of pasta, with contrasts in flavor, texture and temperature. There are cool sauces on hot pasta, cool sauces on cool pasta, and we could hardly feel less lukewarm about any of these new combinations.

LINGUINE WITH TOMATOES AND BASIL

We first had this uncooked pasta sauce when we were guests in a beautiful home on Sardinia. Such a recipe could only be the result of hot, lazy days and abundant ripe tomatoes and basil. The heat of the pasta warms and brings out the flavors of the sauce in a wonderfully subtle way. Delicious and easy.

4 ripe large tomatoes, cut into ½-inch cubes
1 pound Brie cheese, rind removed, torn into irregular pieces
1 cup cleaned fresh basil leaves, cut into strips
3 garlic cloves, peeled and finely minced
1 cup plus 1 tablespoon best-quality olive oil
2½ teaspoons salt
½ teaspoon freshly ground black pepper
1½ pounds linguine
freshly grated imported Parmesan cheese (optional)

1. Combine tomatoes, Brie, basil, garlic, 1 cup olive oil, ½ teaspoon salt and the pepper in a large serving bowl. Prepare at least 2 hours before serving and set aside, covered, at room temperature.

2. Bring 6 quarts water to a boil in a large pot. Add 1 tablespoon olive oil and remaining salt. Add the linguine and boil until tender but still firm, 8 to 10 minutes.

3. Drain pasta and immediately toss with the tomato sauce. Serve at once, passing the peppermill, and grated Parmesan cheese if you like.

4 to 6 portions

SPICY SESAME NOODLES

Our unorthodox but delicious version of a Chinese classic. Use plenty of chili oil.

2 tablespoons salt
1 pound thin linguine or other thin pasta
¼ cup peanut oil
2 cups Sesame Mayonnaise (see page 244)
Szechuan hot chili oil★
8 scallions (green onions), trimmed, cleaned and cut diagonally
  into ½-inch pieces
blanched asparagus tips, broccoli or snow peas (for garnish)

1. Bring 4 quarts of water to a full boil in a large pot, stir in salt, drop in the linguine, and cook until tender but not mushy. Drain, toss in a mixing bowl with the peanut oil, and let cool to room temperature.

2. Whisk together the Sesame Mayonnaise and chili oil to taste in a small bowl. Do not hesitate to make the mayonnaise quite spicy; the noodles will absorb a lot of heat.

3. Add the scallions to the pasta, pour in the sesame mayonnaise, and toss gently but well. Cover and refrigerate until serving time.

4. Toss the noodles again and add additional sesame mayonnaise if they seem dry. Arrange in a shallow serving bowl and garnish with asparagus, broccoli or snow peas if desired. Serve immediately.

6 portions

★available in Oriental groceries and specialty food shops

> ### CONCERT IN THE PARK PICNIC
>
> *Salmon Mousse with*
> *Black bread toasts*
>
> ———
>
> *Veal Roll*
>
> *Asparagus with*
> *Blueberry Vinaigrette*
>
> *Spicy Sesame Noodles*
>
> ———
>
> *Assorted cheeses, Fresh fruit*
>
> *Chocolate Mousse and cookies*

PESTO

Here is our current favorite, a sauce more Mastroianni than DeNiro: suave, mellow, even elegant, and perfect for beginning an important summer dinner. Walnuts and heavy cream sophisticate the basil-garlic duo, and this pesto is equally at home on pasta, fluffed into hot rice, or stirred into homemade mayonnaise as a sauce for cold poached fish or *crudités*.

2 cups fresh basil leaves, thoroughly washed and patted dry
4 good-size garlic cloves, peeled and chopped
1 cup shelled walnuts
1 cup best-quality olive oil
1 cup freshly grated imported Parmesan cheese
¼ cup freshly grated imported Romano cheese
salt and freshly ground black pepper, to taste

1. Combine the basil, garlic and walnuts in the bowl of a food processor — or halve the recipe and use a blender — and chop.

2. Leave the motor running and add the olive oil in a slow, steady stream.

3. Shut the motor off, add the cheeses, a big pinch of salt and a liberal grinding of pepper. Process briefly to combine, then scrape out into a bowl and cover until ready to use.

2 cups, enough to sauce 2 pounds of pasta

PASTA WITH PESTO

1 pound linguine or thick narrow noodles such as fettucine
1½ tablespoons salt
4 quarts water
¼ cup heavy cream
1 cup Pesto (preceding recipe)
freshly ground black pepper
freshly grated imported Parmesan or Romano cheese (optional)

1. Bring water to a boil in a large kettle or stockpot. Add the salt and then add the pasta when the water boils again. Use a wooden fork or spoon to stir pasta until all strands are under water. Boil rapidly until done to taste; we like it tender but not mushy. (To test, occasionally lift and bite a strand.)

2. Stir 2 tablespoons of the hot pasta water and the heavy cream into the pesto. Drain the pasta in a colander and return it to the hot pan. Stir in the pesto and toss well to combine.

3. Serve immediately on warm plates. More freshly ground pepper is welcome, but additional cheese is not really necessary.

6 to 8 moderate first-course portions, 4 generous main-course portions

PESTO PERFECT

The first batch of pesto — that marvelous Genoese basil sauce for pasta — officially welcomes summer back to our kitchen. Like tender shoots of early spring asparagus, or the tangy crunch of an apple as autumn slides into winter, basil, and pesto, are sure signs of seasonal change.

In Genoa the preparation of this sauce is steeped in years of tradition. It must be pounded with a marble pestle in a marble mortar; only the Genoese basil, bathed by salty sea air as it grows, will do; the purest versions contain nothing but basil, cheese, garlic and olive oil.

In truth, this simplest pesto is a revelation — complex, heady, powerful with basil and garlic, only just tamed by the cheese and oil. But summer is too long, basil too plentiful and pesto too good to limit oneself to a single version. Pine nuts and sweet butter have become accepted additions over the years, and we love those versions as well.

PESTO POSSIBILITIES

♥ Mix 2 tablespoons pesto with 2 tablespoons *crème fraîche* or dairy sour cream, and dollop into your favorite summer soup.

♥ Whisk 1 tablespoon pesto into 4 eggs as you scramble them.

♥ Season mayonnaise with a tablespoon or two of pesto when making potato salad.

♥ Brush broiled chicken with pesto to taste about 10 minutes before the end of cooking time. Serve with sautéed tomatoes.

♥ Whisk together 2 tablespoons pesto, 4 tablespoons *crème fraîche* and 1 tablespoon prepared Dijon-style mustard for superb saucing for poached fish.

NUPTIAL BRUNCH

Figs and Prosciutto

Asparagus with Blueberry Vinaigrette

Spinach Pasta with Salmon and Cream Sauce

Raisin Pumpernickel Bread with sweet butter

Campari Ice

134

Italians usually omit grated cheese when serving pasta sauced with seafood. In this case, except for the tablespoon used to thicken the sauce, we agree.

SPINACH PASTA WITH SALMON AND CREAM SAUCE

This elegant dish illustrates the versatility of pasta. It is not particularly Italian, but the subtle flavors and ravishing colors combine to make unique food.

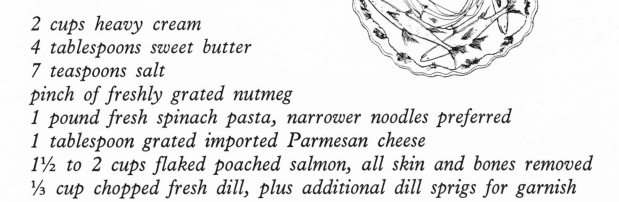

2 cups heavy cream
4 tablespoons sweet butter
7 teaspoons salt
pinch of freshly grated nutmeg
1 pound fresh spinach pasta, narrower noodles preferred
1 tablespoon grated imported Parmesan cheese
1½ to 2 cups flaked poached salmon, all skin and bones removed
⅓ cup chopped fresh dill, plus additional dill sprigs for garnish

1. Bring the cream and half of the butter to a simmer in a small saucepan. Add 1 teaspoon of the salt, and the nutmeg, continue to simmer until cream is reduced by about one third.

Bring 4 quarts water to a boil in a large pot, add remaining 2 tablespoons of salt, and drop in the noodles.

3. Meanwhile, stir grated Parmesan, then the flaked salmon and ⅓ cup chopped dill into the cream, and remove from heat. Remember, fresh pasta is ready in 2 to 3 minutes *at the most.*

4. Drain pasta, return it to the hot pan and toss with remaining butter until butter is melted. Divide pasta equally among 6 heated plates and spoon salmon cream sauce over each portion.

5. Garnish with a sprig of fresh dill and serve at once.
6 first-course portions

PASTA AND SEAFOOD SALAD WITH BASIL

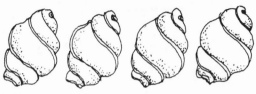

This is perfect summer fare — a casual but dressy one-dish meal that is quick to cook and undemanding to serve. Drop-in guests can give a hand with the chopping or just help themselves to a plateful without fuss or muss. A cool and uncomplicated glass of wine (try one of the California rosés made from Zinfandel or Cabernet grapes) and a piece of crusty bread are all you need to accompany this salad.

1 pound medium-size raw shrimp, shelled and deveined
1 pound bay scallops, rinsed
2 or 3 small squid, dressed (optional)*
½ pound pasta of some interesting shape — shells, spaghetti twists,
   corkscrews, etc.
1 cup tiny peas (defrosted if frozen; rinsed and patted dry if fresh)
½ cup diced sweet red pepper
½ cup minced purple onion
½ cup best-quality olive oil
3 to 4 tablespoons fresh lemon juice
½ cup Basil Purée (see page 51)
salt and freshly ground black pepper, to taste
1 cup imported black olives (Kalamata or Alfonso)

1. Bring a large pot of salted water to a boil, drop in the shrimp and scallops, wait 1 minute, and drain immediately.

2. Cut the bodies of the squid into ½-inch rings. Divide each cluster of tentacles into halves. Bring another pot of salted water to a boil, drop in the squid, and simmer for 5 minutes. Drain.

3. Bring a third pot of salted water to a boil. Drop in the pasta, return to a boil, and cook until tender but not mushy. Drain.

4. Be certain the seafood and pasta are well drained and free of any excess water. Toss them together in a large bowl.

5. Add the peas (no need to cook them), red pepper and onion and toss again.

6. In a small bowl whisk together the olive oil, lemon juice and basil purée and season with salt and pepper. Pour over the salad and toss well to distribute the dressing. Taste and correct seasoning if necessary.

7. Mound the salad on a serving platter and scatter the olives over it. Serve immediately, or cover and refrigerate. Allow salad to return to room temperature before serving.

4 to 6 portions

[*]Omit the squid if you must, but squid gives the salad a special taste, texture and visual appeal for which there is no substitute.

"Summer cooking implies a sense of immediacy, a capacity to capture the essence of the fleeting moment."

— Elizabeth David

THE MAIN COURSE

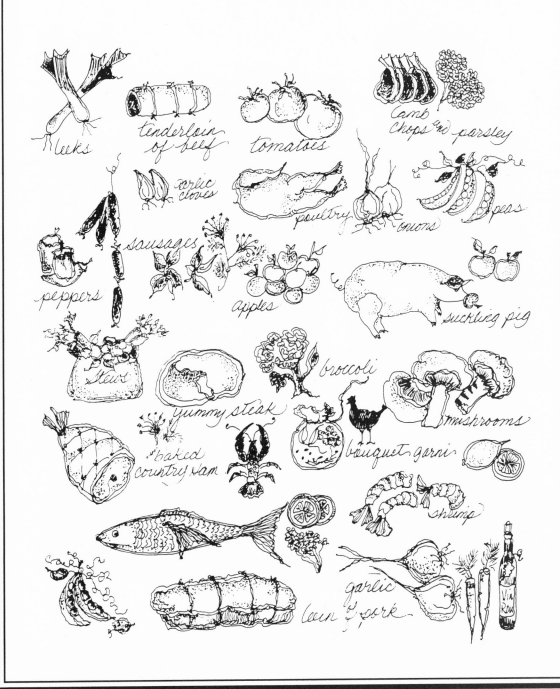

CHICKEN EVERY WAY

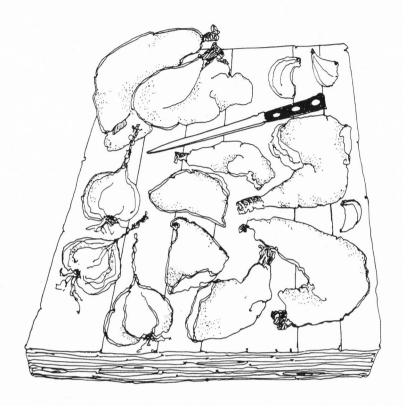

At the turn of the century and for a considerable time afterward, chicken was an expensive treat, served on special occasions and made much of. There were even recipes that extended chicken salads and stews with that economy meat, veal! Times have certainly changed. Chicken today is as easy on the pocketbook as it is on the calorie-counter, and the only danger is that with all the chicken we consume, we might let it become dull. Fortunately, chicken is campatible with so many different seasonings and cooking methods that only the lazy cook risks turning out a boring chicken dish.

There is always a chicken dish *du jour* on the Silver Palate menu, and our never-ending efforts to intrigue our customers have resulted in the following collection of recipes. We think they'll intrigue you too, and prove once again the adaptability of the versatile chicken.

CHICKEN MARBELLA

This was the first main-course dish to be offered at The Silver Palate, and the distinctive colors and flavors of the prunes, olives and capers have kept it a favorite for years. It's good hot or at room temperature. When prepared with small drumsticks and wings, it makes a delicious hors d'oeuvre.

The overnight marination is essential to the moistness of the finished product: the chicken keeps and even improves over several days of refrigeration; it travels well and makes excellent picnic fare.

Since Chicken Marbella is such a spectacular party dish, we give quantities to serve 10 to 12, but the recipe can successfully be divided to make a smaller amount if you wish.

4 chickens, 2½ pounds each, quartered
1 head of garlic, peeled and finely puréed
¼ cup dried oregano
coarse salt and freshly ground black pepper to taste
½ cup red wine vinegar
½ cup olive oil
1 cup pitted prunes
½ cup pitted Spanish green olives
½ cup capers with a bit of juice
6 bay leaves
1 cup brown sugar
1 cup white wine
¼ cup Italian parsley or fresh coriander (cilantro), finely chopped

1. In a large bowl combine chicken quarters, garlic, oregano, pepper and coarse salt to taste, vinegar, olive oil, prunes, olives, capers and juice, and bay leaves. Cover and let marinate, refrigerated, overnight.

2. Preheat oven to 350°F.

3. Arrange chicken in a single layer in one or two large, shallow baking pans and spoon marinade over it evenly. Sprinkle chicken pieces with brown sugar and pour white wine around them.

4. Bake for 50 minutes to 1 hour, basting frequently with pan juices. Chicken is done when thigh pieces, pricked with a fork at their thickest, yield clear yellow (rather than pink) juice.

5. With a slotted spoon transfer chicken, prunes, olives and capers to a serving platter. Moisten with a few spoonfuls of pan juices and sprinkle generously with parsley or cilantro. Pass remaining pan juices in a sauce-boat.

6. To serve Chicken Marbella cold, cool to room temperature in cooking juices before transferring to a serving platter. If chicken has been covered and refrigerated, allow it to return to room temperature before serving. Spoon some of the reserved juice over chicken.

16 pieces, 10 or more portions

COUNTRY WEEKEND LUNCH

Cheese Straws

Crudités and assorted dips

Chicken Marbella

Semolina Bread
Boucheron cheese

Lime Mousse

Chocolate Chip Cookies

THE CHICKEN CHART

BROILERS:
1 to 2½ pounds; young chickens with little fat.

BROILERS / FRYERS:
2½ to 3½ pounds. Butchers use these terms interchangeably. If you prepare them well, these chickens may be cooked either way. Look for yellow fat and plump breasts.

ROASTERS / PULLETS:
3½ to 6½ pounds; good for roasting, baking, barbecuing and quick cooking. Bred for tenderness and very meaty.

HENS AND FOWL:
Up to 8 pounds; best for stock or chicken salad. They require longer and slower cooking but are by far the most flavorful.

✢ FROM THE SILVER PALATE NOTEBOOK

Successful flavoring depends on many things. To appreciate this fully you must experiment. Try some lemon in the rice. Grate an orange on the broccoli. Next time combine meat with fresh fruit. You may feel the need to experiment with small batches at first; as your confidence and your palate develop, you will learn to create boldly, trusting in the results. You will be a cook.

RASPBERRY CHICKEN

Boneless chicken breasts are quick and economical to serve but often dull to eat. In this recipe, ready in minutes, raspberry vinegar lends a bit of welcome tartness, mellowed by chicken stock and heavy cream. A handful of fresh raspberries, poached briefly in the sauce just before serving, adds an elegant note. Wild rice and a simply sautéed green vegetable would be good accompaniments.

2 whole boneless, skinless chicken breasts, about 2 pounds
2 tablespoons sweet butter
¼ cup finely chopped yellow onion
4 tablespoons raspberry vinegar★
¼ cup Chicken Stock (see page 587), or canned chicken broth
¼ cup heavy cream, or Crème Fraîche (see page 582)
1 tablespoon canned crushed tomatoes
16 fresh raspberries (optional)

1. Cut each chicken breast into halves along the breastbone line. Remove the filet mignon, the finger-size muscle on the back of each half, and reserve for another use. Flatten each breast half or *suprême* by pressing it gently with the palm of your hand.

2. Melt the butter in a large skillet. Raise the heat, add the *suprêmes*, and cook for about 3 minutes per side, or until they are lightly colored. Remove from the skillet and reserve.

3. Add the onion to the fat in the pan and cook, covered, over low heat until tender, about 15 minutes.

4. Add the vinegar, raise the heat and cook, uncovered, stirring occasionally, until vinegar is ruduced to a syrupy spoonful. Whisk in the chicken stock, heavy cream or *crème fraîche,* and crushed tomatoes and simmer for 1 minute.

5. Return *suprêmes* to the skillet and simmer them gently in the sauce, basting often, until they are just done and the sauce has been reduced and thickened slightly, about 5 minutes; do not overcook.

6. Remove *suprêmes* with a slotted spoon and arrange on a heated serving platter. Add the raspberries to the sauce in the skillet and cook over low heat for 1 minute. Do not stir the berries with a spoon, merely swirl them in the sauce by shaking the skillet.

7. Pour sauce over *suprêmes* and serve immediately.

2 to 4 portions

*Available in specialty food stores. The intensity of vinegars varies from brand to brand. Be prepared to adjust this quantity to suit your own taste.

SUMMER CHICKEN

We were pleasantly surprised to find that mustard and basil are beautifully compatible in this one-dish meal.

1 roasting chicken, 3½ pounds (save giblets for another use)
1 bunch of fresh basil, washed carefully
5½ cups Chicken Stock (see page 587) or canned chicken broth
1 cup coarsely chopped yellow onions
2 carrots, peeled and chopped
5 parsley sprigs
salt and freshly ground black pepper, to taste
4 small white onions
4 new potatoes, scrubbed
4 medium-size carrots, peeled and cut into 2-inch lengths
¾ pound fresh green beans, cleaned and tipped
6 tablespoons sweet butter
3 tablespoons flour
⅓ cup prepared Dijon-style mustard
⅓ cup Crème Fraîche (see page 582) or heavy cream
2 tablespoons chopped parsley

1. Wash the chicken, pull off all fat that can be removed, stuff the cavity with the basil, and truss. Set the chicken, breast side up, in a heavy saucepan just large enough to hold it comfortably. Pour in the chicken broth (broth need not completely cover the chicken) and bring to a medium boil. Reduce heat to a gentle simmer and skim any accumulated fat or scum.

146

2. Add the chopped onion, chopped carrots and parsley sprigs, and season lightly with salt and pepper. Partially cover, reduce heat, and cook at a gentle simmer for 40 minutes or until chicken juices run a clear yellow when thigh is pricked with a fork.

3. Bring a large pot of salted water to a boil and drop in white onions. Simmer for 10 seconds, lift out with a slotted spoon, and drop into a large bowl of ice water. Next, add the potatoes and cook until tender; drop into the ice water. Repeat this process with the chopped carrots, cooking them until they're tender but crisp, and then with the green beans. Reserve all the vegetables in the ice water.

4. When the chicken is done, remove it from its broth with a slotted spoon, cover, and keep warm.

5. Measure out 2 cups of the chicken broth and bring it to a boil in a small saucepan. In another small pan melt 2 tablespoons of the butter over medium heat. When the butter is foaming, sprinkle in the flour. Cook without browning, stirring constantly, for about 5 minutes. Remove from heat and pour in the boiling chicken broth all at once. The sauce will bubble furiously for a minute. Whisk the sauce as it bubbles and subsides and then return it to low heat. Bring the sauce up to a boil, stirring constantly, and cook for 5 minutes.

6. Remove basil from the chicken's cavity and chop it fine. Whisk the basil, mustard and *crème fraîche* into the sauce, remove sauce from heat, cover, and keep warm.

7. Melt remaining 4 tablespoons butter in a heavy skillet. Drain the blanched vegetables and warm them gently in the butter until hot through, no more than 5 minutes. Season lightly with salt and pepper. Sprinkle with chopped parsley.

8. Carve the chicken into serving pieces and arrange on a platter. Surround chicken with the warmed vegetables, spoon some of the sauce over the chicken, and offer remaining sauce on the side. Serve immediately.

4 portions

"pic' nic, n. (G., *picknick*, Fr. *pique-nique*) 1. an excursion or outing with food usually provided by members of the group and eaten in the open. 2a. A pleasant or amusing experience. b. an easy task or feat."

We think Mr. Webster has defined the word but hasn't done much for the experience. Our rendering of a *pique-nique* includes a group of willing friends, a spontaneous break from the ordinary, and a chance to appreciate simple delightful things.

A picnic need not be lunch in the park. It can be held on the terrace at midnight, watching shooting stars and fireflies; an afternoon gathering by the pool, a luscious breakfast shared with the sunrise. The best picnicking is done with food that looks and tastes delicious, and travels beautifully. Because this portable quality is the true essence of our shop, the recipes in this book are, for the most part, easy to eat, pleasing to the palate and able to survive from the kitchen to the outdoors while still tasting wonderful. Uncomplicated food need not be unimaginative food.

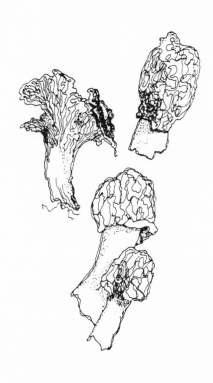

CHICKEN BREASTS BAKED ON A BED OF WILD MUSHROOMS

The rich flavor of wild mushrooms, combined with Port and cream, turns this into a very special main course.

¾ cup Chicken Stock (see page 587) or canned chicken broth
1 ounce dried cèpes, morels or trompettes des morts or a
  combination of all three, thoroughly rinsed under running
  water and drained
½ pound fresh cultivated mushrooms
4 tablespoons sweet butter
¼ cup finely chopped shallots
salt and freshly ground black pepper, to taste
⅓ cup medium Port wine
⅓ cup heavy cream
3 boneless chicken breasts, skinned and halved
chopped parsley (garnish)

1. Bring the chicken stock to a boil in a small saucepan. Pour it over the *cèpes* in a small bowl and let stand for 2 hours.

2. Meanwhile, trim stems from the fresh mushrooms and save stems for another use, or discard. Wipe mushroom caps with a damp paper towel and slice thin.

3. Melt the butter in a skillet. Add the shallots and sauté gently for 5 minutes without browning.

4. Meanwhile, drain the *cèpes*, reserving the liquid, and chop them fine. Add *cèpes* and sliced fresh mushrooms to the skillet, season with salt and pepper, and sauté over medium heat, stirring occasionally, for 10 minutes.

5. Preheat oven to 325°F.

6. Add reserved soaking liquid, the Port and heavy cream to the skillet with the mushrooms and simmer for another 5 minutes, or until slightly thickened.

7. Spoon mushroom mixture into a shallow baking dish. Arrange chicken breast halves in a single layer on top of the mushrooms. Season with salt and pepper to taste and cover the baking dish tightly with a piece of foil.

8. Set dish on the middle level of the oven and bake for 20 minutes, or until chicken breasts are done. Sprinkle with chopped parsley and serve immediately.

6 portions

GLAZED BLUEBERRY CHICKEN

This recipe was developed to showcase our Blueberry Chutney, a very special preserve of fresh blueberries, vinegar, cinnamon, and cloves. Wild rice would be good to serve, as would a buttered green vegetable like asparagus.

1 chicken, 2½ to 3 pounds, cut into quarters
½ cup blueberry vinegar*
1 teaspoon dried thyme
salt and freshly ground black pepper, to taste
⅓ cup Blueberry Chutney*
chopped Italian parsley (garnish)
grated orange zest (optional garnish)

1. Combine chicken quarters, blueberry vinegar and thyme in a bowl and marinate for 2 hours, turning occasionally.
2. Preheat oven to 300°F.
3. Arrange chicken pieces, skin side up, in a flameproof baking dish, reserving the marinade. Season chicken lightly with salt and pepper to taste and coat it with the chutney.
4. Set the pan on the center rack of the oven and bake, uncovered, for about 40 minutes, or until done. You may need to bake the dark meat sections for another 5 to 10 minutes. Transfer chicken to a serving platter, cover, and keep warm.
5. Skim fat from cooking juices and set the baking dish over medium heat. Add the marinade and bring to a boil, stirring and scraping up any browned bits in the pan. Reduce by one-third, or until sauce is lightly thickened. Pour sauce over chicken and garnish with parsley and orange zest. Serve immediately.

2 to 4 portions

*available in specialty food stores

SESAME CHICKEN

1 chicken, 2½ to 3 pounds, quartered
2 teaspoons herbes de Provence
salt and freshly ground black pepper, to taste
½ cup buttermilk
¾ cup unseasoned dry bread crumbs
¾ cup toasted sesame seeds
⅓ cup finely chopped Italian parsley
4 tablespoons sweet butter, melted

1. Arrange the chicken in a bowl just large enough to hold it. Sprinkle on the *herbes de Provence,* season with salt and pepper to taste, and pour the buttermilk over the chicken. Marinate, covered, for 2 to 3 hours, turning occasionally.

2. Preheat oven to 350°F.

3. In a small bowl stir together the bread crumbs, sesame seeds and parsley.

4. Lift chicken pieces from the marinade, one at a time, and roll in the bread-crumb and sesame-seed mixture, coating each piece well. Arrange pieces in a shallow baking dish, and season lightly with salt and pepper.

5. Bake the chicken, basting with melted butter, until it is golden brown and done, 30 to 40 minutes. Dark meat may take a few minutes longer. Serve immediately, or cool to room temperature before eating.

2 to 4 portions

CHUTNEY

Chutneys are descended from the medieval custom of relishes of fruits preserved with sugar, vinegar and spices. The simple notion of grinding a bit of black pepper on melon or strawberries has the same origin. Today chutneys are sweet, tart and complex, full of flavor and chunky in texture.

Many fruits and vegetables, sometimes in combination, make good chutneys; some we've run across include tomato, peach, cherry, fig, date, eggplant, plum, blueberry, cranberry, mango, onion, apple, carrot, tomato-apple and jalapeño.

Be adventurous; don't wait until you're serving curry to enjoy a chutney. They complement food, and stimulate the appetite and taste buds. Try chutney with roast meats or poultry, hot or cold; on a hamburger, in an omelet, or with cheese on a cracker. A chutney can be just the spark needed to pull together a simple broiled dinner, or can become the secret ingredient of a recipe. We think that this is just the beginning of the many flavorful uses of chutney.

"What is sauce for the goose may be sauce for the gander, but it is not necessarily sauce for the chicken, the duck, the turkey or the Guinea hen."

— Alice B. Toklas

mustard

CHICKEN DIJONNAISE

This mustard-flavored chicken is easy and versatile. Although the recipe uses a combination of Dijon-style and coarse mustards, you may substitute any mustard that appeals to your fancy. Since there are hundreds on the market, flavored in countless ways, the possibilities can occupy you for years.

1 chicken, 2½ to 3 pounds, quartered
⅓ cup mustard (we like half Dijon-style and half coarse
  Pommery-style mustard)
freshly ground black pepper, to taste
⅓ cup vermouth or dry white wine
½ cup Crème Fraîche (see page 582) or heavy cream
salt, to taste

1. Coat the chicken with the mustard and set it in a bowl, covered, to marinate at room temperature for 2 hours.
2. Preheat oven to 350°F.
3. Arrange chicken, skin side up, in a flameproof baking dish. Scrape out any mustard remaining in the bowl and spread it evenly over the chicken. Season lightly with pepper and pour the vermouth or wine around the chicken.
4. Set dish on the center rack of the oven and bake, basting occasionally, for 30 to 40 minutes, or until chicken is done. You may have to bake the dark meat sections for another 5 to 10 minutes.
5. Scrape the mustard off the chicken and back into the baking dish. Transfer chicken pieces to a serving platter, cover, and keep warm.
6. Skim as much fat as possible from the cooking juices and set the baking dish over medium heat. Bring to a boil, whisk in the *crème fraîche* or heavy cream, and lower heat. Simmer the sauce for 5 to 10 minutes, or until it is reduced by about one third. Season lightly with salt and pepper. Taste, correct seasoning, and spoon sauce over the chicken. Serve hot or at room temperature.
2 to 4 portions

CHICKEN MONTEREY

Officially this is a fricassee — that is, the chicken is first partially cooked in butter or oil and is then finished in a liquid, in this case a mixture of orange juice, tomatoes and chicken stock. There is a bit of garlic, a touch of rosemary and a colorful garnish of sautéed vegetables. The whole dish is bright and fresh, reminding us of holidays in the sun.

Parsleyed rice, buttered pasta or steamed new potatoes would all be good starchy accompaniments, but you could just offer lots of crusty bread for mopping up the tasty sauce.

5 tablespoons best-quality olive oil
1 chicken, 2½ to 3 pounds, quartered
salt and freshly ground black pepper, to taste
1 cup finely chopped yellow onions
2 carrots, peeled and chopped
4 garlic cloves, peeled and minced
1 cup Chicken Stock (see page 587) or canned chicken broth
½ cup fresh orange juice
½ cup canned crushed tomatoes
1 tablespoon dried rosemary
1 medium-size sweet red pepper, stemmed and cored, cut into julienne
*½ large zucchini and ½ large yellow summer squash, cleaned and
    sliced diagonally*
⅓ cup chopped Italian parsley (garnish)
grated zest of 1 orange (garnish)

1. Heat 3 tablespoons of the oil in a large skillet. Pat the chicken pieces dry, season them with salt and pepper, and cook gently in the oil for 5 minutes. Turn the chicken, season again, then cook for another 5 minutes. Do not attempt to brown chicken or you will overcook it; it should be pale gold. Remove chicken from skillet and reserve.

2. Add the onions, carrots and garlic to the oil remaining in the skillet and cook, covered, over low heat until vegetables are tender, about 25 minutes.

3. Uncover skillet and add the stock, orange juice, tomatoes and rosemary. Season to taste with salt and pepper and simmer the mixture, uncovered, for 15 minutes.

4. Return chicken pieces to the pan and simmer further, 20 to 25 minutes, or until chicken is nearly done. Baste the pieces with the sauce and turn them once at the 15-minute mark. (If you wish, you may complete the recipe to this point the day before serving. Refrigerate chicken in the sauce and reheat gently before proceeding.)

5. Heat remaining 2 tablespoons of olive oil in another skillet and sauté the pepper julienne for 5 minutes. Add sliced zucchini and yellow squash and season with salt and pepper. Raise the heat and toss the vegetables in the oil until they are tender but still firm, another 5 minutes or so.

6. With a slotted spoon, transfer vegetables to the skillet with the chicken and simmer together for 5 minutes. Sprinkle with the chopped parsley and orange zest and serve immediately.

2 to 4 portions

"As for rosemary, I let it run all over my garden walls, not only because my bees love it but because it is the herb sacred to remembrance and to friendship, whence a sprig of it hath a dumb language."

— Sir Thomas More

LEMON CHICKEN

This chicken has a crisp golden crust and the zing of fresh lemon. It's good hot and terrific cold, especially on a picnic.

2 chickens, 2½ pounds each, cut into quarters
2 cups fresh lemon juice
2 cups flour
2 teaspoons salt
2 teaspoons paprika
1 teaspoon freshly ground black pepper
½ cup corn oil
2 tablespoons grated lemon zest
¼ cup brown sugar
¼ cup Chicken Stock (see page 587)
1 teaspoon lemon extract
2 lemons, sliced paper-thin

1. Combine chicken pieces and lemon juice in a bowl just large enough to hold them comfortably. Cover and marinate in the refrigerator overnight, turning occasionally.

2. Drain chicken thoroughly and pat dry. Fill a plastic bag with flour, salt, paprika and black pepper, and shake well to mix. Put 2 pieces of chicken into the bag at a time and shake, coating completely.

3. Preheat oven to 350°F.

4. Heat corn oil in a frying pan or cast-iron Dutch oven until hot and fry chicken pieces, a few at a time, until well browned and crisp. This will take about 10 minutes per batch.

5. Arrange browned chicken in a single layer in a large shallow baking pan. Sprinkle evenly with lemon zest and brown sugar. Mix chicken stock and lemon extract together and pour around chicken pieces. Set a thin lemon slice on top of each piece of chicken.

6. Bake chicken for 35 to 40 minutes, or until tender.

6 or more portions

LEMONS

Lemons remind us of all things cool, fresh and sparkling. You'll find the best flavor and the most juice in the small, round or oval lemons with smooth, unblemished skins. Store lemons at room temperature and you will obtain more juice from them, unless you're planning to keep them for some time. Lemon provides a tart accent in many dishes and slices, wedges or bits of peel add both flavor and color to garnishes. Some stimulating ideas:

♥ Squeeze fresh lemon juice over steamed vegetables before you toss them with butter, or add lemon juice to melted butter and then pour over vegetables.

♥ Sprinkle lemon juice over new potatoes before tossing with butter and fresh dill.

♥ Always serve lemon with shellfish or French fried potatoes.

♥ Serve lemon with most cold or hot soups; it intensifies the flavor.

♥ Add lemon to sour cream for dips; it perks up flavor.

♥ Substitute lemon juice for vinegar in salad dressing.

♥ Drizzle fresh lemon juice over scrambled eggs, then sprinkle with fresh Italian parsley.

♥ Serve lemon and black pepper with oysters, clams or smoked salmon and you're in for a treat.

♥ Tie each lemon half in a cheesecloth bag to accompany fish; the bag traps seeds when lemon is squeezed.

♥ Squeeze lemon over cut-up apples, avocados, mushrooms, bananas or pears so they don't turn brown.

♥ Freeze lemonade ice cubes and add to iced tea, lemonade or white wine spritzers.

♥ Add thinly sliced lemon wedges to a bottle of vodka or gin and put in the freezer. It will be ready to drink in 2 weeks.

♥ Make a lemon pie, lemon sorbet or lemon tart with twice as much lemon as the recipe calls for; you'll be surprised in a delightful way.

♥ Serve lemon sorbet in lemon shells.

♥ Stud a lemon with cloves, covering it completely, and tie with a tartan ribbon to make a long-lasting pomander to freshen your closet.

FRUIT-STUFFED ROCK CORNISH HENS

These small hybrid birds — the product of American ingenuity — have always seemed particularly festive to us. While they are most widely available frozen, fresh are now available as well, and either makes a meal more special. When properly cooked and filled with a flavorful stuffing, they are moist and golden brown, making a stunning and tasty centerpiece.

6 fresh Rock Cornish hens
2 large oranges
½ pound (2 sticks) sweet butter
½ cup yellow onion, peeled and diced
2 tart apples, cored and diced (do not peel)
1 cup seedless green grapes
¼ cup minced Italian parsley
½ cup crumbs, from good-quality French-type bread
¾ teaspoon dried thyme
salt and freshly ground black pepper, to taste
paprika
6 strips of bacon, halved crosswise
1 cup dry sherry or Madeira wine
fresh watercress (garnish)

1. Rinse hens well under cold running water and pat dry.
2. Grate the zest from the oranges (or peel with a zester) and reserve. Cut oranges into halves and rub the cut halves over the insides and outsides of the hens, moistening them with the orange juice. Set hens aside.
3. Melt half of the butter in a skillet. Add diced onion and cook, covered, over low heat until tender and lightly colored, about 15 minutes.
4. Combine apples, grapes, parsley, bread crumbs, reserved orange zest and ½ teaspoon of the thyme in a small bowl; pour the butter and onions over the mixture. Season with salt and pepper and toss gently to combine.
5. Preheat oven to 350°F.
6. Stuff the hens with the stuffing and truss or skewer them shut. Arrange hens in a shallow roasting pan just large enough to hold them,

or use 2 smaller baking dishes, and season the outside of the birds with salt, pepper, the remaining ¼ teaspoon thyme and a sprinkle of paprika. Arrange 2 pieces of bacon in an 'X' on the breast of each hen. Dot with remaining butter, pour the sherry or Madeira into the pan, and set it on the middle level of the oven.

7. Bake for about 1 hour, basting frequently, until hens are golden brown and done. Transfer them to a serving platter and garnish with watercress. Remove grease from sauce in roasting pan and reduce over medium heat to ⅔ the amount. Pass the sauce in a gravy boat.

6 portions

Christmas memories . . . anticipation . . . snow, always, in Michigan . . . a night so clear you can see the Star of Bethlehem . . . favorite relatives . . . hunting in the woods for a tree . . . snacks for Santa's reindeer . . . carols in the snow . . . candlelight services . . . a sleigh ride in the snow . . . and all the good things to eat.

CHRISTMAS DAY MENU

Seafood Pâté

Chicken Liver Pâté with Green Peppercorns

Gougère

Zucchini-Watercress Soup

———

Fruit-Stuffed Cornish Hens
or
Roast Suckling Pig

Nutted Wild Rice

Beet and Apple Purée

———

Chestnut Mousse

Date-Nut Pudding

OUR FAVORITE WAY TO ROAST A TURKEY

We promise wonderful results and a very moist bird.

Cornbread Sausage Stuffing with Apples (recipe follows)
1 turkey, 18 to 22 pounds
2 large oranges, cut into halves
½ pound (2 sticks) sweet butter at room temperature
salt and freshly ground black pepper, to taste
paprika, to taste
4 tablespoons corn oil

1. Make the stuffing for the turkey.
2. Wash the turkey well, inspecting for pinfeathers, and chop off the wing tips, reserving them for later use with giblets in gravy or stock. Dry the turkey inside and out with a kitchen towel.
3. Squeeze the juice from the 2 oranges all over the outside of the bird and rub into the cavity to refreshen. Salt and pepper the cavity to taste. Fill the turkey with the stuffing, not packing too tightly. Sew up the cavity or close with small trussing skewers.
4. Rub the outside of the turkey all over with 1½ sticks of the softened butter and sprinkle generously with salt, pepper and paprika. Drape the turkey with cheesecloth.
5. Place turkey, breast side up, on a rack in a roasting pan.
6. Four to five hours before serving is scheduled, place the turkey in a preheated 325° oven.
7. Melt the remaining 4 tablespoons of butter with 4 tablespoons of corn oil in a saucepan. Lift the cheesecloth from the turkey and baste every 30 minutes, first with butter and oil mixture and later with the turkey's own juices.*

8. Roast for 3½ to 4½ hours or until the thigh juices run clear yellow when pricked with a skewer. There should be no traces of pinkness. The drumstick will move easily in the socket when the turkey is done.

9. When turkey is done, remove to a heated platter and cover with foil. The turkey should stand 30 minutes before carving.

10. Remove stuffing into a bowl. If there is any additional from the recipe, bake it in a covered casserole in a 350° oven, covered with foil, for one half hour before serving.

11. Serve turkey on a large platter. Be sure you have sharp knives and a good carver among the group. Enjoy!

15 to 20 portions

*For a moist bird, frequent basting is essential, so don't forget! Baste every 30 minutes — breast and legs should be a lovely golden color.

Thanksgiving is a purely American holiday, where thanks can be given for, among other things, the abundance of food in this land. To us, Thanksgiving tradition means a turkey and a dazzling array of seasonal trimmings — truly a harvest celebration.

161

CORNBREAD-SAUSAGE STUFFING WITH APPLES

This agreeably all-American stuffing is good with any poultry.

12 tablespoons (1½ sticks) sweet butter
2½ cups finely chopped yellow onions
3 tart apples (Jonathan and Winesap are good), cored and chunked; do not peel
1 pound lightly seasoned bulk sausage (breakfast sausage with sage is best)
3 cups coarsely crumbled cornbread (preferably homemade)
3 cups coarsely crumbled whole-wheat bread
3 cups coarsely crumbled white bread (French or homemade preferred)
2 teaspoons dried thyme
1 teaspoon dried sage
salt and freshly ground black pepper, to taste
½ cup chopped Italian parsley
1½ cups shelled pecan halves

1. Melt half of the butter in a skillet. Add chopped onions and cook over medium heat, partially covered, until tender and lightly colored, about 25 minutes. Transfer onions and butter to a large mixing bowl.

2. Melt remaining butter in the same skillet. Add apple chunks and cook over high heat until lightly colored but not mushy. Transfer apples and butter to the mixing bowl.

3. Crumble the sausage into the skillet and cook over medium heat, stirring, until lightly browned. With a slotted spoon, transfer sausage to the mixing bowl and reserve the rendered fat.

4. Add remaining ingredients to the ingredients in the mixing bowl and combine gently. Cool completely before stuffing the bird; refrigerate if not used promptly.

5. If you do not wish actually to stuff the bird (goose or duck, for example, can make the stuffing greasy), spoon it into a casserole. Cover casserole and set into a large pan. Pour hot water around the casserole to come halfway up the sides. Bake for 30 to 45 minutes at 325°F., basting occasionally with cooking juices from the bird or with the reserved sausage fat if necessary.

Enough stuffing for a 20-pound turkey, to make 12 to 14 portions

THANKSGIVING DAY MENU

Chèvre Tarts

Cheese Straws

Wild Mushroom Soup

———

Puréed Broccoli with Crème Fraîche

Sweet Potato and Carrot Purée

Our Favorite Turkey

Cornbread-Sausage Stuffing with Apples

Cranberry Bread

———

Harvest Tart

Pumpkin Pie

Chocolate Truffles

SWEET AND SAVORY MEATS

At The Silver Palate we have always seasoned entrées with fruit. The richness of some meats is often more fully appreciated with the counterpoint of a fruity tartness.

In fact, sweet and savory meats have an ancient and worldwide tradition. Dishes of the Orient, the Middle East and Africa have always demonstrated the affinity between meats and fruit, often using fruit as much for color and texture as for their natural sweetness. The finished dish is seldom actually sweet; rather the acids and sugars act to bring out the natural flavors of other ingredients in the dish.

In much the same way, mustards, vinegars and chutneys enliven meat dishes, and we use them freely in our cookery.

" 'Roast Beef Medium' is not a food. It is a Philosophy."
— Edna Ferber

FILET OF BEEF

For those times when you want an impressive but essentially conservative main course, this simply roasted filet of beef will fill the bill nicely. Such traditional accompaniments as Sautéed Cherry Tomatoes, asparagus with Hollandaise (see Index for recipes), and a plain baked potato are always appropriate.

1 oven-ready beef filet, about 4½ pounds, wrapped in fat
1 garlic clove, peeled and cut into thin slivers
salt and freshly ground black pepper, to taste

1. Preheat oven to 425°F.
2. With the tip of a sharp knife, cut slits in the meat and insert slivers of the garlic. Season meat generously with salt and pepper, and set it in a shallow roasting pan just large enough to hold the meat comfortably.
3. Bake for 10 minutes. Reduce heat to 350°F. and bake for another

25 minutes for rare meat (120°F. on a meat thermometer), or another 35 minutes for medium (130°F. on a meat thermometer).

4. Remove roast from the oven and let it stand for 10 minutes before slicing. Or cool completely to room temperature and slice for serving cold.

8 to 10 portions

✦ FROM THE SILVER
PALATE NOTEBOOK

A buffet should be bountiful. Make sure the table is generously filled — bowls should be full, breads generously sliced, centerpieces large enough to hold their own, and the table itself of a size to look like the proverbial groaning board without looking overdone.

No event should leave you with an embarrassing amount of leftover food, but no one likes to run out midway through the evening either. If you're cooking your own food, take a chance and prepare extra. If you can serve foods that freeze well, leftovers can be used to feed your family or as a start on your next party.

GLAZED CORNED BEEF

3 pounds corned beef
1 cup dark orange marmalade
4 tablespoons prepared Dijon-style mustard
4 tablespoons brown sugar

1. Place corned beef in a large pot and cover with boiling water. Bring to a boil, lower heat, cover partially and simmer as slowly as possible for about 3 hours, or until very tender when tested with a fork.

2. Preheat oven to 350°F.

3. Mix marmalade, mustard and sugar together in a small bowl.

4. When meat is done, remove from pot and drain. Place meat on an ovenproof serving dish and pour marmalade mixture over it, coating thoroughly.

5. Bake corned beef for 30 minutes, or until glaze is crisp and brown. Serve hot or at room temperature.

6 to 8 portions

PORK CHOPS WITH BLACK CURRANT PRESERVES

This recipe calls for a tart and chunky black currant preserve. Serve two purées with the chops.

¼ cup black currant preserves
1½ tablespoons prepared Dijon-style mustard
6 center-cut pork chops, 1 to 1½ inches thick
salt and freshly ground black pepper, to taste
⅓ cup white wine vinegar
watercress (garnish)

1. Mix the preserves and mustard together in a small bowl. Set aside.
2. Heat a nonstick skillet just large enough to hold the pork chops comfortably, and brown them lightly on both sides. Season with salt and pepper to taste and spoon the currant and mustard mixture evenly over them.
3. Cover chops, reduce heat, and cook for 20 minutes, or until the chops are done. Transfer them to a platter and keep them warm in the oven.
4. Remove excess fat from the skillet. Add the vinegar, set pan over medium heat and bring juices to a boil, stirring and scraping up any brown bits. When the sauce is reduced by about one third, pour it over the chops and serve immediately, garnished with watercress.

3 to 6 portions

BAKED HAM WITH GLAZED APRICOTS

We've baked a glazed ham almost daily since we opened the store. It's a cocktail buffet and picnic favorite and provides endless possibilities for leftovers.

1 ready-to-eat ham with bone in, 12 to 16 pounds
whole cloves, to cover surface of ham
¼ cup prepared Dijon-style mustard
1 cup dark brown sugar
3 cups apple juice
1 pound dried apricots
1 cup Madeira wine

1. Preheat oven to 350°F.
2. Peel skin from ham and trim fat, leaving about a ¼-inch layer to protect meat. With a sharp knife score fat in a diamond pattern.
3. Set ham in a shallow baking pan, insert a whole clove in the crossed point of each diamond, and pat mustard evenly over top and sides of ham. Sprinkle top with brown sugar and pour apple juice into the bottom of the pan.
4. Bake ham for 1½ hours, basting frequently.
5. Meanwhile, combine apricots and Madeira in a small saucepan. Bring to a boil, cover, and remove from heat.
6. At 30 minutes from the end of baking time, add apricots and their liquid to the roasting pan and continue to bake and baste ham.
7. Transfer ham to a large platter. Decorate top of ham with apricots, attaching them with toothpicks. Skim fat from pan juices and pour into a sauceboat. Accompany ham with mustards, chutneys and pan juices.

20 to 25 portions

WELCOME HOME BUFFET

*Fresh purple figs wrapped
in prosciutto with
fresh limes*

Spicy Shrimp

*Seasonal crudités with
Tapenade Dip*

---

*Country Ham with
Glazed Apricots*

*Sweet and Rough
Mustard*

---

*Chocolate Mousse with
Devon cream*

FROM THE *PIPER NIGRUM* VINE:

GREEN PEPPERCORNS: picked while underripe and soft. They are mildly pungent with a bite.

BLACK PEPPERCORNS: picked when more mature and then dried in the sun. They are the strongest in bite and bouquet.

RED PEPPERCORNS: until recently not used and available only in China; developed by being left on the vine even longer.

WHITE PEPPERCORNS: the inside kernels that have been harvested when vine-ripened, then soaked in water and dried. They are not as hot as the black but much more aromatic.

PINK PEPPER BERRIES: grown in Reunion Island, are not really a member of the pepper family at all, but their sweetly mysterious flavor and ravishing pink color have made them the darlings of the *nouvelle cuisine*. Widely accepted in Europe, they are controversial in the U.S.

ROAST LAMB WITH PEPPERCORN CRUST

This mixture of mustard and three peppercorns gives the roast a crisp and piquant crust.

3 tablespoons crushed dried peppercorns, an equal mix of white, black and green
1 tablespoon fresh rosemary leaves, or 1½ teaspoons dried
½ cup fresh mint leaves
5 garlic cloves, crushed
½ cup raspberry vinegar*
¼ cup Oriental soy sauce
½ cup dry red wine
1 boned but untied leg of lamb, about 5 pounds (weighed after boning)
2 tablespoons prepared Dijon-style mustard

1. Combine 1 tablespoon of the crushed peppercorns, the rosemary, mint, garlic, vinegar, soy sauce and red wine in a shallow bowl. Marinate the lamb in the mixture for eight hours, turning occasionally.

2. Remove roast from marinade and drain; reserve marinade. Roll the roast, tying it with kitchen twine.

3. Preheat oven to 350°F.

4. Spread mustard over meat and pat 2 tablespoons of crushed peppercorns into the mustard. Set the roast in a shallow roasting pan just large enough to hold it comfortably and pour reserved marinade carefully around but not over roast.

5. Bake for 1½ hours, or 18 minutes per pound, basting occasionally. Roast will be medium rare. Bake for another 10 to 15 minutes for well-done meat. Let roast stand for 20 minutes before carving. Serve pan juices in gravy boat along with lamb.

6 to 8 portions

*available in specialty food stores

ORIENTAL LAMB CHOPS

3 tablespoons dark Oriental sesame oil★
6 thick lamb chops, shoulder cut, trimmed of excess fat
¾ cup finely chopped yellow onion
3 garlic cloves, peeled and minced
3 tablespoons Oriental soy sauce
3 tablespoons Oriental chili paste★
¾ cup tart orange marmalade
1½ tablespoons rice wine vinegar★
1 tablespoon minced fresh gingerroot

1. Heat the sesame oil in a skillet large enough to hold all the lamb chops. Add chops and brown them lightly on both sides. Transfer chops to paper towels to drain.

2. Add the onion and garlic and cook, covered, over low heat for 20 minutes, or until tender and lightly colored.

3. Add soy sauce, chili paste, marmalade, vinegar, and gingerroot. Simmer for 2 minutes, stirring constantly.

4. Return chops to the skillet, cover, and cook over low heat, turning once, until done, about 7 minutes. Serve immediately, spooning sauce over chops.

3 to 6 portions

★available in Oriental or specialty food stores

The whole roasted animal is in many cultures the epitome of gracious hospitality — it is a tradition that goes back to welcoming the prodigal son by slaughtering the fatted calf for a feast.

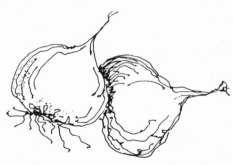

ROAST SUCKLING PIG

There is hardly a more spectacular main course than a roast suckling pig. Given a few days' notice, most butchers can order one for you, and very little additional work is required to produce this unique dish. It is delicious served with Black Bean Soup, Saffron Rice and watercress salad (see Index for recipes).

3 limes, cut into halves
1 suckling pig, 15 pounds, well cleaned
18 garlic cloves, peeled
2 tablespoons dried oregano
⅓ cup capers plus 3 tablespoons caper brine
2 tablespoons olive oil
1 teaspoon salt
1 teaspoon freshly ground black pepper
1 teaspoon curry powder
½ cup firmly packed fresh coriander (cilantro) leaves
watercress (garnish)
kumquats (garnish)
1 tiny apple or a crabapple (garnish)

1. Rub lime halves all over the body of the pig, squeezing lime juice liberally; rub cavity with limes, too.

2. With a knife tip cut slits ¾ inch deep all over body of the pig. (Do not prick the head.) Cut 5 garlic cloves into 8 pieces each and stuff the pieces into the slits in the pig.

3. In a medium-size bowl mix together the remaining 13 garlic cloves, finely minced, the oregano, capers, olive oil, salt, pepper and curry powder. Stuff half of the mixture into the cavity of the pig and rub the remainder all over the outside. Place the coriander inside the cavity. Let the pig rest, covered, in the refrigerator for 24 hours.

4. Preheat oven to 400°F.

5. Place pig on a rack in a large roasting pan and bake for 30 minutes. Turn heat down to 350°F. and roast for 3½ hours, or until juices run clear when pig is pricked with a knife.

6. Place a small apple in the pig's mouth, and serve on a large platter, decorated with watercress and preserved or fresh kumquats.

10 portions

VEAL CHOPS WITH SHERRY AND LEMON MARMALADE

4 tablespoons sweet butter
2 tablespoons vegetable oil
4 loin veal chops, 1 inch thick
salt and freshly ground black pepper, to taste
⅓ cup finely chopped yellow onions
⅓ cup medium-dry sherry wine
⅓ cup Chicken Stock (see page 587)
2 tablespoons lemon marmalade
¼ cup heavy cream or Crème Fraîche (see page 582)
watercress (garnish)

1. Heat the butter and oil in a large skillet until very hot. Add the veal chops and sear them well on both sides, seasoning to taste with salt and pepper.

2. Reduce heat and cook until chops are slightly underdone and still juicy. Remove them from the skillet, cover, and keep warm while making the sauce.

3. Add the onion to the butter and oil remaining in the skillet and cook, covered, over medium heat until tender, about 15 minutes.

4. Add the sherry, stock and marmalade to the skillet and bring to a brisk boil, stirring up any browned bits in the skillet. When the mixture is reduced by one third, whisk in the heavy cream or *crème fraîche* and simmer for another 5 minutes. Taste and correct seasoning.

5. Transfer veal chops to a heated serving platter and spoon some of the sauce over them. Garnish with watercress and serve immediately, accompanied by additional sauce.

4 portions

ROAST SHOULDER OF VEAL

In this recipe, the bacon and wine keep the roast moist, while the mustard adds zest.

4½ pounds boned and tied shoulder of veal,
* weighed after boning*
1 small garlic clove, cut into thin slivers
¼ cup prepared Dijon-style mustard
1 teaspoon dried thyme
salt and freshly ground black pepper, to taste
8 strips of bacon
8 tablespoons (1 stick) sweet butter, at room temperature
¾ cup dry white wine

1. Preheat oven to 350°F.
2. Cut tiny slits in the veal with the tip of a sharp knife and insert garlic slivers. Set roast on rack in a shallow baking pan just large enough to hold it comfortably. Rub mustard all over veal and sprinkle with thyme and salt and pepper to taste.
3. Wrap bacon around roast to cover completely, tucking bacon ends under meat. Spread butter generously over bacon and meat and pour white wine into pan.
4. Bake for 2 hours and 15 minutes, or about 30 minutes per pound, until juices run clear when pricked with skewer. Baste frequently. Let roast stand for 20 minutes before carving. Serve pan juices in gravy boat along with veal.
6 to 8 portions

Of all the courses The Silver Palate provides — literally from soup to nuts — the main course is the most important to our customers. Delicate seafood, hearty stews, succulent roasts and the ever-changing Chicken du Jour take the most time and attention in the kitchen, and are clearly what the too-busy-to-cook hostess is most in need of help with.

The recipes here are a mixed bag, using seasonal vegetables, readily available cuts of meat, and the seasonings and embellishments that we like the most. Menu suggestions are included — recipes for appropriate accompaniments are scattered throughout this book. All are intended to help you plan and cook the most perfect meal possible.

DEGLAZING A PAN

To deglaze a pan, add wine, water or vinegar to a skillet in which food has been browned and stir or scrape up the juices with a whisk or fork. Whisk in butter, herbs or cream, simmer to reduce, and you have a light sauce, ready in minutes.

VEAL SCALLOPS IN MUSTARD-CREAM SAUCE

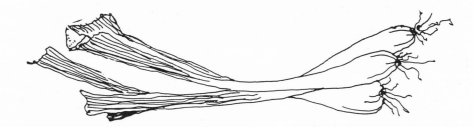

A main course of sautéed veal, sauced with a bit of mustard, white wine and cream, can be ready in minutes. Use your favorite mustard to personalize the dish.

4 tablespoons sweet butter
2 tablespoons vegetable oil
3 scallions (green onions), cleaned and chopped
1½ pounds veal scallops (8 very large scallops, or
    10 to 12 smaller scallops), pounded
salt and freshly ground black pepper, to taste
⅓ cup dry white wine
⅓ cup prepared mustard (avoid "ballpark"-type mustards)
½ cup Crème Fraîche (see page 582) or heavy cream
1 large firm ripe tomato, peeled, seeded and chopped

1. Melt the butter and oil together in a large skillet. Add the scallions and cook over low heat for 5 minutes without browning.

2. Raise the heat, add the scallops, and season to taste with salt and pepper. Cook the scallops for 1 minute per side; do not overcook, and do not worry if they do not actually brown. Remove them from the skillet and keep warm.

3. Add the wine to the skillet and bring it to a boil. Cook until the mixture is reduced to a few syrupy spoonfuls. Whisk in the mustard and the *crème fraîche* or heavy cream and boil for 2 minutes. Taste sauce and correct seasoning.

4. Arrange scallops on a serving platter or on individual plates and spoon the sauce over them. Sprinkle with chopped tomato and serve immediately.

4 to 6 portions

FORK SUPPERS

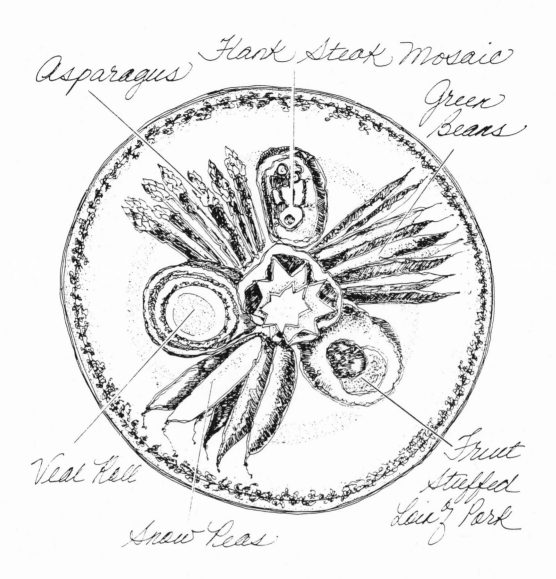

Asparagus

Flank Steak Mosaic

Green Beans

Veal Roll

Snow Peas

Fruit Stuffed Loin of Pork

We have seen many a buffet ruined because an awkward or overly complex dish — often the meat course — was simply impossible to eat from a lap-held plate. Some menus avoid this problem by offering an array of salads or other bite-sized foods, which can often leave one hungry.

With a little thought and planning, however, you can provide a meaty main dish that is simple, elegant, and convenient to eat. The following entrées will fit the bill, and in addition to being tender enough to eat with just a fork, they can all be prepared in advance — a boon to hostess and guest alike.

FLANK STEAK MOSAIC

1 large flank steak, butterflied, 2 to 3 pounds
1 cup red wine
¼ cup Oriental soy sauce
1 garlic clove, minced
2-egg omelet (see page 537), cut into ½-inch strips
½ pound carrots, peeled and cut into julienne
½ pound green beans, trimmed and blanched
pitted green olives
1¾-ounce can pimientos, cut into ¼-inch strips
5 slices of bacon

1. Marinate flank steak in wine, soy sauce and garlic for 2 hours. Remove steak from marinade, pat dry, and lay on a flat surface.

2. Working left to right, arrange 2 rows of omelet strips the length of steak. Top the 2 rows with 2 or 3 layers more of omelet strips. Lay carrots in rows alongside the omelet — 3 wide and 3 high. Repeat with green beans. On other side of the omelet, place 1 row of olives and next to them, 1 row of pimientos, 3 layers high.

3. Roll the steak tightly towards you, tucking meat closely around the vegetables. Wrap bacon around roll and tie securely at ½-inch intervals.

4. Preheat oven to 350°F.

5. Bake the roast for 30 minutes, basting twice with reserved marinade. Put under broiler briefly to brown the bacon. Cool, and cut into ½-inch-thick slices.

6 to 8 portions

Fruit-Stuffed Loin of Pork roast makes a delicious main course for an autumn dinner, served hot with a bit of the pan juices spooned over it. It is also good cold; the rich flavors of the pork and the sweetly tart taste of the fruit are even more apparent. Take it along on a picnic, or slice it thin for elegant sandwiches.

FRUIT-STUFFED LOIN OF PORK

4 pounds boneless pork loin roast, prepared for stuffing
1 cup pitted prunes, approximately
1 cup dried apricots, approximately
1 garlic clove
salt and freshly ground black pepper, to taste
8 tablespoon dried thyme
1 cup Madeira wine
1 tablespoon molasses
watercress (garnish)

1. Preheat oven to 350°F.

2. Using the handle of a wooden spoon, push the dried fruits into the pocket in the roast, alternating prunes and apricots.

3. Cut the garlic into thin slivers. Make deep slits in the roast with the tip of a knife and push the garlic into the slits. Tie roast with twine and rub surface with salt and pepper.

4. Set the roast in a shallow baking pan and smear the butter over the roast. Sprinkle with thyme.

5. Stir Madeira and molasses together in a small bowl and pour over the roast. Set the pan on the middle rack of the oven and bake for 1½ hours (approximately 20 minutes per pound), basting frequently.

6. When roast is done (do not overcook), remove it from the oven and let it stand, loosely covered with foil, for 15 or 20 minutes. Cut into thin slices, arrange slices on a serving platter, and spoon pan juices over them. Garnish platter with watercress and serve immediately.

8 to 10 portions

VEAL ROLL

2 pounds veal scallops, pounded flat
½ pound boiled ham, thinly sliced
olive oil to season veal
juice of 1 lemon
freshly ground black pepper, to taste
½ pound mortadella sausage, thinly sliced
½ pound Genoa salami, thinly sliced
10 hard-cooked eggs
¼ cup minced parsley
¼ cup bread crumbs
2 garlic cloves, minced
salt, to taste
5 slices of bacon
4 cups Quick Tomato Sauce (see page 590)
1 cup dry white wine

1. Preheat oven to 350°F.
2. Unroll an 18-inch length of foil on your working surface.
3. Arrange the veal scallops in a rectangle, 6 x 12 inches, overlapping the scallops as necessary. Arrange the boiled ham in a similar layer over the veal. Sprinkle with oil, lemon juice and black pepper. Repeat with layers of mortadella and salami.
4. Trim the ends of the hard-cooked eggs so that the yolk is exposed. Arrange the eggs in a line lengthwise down the center of the rectangle, being certain the cut edges of the eggs touch closely. Sprinkle parsley down one side of the eggs, and bread crumbs mixed with the garlic down the other side. Drizzle a little oil over the eggs and sprinkle with salt and pepper.
5. Pick up the long edge of the foil and bring it toward you over the eggs. Tuck the meat under the eggs, making a tight roll, and continue to make a roll, ending with the seam side down. Discard the foil, drape the bacon over the roll, and tie securely with kitchen twine at ½-inch intervals.
6. Set the roll in a roasting pan. Mix tomato sauce and wine and pour over the roll. Cook for 1 hour, basting often. Remove from oven and let stand, covered with foil, for 20 minutes.
7. Cut roll into thin slices and serve with the pan juices as a sauce. Pass additional sauce in a gravy boat.
8 to 10 portions

This veal roll, with its own tomato sauce, is a beautiful and unusual main dish. Accompany with a starch such as buttered pasta, and a green vegetable, hot or cold.

✤ FROM THE SILVER
PALATE NOTEBOOK

For buffet meals, tie your eating utensils in pastel napkins with pretty ribbon, and bunch them in a basket. Let it decorate your table and save space, too.

Stack your collection of trays — no matter how eclectic — near the buffet table. It makes it much easier for your guests to relax and enjoy the food without having to balance dishes on their knees.

GAME

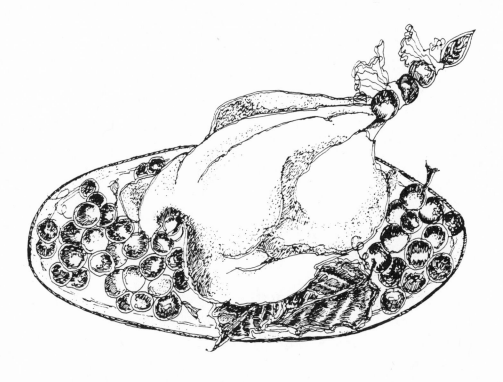

Game was once plentiful in America, and all rural families hunted as a matter of course. Now wild herds are much reduced and hunting is a sport enjoyed by few. Though we still prize game and cook it with respect, we must turn to our butcher to supply the raw materials. The culinary result will lack a truly wild edge, but it also will free the inexperienced cook from some of the pitfalls of game cookery. No more will a tough and impossibly stringy piece of over-the-hill game ruin a long and complex recipe. Now there is no doubt that the hunter will return with supper, and the seasonal limitation is removed — if you want fresh game in spring or summer, you can get it. So, in a different way from our forebears, we give thanks for game and enjoy its rich flavors. The following recipes will help you to celebrate the adventure.

RAGOUT OF RABBIT FORESTIERE

Of course use a fresh domestic rabbit for this recipe if you can, but a good brand of frozen rabbit is available in many supermarkets, and is convenient and affordable. No marinating is needed for the domestic product, and aside from the time to soften the dried mushrooms, the stew proceeds quickly. We suggest serving this with a Leek and Potato Purée (see page 334) and buttered rice or pasta, followed by a green salad and cheese.

Do not attempt this recipe with wild rabbit without expecting to make considerable adjustments in method, seasoning and cooking time.

2½ cups Chicken Stock (see page 587)
1 ounce dried cèpes (dried wild mushrooms)
½ cup best-quality olive oil
2 cups finely chopped yellow onions
3 large carrots, peeled and quartered lengthwise
2 rabbits, a total of 5 to 6 pounds, cut into serving pieces
2 tablespoons sugar
4 tablespoons unbleached, all-purpose flour
salt and freshly ground black pepper, to taste
1 cup dry red wine
1 cup canned crushed tomatoes
1 tablespoon dried thyme
2 bay leaves
6 parsley sprigs
⅓ cup Calvados
1 pound fresh mushrooms
3 tablespoons sweet butter
5 garlic cloves, peeled and chopped

1. If rabbits are frozen, defrost them according to package directions. Heat ¾ cup of the chicken stock to boiling in a saucepan and pour it over the cèpes in a small bowl. Let stand for 2 hours.

2. Heat half of the olive oil in a large stewpot. Add the onions and carrots and cook over medium heat, covered, until tender and lightly colored, about 25 minutes. Remove vegetables with a slotted

spoon, leaving as much cooking oil behind in the pot as possible, and set vegetables aside.

3. Set the stewpot over high heat. Pat the rabbit pieces dry with paper towels and brown them in batches in the hot oil. Turn the pieces frequently, and add additional oil if the pot seems dry. Return all the rabbit pieces to the stewpot, sprinkle the rabbit with the sugar and continue to sauté until evenly browned, another 5 minutes.

4. Turn the heat down and sprinkle rabbit with the flour and with salt and pepper to taste. Continue turning rabbit pieces until the flour is lightly colored, another 5 minutes or so.

5. Add the red wine and stir and scrape up any browned bits in the bottom of the pot. Stir in remining 1¾ cups chicken stock, the crushed tomatoes, thyme, bay leaves and parsley.

6. Warm the Calvados in a small pan and ignite it. When the flame dies down, add Calvados to the stew. Bring to a healthy simmer, cover, and reduce heat. Cook, stirring occasionally, for 30 minutes.

7. Meanwhile, cut stems from the fresh mushrooms and save them for another use. Wipe mushroom caps with a damp paper towel and slice. Carefully lift dried mushrooms from soaking liquid with a slotted spoon. Chop them finely. Let the liquid sit a few moments and then pour it carefully into the stewpot.

8. Melt the butter in a large skillet, add the fresh and dried mushrooms, and sauté over medium heat for 10 minutes. Season with salt and pepper and reserve.

9. Remove rabbit pieces from the stewpot with a slotted spoon and transfer to a plate. Discard the carrots, bay leaves and parsley and purée the sauce with a food processor or a food mill fitted with the fine disc.

10. Return puréed sauce and the rabbit pieces to the stewpot. Add mushrooms and their liquid and the chopped garlic and set over medium heat. Simmer gently for 15 minutes, stirring occasionally. Taste and correct seasoning. Transfer the ragoût to a serving dish and serve immediately.

6 to 8 portions

183

PANCETTA

Pancetta is Italian bacon, cured but not smoked, and quite fatty, available in Italian markets. If you cannot find it, substitute American breakfast bacon; the flavor will be different, but good.

PHEASANT WITH LEEK AND PECAN STUFFING

We think pheasant is one of the most delicious of the domestically raised game birds available to us. It is rich and meaty, with a firm texture no longer found in chicken. If care is taken during roasting, the meat is moist and succulent.

2 young pheasants, about 4 pounds each, thoroughly defrosted if frozen
1 tablespoon olive oil
½ cup finely chopped yellow onion
1 large carrot, peeled and finely chopped
2 tablespoons plus 1 teaspoon dried marjoram
¼ teaspoon dried thyme
1 bay leaf
6 sprigs of Italian parsley
3 cups Chicken Stock (see page 587) or canned chicken broth
salt and freshly ground black pepper, to taste
12 tablespoons (1½ sticks) sweet butter
10 medium-size leeks, white part only, well cleaned and thinly sliced
6 cups crumbs from good-quality white bread
2 cups toasted pecans (see How to Toast Pine Nuts, page 279)
1 cup finely chopped Italian parsley
4 slices of pancetta, 1 ounce each
½ cup heavy cream

1. Rinse the pheasants thoroughly inside and out and pat dry with paper towels. Chop the neck, heart, and gizzard (save the liver for another use).

2. Heat the olive oil in a small saucepan. Brown neck and giblets well in the oil, turning frequently. Add the onion, carrot, and 1 teaspoon

184

of the marjoram. Reduce heat to low and cook, covered, until vegetables are tender, about 25 minutes.

3. Uncover, add the thyme, bay leaf, parsley, and the stock, and season with a pinch of salt and freshly ground black pepper. (Canned broth and *pancetta* are both quite salty; do not salt the sauce again until just before serving.) Bring to a boil, reduce heat and simmer, partially covered, for 45 minutes. Strain the stock, discarding the solids, and reserve.

4. Melt the butter in a skillet. Stir in the sliced leeks and cook, covered, over low heat for 30 minutes, or until leeks are very tender.

5. Toss leeks, including their butter, with bread crumbs, pecans, chopped parsley and remaining 2 tablespoons of marjoram. Season lightly with salt and generously with pepper. Toss again; if the stuffing seems dry, moisten it with ¼ cup or so of the reserved broth.

6. Preheat oven to 375°F.

7. Stuff the pheasants loosely and drape the breasts with the *pancetta*. Tie it in place with kitchen twine and set the pheasants in a shallow roasting pan.

8. Set roasting pan in the middle of the oven and bake for about 1 hour, basting the pheasants occasionally with the fat and juices that accumulate. Pheasants are done when the thighs, pricked with a fork at their thickest, dribble clear yellow juices. Remove the pheasants from the pan, cover with foil, and keep warm.

9. Pour excess fat out of roasting pan. Pour reserved stock and the heavy cream into pan and set over medium heat. Bring to a boil, reduce heat and simmer, stirring and scraping up any browned bits, until sauce is reduced by about one third. Taste and correct seasoning.

10. Carve the pheasants and arrange the meat on a platter. Mound the stuffing in the center and drizzle meat and stuffing with a few spoonfuls of the sauce. Serve immediately, passing remaining sauce in a boat.

6 to 8 portions

VENISON STEW

This rich, complex stew is worthy of your most important holiday celebration. Venison is no longer difficult to come by (we have even seen it cut into stewing pieces and frozen) and for stewing, if you have a choice of cuts, use the chuck or rump — it's the most tender.

MARINADE:

2 cups dry red wine
juice of 1 lemon
juice of 2 limes
2 large bay leaves
2 whole cloves
1 large yellow onion, peeled and sliced
3 carrots, peeled and chopped
top leaves of 2 celery ribs
1 large garlic clove, peeled and crushed
½ teaspoon dried tarragon
pinch of dried thyme
6 whole black peppercorns, crushed
1 juniper berry, crushed
½ teaspoon salt

TO COMPLETE THE STEW:

3 pounds of lean venison cut in 1-inch cubes
8 tablespoons (1 stick) sweet butter (slightly more if needed)
2 tablespoons gin
3 tablespoons lean salt pork, cut into ¼-inch dice
¼ pound fresh mushrooms, as small as possible
salt and freshly ground black pepper, to taste
12 to 18 tiny pearl onions
6 chicken livers

1. Combine marinade ingredients in a large glass bowl and stir well. Add venison, cover, and refrigerate for 1 day. Turn meat 1 or 2 times in the marinade.

2. Remove meat from marinade and dry thoroughly with paper towels. Reserve marinade.

3. Melt 2 tablespoons of the butter in a heavy skillet. Brown the cubed venison a few pieces at a time, and with a slotted spoon transfer them to a bowl. Add additional butter to pan as needed.

4. Transfer all the venison to a flameproof casserole. In a small saucepan, warm the gin, then pour it over the venison and ignite. Shake the casserole slightly until flames die out.

5. Sauté the diced salt pork in a small skillet until golden. With a slotted spoon transfer pork to the casserole.

6. Remove mushroom stems and save for another use or discard. Wipe mushroom caps with a damp paper towel. Melt 4 tablespoons of the butter in a small skillet. Add mushroom caps and season with salt and pepper. Cook, stirring occasionally, until tender, about 5 minutes. Transfer mushrooms and cooking liquid to the casserole.

7. Bring 1 quart salted water to a boil. Drop in the pearl onions and boil for 1 minute. Transfer onions to a bowl of ice water; when cool, peel them and add to the casserole.

8. Strain the marinade and add it to the casserole; stir well. Set casserole over medium heat. Bring to a boil, reduce heat, cover, and simmer for 30 to 40 minutes.

9. Meanwhile, melt remaining 2 tablespoons butter in a small skillet and cook the chicken livers until they are firm but still pink inside, about 5 minutes. Cut into large dice.

10. When venison is tender, add livers to the casserole. Taste, correct seasoning, and serve immediately.

4 to 6 portions

BOUQUET GARNI

This little bouquet of dried and fresh herbs (and sometines spices) is tied around the top with a long kitchen string so that when cooking is completed it is easily lifted out of the pot. There is no set group of herbs which must be used. It depends on the flavor that will most enhance the dish being prepared. Use such spices as peppercorns, whole cloves and cinnamon sticks for hot mulled wine, for instance; other combinations will infuse your soup or casserole. Discard the little bags after use. Start fresh and imaginatively each time a *bouquet garni* is called for.

AN AUTUMN FEAST

Champagne

Smoked caviar

Sugared and spiced nuts

Fresh oysters

Venison Stew

*Chestnut Purée,
Sweet Potato and
Carrot Purée,
Puréed Broccoli with
Crème Fraîche*

---

*Watercress Salad with
Walnut Oil Vinaigrette*

*Stilton Cheese
Port Wine*

Baked Apples

*Chocolate Hazelnut Cake
with Crème Fraîche*

---

*Marc de Bourgogne
Framboise
Armagnac*

CATCH OF THE DAY

The boom in commercial food packing and freezing revolutionized American eating habits — though not always, we have seen, for the better. What we gained in convenience and availability, we lost in variety, and nowhere was this loss more keenly felt than at the fish market. However, increased influence from European chefs and the rise of the American concern about food spurred interest in native fish imaginatively prepared, and superspeed air transport now ensures freshness upon arrival. We are even receiving fish imported from Europe, South Africa and the Pacific. While these can hardly qualify as inexpensive meat substitutes, they are enlarging our awareness of the possibilities of fish cookery as never before. Calories count — and are counted — far more than they used to, and for many people eating light now means eating fish.

SEAFOOD VARIETIES WE PARTICULARLY LIKE:

FRESHWATER:

Bass
Rainbow Trout or German Brown
Perch
Whitefish

SHELLFISH:

Sea Scallops
Bay Scallops — particularly those from
   Long Island's bays
Lobster
Shrimp
Prawns
Oysters
Clams
Langoustines (lobsterettes)
Mussels
Sand Crabs
Sea Urchins
Softshell Crabs
Blueclaw and other hardshell crabs
Crayfish

SALTWATER:

Black Bass
Shad
Skate
Snapper
Salmon
Striped Bass
Bluefish
Cod
Scrod (young cod)
Flounder
Mahimahi (dolphin)
Swordfish
Tilefish
Pompano

FROM EUROPEAN WATERS, BUT
BECOMING AVAILABLE HERE:

Coquilles Saint-Jacques avec Oeufs
   (sea scallops with roe)
Crevette Grise (gray shrimp)
Rouget (red mullet)
Dover Sole

SHRIMP WITH APPLES AND SNOW PEAS

Experiment with the many mustards available and personalize this recipe with your favorite. Served with a bit of fluffy white rice this dish is a perfect first course, while in larger portions it is good as a main course or a luncheon dish. Serve a crisp white wine such as those from the Loire — Muscadet, Pouilly-Fumé, Sancerre or Vouvray.

1 pound snow peas, trimmed and stringed
6 tablespoons sweet butter
2 large, firm, tart apples, peeled, cut into thick slices
2 tablespoons granulated sugar
½ cup finely minced yellow onion
2 pounds mediun-size raw shrimp, shelled and deveined
¾ cup dry white wine or vermouth
⅔ cup prepared Dijon-style mustard (or try tarragon, orange,
   green peppercorn or sherry mustard)
¾ cup heavy cream, or Crème Fraîche (see page 582)

1. Bring a large pot of salted water to a boil and drop in the cleaned snow peas. When tender but still crunchy, after about 3 minutes, drain them and plunge immediately into ice water. This will stop the cooking process and set their bright green color. Reserve.

2. In a large skillet melt 2 tablespoons of the butter and sauté the apple slices over medium heat until tender but not mushy, about 5 minutes. Sprinkle slices with the sugar and raise the heat, rapidly turning apple slices until they are brown and lightly caramelized. Using a spatula, remove slices from the skillet and reserve.

3. In the same skillet melt remaining 4 tablespoons butter and gently cook the minced onion, covered, over medium heat until tender and lightly colored, about 25 minutes.

191

4. Raise the heat, add the shrimp, and stir and toss them rapidly in the butter until they are firm and pink, about 3 minutes. Do not overcook. Remove shrimp from the skillet and reserve.

5. Pour the wine or vermouth into the skillet and over high heat reduce it by two thirds. Turn down the heat and stir in the mustard with a wire whisk. Pour in the cream or *crème fraîche* and simmer uncovered, stirring occasionally, for 15 minutes or until sauce is reduced slightly.

6. Drain snow peas thoroughly and pat dry with paper towels. Add them, along with reserved apples and shrimp, to the mustard-cream sauce and simmer together for 1 minute. Serve immediately.

6 portions as a first course, 4 portions as a main course

SOFTSHELL CRABS AMANDINE

The crabs must be sautéed quickly and served immediately.

6 tablespoons sweet butter
¼ cup sliced blanched almonds
2 or 3 small softshell crabs, dressed
unbleached, all-purpose flour for dredging crabs
juice of ½ lemon
2 tablespoons finely chopped Italian parsley
lemon wedges (garnish)

1. Melt 2 tablespoons of the butter in a small skillet. Add the almonds and sauté, stirring occasionally, until golden brown.

2. Meanwhile, dredge the crabs lightly with flour and shake off excess. Heat remaining butter in another skillet; when it is hot and foaming, add the crabs.

3. Sauté crabs over high heat, turning occasionally with tongs, until crisp and reddish-brown, about 5 minutes.

4. Transfer crabs to a heated plate. Squeeze the lemon juice into the skillet and bring butter and juices to a boil. Add parsley, stir, and pour over crabs.

5. Remove almonds from their butter with a slotted spoon and sprinkle over crabs. Garnish with lemon wedges and serve immediately.

1 portion

HOW TO DRESS A SOFTSHELL CRAB

Our favorite way to dress a softshell crab is to have the fishmonger do it. This is, however, not always possible, and since the task is not all that disagreeable or demanding we think every good cook should learn the basic steps. The delicious end here certainly justifies the means; wouldn't it be a shame to be on the Maryland shore in the springtime, presented with a batch of fresh crabs, and not know where to begin?

Just such a misadventure happened to Julee once, when she invited 12 friends over to celebrate the beginning of the softshell crab season, brought the crabs home, and then realized, as they glared at her from the sink, that they were very much unlike anything she had ever seen on a plate. On inspiration, she called a chef at a restaurant, who took the time to explain the procedure over the phone. For those who are stranded without the aid of an obliging chef, we offer the following procedure.

Rinse the live crabs well under cold water. Snip off their heads approximately ¼ inch behind their eyes. This will kill them instantly and that will be that. Next turn them on their backs and lift and pull away sharply the triangular aprons that are folded on the stomachs like tucked-under tails. Finally peel back the points of the top skin "shells," taking care not to pull them off, and scrape out the spongy gills at each side. Rinse the crabs a final time and pat them dry before grilling, sautéing or broiling.

BLUEFISH BAKED WITH APPLES AND MUSTARD

The oily and robustly flavored bluefish stands up well to the sweet and pungent combination of flavors in this recipe.

4 firm, crisp, tart cooking apples
½ pound plus 4 tablespoons (2½ sticks) sweet butter, chilled
4 bluefish fillets, about 2½ pounds
1 cup coarse mild mustard, approximately
1 cup Fish Stock (see page 588)
2 cups medium-dry white wine, approximately
1 tablespoon minced shallots

1. Preheat oven to 350°F.

2. Peel the apples or not, as you wish, cut them into thin slices, and sauté them in 4 tablespoons of the butter in a skillet over high heat until lightly browned. Reserve.

3. Lay bluefish fillets in a shallow baking dish just large enough to hold them in a single layer. Smear the mustard evenly over the fillets. Spread apples over and around the fish. Pour the fish stock and enough wine around the fillets to come about halfway up their thickness, about ½ cup. The apple slices should be more or less submerged.

4. Set the baking dish in the center of the oven and bake for 8 minutes.

5. While the fish is cooking, combine remaining white wine and the minced shallots in a small skillet and reduce to about a spoonful.

6. Test the fish with a fork. When it is almost, but not quite, done to your liking, remove from the oven.

7. Drain all liquid from the baking dish into the wine-shallot mixture in the small skillet and turn heat on full. Cover the fish and apples with foil and keep warm while finishing the sauce.

8. When the liquid in the skillet is reduced by half, turn the heat to very low. Whisk in remaining 2 sticks of chilled butter, a piece (about a tablespoonful) at a time, always adding the next bit of butter just before the last has been completely incorporated. The sauce will mount and become glossy. When all the butter has been incorporated, turn off the heat and cover the pan.

9. Divide the fillets and apple slices among 4 heated plates, spoon the sauce over all and serve immediately.

4 portions

SWORDFISH STEAKS

Swordfish is deliciously meaty; when cooked with a little care, it need not be dry. We bake it according to the Canadian Fisheries method and surround it with a bit of wine or fish stock as additional insurance. The result is moist and flavorful every time. With a fish this rich a sauce is really unnecessary, but a seasoned butter, melting over the steak as it's brought to table, is a lovely touch. Particularly appropriate are Anchovy Butter and Basil-Mustard Butter (see page 197).

6 swordfish steaks, ½ to ¾ pound each, cut 1 inch thick
1 cup Fish Stock (see page 588) or dry white wine, approximately
salt and freshly ground black pepper, to taste
½ to ¾ cup flavored butter of your choice

1. Preheat oven to 375°F.
2. Arrange swordfish steaks in a single layer in 1 or 2 baking dishes just large enough to hold them comfortably. Pour fish stock or white wine, or a combination of both, around the fish, to a depth equal to half the thickness of the steaks. Season lightly with salt and freshly ground black pepper.
3. Set the dish or dishes on the middle level of the oven and bake for 9 minutes. Check the fish for doneness with a fork, remembering that residual heat will continue to cook the fish even after you take it from the oven; if fish is not ready, bake a moment or two longer and test again.
4. When almost done to your liking, transfer steaks with a spatula to heated plates. Place a tablespoon or two of the flavored butter in the center of each steak and serve immediately.
6 portions

Even a fish story needn't be dull. When you tire of sole fillets and tunafish sandwiches, there is literally a whole ocean full of fish to be discovered. You'll find a wonderful new world of firm-textured, juicy, flavorful fish dishes.

COOKING FRESH FISH

Many Americans overcook fish. The Canadian Fisheries rule of thumb works particularly well, unless your taste runs to really undercooked fish: Lay the fish on its side and measure it with a ruler at its thickest part. Calculate 10 minutes of cooking time, whatever the method, per inch of thickness. Experience will soon guide you; fish continues to cook while it waits for you to complete the sauce, for example.

BAKED STRIPED BASS
WITH FENNEL

When you want to pull out all the stops, this is the most elegant of fish dishes. Serve it with Sautéed Cherry Tomatoes (see page 323) and buttered spinach noodles. Accompany it with an excellent white wine, a first-growth Chablis or a California Chardonnay.

1 large fennel bulb, including stems and feathery leaves
¼ cup best-quality olive oil
2 garlic cloves, peeled and minced
salt and freshly ground black pepper, to taste
¼ cup chopped Italian parsley
1 striped bass, 5 to 7 pounds before dressing,
  backbone removed,★ scaled, head and tail intact
juice of ½ lemon
½ cup dry white wine or vermouth
1 or 2 bunches of fresh watercress (garnish)

1. Preheat oven to 400°F.
2. Cut fennel bulb into slices and the slices into thin strips. Reserve stems and feathery leaves.
3. Heat olive oil in a small skillet and sauté fennel slices and half of the garlic, covered, until just tender, about 10 minutes. With a slotted spoon, transfer fennel to a bowl, season with salt and pepper to taste and add the parsley. Reserve the oil.
4. Arrange the bass in an oiled shallow baking dish and spread it

open. Lay the cooked fennel mixture down the center of the bass and arrange a few of the reserved ferny sprigs on top of the mixture. Sprinkle with lemon juice, close the fish, and tie it together in two or three places with kitchen twine.

5. Season the outside of the fish with salt and pepper and rub it with the remaining garlic. Pour reserved oil over the fish and lay reserved fennel stems on top. Pour white wine or vermouth into the pan.

6. Bake fish on the middle rack of the oven for 10 minutes per inch of thickness, measured at the thickest part. Baste often with accumulated juices from the pan. Bass is done when flesh is opaque and flakes slightly when probed with a fork. Remove strings.

7. Carefully transfer bass to a large serving platter and surround it with fresh watercress. Serve at once.

8 portions

*Your fishmonger will do this for you.

FLAVORED BUTTERS

Try these instead of plain butter in sandwiches and with fish, meat and vegetable dishes. For each flavored butter, either combine the ingredients in the bowl of a food processor fitted with a steel blade and process until smooth, or cream them together by hand in a small bowl. Cover and refrigerate until ready to use. Use a melon-baller, if you like, to make perfect spheres of the butter before chilling.

♥ **ANCHOVY BUTTER:** 8 tablespoons (1 stick) sweet butter, 1 tablespoon capers, drained, 2 tablespoons anchovy paste (or to taste).

♥ **BASIL-MUSTARD BUTTER:** 8 tablespoons (1 stick) sweet butter, ¼ cup prepared Dijon-style mustard, and ¼ cup coarsely chopped fresh basil leaves.

♥ **CURRY-CHUTNEY BUTTER:** 8 tablespoons (1 stick) sweet butter, ¼ cup mango chutney, 1 teaspoon curry powder.

♥ **DILL BUTTER:** 8 tablespoons (1 stick) sweet butter, 3 tablespoons chopped fresh dill, ½ teaspoon lemon juice, ½ teaspoon prepared Dijon-style mustard.

♥ **HERB BUTTER:** 8 tablespoons (1 stick) sweet butter, 1 tablespoon finely chopped fresh herb of your choice.

♥ **RAVIGOTE BUTTER:** 8 tablespoons (1 stick) sweet butter, 1 tablespoon capers, drained, 1 heaping tablespoon each of chopped shallots, chopped fresh parsley, and tarragon (either fresh or preserved, thoroughly rinsed of all vinegar), 1 tablespoon snipped chives, ½ teaspoon lemon juice.

SUNDAY SUMMER SUPPER

Carrot and Orange Soup

---

*Baked Striped Bass
with Fennel*

Bulgur wheat salad

Eggplant Basil Salad

Chocolate Hazelnut Cake

ESCABECHE

This version of South American pickled fish looks complicated, but is assembled with little kitchen time. After this it is marinated for 4 days before you serve it, and will keep for a good 2 weeks afterwards, if well refrigerated. Make it with any firm-fleshed white fish (snapper, tilefish and scrod are good), and serve it with hot bread and white rice. Perfect for a summertime picnic on the porch.

2 cups unbleached, all-purpose flour
4 pounds fish steaks or fillets, ½ inch thick
1½ cups best-quality olive oil
juice of 1½ limes
⅔ cup white wine vinegar
⅔ cup dry white wine
2⅔ cups green beans, cut into julienne
1⅓ cups carrots, cut into julienne
⅓ cup green olives, pitted, with juice
½ cup imported black olives, pitted, without juice
⅓ cup capers
1 medium-size purple onion, cut into thin rounds
1 small white onion, cut into thin rounds
2 green peppers, cut into thin rings
2 sweet red peppers, cut into thin rings
1 tablespoon Oriental oyster sauce
3 tablespoons coarsely chopped fresh coriander (cilantro)
3 tablespoons coarsely chopped fresh dill
1 tablespoon mixed pickling spice
1 teaspoon salt
freshly ground black pepper, to taste
1½ tablespoons brown sugar
3 garlic cloves, peeled and finely chopped

1. Flour the fish lightly. Heat the oil in a large skillet and sauté the fish, in batches if necessary, for 3 to 4 minutes, turning frequently. Fish should be just cooked and starting to brown lightly. Remove from skillet and drain on paper towels.
2. Transfer drained fish to a large bowl. Combine all liquids and

199

seasonings, mix with vegetables, and pour over fish. Cover and refrigerate for 4 days, basting at intervals.

3. Toss again, arrange on a large platter, and garnish with additional chopped parsley. Serve immediately.

12 to 14 portions

COLD POACHED SCALLOPS

Serve the scallops as a first course or as a light main course.

1½ pounds sea scallops
Blueberry Mayonnaise (recipe follows)
fresh blueberries (optional garnish)
fresh mint leaves (optional garnish)

1. Rinse the scallops briefly and place them in a saucepan that holds them comfortably in one layer. Cover with lightly salted water and bring the water to a simmer. Cook gently for 1 minute. Remove saucepan from heat and let scallops cool to room temperature in their poaching liquid.

2. Prepare Blueberry Mayonnaise.

3. Rinse and sort through blueberries if you use them, selecting fat perfect berries only. Rinse sprigs of fresh mint under cold water and pat dry.

4. Drain scallops and arrange them on small plates. Spoon Blueberry Mayonnaise over and around scallops but do not completely mask them. Garnish randomly with selected blueberries and mint sprigs and serve immediately.

4 to 6 portions

Blueberry Mayonnaise is good as a sauce for cold poached fish such as salmon, or on cold chicken. Brands of blueberry vinegar, the essential component, vary in intensity; adjust tartness to suit your own palate.

BLUEBERRY MAYONNAISE

1 whole egg
2 egg yolks
1 tablespoon prepared Dijon-style mustard
¼ cup blueberry vinegar★
salt and freshly ground black pepper, to taste
2 cups corn oil or light salad oil

1. Combine whole egg, extra egg yolks, mustard, vinegar, and salt and pepper to taste in the bowl of a food processor fitted with a steel blade. Process for 1 minute.

2. With the motor running, dribble in the oil in a slow, steady stream.

3. When all oil has been incorporated, shut off motor. Taste mayonnaise and correct seasoning. You may want to add additional blueberry vinegar until the mayonnaise has a sweet-and-sour balance.

4. Transfer to a storage container, cover, and refrigerate.

2½ cups

★available in specialty food shops

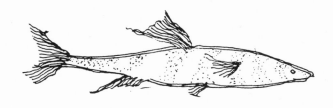

BUYING AND KEEPING FRESH FISH

For Americans used to defrosting a package of sole, the art of dealing with fresh fish can seem as arcane as alchemy. Here are some tips to dispel the confusion:

♥ Most fish are seasonal. Don't insist on a particular type of fish if it is not at its prime. Learn to substitute within fish types.

♥ Whole fish are more perishable, thus they are usually fresher than fillets.

♥ Know your fishmonger. If you have the choice, buy where reputable restaurants get their fish. If you have no choice, learn to shop with an eagle eye; demand increased variety if it seems limited; shout loud and long if fish is over the hill in freshness.

♥ Look your fish squarely in the eye and be sure that eye is bright and firm. The gills should be red, the flesh firm and springy when poked with a finger. Truly fresh fish smell fresh — like the ocean — and are not slimy. Fillets should be firm, without the fishy odor that indicates staleness.

♥ The best way to store fish is on ice — similar to the way the markets do. Bring your fish home immediately, rinse under cold running water, enclose in a plastic bag and immerse in a bowl of ice water. Plan to use the fish, particularly if it is whole, the day purchased.

BAKING IN FOIL

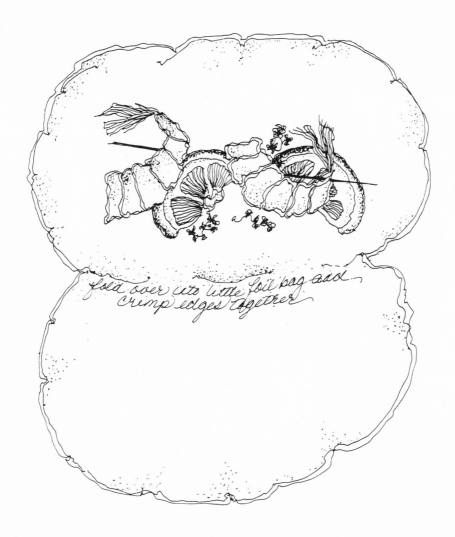

fold over into little foil bag and crimp edges together

Foods baked in foil packets retain the maximum of their natural moisture and flavor. The packets can be arranged and sealed in advance of actual cooking, leaving the hostess free to spend time with her guests. And finally, the silvery envelopes look terrific cut open at the table, releasing their savory steam.

Cut the foil into a large heart shape, or use a simple rectangle. Arrange meat or fish and garnishes inside and fold foil over, sealing well on all sides. When arranging food in packets, do not overlap meat or fish pieces or they will not cook evenly. If the packets are prepared far in advance and refrigerated, be certain to let the foods return to room temperature before cooking. If you prefer to use classic cooking parchment rather than foil, butter it well and reduce cooking times slightly.

LAMB CHOPS WITH MUSHROOMS AND HERBS

1 tablespoon minced garlic
⅓ cup minced fresh mint and parsley, more or less half and half, or to taste
4 tablespoons sweet butter, at room temperature
6 boned loin lamb chops, cut 1½ inches thick, about 6 ounces each, trimmed weight
6 thin lemon slices
6 sprigs of fresh mint
2 to 3 dozen firm white mushroom caps (about 1 pound)
salt and freshly ground black pepper, to taste

1. Preheat oven to 350°F.
2. Mash garlic, herbs, and half of the butter together into a rough paste. Divide the herb butter among the lamb chops, spreading a bit inside the tails and the rest on top. Tie chops into tidy rounds with kitchen twine.
3. Arrange each chop on a piece of foil and place a lemon slice and a mint sprig on top of each. Smear remaining butter over the mushrooms and arrange them evenly around the chops. Season to taste with salt and freshly ground black pepper. Seal the foil packets, and set on a baking sheet.
4. Bake about 20 minutes for medium rare. Transfer packets to serving plates and allow guests to open them at table.
   6 portions

LAMB CHOPS WITH VEGETABLES AND FRUITS

6 boned loin lamb chops, cut 1½ inches thick, about 6 ounces each, trimmed weight
salt and freshly ground black pepper, to taste
3 kiwis, peeled and scooped into balls
2 cups seedless red or green grapes
24 asparagus spears, trimmed, blanched and sliced diagonally
2 thin cucumbers, peeled and scooped into balls
⅓ cup minced fresh mint and parsley, more or less half and half, or to taste

1. Preheat oven to 350°F.
2. Tie chops into neat rounds with kitchen twine. Arrange each on a piece of foil and season to taste with salt and pepper. Scatter fruits and vegetables around chops, dividing equally. Sprinkle chopped mint and parsley over all. Seal the foil packets, and set on a baking sheet.
3. Bake about 20 minutes for medium rare. Transfer packets to serving plates and allow guests to open them at table.

6 portions

LAMB CHOPS

Lamb chops cook to moist perfection in foil packets. The chops should be loin chops, boned but otherwise left in one piece, with the tiny tail intact. After final assembly, secure with toothpick or tie with thin twine. Each of our three versions includes its own vegetables, and no other accompaniment is really necessary, particularly if you begin with a light pasta dish to provide the starch.

LAMB CHOPS WITH ARTICHOKES AND ENDIVE

6 large cooked artichoke hearts, fresh or canned
*6 boned loin lamb chops, cut 1½ inches thick, about 6 ounces
  each, trimmed weight*
salt and freshly ground black pepper, to taste
¾ cup cooked spinach
pinch of freshly grated nutmeg
1 tablespoon finely minced garlic
6 tablespoons sweet butter
6 whole endives, trimmed, cleaned and halved lengthwise
⅓ cup finely chopped Italian parsley

1. Preheat oven to 350°F.
2. Set 1 artichoke heart in the half-circle formed by the tail of each lamb chop, wrap tail around, and secure in place with a short wooden skewer. Season chops and artichokes with salt and freshly ground black pepper.
3. Season spinach to taste with salt, pepper and nutmeg and divide equally in the center of the artichoke hearts.
4. Mash together the garlic and 2 tablespoons of the butter. Spread a bit of garlic butter on top of each lamb chop.
5. Arrange each chop on half of a sheet of foil. Place 2 endive halves next to each chop and dot endive with remaining butter. Season endive with salt and pepper to taste and sprinkle chopped parsley over all. Seal the foil packets, and set on a baking sheet.
6. Bake about 20 minutes for medium rare. Transfer packets to serving plates and allow guests to open them at table.
   6 portions

SKEWERED SHRIMP AND SOLE

6 fillets of flounder or sole, about 3 pounds altogether
18 medium-size raw shrimp, shelled and deveined
24 asparagus tips, blanched
2 limes, thinly sliced
salt and freshly ground black pepper, to taste
4 cucumbers
chopped fresh dill, to taste
4 tablespoons sweet butter

1. Preheat oven to 400°F.
2. Thread sole fillets lengthwise onto wooden skewers, alternating with shrimp, three to a skewer, as if using a needle and thread. Each shrimp will be skewered in a "stitch."
3. Center each sole skewer on a piece of foil and wedge asparagus tips between shrimp and sole. Halve the lime slices and tuck these between shrimp and sole for a decorative effect. Season to taste with salt and freshly ground black pepper.
4. Cut peeled cucumbers with a melon-baller to make as many balls as possible. Scatter cucumber balls over fish and sprinkle with chopped fresh dill to taste. Dot with butter and seal packets. Set on a baking sheet.
5. Bake for 10 minutes, or until done. Transfer packets to serving plates and allow guests to open them at table.

6 portions

One of our favorite restaurants in the world is Elvira's in Nogales, Mexico. It can be truly said that Elvira's is a dive, but in the best sense of the word. Oilcloth covers the tables, a cat wanders through, and genial musicians assault the senses with incomprehensible songs. By way of compensation, the tequila flows freely, the welcome is genuine, and the food delicious.

One of our favorite dishes there is fish baked in foil with a topping of sour cream and onions. It is a simple dish, dressing up the plainest and mildest piece of fish with delicate zest. The Mexican version of sour cream does not separate when heated, much like the *crème fraîche* we have preferred to substitute. Slice the onions paper-thin, and sprinkle the fish with lime juice and chopped cilantro, if you like. Mexican beer or tequila is the perfect accompanying beverage.

SKEWERED SHRIMP AND PROSCIUTTO

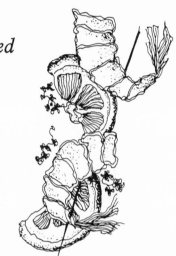

9 thin slices of prosciutto
3 dozen medium-size raw shrimp, shelled and deveined
2 dozen pitted California black olives
18 thin lemon slices (2 to 3 lemons)
⅓ cup finely chopped Italian parsley
2 to 3 garlic cloves, peeled and finely chopped
crushed dried red pepper, to taste
6 tablespoons best-quality olive oil, or more

1. Preheat oven to 350°F.
2. Cut each slice of prosciutto lengthwise into halves and wrap 1 piece of prosciutto around each of 18 shrimp.
3. Slide 2 olives onto one of 6 skewers. Slide a wrapped shrimp onto skewer. Wrap a lemon slice around a plain shrimp and slide onto skewer. Repeat, using 2 more prosciutto-wrapped shrimp and 2 more lemon-wrapped shrimp. End with 2 more olives. Repeat skewering procedure with remaining shrimp, lemons and olives.
4. Lay each skewer on a piece of foil. Sprinkle with parsley, chopped garlic and red pepper to taste. Drizzle each skewer with a tablespoon or so of olive oil and seal the packets. Set on a baking sheet.
5. Bake for 10 minutes, or until shrimp are done. Do not overcook. Transfer packets to plates and allow guests to open them at table.
6 portions

FISH ELVIRA

2 fillets of mild white fish (flounder, sole, etc.), about ¾ inch thick
½ cup Crème Fraîche (see page 582)
1 medium-size white onion, peeled and thinly sliced
salt and freshly ground black pepper, to taste
chopped fresh coriander (cilantro), to taste
1 lime, quartered (garnish)

1. Smear fish fillets with *crème fraîche* and set aside in a dish to marinate at room temperature for 1 hour.
2. Preheat oven to 400°F.
3. Transfer each fish fillet to a piece of foil. Spoon any juices and *crème fraîche* from marinating dish over fish. Cover fillets completely with a thin layer of onion slices. Season to taste with salt and pepper and seal the foil packets. Set on a baking sheet.
4. Bake for 8 to 10 minutes, according to thickness of fish. Transfer packets to plates, slit open, and sprinkle fish with cilantro. Garnish with lime wedges and serve immediately.

2 portions

❖ FROM THE SILVER
PALATE NOTEBOOK

Even if you've prepared everything in advance, try to arrange for the smell of something cooking when guests arrive. Whether it's cloves or herbs simmering in water, the effect is subtly welcoming.

CHICKEN WITH LEMON AND HERBS

*1 cup chopped fresh mint, dill and parsley in about equal
proportions, or to taste*
2 cloves garlic, minced
*6 boned chicken breasts, skinned and halved, about 4½ pounds
altogether*
salt and freshly ground black pepper, to taste
2 lemons
4 tablespoons sweet butter

1. Preheat oven to 350°F.
2. Mix herbs and garlic together in a small bowl. Flatten chicken
breasts by pressing them gently against the work surface with the
palm of your hand. Arrange breast pieces on foil and season with salt
and pepper. Sprinkle herb and garlic mixture over chicken breasts.
3. Slice lemons and arrange 2 to 3 slices over each breast. Dot with
butter and seal the packets. Set on a baking sheet.
4. Set packets in the middle of the oven and bake for 30 minutes.
Transfer to serving plates and allow guests to open packets at table.
  6 portions

THE STEW POT

What can we say about stews that doesn't conjure up remembered scenes and aromas of Saturday afternoons at Grandma's house, or spending a day home from school because a big snowstorm cancelled all classes? Mother and Grandmother made stew in their usual no-nonsense manner. It was filling and economical and used ingredients that were on hand.

We take a bit more care and planning with our stews and ragouts these days, but it's all for the same end. There's something about a stewpot simmering in the kitchen that lets everyone know that a caring cook is in control. Whether you're weathering a storm or coupling the first vegetables of spring in a delicate *navarin,* stews make special memories.

Stews are forgiving food, easygoing and open to improvisation and substitution. They also reduce pressure in the kitchen, since stews are nearly always better made a day or two in advance of serving. The finished product, long simmered and rich flavored, is always a crowd pleaser. Stew says something special to your guests; they feel welcomed, comforted, nourished.

BEEF STEW WITH CUMINSEED

Depending on the rest of the menu, this stew seems Mexican or Mediterranean because it is hearty and intriguingly seasoned with cuminseed, a spice that is a staple in our kitchen.

2 cups unbleached, all-purpose flour
1 tablespoon dried thyme
1 teaspoon salt, plus additional to taste
½ teaspoon freshly ground black pepper, plus additional to taste
3 pounds beef stew meat, in 1-inch cubes
¼ cup olive oil
1 cup dry red wine
1½ cups homemade Beef Stock (see page 586)
1 cup canned crushed tomatoes
2 tablespoons ground cuminseed
1 teaspoon chili powder
1 bay leaf
8 to 12 white pearl onions
6 garlic cloves, peeled and chopped
½ cup chopped Italian parsley, plus additional for garnish
1½ cups green Sicilian olives

   1. Preheat oven to 350°F.
   2. Stir the flour, thyme, 1 teaspoon salt and ½ teaspoon pepper

212

together in a shallow bowl. Turn the cubes of stew meat in the flour to coat well, shake off excess, and transfer to a plate.

3. Heat the olive oil in a heavy kettle. Add the beef cubes, a few at a time, and brown them well on all sides. As they are browned, transfer them to paper towels to drain.

4. When all the meat is browned, discard excess oil but do not wash the kettle. Add the wine, beef stock and crushed tomatoes, and set kettle over medium heat. Bring to a boil, stirring and scraping up the browned bits from the bottom of the pan. Return beef to the kettle, then add cuminseed, chili powder and bay leaf and season to taste with salt and pepper.

5. Cover the kettle and set it on the middle rack of the oven. Bake for 1½ hours, stirring occasionally and regulating the oven temperature to maintain the stew at a steady simmer.

6. Meanwhile, bring a large pot of water to a boil. Cut an X in the root end of each pearl onion and drop them into the boiling water for 1 minute. Drain them and drop them into a bowl of cold water. When completely cool, drain and peel them.

7. After the stew has been in the oven about 1 hour, stir in the onions. Continue to cook the stew, uncovered.

8. After another 15 minutes, stir in the garlic, ½ cup parsley and the olives. Continue to cook, uncovered, until stew is reduced and thickened to your liking and the beef is tender. Transfer to a serving bowl, sprinkle with parsley, and serve immediately.

6 portions

"There is no sight on earth more appealing than the sight of a woman making dinner for someone she loves."
— Thomas Wolfe

BEEF CARBONNADE

Our version of this Belgian beef stew is cooked with sweetly caramelized onions and dark beer. It is the kind of rich, hearty but simple food that is equally appropriate for family or guests. It is especially welcome after an autumn hike, at the end of a long day of skiing, or for a snowbound Sunday supper. Serve *carbonnade* with egg noodles tossed with butter and poppy seeds, sautéed apples and black bread. Serve the same beer you used in the stew.

¼ pound bacon
2 very large yellow onions, 1½ to 2 pounds, peeled and thinly sliced
1 tablespoon granulated sugar
1 cup unbleached, all-purpose flour
1 tablespoon dried thyme
1 teaspoon salt
½ teaspoon freshly ground black pepper
3 pounds beef stew meat (chuck is best), cubed
vegetable oil (optional)
2 cups imported dark beer
chopped parsley (garnish)

1. Coarsely dice the bacon and sauté it in a large skillet until crisp and brown. Remove bacon with a slotted spoon and reserve.

2. Add the onions to the skillet and cook them in the rendered bacon fat until tender, about 20 minutes. Uncover the skillet, raise the heat, and sprinkle the onions with the sugar. Toss and stir them until they are well browned. Transfer onions to a strainer set over a bowl and let stand while you prepare the beef.

3. Stir together on a plate the flour, thyme, salt and pepper, and roll the cubes of meat around in the mixture until well coated. Shake off the excess and set the cubes on another plate.

4. Press the onions gently with the back of a spoon to extract as much of the cooking fat as possible. Transfer fat to a kettle. Add additional fat in the form of vegetable oil if it appears you will not have enough for proper browning of the beef. Be sparing, however, or the *carbonnade* will be greasy.

5. Set the kettle over high heat; when the kettle is very hot, add

6 to 8 beef cubes. Do not crowd them in the kettle or they will not brown properly. Turn the heat down slightly and continue to cook cubes until browned on all sides. Transfer them with a slotted spoon to a clean plate and proceed with the browning until all the meat is done.

6. Preheat oven to 325°F.

7. Pour the beer into the kettle and use a spoon to stir up all the browned bits on the bottom. Return beef cubes to the kettle along with the bacon and sautéed onions. Bring to a simmer on the stove. Cover and set on the middle rack of the oven.

8. Cook for 1½ hours, stirring occasionally, or until stew is reduced and thickened and meat is tender. Regulate the oven temperature as needed to maintain a moderate simmer.

9. Taste and correct seasoning. Turn stew out into a heated serving dish, garnish with chopped parsley, and serve immediately.

6 portions

AUTUMN LUNCHEON

Zucchini-Watercress Soup

Beef Carbonnade

Parsleyed butter noodles

Sweet Potato and Carrot Purée

Arugula Salad with Our Favorite Vinaigrette

Ellen's Apple Tart

POT ROAST

A perfect Sunday supper.

3½ pounds beef shoulder or cross-rib roast, rolled and tied
1 teaspoon freshly ground black pepper, to taste
3 tablespoons best-quality olive oil
1½ to 2 cups Beef Stock (see page 586)
2 cups dry red wine
1 bunch of parsley, chopped fine, plus additional for garnish
1 teaspoon salt
7 whole cloves
2½ cups coarsely chopped yellow onions
2 cups peeled carrot chunks, 1-inch chunks
8 medium-size potatoes, scrubbed and cut into thirds
2 cups canned Italian plum tomatoes, with juice
1 cup diced celery

1. Preheat oven to 350°F.
2. Rub roast with black pepper. Heat olive oil in a heavy flameproof casserole or Dutch oven and sear roast for several minutes on each side, browning well.
3. Pour in stock and wine and add parsley, 1 teaspoon salt, 1 teaspoon black pepper and the whole cloves. Stir in onions, carrots, potatoes, tomatoes and celery. Liquid in casserole should just cover vegetables. Add additional Beef Stock if necessary. Bring to a simmer on top of the stove, cover, and bake in center of oven for 2½ hours.
4. Uncover and cook longer, until meat is tender, about 1½ hours, basting frequently.
5. Transfer roast to a deep serving platter and arrange vegetables around it. Spoon a bit of sauce over all and garnish the platter with parsley. Pass additional sauce in a gravy boat.

6 portions

BEAUJOLAIS

In autumn it is fun to try and catch the first of the "Beaujolais Nouveau" when it appears in stores shortly after the harvest of the first grapes. Americans have joined the French in the race to see how quickly they can make a festivity of the first pressing of the grapes. Even when the wine has lost a bit of its youth, it remains a delight. While Beaujolais wine may not be considered as serious as some of its more upright relatives, its unstuffy character should be given its own place in the sun — maybe at your next picnic.

BEEF STROGANOFF

Our version of this classic is rich and delicious. Serve it with buttered wide noodles and a simple green vegetable. Garnish the plates with Sautéed Cherry Tomatoes (see page 323), and pour a good red wine.

3 cups Crème Fraîche (see page 582)
1½ tablespoons prepared Dijon-style mustard
3 tablespoons tomato paste
3 tablespoons Worchestershire sauce
2 teaspoons imported sweet paprika
¾ teaspoon salt
freshly ground black pepper, to taste
1 teaspoon demiglace*
1 pound medium-size firm white mushrooms
10 tablespoons (1¼ sticks) sweet butter
24 medium-size white pearl onions
3 pounds beef tips (filet)
chopped Italian parsley (garnish)

1. Combine *crème fraîche*, mustard, tomato paste, Worcestershire sauce, paprika, salt, pepper to taste, and demiglace in a medium-size saucepan and simmer slowly for 20 minutes, or until sauce is slightly reduced. Remove from heat and let stand, covered, while completing recipe.

2. Trim stem ends off mushrooms and discard. Wipe mushrooms with a damp paper towel and slice thin. Melt 3 tablespoons of the

butter in a medium-size skillet and sauté mushrooms until tender and golden, about 10 minutes. Transfer to a bowl and reserve.

3. Cut a small X in the root end of each pearl onion. Bring a large kettle of water to a boil and drop in the onions. Blanch for 10 minutes, drain, and rinse under cold running water. Peel the onions. Heat another 2 tablespoons of the butter in the same skillet and sauté the onions, stirring and shaking the skillet often, until they are lightly browned, about 10 minutes. Transfer onions to the bowl with the mushrooms.

4. Cut the meat into thin slices on the diagonal. Heat remaining butter in the skillet and sauté the pieces of filet over high heat until just lightly browned, 3 to 4 minutes. Transfer pieces to a plate as each batch is browned. Recipe can be prepared to this point several hours before serving.

5. To complete, set sauce over medium heat and bring to a simmer. Add mushrooms, onions, and any accumulated juices from the bowl, and simmer for 5 minutes.

6. Add slices of filet and any accumulated juices and simmer just until meat is heated through, about 2 minutes. Serve immediately, garnished with chopped parsley.

6 portions

*available at specialty food shops

✣ FROM THE SILVER PALATE NOTEBOOK

There is one rule in our kitchen, made in the very beginning, which still holds true: When cooking, you must taste. To think that you can follow a recipe and do today what you did yesterday is erroneous. A good cook needs to be able to taste, and trust his or her own judgment. Only through developing taste (and we stress *developing* — no one is born with this kind of a silver spoon) can you begin to trust your cooking self.

Don't be afraid to taste. It is the only way we know to understand food, to know how to experiment, to build our own confidence. Treat it like two pieces of a puzzle; if you try and it doesn't work, what has been lost? If it does, perhaps you can improve upon it the next time. To follow a recipe repeatedly because it is safe, tried, true, and from a reliable source is boring and impersonal. Take our recipes, make them your own, and improve upon them. That will be our greatest pleasure.

BRAISED SHORT RIBS OF BEEF

1 teaspoon freshly ground black pepper, plus additional to sprinkle over ribs before cooking
4 pounds beef short ribs, cut into 2-inch lengths
5 tablespoons best-quality olive oil
8 garlic cloves, peeled and finely chopped
1½ cups canned Italian plum tomatoes, with juice
2 cups sliced carrots, ⅛ inch thick each
3 cups sliced onions
8 whole cloves
½ cup chopped Italian parsley
¾ cup red wine vinegar
3 tablespoons tomato paste
2 tablespoons brown sugar
2 teaspoons salt
¼ teaspoon cayenne pepper
3 cups Beef Stock (see page 586), approximately

1. Sprinkle pepper over short ribs. Heat olive oil in a Dutch oven or casserole. Sear ribs, 3 to 4 at a time, browning well on all sides. As they are browned, drain them on paper towels.

2. Preheat oven to 350°F.

3. Return half of the ribs to the casserole. Sprinkle with half of the garlic. Layer half of each vegetable over the meat. Add 4 cloves and sprinkle with half of the parsley. Repeat with remaining ingredients, ending with a layer of chopped parsley.

4. In a bowl mix together vinegar, tomato paste, brown sugar, salt, 1 teaspoon black pepper and cayenne. Pour over meat and vegetables and then add beef stock just to cover.

5. Cover casserole, set over medium heat, and bring to a boil. Bake in the oven for 1½ hours. Uncover and bake for 1½ hours longer, or until meat is very tender. Taste, correct seasoning, and serve immediately.

6 portions

CHILI FOR A CROWD

From the very beginning of The Silver Palate, Sheila's special chili was a winner. Whether you're a busy cook who likes to freeze food for future meals, or a hostess with a crowd on hand, this southwestern stew is the answer. Offer bowls of sour cream, chopped white onion and grated Cheddar cheese, and let your guests garnish as they please. We like to serve sourdough bread or corn muffins on the side, follow the chili with a plain green salad, and of course serve Mexican beer — try Bohemia, Carta Blanca or the dark Dos Equis.

½ cup best-quality olive oil
1¾ pounds yellow onions, coarsely chopped
2 pounds sweet Italian sausage meat, removed from casings
8 pounds beef chuck, ground
1½ tablespoons freshly ground black pepper
2 cans, 12 ounces each, tomato paste
3 tablespoons minced fresh garlic
3 ounces ground cuminseed
4 ounces plain chili powder
½ cup prepared Dijon-style mustard
4 tablespoons salt
4 tablespoons dried basil
4 tablespoons dried oregano
6 pounds canned Italian plum tomatoes, drained (about 5 cans,
  each 2 pounds, 3 ounces before draining)
½ cup Burgundy wine
¼ cup lemon juice
½ cup chopped fresh dill
½ cup chopped Italian parsley
3 cans, 16 ounces each, dark red kidney beans, drained
4 cans, 5½ ounces each, pitted black olives, drained

1. Heat olive oil in a very large soup kettle. Add onions and cook over low heat, covered, until tender and translucent, about 10 minutes.

2. Crumble the sausage meat and ground chuck into the kettle and cook over medium-high heat, stirring often, until meats are well browned. Spoon out as much excess fat as possible.

3. Over low heat stir in black pepper, tomato paste, garlic, cuminseed, chili powder, mustard, salt, basil and oregano.

4. Add drained tomatoes, Burgundy, lemon juice, dill, parsley and drained kidney beans. Stir well and simmer, uncovered, for another 15 minutes.

5. Taste and correct seasoning. Add olives, simmer for another 5 minutes to heat through, and serve immediately.

35 to 40 portions

SUPER BOWL BUFFET

Chef's Salad

Crusty French bread with herbed butter

Chili for a Crowd, garnished with sour cream, chopped onions, and grated Cheddar cheese

Parsleyed Rice

Brownies

Chocolate Chip Cookies

✤ FROM THE SILVER
PALATE NOTEBOOK

Make entertaining and sharing meals a way of life — as natural and sincere as anything else you do. Entertaining need not be formal or even organized to convey your personal style and feelings. Of primary importance is the bringing together of people you care about, to share food and drink and to have a good time.

SAUSAGE RAGOUT

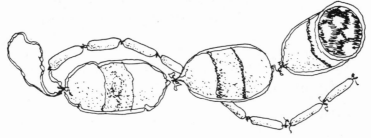

Serve this thick, tomato-rich ragoût with buttered pasta or mashed potatoes and follow it with a tart green salad. A hearty red wine — perhaps the one with which you cooked the ragoût — would be the ideal drink.

1½ pounds sweet Italian sausage
1½ pounds hot Italian sausage
¼ cup best-quality olive oil
1 large yellow onion, peeled and coarsely chopped
3 garlic cloves, peeled and minced
2 green peppers, stemmed, seeded and coarsely chopped
2 sweet red peppers, stemmed, seeded and coarsely chopped
8 fresh Italian plum tomatoes, quartered
1 cup Spicy Tomato Sauce (see page 591)
½ cup dry red wine
½ cup minced Italian parsley, plus additional for garnish
salt and freshly ground black pepper, to taste

1. Cut sausages into ½-inch slices. Heat olive oil in a skillet and add sausage pieces. Cook, stirring occasionally, until sausage pieces are well browned.

2. Add onion and garlic and cook for another 5 minutes. With a slotted spoon transfer meat mixture to a deep casserole.

3. Set casserole over medium heat and add the peppers. Cook, stirring, until peppers are slightly wilted, about 7 minutes.

4. Add tomatoes, Spicy Tomato Sauce, wine and parsley, and season with salt and pepper to taste. Simmer uncovered, stirring occasionally, for 30 minutes.

5. Taste, correct seasoning, and serve immediately, sprinkled with chopped parsley.

6 portions

WINTER PORK AND FRUIT RAGOUT

Serve this delicious casserole with Saffron Rice (see page 592), black beans and a green salad garnished with orange slices.

3 pounds lean boneless pork, cut into 1-inch cubes
2 dozen dried apricot halves
1 cup dark seedless raisins
1 cup dry red wine
1 cup red wine vinegar
3 tablespoons chopped fresh dill
3 tablespoons chopped fresh mint
1 teaspoon ground cuminseed
1 teaspoon freshly ground black pepper
1 tablespoon dried thyme
salt, to taste
⅓ cup best-quality olive oil
4 shallots, peeled and minced
1 cup dry white wine
1 quart Chicken Stock (see page 587)
2 bay leaves
¼ cup honey

1. In a large bowl combine pork, apricots, raisins, red wine, vinegar, dill, mint, cuminseed, pepper, thyme, and salt to taste. Cover and marinate, refrigerated, for 24 hours. Stir occasionally.

2. Remove pork and fruit from marinade. Reserve fruit in a small bowl. Reserve marinade separately. Pat pork dry with paper towels.

3. Heat olive oil in a large skillet and sauté meat, a few pieces at a time, until well browned. With a slotted spoon transfer pork to a deep casserole.

4. Drain oil from skillet, add shallots, and sauté over medium heat for 5 minutes. Add reserved marinade and bring to a boil, scraping up any browned bits remaining in the skillet. Cook for several minutes, until slightly reduced, and add to the casserole.

5. Preheat oven to 350°F.

6. Stir in apricots, raisins, half of the white wine, half of the Chicken Stock, the bay leaves and honey; mix well. Set over medium heat, bring to a boil, cover, and set on the middle rack of the oven.

7. Bake for 1 hour and 15 minutes. Uncover casserole, and add additional wine or stock if meat seems too dry. Bake, uncovered, for another 30 to 45 minutes, or until meat is tender and sauce rich and thick.

6 to 8 portions

HOLIDAY BUFFET

Chicken Liver Pâté with Green Peppercorns, with toasts

Winter Pork and Fruit Ragoût

Sweet Potato and Carrot Purée

Watercress salad with Raspberry Vinaigrette

Chestnut Mousse

Linzertorte

If you are used to thinking of sauerkraut as the obnoxious stuff between the mustard and the hotdog at a baseball game, you have a surprise in store. In this hearty peasant dish, the kraut is rinsed of its salty brine and slowly oven-braised with wine, chicken stock, herbs and spices. Garnish it with an array of sausages and smoked meats, and serve mashed potatoes with lots of butter, black bread and beer. It is a meal fit for family and company alike. Although you can use store-bought sausages and kraut, you really must make the chicken stock — it is the secret of the dish's success.

CHOUCROUTE GARNIE

2 pounds sauerkraut (the kind that comes in plastic bags or refrigerated jars; use canned sauerkraut only as a last resort)
½ pound bacon, coarsely diced
1 large yellow onion, peeled and chopped
3 carrots, peeled and sliced
1 tart cooking apple (Newton, Granny Smith, Winesap), cored and grated; do not peel
1 tablespoon caraway seeds (optional)
10 juniper berries
4 parsley sprigs
6 white peppercorns
2 bay leaves
1 cup dry white wine
4 cups Chicken Stock (see page 587), plus more if needed
1½ pounds sausage (saucisson, spicy bulk breakfast sausage, bratwurst, knackwurst, etc.)
6 smoked pork chops
chopped fresh parsley (garnish)

1. Soak the kraut in a large bowl of cold water for 30 minutes.
2. Meanwhile, fry the bacon in a large skillet. When it renders its fat, after about 5 minutes, add the onion and carrots. Raise the heat and cook, stirring occasionally, until vegetables are about half-

225

cooked and lightly browned. Remove from heat and reserve.

3. Drain the kraut and squeeze out all the water (be thorough!). Spread kraut in a nonaluminum roaster or flame-proof casserole with a tight-fitting lid. Stir in the bacon, bacon fat, sautéed vegetables, grated apple, and caraway seeds if you use them.

4. Tie the juniper berries, parsley, peppercorns and bay leaves in a small cheesecloth bag and bury it in the kraut. Pour in the wine and add enough chicken stock to cover the kraut.

5. Preheat oven to 325°F.

6. Butter a piece of wax paper (do not use foil) and press it, buttered side down, onto the kraut. Set the roaster over medium heat and bring to a simmer, then cover and set in the oven.

7. Cook the kraut for 5 hours, adding additional stock if the dish seems to be drying out. Refrain from adding stock near the end of cooking time, since all liquid must be absorbed by the kraut before serving.

8. If you are using bulk sausage, form it into 6 small patties and brown lightly in a skillet. If you are using link sausages, prick the skins well with a fork and sauté until lightly browned. Discard the rendered fat in any case.

9. About 30 minutes before you estimate the kraut will be done, uncover, lift the wax paper, and distribute the sausages and smoked pork chops over the kraut. Cover and finish cooking. Remove the spice bag and sprinkle with parsley before serving.

6 portions

DILLED BLANQUETTE DE VEAU

Such a rich but delicate dish should be served with nothing but parsleyed new potatoes. The fresh dill makes all the difference.

12 tablespoons (1½ sticks) sweet butter
3 pounds veal, cut into 1-inch cubes
½ cup unbleached, all-purpose flour
1 scant teaspoon freshly grated nutmeg
1½ teaspoons salt
1½ teaspoons freshly ground black pepper
3 cups peeled carrots, sliced diagonally (slices ⅛ inch thick)
3 cups coarsely chopped yellow onions
5 tablespoons finely chopped fresh dill
3 to 4 cups Chicken Stock (see page 587)
¾ cup heavy cream

1. Preheat oven to 350°F.
2. Melt 8 tablespoons (1 stick) of the butter in a heavy flameproof casserole. Add the veal and cook, turning frequently, without browning.
3. Stir 3 tablespoons flour, the nutmeg, salt and pepper together in a small bowl, and sprinkle over the veal. Continue to cook over low heat, stirring, for 5 minutes. Flour and veal should not brown.
4. Add carrots, onions, 3 tablespoons of the dill and enough stock just to cover meat and vegetables. Raise heat to medium, bring to a boil, cover, and bake in the oven for 1½ hours.
5. Remove stew from oven and pour it through a strainer placed over a bowl. Reserve solids and liquid separately.
6. Return casserole to medium heat and melt remaining butter in it. Sprinkle in remaining flour and cook over low heat, whisking constantly, for 5 minutes.
7. Whisk reserved cooking liquid slowly into the butter and flour mixture and bring to a simmer. Cook slowly, stirring constantly, for 5 minutes.
8. Whisk in cream, remaining dill, and additional salt, pepper and nutmeg to taste. Return veal and vegetables to the casserole and simmer together to heat through, about 5 minutes. Transfer to a deep serving dish and serve at once.

6 portions

┌─────────────────────────────────────┐
│ **SUPPER PARTY MENU**

Salmon Mousse with
Green Herb Dipping
Sauce and black Russian
pumpernickel

────────

Dilled Blanquette de Veau

────────

Watercress and Endive Salad
with Walnut Oil Vinaigrette

────────

Chocolate Mousse with
Crème Fraîche
└─────────────────────────────────────┘

PIZZA POT PIE

This hearty casserole features typical pizza ingredients — sausages, mushrooms, and tomato sauce — baked together under a tender pizza crust. It is simple and satisfying, and with a green salad makes a complete meal.

2 pounds sweet Italian sausage, cut into 1-inch pieces
2 pounds hot Italian sausage, cut into 1-inch pieces
4½ cups Spicy Tomato Sauce (see page 591)
2 cups ricotta cheese
½ cup freshly grated imported Parmesan cheese
¾ cup chopped parsley
2½ tablespoons dried oregano
2 eggs
freshly ground black pepper, to taste
4 cups grated mozzarella cheese
Pizza Dough for crust (recipe follows), raised once

1. Preheat oven to 350°F.
2. In a heavy skillet sauté sausages until brown. Drain well and transfer to a bowl. Stir Spicy Tomato Sauce into the sausages and reserve.
3. Mix ricotta, Parmesan, ½ cup of the parsley, 2 tablespoons of the oregano, 1 egg, and freshly ground black pepper to taste.
4. In a rectangular ovenproof dish, about 9 x 13 inches, spread half

228

of the sausage mixture. Dot this with half of the ricotta mixture and sprinkle 2 cups of the mozzarella evenly over the entire surface. Sprinkle with half of the remaining parsley and half of the remaining oregano. Repeat.

5. Roll out three quarters of the dough to a thickness of about ⅓ inch, being certain the dough is about 1 inch larger than the pan all the way around. Transfer dough to top of pizza and tuck in excess all around. Beat remaining egg with 1 tablespoon water and brush some of it on top of crust.

6. Roll out remaining dough and use it to form decorative shapes, cut with cookie cutters if you like. Arrange shapes on top of crust, brush again with beaten egg, and bake for 35 to 45 minutes, or until the top is golden brown and the edges are bubbling.

7. Let pizza stand for 30 minutes before cutting.

8 or more portions.

PIZZA DOUGH

1 package active dry yeast
1 to 1¼ cups lukewarm water (105° to 115°F.)
2⅓ cups unbleached, all-purpose flour
¾ cup cake flour
⅓ teaspoon freshly ground black pepper
1 teaspoon salt
2 tablespoons olive oil

1. In a small bowl, dissolve yeast in ½ cup of the lukewarm water and let stand 10 minutes.

2. In a mixing bowl, mix flours, pepper and salt together.

3. Add dissolved yeast to the dry ingredients with olive oil and ½ cup of remaining water. Mix with a wooden spoon to form a dough, adding a little more water if needed.

4. Remove dough from the bowl to a floured pastry board. Knead for 8 to 10 minutes, or until dough is smooth and pliable. Flour board lightly when dough begins to stick.

5. Wash and dry mixing bowl, and rub it with olive oil. Place dough in the bowl and turn it over to coat it thoroughly. Cover dough with plastic wrap and place in a warm place (75° to 80°F.) for 2 hours, until doubled in bulk.

6. When dough has doubled in bulk, punch it down and knead for 15 seconds. Let it rest under a towel for 10 minutes before proceeding with recipe.

NAVARIN OF LAMB

Our *navarin*, made with snow peas, is light and very beautiful.

3 tablespoons best-quality olive oil
1 tablespoon sweet butter
3 pounds boned lamb, cut into 1-inch cubes for stew
18 medium-size pearl onions
¾ pound snow peas, trimmed and cleaned
½ cup Cognac
¼ cup sherry vinegar
2 tablespoons potato starch
2 tablespoons red currant jelly
2 tablespoons tomato paste
2 cups rich Beef Stock (see page 586)
1 cup dry red wine
1 medium-size yellow onion, thinly sliced
4 large carrots, peeled and cut into 1-inch lengths
5 garlic cloves, peeled and crushed
¼ cup chopped fresh parsley (reserve a bit for garnish)
1 teaspoon dried rosemary
1 teaspoon dried thyme
1 teaspoon salt
1 teaspoon freshly ground black pepper
1 bay leaf

1. In a heavy skillet, heat olive oil and butter. Over medium heat, brown lamb, a few pieces at a time. Transfer with a slotted spoon to a deep ovenproof casserole.

2. Bring 2 quarts of salted water to a boil. Cut a shallow ✕ in the root end of each pearl onion and drop them into the water. Cook until tender but firm, 10 minutes. Drain, transfer to a small bowl, and cover with cold water for 10 minutes. Drain, peel, and reserve.

3. Bring another 2 quarts of salted water to a boil. Drop in the snow peas and cook for 1 minute. Drain and plunge into ice-cold water. Let stand until cool, drain, pat dry, and reserve.

4. When all lamb is browned, turn off heat under skillet. Drain the oil and return all the lamb to skillet.

5. Preheat oven to 350°F.

6. Heat the Cognac in a small saucepan. Set skillet with lamb over low heat and pour in Cognac. Ignite Cognac with a match and let it flame for 30 seconds. Turn off heat. With a slotted spoon return meat to the casserole.

7. Add vinegar, potato starch, currant jelly, tomato paste, beef stock and red wine to the skillet and stir well. Set over high heat and bring to a boil, stirring constantly, for 5 minutes.

8. Add sliced onion, carrots, garlic, parsley, rosemary, thyme, salt, pepper and bay leaf to the casserole. Pour sauce over all, stir well, and cover.

9. Bake for 1½ hours, uncovering casserole for last 15 minutes of baking.

10. Toss in snow peas and pearl onions and serve garnished with chopped parsley.

6 portions

COOKING WITH HERBS

Herbs have been used throughout the ages to flavor foods, to cure ills, and to make cosmetics, dyes and even insect repellents. Just as each herb once had a symbolic meaning (remembrance, purity, etc.), each now has a culinary identity in our kitchen.

The culinary basics are thyme, parsley, bay (together, the classic *bouquet garni*), plus tarragon, basil, dill, chives, mint and oregano.

Be cautious when buying dried herbs. They lose flavor rapidly when exposed to light, air or heat and may be tasteless. Don't hesitate to throw out a jar of herbs that you've left untouched on your shelf for too long. When in doubt, sniff. A tired herb won't do much for your recipe anyway.

" 'Classic' — a book which people praise and don't read."
— Mark Twain

231

OSSO BUCO

Serve the meaty veal shanks with Saffron Rice (see page 592) into which you have thrown a handful of peas.

1 cup unbleached, all-purpose flour
salt and freshly ground black pepper for seasoning, and to taste
16 sections of veal shank, 10 to 12 pounds, 2 inches thick
½ cup best-quality olive oil
4 ounces (1 stick) sweet butter
2 medium-size yellow onions, coarsely chopped
6 large garlic cloves, peeled and chopped
½ teaspoon dried basil
½ teaspoon dried oregano
28 ounces canned Italian plum tomatoes, drained
2 cups dry white wine
2 cups Beef Stock (see page 586)
¾ cup chopped Italian parsley
grated zest of 2 lemons

1. Season the flour with salt and pepper and dredge the pieces of veal shank well. Heat oil and butter together in a large casserole or Dutch oven and sear the veal, browning well on all sides. Transfer veal to paper towels to drain.

2. Add onions, garlic, basil and oregano to casserole and cook, stirring occasionally, for 10 minutes.

3. Add tomatoes, and salt and pepper to taste, and cook for another 10 minutes. Skim excess fat.

4. Add wine and bring to a boil. Reduce heat and simmer uncovered for 15 minutes.

5. Preheat oven to 350°F.

6. Return veal shanks to the casserole and add beef stock just to cover. Cover casserole and bake for 1½ hours. Remove lid and bake uncovered for another 30 minutes, until veal is very tender.

7. Sprinkle with chopped parsley and grated lemon zest and serve immediately.

6 to 8 portions

Some of these stews could be called classics, but we've made them with lighter sauces and abundant vegetables so that they fit right in with contemporary cooking. Stews are perfect entertaining fare. They have always been part of our repertoire, and are only becoming more popular as time goes by.

OXTAIL STEW

Americans are not as fond of oxtail as Europeans are. But if you, like us, enjoy a chewy, meaty, gelatinous bit of flavorful beef once in a while, this stew is for you. It is a complete meal, needing only a light first course (marinated shrimp or raw oysters, for example) and a green salad or a vegetable in vinaigrette afterwards.

2 oxtails, about 5 pounds, cut into 2-inch pieces
¾ cup unbleached, all-purpose flour
3 tablespoons best-quality olive oil
3 cups Beef Stock (see page 586)
1 cup Burgundy wine
1 cup tomato juice
3 tablespoons tomato paste
2 garlic cloves, minced
1 bay leaf
1 teaspoon dried thyme
½ teaspoon grated nutmeg
1 teaspoon salt
1 teaspoon freshly ground black pepper
2 cups coarsely chopped yellow onions
1 cup diced celery
1 cup carrot rounds, ⅛ inch thick each
8 medium-size potatoes, cut into thirds
chopped fresh parsley (garnish)

1. Dredge oxtails with flour until thoroughly coated. Shake off excess.
2. Heat oil in a heavy Dutch oven and brown the oxtails well in several batches, setting each batch aside until all are browned; return all oxtails to pot.

3. Add stock, wine, tomato juice and tomato paste. Stir in garlic, bay leaf, thyme, nutmeg, salt and pepper. Add vegetables, immersing them well in the liquid.

4. Set Dutch oven over medium heat. Bring to a boil, cover, reduce heat, and simmer for 2 hours, or until oxtails are very tender. Taste and correct seasoning. Skim fat from sauce, garnish with parsley, and serve immediately.

4 to 6 portions

"There is an emanation from the heart in genuine hospitality which can not be described but is immediately felt, and puts the stranger at once at his ease."

— Washington Irving

GREAT GARDEN VEGETABLES

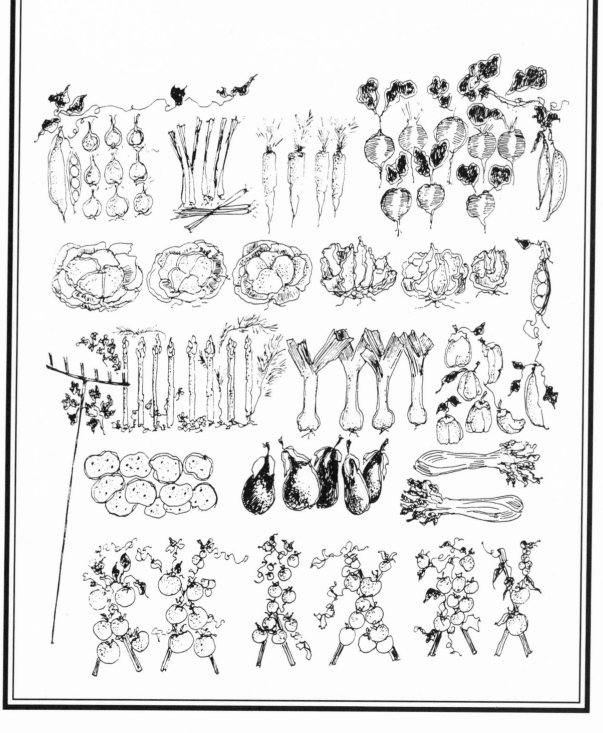

ARTICHOKES

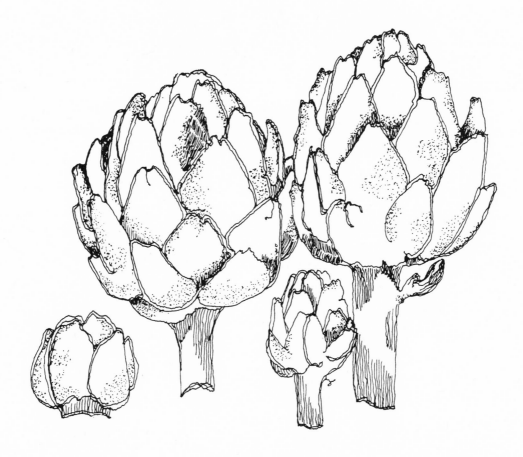

Artichokes intimidate. They are members of the thistle family and seem armored, behind their spiky leaves and fuzzy choke, against our intrusion. Beyond this barricade, however, is the tasty prize — a sweet and tender heart.

The ancient artichoke has been grown in the Mediterranean basin for centuries and is now cultivated in coastal California. It's available year-round, but is at its best in late spring, and has become a standard item on restaurant menus and in home kitchens.

Choose only firm, young and unspotted artichokes. Although Americans always seem to prefer their vegetables huge, the small- to medium-size artichokes have better flavor. Most stores will sell artichokes individually rather than by the pound.

Trim off the stem, and use kitchen scissors to cut the spiky points off the outside leaves. Rinse under cold water. Cook in boiling salted water until done, about 30 to 40 minutes, or until a few test leaves pull out easily.

ONE-STEP ARTICHOKES

These artichokes are easy to prepare and add a colorful note as well. Since they're as good cold as hot, plan to make them ahead. We like to take them on picnics with Lemon Chicken and Cracked Wheat Salad (see Index for recipes).

6 whole artichokes, trimmed
3 carrots, peeled and finely diced
1 medium-size yellow onion, peeled and finely diced
½ cup olive oil
¼ cup chopped fresh parsley (reserve a bit for garnish)
¼ cup lemon juice
1 tablespoon dried oregano
1 tablespoon dried basil
1 teaspoon freshly ground black pepper
½ teaspoon salt

1. Place artichokes in deep heavy pot and just cover with water. Add remaining ingredients. Cook, partially covered, at a gentle boil until leaves pull away easily, 40 minutes.

2. Transfer artichokes to a large serving platter. Strain the cooking liquid and strew the vegetables and herbs over the artichokes. Serve hot, or cool to room temperature.

6 portions

HERB MAYONNAISE

Instead of hollandaise to sauce these thistles, try this herb mayonnaise, perfect on cold artichokes served as a summertime first course.

1 cup Homemade Mayonnaise (see page 582)
1 cup watercress leaves, rinsed and dried
¼ cup chopped Italian parsley
¼ cup snipped fresh chives

Combine all ingredients in the bowl of a food processor fitted with a steel blade. Process until smooth; do not overprocess.

1¼ cups

LEMON BUTTER

For a light and piquant accompaniment to steamed or boiled fresh, green vegetables, melt 8 tablespoons (1 stick) sweet butter with the juice of 2 lemons and 2 tablespoons freshly chopped Italian parsley.

STUFFING ARTICHOKES

Once artichokes are cooked and the tangle of hairs known as the "choke" is removed, a cavity remains that is a natural container for a wide variety of savory fillings.

For the simplest kind, you can spoon Sauce Hollandaise into the cavity. Other stuffing possibilities include Shrimp and Grape Salad with Dill, Shrimp and Artichoke Salad (minus the artichoke hearts), Rice and Vegetable Salad (see Index for recipes).

STUFFED ARTICHOKES FONTECCHIO

A specialty of our Italian chef, these meaty stuffed artichokes are good hot or cold.

4 large artichokes, trimmed
juice of 2 lemons
½ cup best-quality olive oil
1 large yellow onion, peeled and finely chopped
4 garlic cloves, peeled and finely chopped
¼ cup finely chopped Italian parsley
½ pound sweet Italian sausage, removed from casing
2 cups fine dry bread crumbs
1 cup Chicken Stock (see page 587)
½ teaspoon dried oregano
salt, to taste
½ teaspoon freshly ground black pepper
¼ cup grated imported Romano cheese
2 eggs

1. Trim stems of artichokes so that they will sit upright. Bring a large pot of salted water to a boil. Add the lemon juice, drop in the artichokes, and cook for 20 to 30 minutes, or until a few leaves pull out with only slight resistance. (You will cook the artichokes again later in the recipe; do not overcook now.) Drain artichokes, invert them, and cool completely.

2. Heat half of the oil in a skillet. Add onion, garlic and parsley, and cook over low heat for 15 minutes.

3. Add sausage and cook for another 15 minutes, stirring to break up lumps, or until sausage is mostly, but not completely, cooked.

4. Transfer sausage mixture to a mixing bowl and add bread crumbs, chicken stock, oregano, salt to taste, black pepper and Romano cheese. Toss gently and cool to room temperature.

5. Beat the eggs lightly and stir them into the cooled stuffing.

6. Preheat oven to 350°F.

7. Carefully spread open the cooled and drained artichokes and remove the choke from each with a spoon. Fill the cavities with stuffing, and force any remaining stuffing down inside the outside leaves. Reform the artichoke shape as much as possible.

8. Arrange stuffed artichokes in a shallow baking dish; drizzle them with remaining olive oil and pour 1 cup water into the dish. Cover tightly and bake for 40 minutes.

9. Remove artichokes from oven and serve hot with tomato sauce; or cool to room temperature and garnish with chopped parsley and wedges of fresh lemon.

4 portions

ASPARAGUS

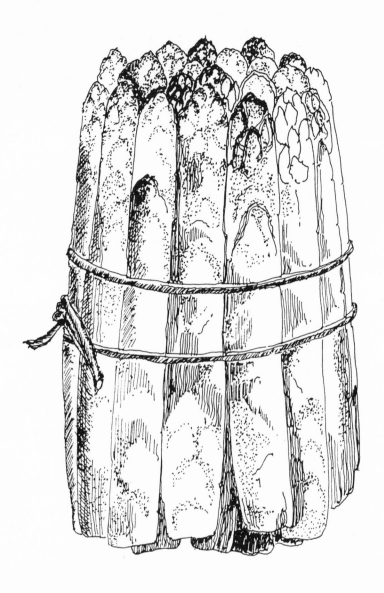

The spring asparagus hunt can take us to the fields, our gardens, or the market, but it is always a joy. The thrill of sighting them, pencil-thin and tight-tipped, gives way to the joy of abundance, followed all too soon by the reluctant compromise of our standards until they're too thick to consider at all. As we carry home our tiny collection of spears, we reflect that in Russia asparagus is so plentiful that cows in pastures eat it all day long. How lucky they are!

Once found, will our asparagus become soup, pasta sauce, salad, soufflé or — best of all — nature's most elegant finger food? There are many wonderful choices to make during the asparagus celebration. And we love the challenge!

STRAIGHT TALK ABOUT ASPARAGUS

Much advice is given regarding the cooking of asparagus; most of it can be ignored. This best of all possible vegetables needs only the simplest kind of attention to bring out and preserve its goodness.

Choose thin or thick spears, as you like. They should be firm and green with tightly closed tips. Do not plan on storing uncooked asparagus for more than 24 hours. Refrigerate it if you must keep it.

Take each spear by its ends and bend gently in half; it will snap approximately at the point where tenderness begins. Reserve the woody stem ends for another use, such as soup, or discard them. Rinse the tip ends under cold running water. If you would like to tie the asparagus into convenient serving-size bundles, do so now, using plain kitchen twine. (Include a few extra spears to use in testing doneness.)

Bring a large kettle of salted water to a full rolling boil. Drop in the asparagus spears or bundles, let the water return to a boil, and cook uncovered to desired doneness. You have some flexibility here as long as you don't overcook the asparagus. Occasionally fish out a spear and bite it (not an unpleasant task) to test if it's ready. This may seem a vague guide, but you'll soon learn that such variables as thickness of stalk make you, and not time, the final judge. If you'll be reheating the asparagus later, you'll want the cooking to stop when it is still fairly crisp; if you're serving it cold with dips, it should be tender but not droopy; if you want to serve it cold in, say, a vinaigrette, it can be quite tender, as long as the spears are not mushy.

Have a large bowl of ice water nearby. When the asparagus is perfect, transfer it with tongs to the ice water. This stops the cooking and sets the brilliant green color.

Let stand until thoroughly cool, drain, and pat dry. Cover until ready to use, refrigerating if serving time is several hours off. Asparagus is best eaten the same day as cooked, but will keep for another day, losing only a little of its perfection in your refrigerator.

"Do that in less time than it takes to cook asparagus."
— A Roman Expression

MAYONNAISES FOR ASPARAGUS

Here is a trio of our favorite mayonnaises, light enough not to disguise the wonder of this long vegetable. Arrange asparagus tips for dipping upright in a small basket, as if they had just arrived from the market. As a first course, serve 4 to 6 stalks on a small plate; lightly drizzle 3 to 4 tablespoons of dressing across the center of the asparagus and sprinkle with chopped parsley or other appropriate garnish.

SESAME MAYONNAISE

1 whole egg
2 egg yolks
2½ tablespoons rice vinegar*
2½ tablespoons Oriental soy sauce
3 tablespoons prepared Dijon-style mustard
¼ cup dark Oriental sesame oil*
2½ cups corn oil
Szechuan-style hot and spicy oil (optional)*
grated fresh orange rind (optional)

1. In a food processor fitted with a steel blade, process the whole egg, egg yolks, vinegar, soy sauce and mustard for 1 minute.
2. With the motor still running, dribble in the sesame oil and then the corn oil in a slow, steady stream.
3. Season with drops of the hot and spicy oil if you use it, and scrape the mayonnaise out into a bowl. Cover and refrigerate until ready to use.
4. Garnish with orange rind, if you use it, before serving.
About 3½ cups

*available in Oriental groceries and other specialty food shops

MAYONNAISE NICOISE

1 cup Homemade Mayonnaise (see page 582)
1 tablespoon capers, drained, plus additional to taste
1 tablespoon tomato paste
1 tablespoon anchovy paste
1 garlic clove, peeled and minced
large pinch of oregano

1. Combine all ingredients in the bowl of a food processor fitted with a steel blade.
2. Process until smooth, then stir in additional capers to taste.
1¼ cups

GREEN HERB DIPPING SAUCE

½ bunch of Italian parsley
½ bunch of fresh dill
½ bunch of watercress
¾ cup drained, cooked fresh spinach, all liquid squeezed out
2 scallions (green onions), tender greens included, sliced thin
2 cups Homemade Mayonnaise (see page 582)
1 cup dairy sour cream
salt and freshly ground black pepper, to taste

1. In a food processor fitted with a steel blade, place parsley, dill and watercress. Chop fine and transfer to a bowl.
2. Process spinach in the same way and add to herb mixture.
3. Combine herbs with scallions, mayonnaise and sour cream, folding together gently. Add salt and pepper to taste. Refrigerate until ready to use.
4 cups

Asparagus makes a natural, edible paintbrush. Serve tender spears alongside your soft-cooked breakfast egg. Dunk asparagus into yolk, stir, eat. Repeat until happy.

ASPARAGUS SAUCE

12 asparagus spears, trimmed
1½ tablespoons sweet butter
4 scallions (green onions), white and green parts, chopped
salt and freshly ground black pepper, to taste
pinch of granulated sugar
2 tablespoons heavy cream

1. Cut asparagus into 1-inch pieces. Parboil in a pot of boiling salted water until just tender, about 8 minutes.

2. Melt butter in a skillet. Add asparagus, chopped scallions, seasoning to taste with salt, pepper and sugar. Cook, stirring, over medium heat until scallions are tender, about 5 minutes.

3. Purée mixture in a food processor or push through a food mill. Place purée in a saucepan, add the cream, and keep warm until needed.

4 portions

AN ASPARAGUS MENU

Asparagus with Sesame
Mayonnaise

Asparagus with
Asparagus Sauce

Asparagus Strudel with
Tomato Coulis

Asparagus-Parmesan
Soufflé

Chocolate Mousse

Devon cream

Fresh strawberries

An early morning asparagus hunt, a generous basketful of prime spring bounty, a dozen eggs. Why wait for dinner when the asparagus can be ready before the sun is up?

VINAIGRETTES FOR ASPARAGUS

BLUEBERRY VINAIGRETTE

⅓ cup olive oil
½ cup blueberry vinegar with blueberries
¾ teaspoon salt
¾ teaspoon freshly ground black pepper
1-inch cinnamon stick
¼ cup fresh blueberries, or unsweetened frozen, thawed

Combine all ingredients in a jar. Shake well. Make at least 1 hour before using. Shake again before serving.

1 cup

OUR FAVORITE VINAIGRETTE

1 tablespoon prepared Dijon-style mustard
4 tablespoons red wine vinegar
1 teaspoon granulated sugar
½ teaspoon salt
½ teaspoon freshly ground black pepper
minced parsley and/or snipped fresh chives, to taste
½ cup olive oil

1. Measure mustard into a bowl. Whisk in vinegar, sugar, salt, pepper and herbs to taste.
2. Continue to whisk mixture while slowly dribbling in olive oil until mixture thickens. Adjust seasoning to taste. Cover until ready to use. (Vinaigrette is best if made just before it is to be used.) If necessary, whisk again before serving.

1 cup

ASPARAGUS WITH PROSCIUTTO

4 ounces whipped cream cheese
¼ teaspoon finely minced garlic
pinch of salt
pinch of freshly ground black pepper
12 thin slices of prosciutto, cut crosswise into halves
24 asparagus spears, cut to 4 inches, lightly cooked

1. Combine whipped cream cheese with garlic, salt and pepper.
2. Spread each half slice of prosciutto with some of the cheese mixture and roll around an asparagus spear. Arrange on baking sheet.
3. Heat in a preheated 350°F. oven for 3 to 4 minutes, until heated through. Serve immediately.

24 spears, 6 to 8 portions

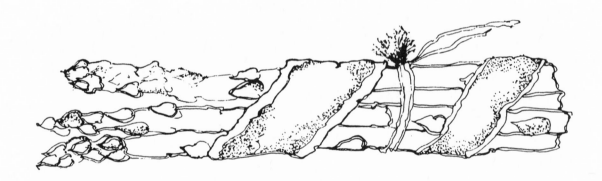

In the earliest days of The Silver Palate, we raided Sheila's asparagus patch in the country and dedicated our day's efforts to an Asparagus Celebration. We felt, and our customers agreed, that you can never, ever, have too much of a good thing.

ASPARAGUS STRUDEL

¾ *pound asparagus, trimmed and cut into 1-inch lengths*
2 medium-size leeks, white parts only, thinly sliced and washed well
1 tablespoon chopped shallot
½ pound plus 4 tablespoons (2½ sticks) sweet butter, melted
½ pound Gruyère cheese, grated
2 ounces sliced almonds, toasted
3 eggs
2 tablespoons chopped fresh mint
2 tablespoons chopped fresh parsley
4 tablespoons chopped fresh dill
2 tablespoons snipped fresh chives
1 teaspoon salt
½ teaspoon freshly ground black pepper
½ teaspoon paprika
dash of cayenne pepper
2 tablespoons fresh lemon juice
12 leaves of packaged phyllo pastry, thawed if necessary

1. Blanch asparagus in large pot of boiling water for 3 minutes. Drain and pat dry. Place in a bowl.

2. Sauté leeks with shallot in 4 tablespoons of the butter until transparent. Add to the bowl of asparagus.

3. Add all other ingredients except remaining melted butter and phyllo. Toss together.

4. Preheat oven to 350°F.

5. Butter a cookie sheet with melted butter. Lay 1 leaf of phyllo on work surface and quickly brush with melted butter. Continue until you have 6 layers, buttering each one thoroughly.

6. Place half of the asparagus mixture along one short end, tuck ends in, and roll up jelly-roll fashion. Place on large baking sheet. Proceed to make second strudel with remaining phyllo, butter, and filling and place it on the baking sheet, leaving ample space between the rolls. Brush tops of rolls with any remaining butter.

7. Bake for 40 to 45 minutes, until golden. Cool slightly and slice into 2-inch pieces.

8. Serve as a first course with fresh Tomato Coulis (see page 324).
8 portions

The food mill is really essential for this recipe. A food processor won't adequately purée the asparagus fibers, and forcing the soup through a sieve will take hours. If you don't have a food mill, an inexpensive and incredibly handy little gadget, consider investing in one.

CREAM OF ASPARAGUS SOUP

Our favorite asparagus soup, tasting purely and simply of asparagus and nothing else. This recipe is a good way to use the thick and woody asparagus that appears late in the season. The soup is fabulous cold, but it's also pretty wonderful hot: play your cards right and you can have it both ways; the recipe makes a generous 2½ quarts.

4 cups chopped yellow onions, about 4 large onions
8 tablespoons (1 stick) sweet butter
2 quarts Chicken Stock (see page 587), thoroughly defatted
2 pounds asparagus
½ cup heavy cream or buttermilk (for cold soup)
salt and freshly ground black pepper, to taste

1. Melt the butter in a large pot and simmer the onions until very soft and golden, about 25 minutes, stirring often.
2. Add the chicken stock and bring to a boil.
3. Meanwhile, trim the tips from the asparagus and reserve. Cut about 1 inch from the butt ends of the asparagus spears; don't try to remove all of the tough parts, just the very woody ends. Chop spears into ½-inch pieces and drop into the boiling chicken stock, cover, reduce heat, and simmer for 45 minutes, or until asparagus is very soft.
4. Force the soup, broth and all, through the medium disc of a food mill. Return purée to the pot, add the reserved asparagus tips, and simmer until they are tender but still firm, 5 to 10 minutes. If serving the soup hot, season with salt and pepper and serve.
5. If serving the soup cold, remove from heat, cool, stir in the cream or buttermilk, and refrigerate covered. Season to taste with salt and pepper. Serve very cold.
8 to 10 portions

CONSOMME WITH ASPARAGUS
AND DILL

7 cups Chicken Stock (see page 587), well concentrated
3 egg whites
2 cups raw asparagus tips
fresh dill (garnish)

1. To clarify the stock: Beat 1 cup stock in a bowl with the egg whites. Bring remaining stock to a boil in a saucepan.

2. Dribble the hot stock into the egg-white mixture, beating constantly with a whisk.

3. Return all stock to the saucepan and bring to a simmer over moderate heat, stirring gently with the whisk at all times.

4. When stock reaches a simmer, stop stirring and reduce heat to absolute minimum; liquid must just "shiver" for 20 minutes.

5. Meanwhile, set a sieve or colander over a bowl and line with several layers of damp cheesecloth or paper towels. Set the saucepan of stock next to the bowl and gently ladle broth and egg whites into the sieve, keeping whites intact as much as possible. The egg whites and particles from the stock will remain behind in the strainer. The resulting stock will be transparent and golden.

6. Put stock in a clean pan and bring to a boil. Drop in the asparagus and cook until just tender, less than 5 minutes. Ladle into serving bowls, and garnish with chopped fresh dill.

7 to 8 portions

As good as asparagus is cold, it is equally delicious hot. Asparagus cloaked in a lemony Sauce Hollandaise (see page 583) is a pairing made in heaven. Asparagus in butter, with or without a shower of your favorite herb chopped over all, is simple perfection. Other partnerships are equally successful.

ASPARAGUS-PARMESAN SOUFFLE

2 cups 1-inch pieces of asparagus tips and tender stems
4 tablespoons sweet butter
½ cup finely chopped yellow onion
1 cup milk
3 tablespoons unbleached, all-purpose flour
4 egg yolks
⅔ cup freshly grated imported Parmesan cheese
salt and freshly ground black pepper, to taste
nutmeg, to taste
5 egg whites
cream of tartar or lemon juice

1. Preheat oven to 425°F.
2. Bring a kettle of salted water to a boil, drop in the pieces of asparagus, and cook until tender but not mushy. Drain and plunge into ice water. When cool, drain, and purée in a food processor.
3. Melt butter in a heavy saucepan, and sauté the onion, partially covered, until tender and lightly colored, about 25 minutes. In a second saucepan, bring the milk to a boil.
4. Sprinkle the flour over the onion and butter and, stirring constantly, cook gently for 5 minutes.
5. Shut off heat and pour in the boiling milk all at once. Beat vigorously with a whisk as the mixture bubbles, and then set the pan over medium heat. Bring sauce to a boil, stirring constantly, and let it boil for 3 minutes.
6. Remove from heat. Stir in egg yolks, one at a time. Then stir in the asparagus purée, ⅓ cup of the Parmesan, and salt, pepper and nutmeg to taste. Taste and correct seasoning. Butter a 1-quart soufflé dish and sprinkle with remaining Parmesan. Shake out excess cheese and reserve it.
7. Beat egg whites until foamy. Add a pinch of salt and either a pinch of cream of tartar or a few drops of lemon juice and continue to beat until the whites form stiff peaks.
8. Scoop out about a third of the whites and stir them thoroughly into the asparagus-egg mixture. Scrape remaining beaten whites onto asparagus mixture and fold in just until incorporated; don't overmix.

9. Pour the soufflé mixture into prepared dish and rap dish on a work surface to eliminate air bubbles. Sprinkle top with reserved Parmesan. Set in the center of the preheated oven; reduce heat to 375°F.

10. Bake for 20 minutes without opening the oven door, then check the soufflé. It should be browning nicely and should have risen 2 inches above the rim of the dish. Let it bake for another 15 or even 20 minutes if you like a very well-done soufflé. Serve immediately.

4 to 5 portions as a first course, 3 portions as a main course

AN ASPARAGUS OMELET

Simple things like eggs and butter emphasize the simple goodness of asparagus. Cook the asparagus lightly, warm it in plenty of butter, and arrange across a plain omelet before folding.

ASPARAGUS AND EGG SALAD

Asparagus and eggs again, this time a glorified version of an old favorite, egg salad. Lots of eggs, lots of good mayonnaise, onion if you like, and an indispensable touch of mustard. Stir in tender asparagus tips, or strew them with a lavish hand over the completed salad. Dill — lots of it — is a welcome addition.

POACHED EGGS ON ASPARAGUS

For a perfect breakfast or brunch place 2 poached eggs on top of 6 blanched asparagus spears for each helping. Cover with Sauce Hollandaise (see page 583) and serve. If you can catch a brook trout and sauté it, you have the ultimate dish!

ASPARAGUS EN CROUTE

12 slices of good-quality white sandwich bread
½ pound Jarlsberg or other Swiss-type cheese
½ cup prepared Dijon-style mustard
12 asparagus spears, cooked
4 tablespoons melted sweet butter, approximately

1. Roll slices of bread as thin as possible with a rolling pin; trim crusts. You will have pieces of bread 3 to 3½ inches square.

2. Lay squares out on a work surface and cover with a damp towel for 10 minutes.

3. Cut cheese into fingers, more or less the size of the asparagus spears.

4. Spread each bread square evenly with mustard. Lay an asparagus spear and a strip of cheese on each bread square and roll up. Place seam side down on a buttered baking sheet.

5. Brush rolls with melted butter. Bake in the upper third of a 450°F. oven for 10 minutes, or until brown and bubbling. Serve immediately.

12 rolls, 4 to 6 portions

BEANS

Beans and their leguminous kin, like others of the world's staple foods, are social climbers, their presence on elegant menus and in important kitchens belying their simple origins. Beans are available, affordable, and high in valuable proteins. In short, the possibilities are limited only if you underestimate the humble bean.

DRIED BEANS AND PEAS

Buy dried beans from a packer whose name you know and trust, or seek out a store that offers its beans loose in bulk. Rinse them in a strainer under cold running water and sort through the beans to remove any pebbles or other foreign matter you may find. Depending on the recipe, the beans may need to be soaked overnight. After they are rinsed, transfer them to a bowl and add enough cold water to cover the beans by at least 3 inches; most dried beans will absorb this much water overnight.

BLACK-EYED PEAS: Small oval legumes (not a true bean), with a black or yellow spot; a favorite in the South.

BLACK(OR BLACK TURTLE) BEANS: Small, mild-flavored, black-skinned; used in Mexican and South American cuisines.

CANNELLINI: Also called white kidney beans; used in salads and soups, particularly in Italy, and are often puréed.

CRANBERRY BEANS: Small, oval beans with pink markings; featured in New England cooking — remember succotash?

FAVA BEANS: Known also as broad beans; large, brown, shaped a bit like limas.

FLAGEOLETS: Small, oval, delicately flavored green beans; when found these should be treasured.

GARBANZOS: Also called chick-peas, cream-colored or brownish, with a nutlike flavor, round and firm-textured; often used in East Indian, Latin American and Middle Eastern cuisines.

KIDNEY BEANS: Oval pink or dark-red beans; great in soups, stews and chilies.

LENTILS: Small, round and flat legumes — one of our favorites for casseroles and salads; usually greenish tan, brown or reddish orange.

LIMA BEANS: Mild-flavored, these flat round beans, often called butter beans, are used in soups or in combinations with pork.

PINK BEANS: Small, brownish red beans; often replace cranberry or pinto beans.

PINTO BEANS: Pale pink and speckled with brown; great in Western and Mexican cooking.

RED BEANS: Smaller than kidney, pinto or pink beans, these are often used in Oriental cookery.

SOYBEANS: Small, pea-shaped and light tan; an Oriental staple, used in the East for centuries, and now favorites in the West.

SPLIT PEAS: Both green and yellow. Soup standbys.

WHITE BEANS: Beans of varying sizes, delicately flavored; they include Great Northerns, white kidney (cannellini) and marrow beans, and navy beans and white pea beans, both of Boston fame.

COOKING FRESH GREEN BEANS

Buy about ¼ pound beans per person. Snap off the tips of the beans and pull away any strings. (It seems to us that fewer and fewer string beans actually have strings; that feature has been largely bred out. Always check a few, just to make sure, since the strings make for unpleasant eating.)

Bring a large pot of water, to which you have added some salt to taste, to a full rolling boil. Drop in all the beans at once, taking care to leave the heat at its highest since you want the water to return to the boil as quickly as possible. Do not cover the pot. Stir the beans occasionally so they'll cook evenly. The beans may be done in as few as 5 minutes or may take as long as 15. Keep testing until the desired "crunch" is obtained. (Note: beans *should* have a crunchy texture; a silent bean is an overcooked bean.)

Have ready a large bowl of ice water. When the beans are cooked to taste, drain them and toss them immediately into the ice water. This will stop the cooking process and set the bright green color. Let beans stand in the water until completely cool. Drain them and pat dry. Refrigerate beans, covered, until they are used for a platter of *crudités* or tossed with vinaigrette or rewarmed in butter.

GREEN BEANS WITH TOMATOES

This dish, in which the raw beans are sautéed, calls for the thinnest and tenderest green beans you can find. It is bright, fresh and crisp, and can be eaten hot or at room temperature.

⅓ cup olive oil
1½ pounds green beans
2 garlic cloves, peeled and chopped
1 medium-size yellow onion, peeled and cut into thin rings
4 small ripe tomatoes, about 1 pound, peeled, seeded and roughly chopped
¼ cup chopped Italian parsley
4½ tablespoons red wine vinegar
1½ teaspoons dried oregano
½ teaspoon salt
½ teaspoon freshly ground black pepper

1. Heat the olive oil in a heavy skillet, add the beans and cook, stirring and tossing constantly, until beans are about half-cooked and become bright green.

2. Reduce heat and add garlic and onion. Cook, stirring, for 1 minute.

3. Add tomatoes, parsley, vinegar, oregano, salt and pepper, and continue to cook, tossing occasionally, for about another 5 minutes, or until sauce is slightly reduced. Serve immediately, or cool and serve at room temperature.

4 to 6 portions

AUTUMN DUCK SALAD WITH GREEN BEANS

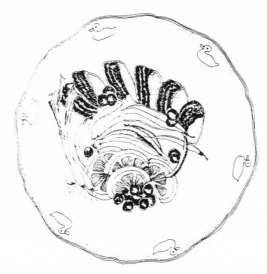

This main-course salad is a beauty any time of the year.

2 ducks, each 4½ to 5 pounds, defrosted or fresh
salt
2 cups orange juice
½ cup granulated sugar
½ pound fresh cranberries (about 2 cups)
1½ pounds green beans, trimmed and blanched
1 cup shelled pecans
4 or 5 fresh clementines or tangerines, peeled and sectioned, or
  1 cup canned mandarin orange sections, drained
Raspberry Vinaigrette (see page 390)
3 scallions (green onions), thinly sliced

1. Reserve duck giblets for another use. Trim away wing tips and remove all fat from duck cavities. Salt ducks inside and out and place breast side up in a shallow baking dish just large enough to hold them comfortably. Let ducks come to room temperature, about 45 minutes.
2. Preheat oven to 450°F.
3. Set ducks on middle rack of the oven and roast for 15 minutes. Reduce heat to 375°F. and continue to roast, draining accumulated fat frequently. Ducks will be medium rare after another 20 to 30 minutes, well done after another 35 to 40 minutes.

258

4. Cool ducks. Skin them and remove each breast half in one piece. (Save legs and thighs for chef's lunch.) Using a thin, very sharp knife, slice the breast meat into long, thin pieces. Reserve.

5. Stir together orange juice, sugar and cranberries. Set over medium heat and bring to a boil, skimming any foam that accumulates. Remove from heat as soon as first berries burst, and let berries cool in the juice. Drain and reserve berries. Reserve cooking syrup for another use.

6. Divide duck strips and green beans equally among 6 plates, arranging like spokes of a wheel.

7. Combine cranberries, pecans and orange sections, and divide equally among the 6 plates, mounding the center of the "wheel."

8. Drizzle salad with raspberry vinaigrette to taste and sprinkle sliced scallions over all. Serve immediately.

6 portions

Note: Cooking syrup from step 5 can be frozen into a delightful sorbet.

SUGAR SNAP PEAS

Sugar snaps are the sweetest of young peas. Lightly wash and dry them, discarding anything that is not green. Sauté in melted butter for 3 minutes just before serving.

✤ FROM THE SILVER PALATE NOTEBOOK

The dramatic balance you strike between color, texture, flavor and temperature says much about your style. Make these elements important to the hour, the setting and the guests.

Strive to make food picture perfect. The effort — and it takes planning, thought, judgment — is worth it.

BUTTERED GREEN BEANS
WITH CASHEWS

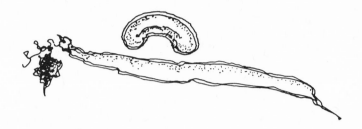

The green bean gets a little dressed up for company.

1½ pounds green beans
3 tablespoons sweet butter, melted
¾ teaspoon salt
½ teaspoon freshly ground black pepper
¼ cup finely chopped parsley
1 cup cashews

1. Blanch the green beans in boiling salted water.
2. While beans are cooking, melt the butter and add salt, pepper and parsley. Stir to mix.
3. Drain beans and place in a warm bowl. Sprinkle cashews on top and then pour butter mixture over the beans. Toss well. Arrange in a serving dish and serve immediately.
   6 portions

Variation: This recipe can be made with pecans, almonds, hazelnuts, pine nuts or any other favorite nut.

BLACK BEAN SOUP

1 cup olive oil

3 cups diced yellow onions

8 garlic cloves, peeled and crushed

2 pounds black turtle beans, soaked in water overnight

1 meaty ham bone or smoked ham hock

6 quarts water

2 tablespoons plus 1 teaspoon ground cuminseed

1 tablespoon dried oregano

3 bay leaves

1 tablespoon salt

2 teaspoons freshly ground black pepper

pinch of cayenne pepper

6 tablespoons chopped parsley

1 medium-size sweet red pepper, diced

¼ cup dry sherry wine

1 tablespoon brown sugar

1 tablespoon lemon juice

1 to 2 cups Crème Fraîche (see page 582) or dairy sour cream

1. Heat the oil in a soup pot. Add the onions and garlic and cook over low heat until vegetables are tender, about 10 minutes.

2. Drain the beans and add them, the ham bone or ham hock, and the 6 quarts water to the pot. Stir in 2 tablespoons of the cuminseed, the oregano, bay leaves, salt, pepper, cayenne and 2 tablespoons of the parsley. Bring to a boil, reduce heat and cook, uncovered, until beans are very tender and liquid is reduced by about three quarters. This will take 1½ to 2 hours.

3. Transfer ham bone or hock to a plate and cool slightly. Pull off any remaining meat with your fingers, and shred finely. Return meat to the pot.

4. Stir in remaining parsley, sweet red pepper, remaining cuminseed, sherry, brown sugar and lemon juice. Simmer for another 30 minutes, stirring frequently. Taste, correct seasoning and serve very hot, garnished with a dollop of crème fraîche.

10 to 12 small portions

LENTIL SOUP

¼ *pound slab bacon*
2 cups finely chopped yellow onions
2 carrots, peeled and finely chopped
3 large garlic cloves, peeled and chopped
7 cups Chicken Stock (see page 587) or Beef Stock (see page 586)
1 teaspoon dried thyme
¼ *teaspoon celery seeds*
2 bay leaves
salt and freshly ground black pepper, to taste
1½ cups brown lentils

1. Finely cube the bacon and sauté in a soup pot over medium heat until crisp. Remove bacon with a slotted spoon and reserve.

2. Add onions, carrots and garlic and sauté in the bacon fat over low heat, covered, until tender and golden, about 25 minutes.

3. Add the chicken or beef stock, thyme, celery seeds, bay leaves, a grinding of fresh pepper (no salt until later) and the lentils. Bring to a boil, reduce heat, and cover. Simmer until lentils are very tender, about 40 minutes.

4. Discard bay leaves and purée half of the soup in a food processor fitted with a steel blade, or force through the medium disc of a food mill. Return puréed soup to the pot.

5. Taste and correct seasoning, adding salt if necessary. Stir in the reserved crisp bacon and simmer briefly before serving.

6 to 8 portions

ABOUT CASSOULET

Cassoulet, like other hearty dishes that come to mind — bouillabaisse, chili, onion soup — is peasant fare. Despite the controversies that rage regarding the proper preparation of these one-pot meals, everyone agrees that they are hearty, nourishing, essentially *simple* foods, elevated to greatness by the skill of the cook and the matchless combination of ingredients that he or she chooses to employ.

Cassoulet is a specialty of the Languedoc, the southwestern region of France between Spain and Provence. Three towns — Toulouse, Castelnaudary and Carcassonne — claim to make *le vrai cassoulet*. The battle over authenticity can grow very heated, indeed, and to the combatants the distinctions are vast. For our purposes, suffice it to say that cassoulet is a dish of white beans and meats, simmered long together, as rich and fragrant a pot of baked beans as you're ever likely to eat. *Confit d'oie* (preserved goose) may or may not be present, and lamb (or mutton) can also come or go from your cassoulet. Pork, often including pork sausages, is the common denominator, along with the beans of course, and a very commendable meal can be made of just such a dish.

To get a taste of the real thing, however, we suggest the following recipe: some pork, a little lamb, garlic sausages and, in place of the preserved goose, a duck. This is our version, slightly streamlined, but nevertheless authentic. Cassoulet is neither quick nor inexpensive to prepare. It is not a dish for only the most experienced cook, though, and the various cooking steps can be spread over 3 or 4 days. Serve it as the centerpiece of an important buffet (it always impresses), or offer it to a group of close, food-loving friends as a hearty midwinter lunch to be followed by a nap. (A story is told of a sign in the door of a shop: "Closed on account of a cassoulet.")

While cassoulet is a meal in itself, a light appetizer (oysters, say, or a consommé) is not out of place; a simple green salad and a dessert of fresh fruit would be welcome. Serve a dry wine — a full-bodied red, white or even a rosé. Regional wines that would be especially appropriate include Fitou, Corbières, or Côtes du Roussillon. Afterwards, you'll want to serve a good *digestif*. An Armagnac from the neighboring region of Gascony would do the job nicely, as would a fiery Calvados, or even a Green Chartreuse. And afterwards, of course, the nap.

CASSOULET

2 pounds dried white beans (Great Northern, or try half
   Great Northern, half dried flageolets), soaked overnight
½ pound fresh pork rind
1 duckling, 4½ to 5 pounds
salt and freshly ground black pepper, to taste
1 pound (more or less) lamb bones
2¼ pounds lamb stew meat, cut into 1-inch cubes
2 pounds boneless pork shoulder, cut into 1-inch cubes
1½ tablespoons dried thyme
1 teaspoon ground allspice
1 or 2 tablespoons olive oil, if needed
⅓ cup rendered bacon fat
2 cups chopped yellow onions
3 large carrots, peeled and chopped
2 cups dry white vermouth
6 ounces tomato paste
5 cups Beef Stock (see page 586) or canned beef broth
9 large garlic cloves, peeled
5 bay leaves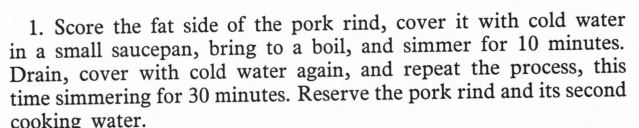
1½ pounds fresh garlic sausage or kielbasa
1 pound salt pork
4 cups bread crumbs mixed with 1 cup chopped parsley

1. Score the fat side of the pork rind, cover it with cold water
in a small saucepan, bring to a boil, and simmer for 10 minutes.
Drain, cover with cold water again, and repeat the process, this
time simmering for 30 minutes. Reserve the pork rind and its second
cooking water.

2. Drain the beans and place them in an 8-quart oven-proof pot
with a lid. Cover them with water by at least 3 inches, and bring
to a boil. Reduce heat and cook briskly, uncovered, for 15 minutes.
Remove pot from heat and let beans stand in the cooking liquid.

3. Cut off wing tips of duck and set them aside, along with neck,
heart and gizzard. (Save liver for another use.) Pull all the fat out
of the duck, and season the cavity with salt and pepper. Put the duck
in a small roasting pan. Put the lamb bones in a second small pan

and roast, along with the duck, in a preheated 450°F. oven for 45 minutes. Drain accumulated fat frequently. Remove from oven after cooking time; duck should still be slightly underdone; lamb bones should be well browned; reserve lamb bones. Drain juices from duck cavity into a large bowl and reserve. Cool, cover and refrigerate duck.

4. In a heavy skillet, brown the cubed lamb in batches, seasoning to taste with salt and pepper. Do not crowd the pan. Remove browned lamb to the large bowl and reserve.

5. Without cleaning the skillet, sauté the pork cubes and the reserved duck giblets and wing tips in the same fashion, seasoning with salt, pepper, 1 teaspoon of the thyme and the allspice. You may need to add a tablespoon or two of olive oil if the skillet is particularly dry at this point. Reserve the browned pork in the same bowl with the lamb.

6. Do not clean the skillet. Melt the rendered bacon fat in the skillet and sauté the onions and carrots for about 20 minutes, stirring, or until tender. Add to the pot with the beans.

7. Add the vermouth, along with the meat juices accumulated in the large bowl, to the skillet. Bring to a boil. Lower heat slightly and cook briskly, stirring, until vermouth is slightly reduced and all browned cooking particles remaining in the skillet have dissolved. Pour the vermouth into the beans.

8. Stir in the tomato paste, the pork rind cooking liquid, the beef broth, remaining thyme, 6 of the garlic cloves, chopped, and the bay leaves. Add additional water if necessary; liquid should just cover the beans. Put the pork rind, fat side down, on top of the beans, and cover the pot.

9. Bake in the center of a preheated 350°F. oven for 2 to 2½ hours, or until beans are completely tender. Remove and cool to room temperature, uncovered, stirring occasionally. Cover and refrigerate overnight.

10. The next day, prick the skin of the garlic sausage all over with a fork and simmer in a pan of water for 30 minutes. Drain and reserve.

11. Put the salt pork in a pan of cold water, bring to a boil, and cook for 10 minutes. Drain, cover with cold water and repeat, reserving salt pork in its cooking water.

12. Remove the pot of beans from the refrigerator. Discard the lamb bones, the bay leaves, the duck neck and wing tips, and — if you can find them — the heart and gizzard.

13. Drain the salt pork; cut off the rind and discard it. Chop the salt pork into cubes and place in the bowl of a food processor fitted with a steel blade. Purée to a paste, dropping the 3 remaining peeled garlic cloves through the feed tube while the motor is running. Stir the paste into the beans.

14. Skin the duck, pull all meat from the bones, and cut into chunks. Stir duck into the beans. Skin the garlic sausage and cut into rounds; stir into the beans.

15. The beans will now cook for another 1½ hours. If they are too dry (it is preferable that they be too moist), stir in another cup or two of warm water. Smooth the top of the beans and sprinkle heavily with half of the bread-crumb and parsley mixture.

16. Bake, uncovered, in a preheated 325°F. oven for 45 minutes. Remove from oven, stir the top crust into the beans, sprinkle on the remaining bread crumbs and parsley, and bake further — for another 45 minutes, or until crust has formed and browned well. Serve immediately.

12 portions

✦ FROM THE SILVER PALATE NOTEBOOK

Collect and use recipes that are good cold or at room temperature, or those which taste best prepared a day or two ahead. Avoid last-minute kitchen dramas.

If time is limited, choose a menu that is more assembling than cooking — an antipasto or a charcuterie board, for example.

Always be prepared for an expanded guest list — just in case. And always be gracious about it.

WHITE BEAN AND SAUSAGE SOUP WITH PEPPERS

This soup is a sturdy one-dish meal. Vary the type of sausage as you like — by using pepperoni, knackwurst, or another favorite sausage.

4 tablespoons sweet butter
2 cups finely chopped yellow onions
2 carrots, peeled and chopped
3 garlic cloves, peeled and minced
6 parsley sprigs
1 teaspoon dried thyme
1 bay leaf
4 cups Chicken Stock (see page 587)
1¼ cups dried white beans, soaked overnight
1 sweet red and 1 green pepper
2 tablespoons olive oil
½ pound precooked kielbasa
salt and freshly ground black pepper, to taste

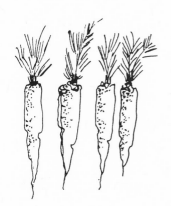

1. Melt the butter in a pot. Add onions, carrots and garlic and cook, covered, over low heat until vegetables are tender and lightly colored, about 25 minutes.

2. Add parsley, thyme and bay leaf and pour in the stock. Drain the beans and stir them into the pot. Bring to a boil, reduce heat and simmer, partially covered, until beans are very tender, 45 minutes to 1 hour.

3. Pour the soup through a strainer, reserving the stock; discard the bay leaf, and transfer the solids to the bowl of a food processor fitted with a steel blade, or use a food mill fitted with a medium disc. Add 1 cup of the cooking stock if using the processor and process until smooth.

4. Return puréed soup to the pot and stir in additional cooking liquid, 2 to 3 cups, until the soup is of the desired consistency.

5. Cut away stems and ribs of the peppers and dice them. Heat olive oil in a small skillet, add peppers and sauté over low heat, stirring occasionally, until tender but still crunchy, about 15 minutes.

Transfer peppers to the soup with a slotted spoon.

6. Skin the kielbasa if necessary, dice it, and add it to the soup. Set over medium heat and cook, partially covered, until heated through, about 15 minutes. Season to taste. Serve immediately.

4 to 6 portions

LENTIL AND WALNUT SALAD

A good lentil salad makes an excellent first course, and this is one of the best we have ever tasted.

2½ cups dried lentils
3 carrots, peeled and quartered
1 medium-size yellow onion, peeled
3 cloves
1½ quarts Chicken Stock (see page 587) or canned chicken broth
1 bay leaf
2 teaspoons dried thyme
⅓ cup white wine vinegar
3 garlic cloves, peeled
½ cup walnut oil
salt and freshly ground black pepper, to taste
1 cup thinly sliced scallions (green onions), with green tops
1 cup shelled walnut halves
chopped Italian parsley (garnish)

1. Rinse the lentils and sort through them carefully, discarding any pebbles you may find.

2. Transfer lentils to a large pot and add the carrots, the onion stuck with the cloves, chicken stock, bay leaf and thyme. Set over moderate heat and bring to a boil. Reduce to a simmer, skim any foam that may appear, cover, and cook for about 25 minutes (lentil cooking time varies widely), or until lentils are tender but still hold their shape. Do not over-cook.

3. While lentils are cooking, combine vinegar, garlic and walnut oil in a blender or in the bowl of a food processor fitted with a steel blade, and process until smooth and creamy.

4. When lentils are done, drain them, discard the carrots, onion,

cloves and bay leaf, and pour lentils into a mixing bowl. Rewhisk dressing and pour it over the still-hot lentils. Toss gently, season generously with salt and pepper and let salad cool to room temperature. Toss again, cover, and refrigerate overnight.

5. Just before serving, add scallions and walnuts. Add an additional tablespoon or two of vinegar or walnut oil if you like, and toss gently. Sprinkle heavily with chopped parsley and serve, accompanied by a peppermill.

6 to 8 portions as a first course

CARROTS

The versatile carrot is a year-round kitchen staple. Its natural sweetness flavors soups and stocks; it is delicious alone either raw and crunchy or just lightly cooked. Carrots are intriguing when combined with stronger flavors; they add color and texture to any dish and are an especially tasty accompaniment to meat and salad dishes.

GINGER CANDIED CARROTS

Sweet and spicy — a good way to prepare carrots any time of the year.

12 medium-size carrots, peeled and cut into 1-inch lengths
4 tablespoons sweet butter, melted
¼ cup brown sugar
1½ teaspoons ground ginger
½ teaspoon caraway seeds

1. Place carrot pieces in a saucepan and add cold water to cover. Cook carrots until tender, 25 to 30 minutes.
2. Melt butter in a small saucepan. Add brown sugar, ginger and caraway seeds. Mix and set aside.
3. When carrots are done, drain and return to the pot. Pour butter mixture over them and cook over low heat for 5 minutes, stirring occasionally.
4. Transfer to a serving dish and serve immediately.
6 portions

In the English court of the 1700's and early 1800's, carrots were a novelty. They were prized for their delicate green foliage, worn like feathers in elegant ladies' hats.

HUNTER'S STYLE CARROTS

A perfect autumn side dish. Serve the carrots with duck, goose, lamb or any other strong meat. As a variation, sprinkle them with Parmesan cheese just before serving.

½ ounce dried wild mushrooms
½ cup Madeira wine
3 tablespoons best-quality olive oil
1½ pounds thin carrots, peeled and cut diagonally into ½-inch pieces
pinch of salt
1 ounce thinly sliced prosciutto, cut into fine julienne
2 large garlic cloves, peeled and finely chopped
3 tablespoons coarsely chopped Italian parsley
freshly ground black pepper, to taste

1. Wash the mushrooms well in a sieve under running water, then soak them in the Madeira for 2 hours. Drain mushrooms, reserving any liquid, and chop mushrooms fine. Set aside.
2. Heat the oil in a large skillet. Add the carrots and cook over medium heat for 10 minutes, stirring occasionally. Season with a pinch of salt.
3. Add chopped wild mushrooms and any of the Madeira they have not absorbed. Continue to sauté, stirring and tossing until the carrots begin to brown lightly, another 10 minutes or so.
4. Add prosciutto and cook for another minute, or until prosciutto is just heated through.
5. Stir in garlic and parsley, grind black pepper over all, and turn the carrots out into a heated vegetable dish. Serve immediately.

4 to 6 portions

WINTER VEGETABLE SALAD

This crisp salad, with its tarragon- and mustard-spiked dressing, is a Silver Palate standard featuring a quartet of readily available winter vegetables, including the trusty carrot. The salad keeps well and improves if refrigerated overnight before serving.

1 large bunch of broccoli, about 3½ pounds, trimmed and
   separated into small florets*
1 large head of cauliflower, about 3½ pounds, trimmed and
   separated into florets
3 medium-size carrots, peeled and sliced into ¼-inch rounds
10 ounces frozen sweet green peas
¾ cup prepared Dijon-style mustard
¾ cup dairy sour cream
¾ cup Homemade Mayonnaise (see page 582)
2 teaspoons celery seeds
2 tablespoons dried tarragon, crumbled
½ cup finely chopped Italian parsley
freshly ground black pepper, to taste

1. Bring a large kettle of salted water to a boil. Drop broccoli into boiling water, let water return to the boil, and cook for 1 minute. Lift from water with a slotted spoon or skimmer and drop immediately into a bowl of ice water. Keep kettle over heat.

2. Drop cauliflower into boiling water, let water return to boil, and cook for 2 minutes. Transfer to a bowl of ice water.

3. Repeat the blanching process with the carrots and the peas in turn, using same pot of water, boiling each 1 minute.

4. Drain all vegetables thoroughly, making sure they are dry, and toss together in a large mixing bowl.

5. Whisk remaining ingredients together in another bowl and pour over vegetables. Toss together gently but thoroughly, cover, and chill until serving time.

6 or more portions

*reserve stems for another use

Variety and contrast are the spice of good party arranging. Don't hesitate to combine your favorite tablecloths, serving pieces and flower bowls, even if they aren't color and pattern coordinated. Contrast antique serving pieces with high-technology plastic plates and utensils; combine new baskets and old. If you find them attractive, in combination they express your taste in the most direct and personal way possible.

RASPBERRY-MARINATED CARROTS

Tartly sweet and spicy. Serve with pâté or as part of an antipasto.

1½ pounds carrots
⅓ cup raspberry vinegar
½ cup best-quality olive oil, approximately
freshly ground black pepper, to taste

1. Peel the carrots and cut them into "coins" ⅛ inch thick. Bring a pot of salted water to a boil and drop in the carrots, cooking them until nearly tender, about 6 minutes. They should retain a slight crunch.

2. Drain the carrots, drop them into a bowl, and sprinkle them with the raspberry vinegar; you must do this while the carrots are still hot. Add enough olive oil to cover the carrots and toss well. Refrigerate at least overnight, although the carrots will keep (and even improve) for several days.

3. To serve, bring carrots to room temperature and lift them from their marinade with a slotted spoon; it is not necessary to drain them completely; some vinegar and oil should still coat the carrots. Season generously with black pepper to taste.

6 portions

CAROTTES RAPEES

A crisp and colorful carrot salad in the French manner.

3 large carrots, trimmed and peeled
½ cup dried currants
juice of 1 medium-size lemon
juice of 1 medium-size orange
¼ cup vegetable oil
¼ cup chopped fresh mint
⅛ teaspoon freshly ground black pepper

1. Coarsely shred carrots, using a food processor or a mandoline.
2. Toss carrots in a mixing bowl together with remaining ingredients. Cover and refrigerate. Serve very cold.
4 to 6 portions, as part of an hors d'oeuvre selection

A MEADOW PICNIC

Pâté de Campagne

Raspberry
Marinated Carrots

French Potato Salad

Ratatouille

Lemon Chicken

Apple Raisin Cake

EGGPLANT

Eggplant originated in tropical Asia and was gradually adopted by Near-Eastern and Mediterranean cuisines, where it is now very much at home.

These rich, dark purple vegetables look mysterious; their flavor is subtle and elusive. Eggplant is at its best when combined with stronger-flavored vegetables and seasonings.

COOKING EGGPLANT

Eggplant is a Silver Palate favorite because it is so versatile and is available year-round. Buy only those eggplants that are firm, shiny and free from wrinkles and blemishes. Store them for no more than a day or two.

Eggplant contains a lot of moisture which can be bitter. It has a tendency to soak up tremendous amounts of oil or butter when sautéed. Salting, or occasionally blanching, will eliminate both problems. Cut the eggplant as directed in each recipe; there is usually no need to peel it. Layer into a colander, salting generously as you go. The eggplant should stand for about 1 hour while it exudes its juices. Rinse off the salt and pat it thoroughly dry on paper towels before proceeding with the recipe. Blanching for a minute or two in boiling salted water is faster; while more tender eggplant is the result, it can reduce the vegetable's already subtle flavor.

When sautéing eggplant, use only as much oil as directed in the recipe, or the minimum necessary to coat the skillet, and be sure skillet is quite hot before the eggplant is added. Toss or turn the eggplant pieces as you add them to coat all sides evenly with oil. *Do not add any more oil!* Even after the salting procedure, eggplant can absorb an amazing amount of oil and the resulting dish could be greasy. If the skillet seems dry, merely stir or turn the eggplant more frequently until properly browned. Drain on paper towels and proceed with the recipe.

EGGPLANT SALAD WITH BASIL

A beautiful summer salad.

3 medium-size eggplants, about 4½ pounds in all, cut into
  1½-inch cubes (do not peel)
1 cup best-quality olive oil
1 tablespoon coarse salt
4 garlic cloves, peeled and minced
2 large yellow onions, peeled, halved and thinly sliced
freshly ground black pepper, to taste
1 cup chopped fresh basil leaves, coarsely chopped
juice of 2 lemons

1. Preheat oven to 400°F.
2. Line a roasting pan with foil and add eggplant. Toss with half of the olive oil, the coarse salt and the minced garlic. Bake for about 35 minutes, until the eggplant is soft but not mushy. Cool slightly and transfer to a large bowl.
3. Heat remaining olive oil in a large skillet. Add sliced onions and cook, covered, over low heat until tender, about 15 minutes. Add onions to the eggplant.
4. Season generously with black pepper; add fresh basil and lemon juice. Toss together. Adjust seasonings and serve at room temperature.

6 to 8 portions

PEASANT CAVIAR

Serve this well chilled as a first course or as part of an hors d'oeuvre selection, with crisp dry toast or hot triangles of pita bread.

2 small eggplants, about 2 pounds in all
4 garlic cloves, or more, peeled and slivered
salt and freshly ground black pepper, to taste
1 teaspoon soy sauce
4 tablespoons best-quality olive oil
1 medium-size tomato, peeled, seeded and chopped
¼ cup golden raisins
¼ cup toasted pine nuts*
chopped fresh Italian parsley (garnish)

1. Cut the eggplants lengthwise into halves and make several deep slits in the flesh; be careful not to pierce the skin. Insert the garlic slivers into the cuts. Lightly sprinkle the cut surfaces with salt, and place halves on a baking sheet. Bake in a preheated 350°F. oven for 1 hour.

2. Remove eggplants, cool slightly, and invert on paper towels. As the eggplants finish cooling, squeeze them gently to eliminate any excess liquid. Scrape the eggplant flesh and the cooked garlic out of the skins into a small mixing bowl and mash with a fork.

3. Season to taste with salt and pepper, stir in the soy sauce, olive oil, chopped tomato, and raisins; cover and refrigerate overnight.

4. Just before serving, stir the peasant caviar well, taste, and correct seasoning. Stir in the pine nuts and sprinkle generously with chopped fresh parsley. Serve immediately.

2 cups, 4 portions as a first course

*To toast pine nuts, spread them in a single layer on a baking sheet; place in a preheated 400°F. oven for 5 to 7 minutes. Stir once or twice during baking. Remove immediately when well browned and transfer to a cool plate; otherwise the heat from the baking sheet may cause them to burn. Toasted nuts can be frozen for long-term storage.

BASIL

Basil has long been a symbol of royalty. Legends tell that once only kings with golden sickles were allowed to cut the fragrant herb. To us, basil has always signified the rich warm fertility of summer. This generous plant, pinched back frequently to keep it short and bushy, will give pleasure from midsummer to the first frost.

If we have a favorite herb, basil is it, and the passing of summer always brings a qualm of panic. Dried basil is useful in its way, but nothing like the fresh, which seems to insinuate itself into our cooking more with each passing year.

Fortunately, the season for fresh basil can be extended in several ways. Freshly washed and carefully dried leaves of fresh basil can be puréed in the food processor with enough olive oil to make a smooth paste. We put the paste in small plastic containers and freeze. Pesto — the basil sauce for pasta — can also be frozen.

Pack washed and well-dried fresh basil leaves into a jar and add olive or salad oil to cover. Tightly capped and refrigerated, the leaves will keep for at least 6 months, and flavor the oil a bit as well. If you've thought to use a decorative jar, this makes a nice present at holiday time.

As a last resort, try this trick: Soak dried basil in a little wine or spirits — vermouth is good, but Strega, vodka and white wine have also been suggested — for several days. Drain and chop the reconstituted basil together with an equal amount of fresh parsley. Use the resulting mixture in recipes calling for fresh basil. Close your eyes and you can almost hear the crickets.

RATATOUILLE

2 cups best-quality olive oil
4 small eggplants, about 4 pounds in all, cut into 1½-inch cubes
2 teaspoons salt
1½ pounds white onions, peeled and coarsely chopped
7 medium-size zucchini, washed, trimmed, quartered lengthwise
*   and cut into 2-inch strips*
2 medium-size sweet red peppers, stemmed, seeded, cut
*   into ½-inch strips*
2 medium-size green bell peppers, stemmed, seeded, cut
*   into ½-inch strips*
2 tablespoons minced garlic
3 cans (16 ounces each) Italian peeled plum tomatoes, drained
1 can (6 ounces) tomato paste
¼ cup chopped fresh Italian parsley
¼ cup chopped fresh dill
2 tablespoons dried basil
2 tablespoons dried oregano
freshly ground black pepper, to taste

1. Preheat oven to 400°F.

2. Line a large roasting pan with foil and pour in 1 cup of the olive oil. Add the eggplant, sprinkle it with the salt, and toss well. Cover pan tightly with foil and bake for 35 minutes, until eggplant is done but not mushy. Uncover and set aside.

3. In a large skillet or in 2 smaller skillets, heat remaining oil. Sauté onions, zucchini, red and green peppers and garlic over medium heat until wilted and lightly colored, about 20 minutes. Add tomatoes, tomato paste, parsley, dill, basil, oregano and black pepper. Simmer for 10 minutes, stirring occasionally.

4. Add eggplant mixture and simmer for another 10 minutes. Taste and correct seasoning. Serve hot or at room temperature.

12 portions

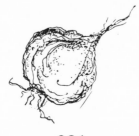

EGGPLANT WITH HERBS

This is a simple thing, but good.

1 tablespoon minced fresh basil, thyme, rosemary or oregano
1 tablespoon minced fresh parsley
1 large garlic clove, peeled and minced
1 medium-size eggplant, about 1 pound
salt and freshly ground black pepper, to taste
2 tablespoons olive oil

1. Preheat oven to 350°F.
2. Mix together the minced basil, parsley and garlic.
3. Cut the eggplant into halves. Cut several slits in the eggplant flesh, being careful not to cut through the skin. Push the herb and garlic mixture into the slits. Season eggplant with salt and pepper, and drizzle with olive oil, about 1 tablespoon per half.
4. Bake eggplant halves for 30 minutes. Serve hot or, even better, at room temperature, sprinkled with additional chopped fresh herbs.
   2 portions

OIL-ROASTED SUMMER VEGETABLES

In this method of cooking vegetables, the oil keeps them from drying out while the salt draws out their natural moisture, concentrating the flavors of the vegetables. They emerge looking limp and shiny and tasting fabulous — sweet and intense.

Although you can serve this hot, the flavors of the vegetables are even more apparent at room temperature. They are perfect served with grilled or roast chicken, meat or fish.

6 baby zucchini, about 3 inches long
6 baby eggplants, about 3 inches long
1 pound fresh green beans, cleaned and tipped
6 new potatoes, scrubbed
⅓ cup best-quality olive oil, approximately
2 tablespoons coarse salt, approximately

1. Preheat oven to 375°F.
2. Wash and dry vegetables, leaving stems intact, and arrange them in a shallow baking dish just large enough to hold them in a single layer.
3. Drizzle with the olive oil, then sprinkle coarse salt over all. (While it is possible to oversalt the dish, it can stand more salt than you might think; we use about 2 tablespoons.)
4. Set the baking dish in the center of the oven and bake until brown and slightly shriveled. Vegetables will not all cook at the same rate. Zucchini and eggplant will be done in 30 minutes or so; potatoes can take an hour. Remove individual vegetables as they become tender and arrange them on a serving plate.
5. Cool to room temperature and serve at your leisure.
6 portions

"If I had to choose just one plant for the whole herb garden,
I should be content with basil."
— **Elizabeth David**

When cooking combinations of vegetables, aim for a variety of colors as well as tastes and textures. Our recipe for Oil-Roasted Summer Vegetables calls for eggplant, zucchini, green beans and new potatoes — try substituting carrots, baby artichokes, and strips of red and green pepper.

FRESH HERBS

Fresh herbs are a necessity to many; others spend a lifetime cooking well without them. If you must have them, try growing your own. We have friends, quite unobsessed otherwise, who grow herbs near the bathtub, in window boxes, near the garbage cans or in the cracks in the patio. These are the folks who ask us to bring, when we return from Paris, not chocolates or perfume but obscure seedlings and seeds. For them we visit the Quai de la Megisserie, along the banks of the Seine, where we find the herbs our friends desire.

Be prudent when substituting fresh herbs for dried, and vice versa. The usual formula is to use 2 to 3 times as much fresh as dried, but your taste buds must be the final arbiter.

EGGPLANT PARMIGIANA

Fresher and lighter than the usual version.

2 small eggplants, about 2 pounds in all
salt for draining eggplant
2 cups ricotta cheese
2 eggs
¼ cup grated imported Parmesan cheese
1 cup chopped Italian parsley
salt and freshly ground black pepper, to taste
½ cup olive oil, approximately
2 cups Quick Tomato Sauce (see page 590)
½ pound whole-milk mozzarella cheese, grated

1. Slice the eggplant into ½-inch-thick pieces and layer in a colander, salting the slices heavily as you go. Set aside for 30 minutes.

2. Combine the ricotta, eggs, Parmesan and chopped parsley. Season to taste with salt and pepper.

3. Rinse eggplant slices well and pat dry on paper towels. Heat 2 tablespoons olive oil in a large skillet until it begins to smoke. Add a single layer of eggplant slices with no overlapping. Turn the slices quickly to coat both sides lightly with oil; reduce heat slightly. Fry the eggplant until lightly browned on both sides. (Do not add more oil after eggplant is in the skillet.) When slices are browned, remove to paper towels to drain. Pour 2 tablespoons more oil into the skillet and cook another layer of eggplant. Repeat until all eggplant pieces are done.

4. Spread ½ cup tomato sauce over the bottom of an oval gratin dish measuring 9 x 12 inches. Arrange a layer of eggplant slices over the sauce. Top each eggplant slice with a tablespoon of ricotta mixture and sprinkle about ⅓ of the grated mozzarella over the layer. Repeat, arranging the next layer of eggplant slices to cover the gaps between the slices in the first layer. Add more ricotta mixture and mozzarella. Add a final layer of eggplant, cover it well with remaining tomato sauce, and spoon remaining ricotta mixture down the center of the dish. Sprinkle remaining mozzarella over the exposed tomato sauce.

5. Set dish on the middle rack of the preheated 400°F. oven and bake for 25 to 30 minutes, or until well browned and bubbling. Let stand for 10 minutes before serving.

4 to 6 portions

MUSHROOMS

Mushrooms miraculously appear overnight in the most mysterious places. They have been the subject of legends and folklore for centuries. They were once thought to be the result of thunder, since they appeared after rainstorms, and they still seem to many people as magical as elves, gnomes, fairies and hobbits. The ancient Greeks thought them "food for the gods." We make a bit of a ceremony about them as well.

THE DOMESTIC MUSHROOM

Only one genus of mushroom *(Agaricus)* is responsible for most of the mushrooms grown commercially in the United States. Though they lack some of the earthy intensity of their choicest cousins grown in the wild, tons of them are consumed yearly. Their availability and versatility make them indispensable and they're full of vitamins, too. Best of all, they combine beautifully with dried wild mushrooms, and allow us to extend those precious morsels economically.

THE WILD MUSHROOM

Since almost countless species of wild mushrooms grow on this earth, hunting them is hardly the esoteric pursuit it is often made out to be. Of course you must know your onions, so to speak, since some mushroom species are poisonous, but courses and guidebooks abound, and the beginning mushroom hunters who learn their lessons and observe their sensible precautions need not fear. Do be cautious and follow the example of the experts: never eat a mushroom not positively identified as safe.

In certain regions of the U.S., spring still signals the start of the mushroom hunt, and entire families will happily forage for basketfuls to be rushed home and consumed at once, with nothing more than bread to mop up the juices. Chief among the spring mushrooms is the morel, which often grows under oak and apple trees from Connecticut to Oregon. Fresh morels, like other fresh wild mushrooms, can be very sandy and need to be washed carefully. Slice them thin and sauté long and slowly in butter with a touch of garlic. Add cream or sherry, if you like; scramble them with eggs or stuff them into a chicken. Once you've tasted their buttery flavor, you too will be part of the mushroom hunt.

If wandering in the woods is not your thing, however, don't despair. The taste of wild mushrooms can still be yours, captured in dried form. Several kinds of these are available, usually imported from Europe. When they are properly reconstituted by soaking, the flavor and texture are as good — though different — as those of the fresh.

Buy from a reputable dealer, and preferably one who offers his wares in bulk; dried mushrooms can be invaded by worms and other insects and a wary shopper will examine them closely. Rinse them thoroughly under cold running water and soak them in water, or, more wisely, a liquid that you will be able to incorporate into the recipe, thus saving every bit of elusive flavor. Madeira or Port and chicken stock are the two best choices; lemon juice is good where appropriate.

After soaking, dried mushrooms are usually chopped and sautéed in butter to bring out their full flavor before going into the dish. We have learned to combine an ounce or two of dried with a pound or more of sautéed sliced cultivated mushrooms; the exchange of flavors and textures benefits both, and the result is a generous quantity of wild mushroom flavor with a minimum of expense.

Some of our favorite mushrooms, often available fresh as well as dried, include the following:

CEPES/PORCINI: *Cèpes* are imported dried or canned from France, where they grow in oak, chestnut and beech forests. *Porcini* (or "little pigs") are the same mushroom, a kind of boletus; they come to us from Italy. *Cèpes* and *porcini* impart rich deep flavor to game and poultry dishes and to sauces.

CHANTERELLES: Often called "little goblets." they are dainty and reddish yellow, with a cup shape and a slight apricot taste.
GIROLLES: These golden mushrooms sparkle in forests of deciduous trees. They are delicately shaped, reminding us of morning glories; lovely sautéed in an omelet.

288

MORELS: These come from Europe, too, and are widely available; they are the only fungus to approach the intensity of bouquet of the truffle. After soaking, sauté long and slowly.

ORANGE MUSHROOMS: Caesar's mushroom. Reddish with yellow gills; excellent flavor.

OYSTER MUSHROOMS: White and delicate, this mushroom is often called "weeper" because of the liquid it produces when sautéed fresh.

TROMPETTES DES MORTS (Horns of Plenty): These black, trumpet-shaped mushrooms border the vineyards in France. Softened in wine and stuffed into meats, dried trompettes give a taste that suggests truffles.

TRUFFLES: The most highly prized of the earth's edible fungi. Their mystery and delicate flavor make grown people a little crazy. They have always been expensive, and must be eaten fresh if all the fuss is to make sense.

Dark, rich truffles are hunted in France, largely in the Périgord, an ancient region where the truffle was once considered a pest. They grow under oak trees and are hunted in the fall with trained hounds or pigs that have been given food mixed with truffles.

In late fall and winter they are available fresh in this country, and, though expensive, their penetrating flavor makes them go a long way. Truffles are also sold in cans or jars; these are expensive, too, but nearly always flavorless, and we, like Colette, would rather do without.

Italian white truffles from Piedmont are more pungently flavored than the black and are equally expensive. It is delicious to have one finely shaved over a dish of pasta or scrambled eggs; the truly devoted slice them and warm them briefly in butter.

WOODSY WILD MUSHROOM SAUTE

Serve this as an earthy side dish to pork or game.

1 ounce dried cèpes★
4 ounces fresh morels or 1 ounce dried★
1 ounce dried trompettes des morts★
1½ cups Madeira wine
2 pounds large fresh mushrooms
6 tablespoons sweet butter
¼ cup chopped shallots
4 garlic cloves, very finely minced
½ cup chopped fresh parsley
½ teaspoon salt
freshly ground black pepper, to taste
juice of 1 lemon

1. Rinse dried mushrooms under cold running water in a small strainer until they are free of all dirt and grit.

2. Combine dried mushrooms and Madeira in a small bowl, cover, and let stand for 1 hour, stirring occasionally.

3. Wipe fresh mushrooms with a damp paper towel. Cut off stems and save for another use. Slice mushroom caps in half.

4. Melt half of the butter in a large skillet and add the halved fresh mushrooms. Cook, stirring, over high heat for 5 minutes.

5. Lift the dried mushrooms carefully from the bowl with a slotted spoon. Coarsely chop the dried mushrooms and add them, the remaining butter, shallots, garlic and parsley to the skillet and cook over low heat for another 10 minutes, stirring occasionally. Pour the Madeira carefully into the skillet, leaving any sediment behind.

6. Season to taste with salt and pepper, turn out into a heated vegetable dish, and sprinkle with fresh lemon juice. Serve immediately.

8 to 10 portions

★available at specialty food shops

DUXELLES

This reduced preparation of minced mushrooms is endlessly useful. It can become a stuffing for mushrooms, chicken breasts or an omelet; it can be stirred into scrambled eggs; a spoonful or two will add intensity to soup or sauce; a simply roasted piece of chicken can be transformed into something special by a pan deglazing of cream into which a spoonful of *duxelles* is stirred. Our version includes both cultivated and dried wild mushrooms for extra flavor.

The recipe here can easily be halved, but since *duxelles* freezes well, it is less work to make the larger amount.

1 to 2 ounces dried wild mushrooms (cèpes, morels,
   trompettes des morts or a mixture)
½ cup Madeira wine
2½ to 3 pounds firm fresh mushrooms
8 tablespoons (1 stick) sweet butter
2 large shallots, peeled and finely chopped
1 cup finely chopped yellow onions
1 teaspoon dried thyme
1½ teaspoons salt
pinch of grated nutmeg
freshly ground black pepper, to taste
½ cup finely chopped Italian parsley

1. Rinse the mushrooms under cold running water in a strainer. Drain and place them in a small bowl. Add the Madeira and let stand until mushrooms are soft, at least 1 hour.

2. Wipe the fresh mushrooms with damp paper towels and trim the stem ends. Mince the mushrooms. (A food processor fitted with a steel blade is ideal for this.)

3. Melt the butter in a large skillet. Add shallots and onions and cook, covered, over low heat until tender and lightly colored, about 25 minutes.

4. Add minced fresh mushrooms to the skillet, raise the heat and cook, stirring, until they render their juices, about 5 minutes. Add the thyme, salt, nutmeg, and black pepper to taste.

5. Meanwhile, transfer the reconstituted wild mushrooms to the food

processor, lifting them from the Madeira with a slotted spoon. Carefully pour the wine over them, discarding any sediment in the bowl, and purée until very smooth. Add them to the skillet. Reduce the heat and cook, stirring occasionally, until *duxelles* is reduced and thickened, about 40 minutes. Near the end of this cooking time the mixture will become dry; stir constantly to prevent scorching.

6. Remove pan from the heat. Taste *duxelles* and correct seasoning. Stir in the chopped parsley, cool to room temperature, and cover before refrigerating or freezing.

About 1 quart

A FRENCH BRUNCH

Croissants with sweet butter and preserves

———

Black Forest Crêpe Torte and Woodsy Wild Mushrooms

———

Fresh fruit basket

Chèvre cheeses

———

Café au lait

MUSHROOM SERENDIPITIES

One of the joys of earning a bit of name recognition in this business is the amazing number of culinary offerings that find their way to us. One of the most pleasant occurred the day we were finishing this chapter on mushrooms: a phone caller from Connecticut had several pounds of Hen- and Chicken-of-the-Woods to offer us. These were wild mushrooms that grow on trees and we had never tasted them, so we jumped at the chance.

After assuring ourselves of the gentleman's mycological credentials, we rushed to the kitchen to examine our prize. They were fantastically beautiful; sliced and sautéed in butter a few minutes later, they tasted wonderful too.

We have preached throughout this chapter that, for many, fresh wild mushrooms are a way of life. This episode only convinced us that more and more people are becoming aware of the mushroom possibilities that await them in nearly every part of the country.

WILD MUSHROOM SOUP

A rich and earthy beginning to a fall or winter meal, or a meal in itself. This has been made at The Silver Palate's kitchen for several years and always brings rave reviews.

2 ounces dried cèpes, morels or chanterelles
¾ cup Madeira wine
8 tablespoons (1 stick) sweet butter
2 cups finely chopped yellow onions
2 pounds fresh mushrooms
salt and freshly ground black pepper, to taste
4 cups Chicken Stock (see page 587)
1 pint heavy cream (optional)

1. Rinse the dried mushrooms well in a sieve under cold running water and soak them in the Madeira for 1 hour, stirring occasionally.

2. Melt the butter in a soup pot. Add the onions and cook, covered, over low heat until they are tender and lightly colored, about 15 minutes, stirring occasionally.

3. Trim stems from the fresh mushrooms and save for another use. Wipe caps with a damp cloth and slice thin. Add caps to the soup pot, season to taste with salt and pepper, and cook over low heat, uncovered, stirring frequently, for 15 minutes.

4. Carefully lift mushrooms from bowl with a slotted spoon and transfer to soup pot. Let Madeira settle a moment and then pour carefully into soup pot, leaving sediment behind.

5. Add the chicken stock and bring to a boil. Reduce heat, cover, and simmer for 45 minutes, or until dried mushrooms are very tender.

6. Strain the soup and transfer the solids to the bowl of a food processor fitted with a steel blade. Add 1 cup of the liquid and purée until very smooth.

7. Return purée to the soup pot along with remaining liquid and set over medium heat. Taste, correct seasoning, and thin the soup slightly with heavy cream if it seems too thick. Heat until steaming and serve immediately.

6 to 8 portions

"If I can't have too many truffles, I'll do without truffles."
— Colette

TRUFFLES AND AVOCADOS

Peel and slice an avocado, toss lightly in lemon juice, drain, and cover with olive oil and a shaved raw or tinned truffle. Let stand for 1 hour. Serve on a bed of fresh watercress. Luxurious and buttery. Pass the peppermill.

TRUFFLES AND POTATOES

Combine these two wonders from underground: sliced potatoes, sautéed in lots of butter until tender, and tossed when done with shaved raw or tinned black truffle — about 1 truffle for every 6 potatoes. Grind pepper liberally over all and live it up.

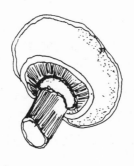

CREAMED MUSHROOMS

Perfect folded into crêpes or as an omelet filling, and particularly good spooned over buttered sourdough toast.

2 pounds firm fresh white mushrooms
4 tablespoons sweet butter
1 teaspoon salt
¼ teaspoon freshly ground black pepper
pinch of grated nutmeg
⅓ cup heavy cream
2 tablespoons Madeira wine
1 tablespoon imported soy sauce
½ cup finely chopped Italian parsley

1. Wipe the mushrooms with a damp paper towel and trim the stem ends. Cut the mushrooms into thick slices.

2. Melt the butter in a large skillet. Add the mushrooms, raise the heat, and toss and stir until mushrooms render their juices, about 5 minutes.

3. Lower the heat, season mushrooms with salt, pepper and nutmeg, and cook uncovered for another 5 minutes.

4. With a slotted spoon, transfer mushrooms to a bowl. Add the cream, Madeira and soy sauce to the juices in the skillet and bring to a boil. Cook until reduced by about half.

5. Return mushrooms to the skillet and simmer for another minute or two to heat through. Stir in the parsley and serve immediately.

About 2 cups, serving 4, depending on use

MARINATED MUSHROOMS WITH RED WINE AND FENNEL

Present the mushrooms in a bowl surrounded by squares of black bread, spread, if you like, with butter and sprinkled with parsley. Scoop the mushrooms onto the bread squares and enjoy.

¼ cup best-quality olive oil
1½ pounds medium-size fresh mushrooms, stems removed
  (reserve for another use) and wiped clean
salt and freshly ground black pepper, to taste
1 medium yellow onion, peeled and sliced into thin rings
4 to 6 garlic cloves, peeled and chopped
1 tablespoon fennel seeds
1 tablespoon dried basil
2 teaspoons dried marjoram
1 cup canned Italian peeled plum tomatoes, drained and chopped
1 cup hearty red wine
¼ cup Balsamic Vinegar (see page 357)
1 teaspoon salt
freshly ground black pepper, to taste
chopped Italian parsley (garnish)

1. Heat the oil in a heavy saucepan. Add the mushrooms and cook, stirring frequently, for 5 minutes. Salt and pepper the mushrooms, and cook further, for 2 to 3 minutes. Remove mushrooms with a slotted spoon and reserve.

2. Cook the onion and garlic in the oil remaining in the pan over low heat for 15 minutes. Onions should still have some "crunch."

3. Add fennel seeds, basil and marjoram and cook for another 5 minutes, stirring occasionally.

4. Add tomatoes, wine and vinegar to the pan, season with 1 teaspoon salt and pepper to taste, and simmer for 15 minutes, or until slightly reduced.

5. Return mushrooms to the pan, simmer for 5 minutes, and remove from heat. Let cool to room temperature, stirring occasionally, then cover and refrigerate. Marinate for at least 24 hours before serving.

6. Sprinkle heavily with chopped fresh parsley before serving.

4 to 6 portions

GAZEBO PICNIC

Layered Vegetable Terrine
with Tomato Coulis

———

Sliced Filet of Beef with
horseradish sauce

Marinated Mushrooms with
Red Wine and Fennel

———

Cracked Wheat Salad

French Bread

———

Pears poached in
white wine

Black Walnut Cookies

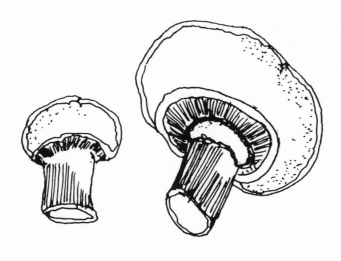

POTATOES

The potato, available worldwide, is a most comforting vegetable. It has held nations together in times of war and famine, and even today there are places where potatoes are eaten three times a day. Grown as it is in almost every state of the Union, the potato is considered somewhat common by some. We don't think so.

DILLED NEW POTATOES

24 tiny new potatoes
8 tablespoons (1 stick) sweet butter
salt and freshly ground black pepper, to taste
6 tablespoons chopped fresh dill

1. Scrub potatoes and dry. Melt butter in a heavy flameproof casserole with a tight-fitting cover. Add potatoes and season with salt and pepper to taste. Coat with butter.
2. Cover and cook over low heat for 30 to 45 minutes. Shake casserole occasionally. Potatoes are done when they can be pierced with the tip of a sharp knife.
3. Toss with dill and serve at once.
4 to 6 portions

THE WELL-DRESSED NEW POTATO

In any season at The Silver Palate, the tiny new potato is cooked with its jacket on. Scientists tell us the potato retains more vitamins that way. Our eye tells us that the delicate pink or tan of the potato skins makes every dish prettier. Since no one wants to peel the little devils, it saves time too.

Other potatoes — the larger ones used for slicing or mashing — are peeled, letting the fluffy white insides stand on their own merits.

ORANGE MASHED POTATOES

The earthy neutrality of mashed potatoes makes them compatible with a wide range of partners — herbs, vinegars, cheeses, other vegetables, and even citrus, as here. Use your imagination for these white clouds, as we have done in the following recipe.

3 pounds potatoes
2 cups finely chopped yellow onions
4 tablespoons sweet butter
½ cup Crème Fraîche (see page 582)
¾ cup fresh orange juice
grated fresh orange zest (garnish)

1. Peel and quarter the potatoes and drop them into a large pot of cold salted water. Bring to a moderate boil and cook until potatoes are very tender, 30 minutes or so.
2. Meanwhile, in another pan, cook the onions in the butter, covered, until very tender and lightly colored, about 25 minutes.
3. Drain and mash the potatoes and stir in the onions and their cooking butter. (Or force potatoes, onions and butter through the medium disc of a food mill.)
4. Stir in the *crème fraîche* and orange juice and beat the potatoes with a wire whisk until fluffy. Turn into a heated serving dish and garnish with fresh orange zest to taste. Serve immediately.

6 portions

SWISS POTATO GRATIN

2 pounds red-skinned boiling potatoes
1 cup ricotta cheese
¾ cup chopped parsley
salt and freshly ground black pepper, to taste
nutmeg, to taste
1 egg
1 cup heavy cream (approximately)
sweet butter for greasing baking dish
¼ pound Gruyère cheese, grated (about 1 cup)

1. Wash potatoes well and trim away any discolored spots or eyes. (You may peel potatoes if you like.) Slice thin and drop into a pot of cold, heavily salted water. Set over high heat and bring to a boil. Boil potatoes for 1 minute, drain, and rinse with cold water. Drain again and pat dry.

2. Combine ricotta and parsley and season generously with salt, pepper and nutmeg.

3. Beat the egg briefly and add enough heavy cream to make 1 cup of liquid. Season with salt, pepper and nutmeg.

4. Lightly butter a shallow, oval gratin dish measuring 9 x 12 inches. Arrange a layer of slightly overlapping potato slices in the dish. Dot with about one third of the ricotta mixture; sprinkle with one third of the Gruyère. Repeat, using all of the ingredients and ending with a potato layer.

5. Gently pour the egg and cream mixture into the dish, lifting potato slices with a fork if necessary to allow the cream to spread evenly among them.

6. Bake on the center rack of a preheated 350°F. oven for 35 to 45 minutes, or until potatoes are tender and the cheese is browned and bubbling. Let sit for about 10 minutes before serving.

4 portions

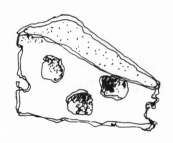

STUFFED POTATOES

Bake and stuff the largest potato you can find, and you have a savory and elegant luncheon main course or late-night snack that is special and comforting at the same time.

While you can stuff a memorable potato with practically anything you find in cupboard and refrigerator, here are two of our favorite fillings to get you started.

TWICE-BAKED POTATOES WITH LOBSTER

4 large baking potatoes
salt and freshly ground black pepper, to taste
4 tablespoons sweet butter
½ cup chopped yellow onion
½ cup finely chopped fresh mushrooms
2 cups cooked lobster (or crab) meat
1 cup dry white vermouth
½ cup Crème Fraîche (see page 582)
½ cup grated Jarlsberg cheese, plus additional cheese for
  topping potatoes
1 to 2 tablespoons heavy cream (optional)

1. Scrub and dry the potatoes. Cut a small, deep slit in the top of each potato. Set potatoes on the middle rack of a preheated 375°F. oven and bake for about 1 hour, or until potatoes are tender when pierced with a fork.

2. Let potatoes cool slightly, cut off and discard the tops, and scrape the potato pulp into a bowl. Do not scrape so deeply that you tear the potato skin. Salt and pepper the potato shells; reserve. Mash the potato pulp; reserve.

3. Melt the butter in a small skillet and sauté the chopped onion, covered, until tender and lightly colored, about 25 minutes. Add the mushrooms and sauté for another 5 minutes. Stir in the lobster or crab. Season with salt and pepper, add the vermouth, then raise heat to a boil. Stir frequently over high heat until all liquid has boiled away. Stir in *crème fraîche* and remove from heat.

4. Combine lobster mixture with the reserved mashed potato pulp

and ½ cup Jarlsberg. Taste, correct seasoning; add heavy cream if the mixture seems too dry.

5. Stuff the mixture into the reserved potato skins; mound the filling slightly. Sprinkle additional grated cheese on top and place on baking sheet.

6. Bake again, at 400°F., until potatoes are hot and cheese is bubbling. Serve immediately.

4 portions

TWICE-BAKED POTATOES WITH CHEESE AND CHILIES

4 large baking potatoes
salt and freshly ground black pepper, to taste
4 tablespoons chopped imported black olives
½ cup diced canned mild green chili peppers
4 to 6 tablespoons heavy cream
½ cup grated sharp Cheddar cheese, plus additional cheese for
   topping potatoes
½ cup sour cream (garnish)
whole imported black olives (optional garnish)

1. Scrub and dry the potatoes. Cut a small, deep slit in the top of each potato. Set potatoes on the middle rack of a preheated 375°F. oven and bake for about 1 hour, or until potatoes are tender when pierced with a fork.

2. Let potatoes cool slightly, cut off the tops, and scrape the potato pulp into a bowl. Do not scrape so deeply that you tear the potato skin. Salt and pepper the potato shells; reserve.

3. Mash the potato pulp and stir in chopped olives, diced green chilies, and enough heavy cream to give the mixture the desired consistency. Season to taste with salt and pepper, and stir in ½ cup grated cheese.

4. Divide the potato mixture equally among the shells, mounding the filling slightly. Sprinkle with additional grated cheese and place on baking sheet.

5. Bake again, at 400°F., until potatoes are hot and cheese is bubbling.

6. Top each potato with a generous dollop of sour cream, and add a black olive if you like. Serve immediately.

4 portions

"Let the sky rain potatoes."
— *The Merry Wives of Windsor,*
William Shakespeare

The largest concentration of potato growers and lovers on earth can be found on the south fork of Long Island. It is there in Water Mill, Sagaponack and Bridgehampton that moneyed families, artists, expatriate Europeans and beach bums scramble to buy homesites on land that only recently was used as potato fields. The home of potato farmers and fishermen has become a weekend and summer resort of incredible chic. Land prices have soared, but between the classy getaway homes, affordable potatoes are still grown. We hurry to enjoy them now, before they, too, become too dear.

SOME GOOD EXCUSES FOR A PICNIC

bicycling
bird watching
trout fishing
hunting for wild mushrooms
watching the autumn foliage turn
looking for shooting stars
at the beach
canoeing
skiing cross-country or downhill
the Fourth of July
listening to the Philharmonic
fireworks anytime
a birthday
after a tennis match
half time of the big game
while driving cross-country
at the summit of the mountain

303

while antique-hunting
during a James Joyce reading
cleaning out closets with a friend
organizing photo albums
during a day at the zoo
studying for finals
washing the family car
a backgammon tournament
a session of constructive criticism
annual budget time
studying for the SAT
while working on a Saturday
in a hot air balloon
after watching or running the marathon

FRENCH POTATO SALAD WITH BACON

8 or 9 new potatoes, 1 pound
¼ pound bacon
¼ cup finely chopped shallots
¼ cup red wine vinegar
2 tablespoons olive oil
salt and freshly ground black pepper, to taste
¼ cup chopped purple onion
½ cup chopped parsley

1. Scrub the potatoes under running water with a soft brush. Quarter them and drop them into a kettle of cold, salted water. Bring to a boil and cook until tender but still firm, 8 to 10 minutes after the water reaches a boil.

2. Meanwhile, chop the bacon and sauté in a small skillet until crisp. Remove bacon and reserve.

3. In the bacon fat remaining in the skillet, sauté chopped shallots until tender but not at all browned, 5 minutes or so. Reserve shallots and fat.

4. When the potatoes are done, drain them and drop them into a mixing bowl.

5. Pour vinegar, olive oil, shallots and reserved bacon fat over the still-hot potatoes. Season with salt and pepper to taste, and gently

toss. Add purple onion and parsley and toss again. Cool to room temperature, cover, and refrigerate.

6. Before serving bring back to room temperature, toss, correct seasoning and add additional oil and vinegar if the salad seems dry. Sprinkle reserved crisp bacon on top.

4 portions

AMERICAN PICNIC POTATO SALAD

4 pounds boiling potatoes, peeled
½ cup white wine vinegar
½ cup olive oil
1 teaspoon salt
¼ teaspoon freshly ground black pepper
1 cup thinly sliced purple onions
1 cup celery strips, 1 inch long, ¼ inch wide
3 medium-size cucumbers, peeled, seeded and sliced
2 cups Hellmann's mayonnaise, plus more if needed
5 tablespoons prepared Dijon-style or herb mustard
  (dill, tarragon or basil)
20 hard-cooked eggs, peeled and quartered
1 cup chopped Italian parsley

1. Drop the potatoes as you peel them into a kettle of cold, salted water. Bring to a boil and cook until tender but still firm.

2. When done, drain the potatoes and drop them into a mixing bowl; roughly slice them. Sprinkle the still-hot potatoes with vinegar, olive oil, salt and pepper.

3. Add the onions, celery, cucumbers, mayonnaise and mustard; toss gently to combine.

4. Add quartered eggs and parsley and toss again. Cool to room temperature, cover, and refrigerate overnight. Before serving, toss again, correct seasoning and add more mayonnaise if needed.

20 portions

How many potato salads should a cookbook have? We stopped with three, not because we ran out of ideas, but because we ran out of room.

SCANDINAVIAN POTATO SALAD

8 or 9 new potatoes (about 1 pound)
salt and freshly ground black pepper, to taste
1 cup dairy sour cream
⅓ cup chopped purple onion
⅓ cup chopped fresh dill

1. Scrub the potatoes with a soft brush under running water. Quarter them and drop them into a kettle of cold salted water. Bring to a boil and cook until tender but still firm, for 8 to 10 minutes after the water reaches a boil.
2. When the potatoes are done, drain them and place them in a mixing bowl.
3. Season with salt and pepper to taste, add sour cream to the still-hot potatoes, and toss gently. Add chopped onion and dill, toss again, and cool to room temperature before refrigerating at least 4 hours.
4. Before serving, toss again, correct seasoning and add more sour cream if salad seems dry.

4 portions

DILL

Dill was first discovered in England in 1597. Its name is taken from the Saxon "dillan," meaning "to lull," since its reeds were used to soothe babies to sleep.

SCALLIONS, LEEKS, GARLIC, SHALLOTS AND ONIONS

These lusty members of the onion family have been frowned on by polite society for centuries. Their taste and smell have been considered common, and indeed their very availability has made them the cornerstones of peasant cooking the world over.

Though still thought of as "stinky," the members of the family are seen by wise cooks for what they are — flavor-makers in the best sense of the word, adding richness and zest to otherwise bland dishes.

BRAISED SCALLIONS IN MUSTARD SAUCE

The simple scallion, treated with imagination and respect, can become a dressy hot vegetable. Here it is braised with aromatic vegetables and chicken stock and sauced with cream and a bit of mustard. This is rich and is best with simply roasted beef or veal, or as a first course over toast points.

20 to 24 large scallions (green onions)
1 tablespoon sweet butter
1 celery rib, cleaned and chopped
1 carrot, peeled and chopped
1 teaspoon dried thyme
1 bay leaf
2 parsley sprigs
freshly ground black pepper, to taste
1½ cups Chicken Stock (see page 587) or canned chicken broth
¼ cup prepared Dijon-style mustard
½ cup heavy cream or Crème Fraîche (see page 582)
salt (optional)

1. Trim and clean the scallions and cut away all but about 1 inch of the green tops. Save tops for another use if you like.

2. In a skillet large enough to hold the scallions later, melt the butter and cook the celery and carrot over low heat, covered, until tender and lightly colored, about 20 minutes.

3. Add the thyme, bay leaf, parsley, black pepper to taste, and chicken stock. Simmer together, partially covered, for 15 minutes. Add no salt at this point; you will correct seasoning as necessary when the dish is completed.

4. Add the scallions to the broth and simmer, uncovered, for about 5 minutes, until barely tender. Do not overcook. Remove scallions with a slotted spoon and reserve.

5. Strain the liquid, discard the solids, measure out ½ cup, and return it to the skillet. Whisk in the mustard and the heavy cream or *crème fraîche*. Set skillet over medium heat and simmer, stirring occasionally,

for 10 minutes, or until sauce is reduced by about one third. Taste and correct seasoning.

6. Return scallions to the skillet for 1 minute to warm them through before serving immediately.

4 to 6 portions

SCALLIONS

Scallions are usually only baby or teenage onions, and they can be sweetly mild or bitingly strong, depending on which onion variety they belong to. They make good if pungent eating just dipped into coarse salt. They add crunch, color and flavor to soups and salads, and can be used as garnishes in a variety of ways. We love tiny green rings of scallion tops in cool white soups. We sprinkle the chopped white and green scallion bits lavishly over pasta and seafood salads. Fine scallion julienne, scallion brushes, and whole green scallions — all are used at The Silver Palate.

LEEKS

Leeks, with their thick white bodies and broad green leaves, grow like and resemble onions, although they have a mild, almost sweet flavor that is all their own. In Europe leeks are plentiful and cheap, and are called "The asparagus of the poor." They were once difficult to find in this country, and though they are more available than they used to be, they are still expensive. Nevertheless, leeks are essential in the soup or stockpot, adding a depth of flavor not achieved by onions alone. As a vegetable served on their own, leeks can be braised and eaten hot or cold — a favorite first course in French bistros. Sliced and gently sautéed in butter, they become a delicious filling for an omelet or quiche. Like all members of the onion tribe, leeks are pleasantly easy to grow; you'll come to love and rely on this homely vegetable.

Clean leeks carefully, since they often contain a lot of sand. Cut off the root and most, but not all, of the green top. Cut the resulting white part into halves the long way, separate the layers, and wash thoroughly under cold running water. Pat dry before using.

LEEKS NICOISE

Serve these leeks as a sit-down first course, or as part of an alfresco meal.

12 leeks, each 1½ inches in diameter
¼ cup best-quality olive oil
1 large garlic clove, peeled and finely minced
3 ripe tomatoes, cut into eighths
½ cup Niçoise olives
2 teaspoons dried basil or 1½ tablespoons chopped fresh basil
2 tablespoons chopped parsley
freshly ground black pepper

1. Leave the roots on the leeks for now, but trim away 2 or 3 inches of the toughest tips of the green leaves. Split the leeks down to but not completely through the root end, separate the layers, and wash the leeks carefully under running water; they'll be sandy.

2. Bring a large kettle of salted water to a boil and add the leeks. Cook just until the white part is tender. Drain the leeks and reserve.

3. Heat the olive oil in a large skillet. Add the garlic and cook over low heat for 3 minutes. Pat leeks dry on paper towels, trim off the roots, and add leeks to the skillet. Cook over low heat for 5 minutes.

4. Stir in tomatoes, Niçoise olives, basil, parsley, and black pepper to taste and heat together, covered, for 3 to 5 minutes.

5. Transfer leeks to a serving platter, pour contents of skillet over them, and cool to room temperature before serving.

6 portions

310

TARTE SAINT-GERMAIN

The lowly leek is the star in this glamorous tart.

4 tablespoons sweet butter
6 leeks, trimmed, well-washed and thinly sliced
2 eggs
2 egg yolks
1 cup light cream
1 cup heavy cream
salt and freshly ground black pepper, to taste
freshly grated nutmeg (optional)
1 9-inch shell of Pâte Brisée (see page 573), partially baked*
½ cup grated Gruyère cheese

1. Melt the butter in a skillet. Add sliced leeks and cook, covered, over low heat for about 30 minutes, or until leeks are tender and lightly colored. Stir frequently or leeks may scorch. Remove from heat and cool slightly.

2. Whisk eggs, yolks, and light and heavy cream together in a bowl and season to taste with salt and pepper. Add a grating of nutmeg, if you like.

3. Preheat oven to 300°F.

4. Spoon cooled leek mixture into partially baked tart shell. Add cream and egg mixture to fill the tart to within ½ inch of the top. Sprinkle the Gruyère evenly over the tart.

5. Set the tart on the middle level of the preheated oven and bake for 35 to 45 minutes, or until top is well browned and filling is completely set.

6. Cool for 10 minutes. Cut into wedges and serve warm.

4 main-course portions, or 6 appetizer portions

*use a quiche pan approximately 2 inches deep

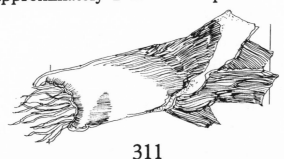

In our never-ending search for dishes to season with garlic, we discovered that a piece of corned beef, simmered until tender and then cooled to room temperature, is delicious with Aïoli Sauce. French Potato Salad and Ratatouille complete this menu for garlic lovers (see Index for recipes).

BAKED GARLIC

This vegetable side dish is not for garlic lovers only; we hope you'll take our word that after an hour in the oven garlic is soft, sweet and mellow. We feel certain that you'll become a convert.

In smaller quantities the roasted cloves make a splendid garnish for plain roasted or grilled meats.

6 whole heads of garlic
4 tablespoons sweet butter
⅓ cup Chicken Stock (see page 587)
coarse salt to taste
freshly ground black pepper, to taste

1. Preheat oven to 350°F.
2. Remove the papery outer skin from the garlic heads, leaving the clusters of cloves intact.
3. Arrange the heads in a baking dish just large enough to hold them comfortably. Add the butter and stock to the pan and set it in the middle level of the oven.
4. Bake for 1 hour, basting every 10 minutes or so, until garlic heads are golden brown and tender. Season to taste with coarse salt and freshly ground black pepper. Serve immediately.
   6 heads, 2 to 6 portions

DUCK WITH FORTY CLOVES OF GARLIC

Garlic lovers as well as those who are not so sure will be surprised at the mellow sweetness a long, slow baking imparts to these 40 garlic cloves. The duck is perfumed with the heady aroma, and the sauce, finished with sherry vinegar and Cassis, is sweetly tart and nutty. The perfect accompaniments are wild rice, chestnut purée and your best Bordeaux.

1 duck, 4½ to 5 pounds, fresh or thoroughly defrosted
salt and freshly ground black pepper, to taste
2 tablespoons vegetable oil
1 cup finely chopped yellow onions
2 carrots, peeled and finely diced
1½ cups Chicken Stock (see page 587) or canned chicken broth
1 teaspoon dried thyme
3 parsley sprigs
1 bay leaf
40 large garlic cloves
2 tablespoons sherry vinegar
1 tablespoon Crème de Cassis (black currant liqueur)
8 tablespoons (1 stick) sweet butter, chilled
chopped parsley (garnish)

1. Remove neck and giblets from the duck; save the liver for another use. Chop neck, heart and gizzard. Cut off wing tips. Remove all possible fat from the duck's cavity and prick the skin all over with a fork. Salt the inside and outside of the duck and set it in a shallow baking pan just large enough to hold it comfortably. Set aside.

2. Heat the vegetable oil in a small saucepan, add chopped giblets and wing tips, and brown over high heat. Season with salt and pepper, reduce heat, and add the onions and carrots. Cover and cook until vegetables are tender and lightly colored, about 20 minutes.

3. Add the chicken stock, thyme, parsley and bay leaf, season with salt and pepper, and bring to a boil. Reduce heat, partially cover, and simmer while the duck roasts.

4. Preheat oven to 450°F.

5. Separate the heads of garlic into cloves, discarding the papery skin from the heads; do not peel the cloves. Select about 6 of the largest cloves and stuff them into the duck. Arrange the rest of the garlic around the duck.

6. Set the pan on the middle level of the oven. After 15 minutes turn the temperature down to 375°F. and roast the bird for another 35 minutes for medium rare; 5 to 10 minutes more for juicy and still slightly pink. We do not recommend cooking duck "well done." Transfer duck to a platter, cover with foil, and keep warm.

7. Strain the broth, discard the solids, and measure the broth. You should have ½ cup. If you have less, don't worry. If you have more, return it to the saucepan and cook briskly for 5 minutes or so to reduce it.

8. Lift the garlic cloves from the cooking fat with a slotted spoon and force them through the medium disc of a food mill. Reserve the puréed garlic and discard the skins.

9. When the broth is properly reduced, add the vinegar and Cassis, bring to a boil, and reduce the mixture by one third. Whisk in the garlic purée and remove the pan from the heat.

10. Cut the chilled butter into 10 pieces and whisk the butter, piece by piece, into the hot sauce, always adding another piece of butter before the previous one is entirely absorbed. The sauce will begin to look creamy and thicken slightly. Cover the saucepan and set it in a warm (not hot) place.

11. Carve the duck into 4 serving pieces and divide them between 2 warmed plates. Add the accompaniments you have chosen. Spoon some of the sauce over the duck, and transfer the rest to a sauceboat. Retrieve the garlic cloves remaining inside the carcass and use them to garnish the sauced duck. Sprinkle with parsley. Serve immediately.

2 portions

GARLIC

Garlic, used since ancient times by the Chinese, Egyptians and Hebrews, is the strongest-flavored member of the onion group. As a seasoning and as a reputed medicine, it has exerted a powerful influence (in more ways than one) over people around the world. Garlic was once used to ward off evil; it is still believed to prevent colds.

Garlic lovers are in luck these days. The hot and spicy flavors of Szechuan cooking, and the intriguing combinations of Italian cuisine, both relying heavily on garlic, are currently in vogue. The formerly frowned-upon garlic could hardly be more fashionable.

Garlic should be firm and crisp; soft, yellowed cloves or those which are showing green sprouts should be discarded. The fresher the garlic, the milder the taste. Therefore, buy only the quantity you will use promptly and store it at room temperature (it mildews in the refrigerator).

Garlic may be mild (like elephant garlic, whose cloves are huge) or strong, like the rose-colored variety. In between are white- or violet-skinned heads. Raw garlic, minced or forced through a press, retains its pungent flavor and odor. Cooked garlic, on the other hand, becomes more subtle the longer it is exposed to heat. Bruised or sliced and added at the last minute to sautéed vegetables or sauces, it is excitingly vibrant. Slivered and pushed into slits in a roast, it pungently permeates the meat.

When long cooked in a sauce or stew, garlic flavor dissipates, contributing to the general savor but losing its individual identity. Whole garlic cloves, roasted in their skins, are a delicious side dish; chestnutlike, sweet and buttery, they are the perfect accompaniment to simply grilled or roasted meats.

If after all this you are curious but still hesitant, we pass along one final tip: chewing a bit of fresh parsley or mint will sweeten the breath and help to eliminate traces of garlic just eaten.

RED SNAPPER WITH BUTTER AND SHALLOT SAUCE

In this elegant dish, the hot fillets of red snapper transform the raw spinach into something tender and wonderful. The sauce, a fragile binding of raspberry vinegar, shallots and butter, is delicately pink and tart. Begin the meal with a pasta dish and serve the main course ungarnished; it is beautiful by itself.

⅓ cup raspberry vinegar
2 tablespoons finely minced shallots
2 red snapper fillets, ¾ pound each
⅓ cup Fish Stock (see page 588)
⅓ cup dry white wine or vermouth
salt and freshly ground black pepper, to taste
½ pound (2 sticks) chilled sweet butter, cut into small pieces
1 tablespoon Crème Fraîche (see page 582)
3 cups finely shredded raw spinach

1. Preheat oven to 400°F.
2. Combine vinegar and shallots in a small heavy saucepan. Bring to a boil, lower heat slightly, and simmer until vinegar is reduced to about 2 tablespoons. Set aside.
3. Arrange snapper fillets in a shallow baking dish just large enough to hold them without overlapping. Pour the fish stock and the wine over the fillets, season with salt and pepper, and set dish on the middle rack of the oven. Bake for 8 to 10 minutes; fish should be just slightly underdone since it will continue to cook due to residual heat. Cover with foil and keep warm.
4. Meanwhile, heat the vinegar and shallot mixture again and, over very low heat, whisk in the chilled butter bit by bit, always adding another piece before the preceding piece is completely absorbed. The sauce will mount and become creamy and glossy. Remove sauce from heat, whisk in the *crème fraîche,* and set the sauce aside, covered.
5. Divide the spinach equally between 2 plates. Using a spatula, transfer a fillet to each plate, centering it on the spinach. Spoon the raspberry butter sauce over the fish and serve immediately.

2 portions

"There is no such thing as a little garlic."
— **Arthur Baer**

SHALLOTS

When we opened The Silver Palate a few years ago, we had to scramble for shallots. Our sole source was a supplier in New Jersey who made only infrequent trips to the city. What a wonder, then, that now we can order them from our produce man as easily as we order celery. In fact, we've spotted them in markets around the country, further evidence of the increasing availability of hard-to-find ingredients.

The delicate but distinctive flavor of shallots falls somewhere between that of garlic and onions, and yet is more sophisticated than either. There are three kinds of shallots: red, greenish-white, and the purple which is considered to be the best. They are used most often raw in salads or cooked in dishes where a subtle but emphatic onion touch is needed — the great sauces of the French *haute cuisine,* for example. They are versatile favorites in our kitchen; we think if you try them you'll like them too.

ONIONS

Teary eyes are a small price to pay for the countless ways that onions enrich our food. The pantry is never without them, and we reach for an onion almost as automatically as we reach for a knife when we begin to cook.

The strength of the onion depends on the variety and its origin; the warmer the climate, the sweeter the onion.

The sweet yellow Spanish, the sharp white, the mild Italian or purple, and the Bermuda onion all play their part in the food we make for our store. At home, out reliance on this flavorful vegetable is hardly less. Since we have learned that chilled onions cause fewer tears than those at room temperature, we hardly ever cry.

PEARLY VEAL AND ONION STEW

This light, herb- and wine-flavored stew gains flavor from onions, and is garnished with them as well. Serve it with parsleyed rice or buttered noodles.

¼ to ½ cup best-quality olive oil
3 pounds boneless veal stew meat, cut into 1-inch cubes
4 tablespoons potato starch or flour
10 large garlic cloves, peeled and chopped
3 cups Chicken Stock (see page 587)
1½ cups white wine
1 tablespoon fresh or 1 teaspoon dried rosemary
1 teaspoon dried oregano
1 teaspoon salt
½ teaspoon pepper
2 pounds white pearl onions
chopped fresh parsley (garnish)

1. Heat ¼ cup olive oil in a deep, heavy, flameproof casserole and brown the veal, a few pieces at a time, adding more oil as necessary. Remove with a slotted spoon and transfer to a bowl. When all the pieces are browned, sprinkle on the potato starch and toss to coat. Reserve.

2. In the same oil cook the garlic over low heat until lightly browned. Preheat oven to 325°F.

3. Return veal to the casserole, and add chicken stock, white wine, rosemary, oregano, and salt and pepper. Bring to a simmer on top of the stove. Cover the casserole and set it in the middle level of the oven. Bake for 1 hour, stirring occasionally.

4. Meanwhile, cut a small X in the root end of each pearl onion, being careful not to cut completely through the root end so onions will not fall apart in the stew. Bring a pan of salted water to a boil, drop in the onions, and cook until tender, about 15 minutes. Drain them and plunge immediately into cold water. When onions are cool enough to handle, peel them.

5. Uncover casserole and taste the stew; correct seasoning if necessary. Stir in the onions, and cook for another 20 minutes, uncovering the stew for the last 10 minutes of the cooking time. Sprinkle with chopped parsley and serve immediately.

8 to 10 portions

"The sliced onions give of their essence after a brew and become the ambrosia for gods and men."
— Jane Bothwell

CHIVES

Chives are the tenderest and mildest member of the onion family and are a joy to look at and to cook with. We love their bright green tubular leaves and lavender thistlelike flowers on our windowsill.

We always use scissors to snip chives (chopping crushes out the juices) and sprinkle them wherever we need a bit of green or a garnish with more flavor than parsley. We couldn't make vichyssoise without chives. We love to scramble them into eggs; they make that simple dish very special.

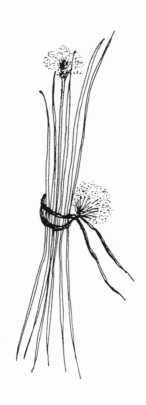

SIX-ONION SOUP

The whole array of onions is present in this rich and creamy soup. Float croutons of toasted French bread on the soup and add a sprinkling of chives.

4 tablespoons sweet butter
2 cups finely chopped yellow onions
4 large leeks, white parts only, well cleaned and thinly sliced
½ cup chopped shallots
4 to 6 garlic cloves, peeled and minced
4 cups Chicken Stock (see page 587)
1 teaspoon dried thyme
1 bay leaf
salt and freshly ground black pepper, to taste
1 cup heavy cream
3 scallions (green onions), trimmed, cleaned, and diagonally cut
  into ½-inch pieces
toasted French bread croutons (garnish, see page 101)
snipped fresh chives (garnish)

1. Melt the butter in a pot. Add the onions, leeks, shallots and garlic and cook, covered, over low heat until vegetables are tender and lightly colored, about 25 minutes.

2. Add the stock, thyme and bay leaf, and season to taste with salt and pepper. Bring to a boil, reduce heat, and cook, partially covered, for 20 minutes.

3. Pour the soup through a strainer set over a bowl, transfer the solids and 1 cup of the liquid to the bowl of a food processor fitted with a steel blade (or use a food mill fitted with the medium disc), and purée.

4. Return the purée and remaining 3 cups of liquid to the pot and set over medium heat. Whisk in the heavy cream and bring to a simmer. Add the scallions and simmer for another 5 minutes, or until they are tender.

5. Ladle into heated bowls and garnish with croutons of toasted French bread and snipped fresh chives.

4 to 6 portions

TOMATOES

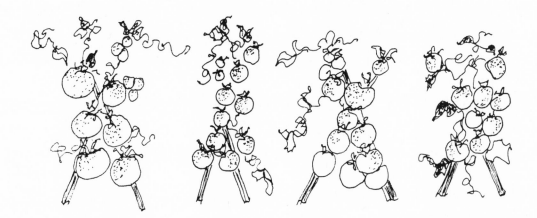

Vine-ripened tomatoes are one of summer's chief joys. Treasure them eaten out of hand with a sprinkling of salt, or thickly sliced and marinated with fresh herbs and olive oil just long enough to heighten the flavors of all three — pure pleasure.

Turn these beauties into Tomato Sauce (see page 590) and freeze in plastic containers; you'll have a taste of summer available all winter long.

During the rest of the year we recommend avoiding the tasteless hothouse tomatoes available in supermarkets. Far better are canned Italian plum tomatoes, which have been picked and preserved at their peak of freshness. Stock them as pantry staples and use them freely.

TOMATO TYPES

ITALIAN PLUM TOMATOES are the essential cooking tomatoes. Canned or fresh, these small chunky tomatoes are full of flavor and low on interior moisture, making them perfect for sauces. At their best, usually sun-ripened and still warm from the garden, they make magnificent eating without adornment.

CHERRY TOMATOES are indispensable at The Silver Palate. As a bright and colorful garnish, a container for delicious fillings or a hot vegetable, they are unsurpassed. Properly ripened and flavorful cherry tomatoes are available year-round, if you look for them; they are one of the busy cook's best friends.

"BEEFSTEAK" TOMATOES are America's favorite, and these big, thick and meaty tomatoes are truly "American style." Cut them into wedges for a simple salad, stuff and bake them, or just slice them onto a burger. The tomato lover must be wary, however, since these tomatoes are often grown in greenhouses or hydroponically, and can look spectacular but taste like wet cardboard. Shop carefully, or grow your own and don't hesitate to let them ripen a day or two more on a sunny windowsill.

YELLOW TOMATOES are sweeter and less acidic than the red, and can be lovely in salads or in sauces. They are not common, and thus not found in many markets, but seeds are available and they are easy to grow.

GREEN TOMATOES are delicious. If you hate to leave them to rot on the vine after frost, pick them before frost strikes and utilize them in a dozen ways — in jams, fried and served with brown sugar and cream, or grilled outdoors during a barbecue.

ELECTION NIGHT CELEBRATION SUPPER

Raw oysters on the half shell with Shallot Sauce

Pasta with Lobster and Tarragon

Roast Filet of Beef

Sautéed Cherry Tomatoes

Raspberries and Crème Fraîche

Black Walnut Cookies

SAUTEED CHERRY TOMATOES

This is one of the best vegetable side dishes we know. The few minutes of heat accentuate the cherry tomatoes' natural sweetness, a sprinkling of herbs integrates them into the rest of the menu, and the shiny red globes are an attractive garnish.

You can sauté a little garlic in the butter before adding the tomatoes, or sprinkle them with fresh or dried basil, tarragon or rosemary. Parmesan cheese is nice too. Remember, your goal is just to enhance the tomato flavor with heat — they should not cook and should never burst or become mushy.

6 tablespoons sweet butter (or half butter, half olive oil)
3 pints cherry tomatoes, stemmed, rinsed, and dried
salt and freshly ground black pepper, to taste

1. Melt the butter in a heavy skillet. Add the tomatoes and raise the heat.
2. Shake and roll the tomatoes around in the butter until they are shiny and heated through, no more than 5 minutes. Do not overcook.
3. Season to taste with salt and freshly ground black pepper. Serve immediately.
   6 portions

COULIS

A *coulis* is simply a reduced purée or sauce, often of vegetables. The best known and most useful is the tomato *coulis*. It must be made with only the freshest vine-ripened tomatoes. It can be seasoned with herbs, spices or garlic as required by the recipe it is to be used with.

The *coulis* can be served hot or cold, as a sauce for such dishes as the Vegetable Pâté or Seafood Terrine.

Spoon a puddle of *coulis* onto a small plate and set the serving of food in the middle of the pool. Garnish as directed in recipe.

TOMATO COULIS

6 pounds vine-ripened tomatoes (about 12 good-size tomatoes)
2 tablespoons sweet butter
2 tablespoons best-quality olive oil
2 cups finely chopped yellow onions
salt and freshly ground black pepper, to taste
1 cup of Italian parsley, chopped

1. Bring a large kettle of salted water to a rolling boil. Drop tomatoes into the boiling water one at a time and leave each for 10 to 15 seconds. Remove with a slotted spoon and drop into a bowl of cold water. Proceed until all the tomatoes have been scalded, then drain them.

2. The tomatoes will now peel easily. Remove peels and stems, cut the tomatoes horizontally into halves, and use the handle-end of a teaspoon to scoop out the seeds and liquid inside the tomatoes. Coarsely chop tomatoes and reserve.

3. Heat the butter and the oil together in a heavy kettle. Add the chopped onions, cover, and cook over low heat until onions are tender and lightly colored, about 25 minutes.

4. Stir in chopped tomatoes and bring to a boil. Season with salt and freshly ground black pepper. Reduce heat and simmer, uncovered, for about 40 minutes, or until *coulis* is somewhat reduced and thickened.

5. Transfer *coulis* to the bowl of a food processor fitted with a steel blade, or use a food mill fitted with the medium disc, and purée.

6. Return *coulis* to the kettle, add the chopped parsley, and simmer for 5 minutes, or longer if you think you would like a thicker purée.
   About 2 quarts

Our favorite variation: Add 3 medium-size garlic cloves, minced, to the kettle along with the onion. Add ¼ cup Basil Purée (see page 51) to the tomato mixture just before puréeing it.

TOMATO DILL SOUP

Our store's most popular soup is based on the rich flavor of the plum tomato. Take our advice and make it only when you have fresh dill; the dried variety just won't do.

8 tablespoons (1 stick) sweet butter
3 cups yellow onions, peeled and sliced
2 garlic cloves, peeled and minced
1 bunch of fresh dill, finely chopped, plus dill sprigs for garnish
salt and freshly ground black pepper, to taste
2 quarts Chicken Stock (see page 587)
3 pounds Italian plum tomatoes, drained and seeded
1 teaspoon ground allspice
pinch of sugar
grated zest of 1 small orange
1 cup dairy sour cream (garnish)

1. Melt butter in a soup pot. Add onions and cook over low heat, covered, until tender, about 20 minutes. Add garlic and cook for another 5 minutes.

2. Add half of the dill, season to taste with salt and pepper, and cook uncovered for another 15 minutes.

3. Add chicken stock, tomatoes, allspice and pinch of sugar. Bring to a boil, reduce heat, cover, and simmer for 45 minutes. Add orange zest, remove from heat, and cool slightly.

4. Transfer soup in batches to the bowl of a food processor fitted with a steel blade, or use a food mill fitted with the medium disc. Purée the soup.

5. Return soup to the pot, add remaining dill, and simmer for 5 minutes. Serve immediately; or cool and refrigerate, covered, overnight.

6. Taste and correct seasoning. Garnish soup, hot or cold, with a dollop of sour cream and a sprig of dill.

8 to 10 portions

The search for the perfect vegetable drives some of us to walk the city, investigating every produce stand we can find (in New York there is at least one per block), and cajoling, berating and attempting to bribe a variety of vendors, large and small. Often the search is spectacularly rewarding, even if it does mean we have a different source for every vegetable on our list.

For others the search can become such a passion that nothing will do but growing their own. Organically raised vegetables, picked at the peak of perfection in your own backyard, are foods you can trust.

Not all home gardening is done in backyards, however. We know those who use terraces, window boxes, rooftops and fire escapes. All you need are seeds, sunlight, water, soil with good drainage, and the passionate interest in vegetables to see you through. Watching and watering as your prizes grow will be an astonishingly relaxing and rewarding experience.

STUFFED TOMATOES

A hollowed-out ripe tomato makes a naturally delicious cup for a salad or other cold food, and has the additional virtue of being easy to handle. On the buffet table, tomatoes offer perfect portion control, and they look terrific as well.

The technique is simple. Select large symmetrical tomatoes, the riper the better. Cut off the tops with a serrated knife and reserve tops. Use the handle-end of a teaspoon to scrape out all the seeds, juice and partitions, leaving a shell (be careful not to pierce the sides). Salt the cavities and set the tomatoes upside down on a paper towel for 30 minutes.

Blot tomato cavities with a paper towel and fill them with your selected stuffing, mounding it slightly. Set the reserved caps back on top at a jaunty angle; refrigerate until serving time.

Depending on the size of the tomatoes, each will hold ½ to ¾ cup stuffing. You can use your imagination endlessly here, but some of our favorite stuffings include Tarragon Chicken Salad, Shrimp and Grape Salad, either of the arugula salads, or Rice and Vegetable Salad (see Index for recipes).

SPINACH-AND RICOTTA-STUFFED TOMATOES

8 ripe red tomatoes, the best you can find
salt for draining tomatoes
3 tablespoons best-quality olive oil
1 cup finely chopped yellow onions
10 ounces frozen spinach, defrosted, drained, and squeezed dry
salt and freshly ground black pepper, to taste
nutmeg, to taste
1 cup ricotta cheese
2 egg yolks
½ cup toasted pine nuts (see page 279)
¼ cup grated imported Parmesan cheese, plus additional
  cheese to top tomatoes
½ cup chopped Italian parsley

1. Wash and dry the tomatoes and cut off their tops. With the handle end of a small spoon, scrape out seeds and partitions, being careful not to pierce the sides of tomatoes. Salt the cavities and set tomatoes upside down on a paper towel to drain for 30 minutes.

2. Heat the olive oil in a skillet, add the onions and cook, covered, over low heat until tender and lightly colored, about 25 minutes.

3. Chop the spinach and add it to the skillet. Combine onions and spinach thoroughly, season to taste with salt, pepper and nutmeg, and cover. Cook over low heat, stirring occasionally, for 10 minutes. Do not let the mixture scorch.

4. Beat ricotta and egg yolks together thoroughly in a mixing bowl. Add spinach mixture, pine nuts, ¼ cup of the Parmesan and the parsley, and season to taste with salt and pepper.

5. Gently blot tomato cavities dry with a paper towel and spoon an equal share of the spinach mixture into each one. Top each tomato with a sprinkle of additional Parmesan.

6. Arrange tomatoes in a shallow baking dish and set in the upper third of a preheated 350°F. oven. Bake until tops are well browned and filling is hot and bubbly, about 20 minutes. Serve immediately.

8 portions

"What is paradise? but a garden, an orchard of trees and herbs full of pleasure and nothing there but delights."
— William Lawson, 1687

STUFFED CHERRY TOMATOES

Stuffed cherry tomatoes are a bit more work than large ones, but they have the same virtues: They add color to an hors d'oeuvre platter, are easy to handle, and are perfect portion controls. Prepare them in the same way as the shells for Cold Stuffed Tomatoes, although you will have to be even more careful not to tear the sides. Discard the caps in this case. Salt and drain the tomatoes for 30 minutes, and stuff with the filling of your choice.

Each tomato will hold about 1 tablespoon of filling. Try Salmon Mousse, Tapenade Dip, Pesto Mayonnaise, or Taramosalata (see Index for recipes); or mash a bit of soft fresh chèvre cheese such as Montrachet. Garnish each tomato with a sprig of fresh dill or parsley or a basil leaf. Chill until serving time.

LAYERED MOZZARELLA AND TOMATO SALAD

Could any salad be simpler? or better?

4 large ripe tomatoes, cut into ¼-inch slices
2 pounds fresh mozzarella cheese, cut into ¼-inch slices
¼ cup chopped fresh basil
¼ cup chopped Italian parsley
½ cup Niçoise olives
½ cup Our Favorite Vinaigrette (see page 247)
freshly ground black pepper, to taste

1. On a large serving platter, alternate overlapping slices of tomato and mozzarella cheese.
2. Sprinkle basil, parsley and black olives over all.
3. Drizzle vinaigrette over salad and grind black pepper on generously. Serve at room temperature.
6 portions

VEGETABLE PUREES

The chefs of the *nouvelle cuisine,* in their search for techniques that rearrange our awareness of the familiar, have revived the homey purée. When a vegetable is presented to us with its texture and sometimes its colors altered, we are forced to concentrate on its flavor. At the same time purées are rich, comforting and undemanding. Combinations can be exhilarating, and when two or three purées are presented on the same plate, complementing each other as well as the entrée, the effect is dazzling.

CHESTNUT AND POTATO PUREE

A rich and perfect accompaniment to roast beef, pork or game.

1¾ cups potatoes, peeled and roughly diced
1½ pounds canned unsweetened chestnut purée*
12 tablespoons (1½ sticks) sweet butter, at room temperature
⅓ cup Crème Fraîche (see page 582)
1 egg
1 egg yolk
4 tablespoons Calvados
1 teaspoon ground cardamom
1½ teaspoons salt
pinch of cayenne pepper

1. Cover potatoes with 2 quarts salted water and cook until tender. Drain well.

2. In a food processor fitted with a steel blade process chestnut purée until smooth. Transfer to a mixing bowl.

3. Mash the drained potatoes until smooth with 8 tablespoons (1 stick) of the butter. Transfer to the bowl with the chestnut purée.

4. Whisk in *crème fraîche*, the whole egg and extra yolk, the Calvados, cardamom, 1½ teaspoons salt and the cayenne pepper.

5. Smear a 1½-quart soufflé dish with some of remaining 4 tablespoons of butter and spoon purée into it. Dot top with remaining butter. Bake in a preheated 350°F. oven for 25 minutes before serving.

6. The dish can be made ahead and refrigerated, then baked just before serving.

6 portions

[*]available at specialty food shops

CHESTNUTS

If you've never roasted chestnuts, take a lesson from the street vendors of Paris and New York, who know that crowds will gather whenever the vendors begin to sell their wares. Roasted over an open fire, chestnuts are absolutely delicious. In the kitchen, you'll be pleased with the way their sweet, nutty flavor enhances a menu.

Preheat oven to 400°F. Cut 2 slashes in the flat side of each chestnut. Arrange nuts in a single layer on a baking sheet and bake for 4 or 5 minutes, turning once. Peel with the help of a small sharp knife, and eat. Traditionally, eat chestnuts while still very hot; you should burn your fingers just a bit if the chestnuts are to taste their best.

Don't wait for Christmas to have chestnuts. They're excellent with poultry or game all fall and winter.

BEET AND APPLE PUREE

Serve this delicious, brightly colored purée hot with pork, duck, goose or ham, or cold with hot grilled sausages.

5 medium-size beets (about 2 pounds)
2 tablespoons salt
8 tablespoons (1 stick) sweet butter
1 cup finely chopped yellow onions
4 tart apples (about 1½ pounds)
1 tablespoon granulated sugar
½ teaspoon salt
¼ cup raspberry vinegar*
chopped fresh dill (optional)

1. Trim away all but 1 inch of green tops from the beets, leaving skins and roots; scrub well. Cover beets with cold water in a large pot, add 2 tablespoons salt, and bring to a boil. Reduce heat and simmer, partially covered, until beets are tender, about 40 minutes to an hour. Add additional water if necessary to ensure that the beets remain covered. Drain the beets as they are done, cool slightly, and slip off tips, skins, and roots.

2. Melt the butter in a medium-size saucepan. Add the onions and cook, covered, over medium heat until tender and lightly colored, about 25 minutes.

3. Peel, core, and chop the apples and add them to the onions. Add sugar, salt and raspberry vinegar, and simmer, uncovered, for 15 to 20 minutes, or until apples and onions are very tender.

4. Transfer apple mixture to the bowl of a food processor fitted with a steel blade, or use a food mill. Chop the beets and add them to the bowl. Process until smooth.

5. Return purée to the saucepan and reheat, stirring constantly. Taste and correct seasoning. Serve immediately, or set aside to cool to room temperature, cover, chill, and serve very cold.

6 portions

PUREED BROCCOLI WITH CREME FRAICHE

A green and hearty purée, good with nearly every entrée in the book.

2 bunches of broccoli, about 5 pounds, trimmed and chopped,
  including peeled stems
1 cup Crème Fraîche (see page 582)
4 tablespoons dairy sour cream
⅔ cup freshly grated imported Parmesan cheese
½ teaspoon freshly grated nutmeg
½ teaspoon freshly ground black pepper
salt, to taste
2 tablespoons sweet butter

1. Chop broccoli, leaving 8 small flowerets whole, and drop chopped broccoli and whole flowerets into 4 quarts of boiling salted water. Cook until just tender, about 8 minutes.

2. Transfer broccoli, reserving 8 flowerets, to a food processor. Add *crème fraîche* and purée thoroughly. Preheat oven to 350°F.

3. Scrape purée into a bowl and stir in sour cream, Parmesan, nutmeg, pepper, and salt to taste. Mix well.

4. Mound in an ovenproof serving dish, dot with butter and bake in preheated oven for 25 minutes, or until purée is steaming hot.

5. Garnish with reserved flowerets and serve immediately.

6 portions

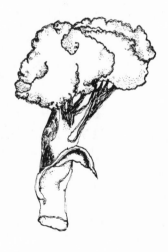

NEW YEARS'S EVE MENU

Sweet Black Cherry Soup

Oysters and Spinach

Fresh fois gras and toasts

Lamb with Peppercorn Crust

Chestnut Purée, Puréed Broccoli with Crème Fraîche, Leek and Potato Purée

---

Watercress, endive and mandarin orange salad with Champagne Vinaigrette

---

Lemon Ice

Decadent Chocolate Cake

❖ FROM THE SILVER
PALATE NOTEBOOK

Analyze traffic patterns based on previous parties or on other parties you've recently attended. A truism: if guests can find the kitchen, they'll gather there. Walk through the evening in your mind, looking for snags, loop-holes, omissions.

Always make sure you have provided room for guests to leave coats, and to be able to find them easily, too.

LEEK AND POTATO PUREE

Two of our favorite earthy vegetables combine in a rich and soothing purée.

6 large leeks
2 pounds red-skinned potatoes
12 tablespoons (1½ sticks) sweet butter
2 garlic cloves, minced
½ cup heavy cream
salt and freshly ground black pepper, to taste

1. Trim roots and most, but not all, of the green leaves from leeks, leaving each leek about 7 inches long. Split down to but not through the base and wash thoroughly.

2. Bring 3 quarts salted water to a boil in a pot, add leeks, and cook until tender, about 15 minutes. Drain and chop.

3. Meanwhile, peel the potatoes. Cover them with cold water in another pot. Add salt and bring to a boil. Reduce heat and cook until potatoes are very tender, 20 to 40 minutes, depending on the size. Drain and reserve.

4. Melt 3 tablespoons of the butter in a skillet. Add the garlic and cook over low heat until lightly colored, about 15 minutes. Add leeks and an additional 3 tablespoons butter and continue to cook, stirring occasionally, for 15 minutes.

5. Transfer leeks-and-butter mixture to the bowl of a food processor fitted with a steel blade, and purée until smooth.

6. Mash the potatoes, adding heavy cream as needed. Stir in the leek purée and remaining 6 tablespoons butter; season with salt and pepper. Reheat gently until steaming. Serve immediately.

6 portions

SWEET POTATO AND CARROT PUREE

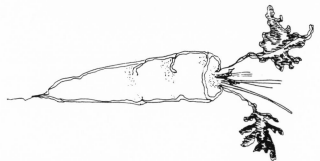

4 large sweet potatoes (about 2 pounds), of a moist variety
1 pound carrots
2½ cups water
1 tablespoon granulated sugar
12 tablespoons (1½ sticks) sweet butter, softened
salt and freshly ground black pepper, to taste
½ cup Crème Fraîche (see page 582)
½ teaspoon freshly grated nutmeg
dash of cayenne pepper (optional)

1. Scrub potatoes and cut a small, deep slit in the top of each. Set on the center rack of a preheated 375°F. oven and bake for about 1 hour, or until potatoes are tender when pierced with a fork.

2. Meanwhile, peel and trim the carrots and cut them into 1-inch lengths. Put them in a saucepan and add the water, sugar, 2 tablespoons of the butter, and salt and pepper to taste. Set over medium heat, bring to a boil, and cook uncovered until water has evaporated and carrots begin to sizzle in the butter, about 30 minutes. The carrots should be tender. If not, add a little additional water and cook until carrots are done and all liquid has evaporated.

3. Scrape out the flesh of sweet potatoes and combine with carrots in the bowl of a food processor fitted with a steel blade. Add remaining butter and *crème fraîche* and process until very smooth.

4. Add nutmeg, and season to taste with salt and pepper. Add cayenne, if desired, and process briefly to blend.

5. To reheat, transfer to an ovenproof serving dish and cover with foil. Heat in a preheated 350°F. oven for about 25 minutes, or until steaming hot.

6 portions

SALADS

SIGNIFICANT SALADS

Salads have new importance, yet the key to their success still rests in their simplicity. The salad bowl is no place to mix metaphors or too many good ideas. Stick to a single theme; the best salads are conceived so that the partnerships work together wonderfully while still preserving the integrity of the individual ingredients. This can even encompass the use of two dressings, the first to coat the greens, the second to enhance the keynote flavor.

In no other course is there so wide a range of individuality, and there is no single step in the preparation of a salad which is unimportant.

AVOCADO AND HAM SALAD

A colorful, zesty combination.

1 cup lemon juice
¼ cup water
4 ripe avocados, halved and peeled
2 heads of red-leaf lettuce or Boston lettuce, leaves separated, washed and patted dry
3 pounds baked ham, cut into ¼-inch slices and then into 2-inch strips (make them a bit rough looking)
8 medium-size tomatoes, cut into quarters
1 purple onion, peeled and cut into thin rings
1 cup Lemon Vinaigrette (recipe follows)
salt and freshly ground black pepper, to taste
¼ cup chopped parsley
1 bunch of watercress, washed and dried (garnish)

1. Mix lemon juice and water together in a small bowl. Slice peeled avocado and dip into lemon-juice mixture. Drain.

2. Line a large serving platter with lettuce leaves. Arrange avocados, ham, tomatoes and onion rings in a decorative spiral fashion on lettuce leaves.

3. Drizzle salad with Lemon Vinaigrette. Season with salt and pepper and sprinkle with chopped parsley.

4. Garnish with watercress and serve immediately.

8 portions

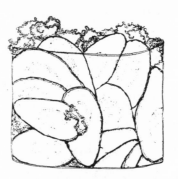

LEMON VINAIGRETTE

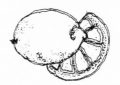

1 cup best-quality olive oil
⅔ cup lemon juice
½ cup snipped fresh chives
2 tablespoons finely minced shallots
2 tablespoons prepared Dijon-style mustard
salt and freshly ground black pepper, to taste

Combine all ingredients, with seasoning to taste, in a covered container and shake well until blended. Serve immediately.

About 1¾ cups

"If you are lazy and dump everything together, they won't come out as well as if you add one thing at a time. It's like everything else; no shortcuts without compromising quality."
— **Lionel Poilâne**

CHEF'S SALAD

This can be a spectacular salad if you discard the idea of making it with odds and ends. Use only the freshest of vegetables and take the time to julienne them beautifully. It's all in the hands of the chef.

1 large head of red-leaf lettuce, leaves separated, washed and dried
2 medium-size heads of romaine lettuce, leaves separated, washed
 and dried
1 bunch of watercress, stems removed, washed and dried
1 large cucumber, peeled, halved lengthwise, seeded and sliced
 into crescents
6 tomatoes, each cut into 6 wedges
½ green pepper, stemmed, cored, cut into julienne
½ sweet red pepper, stemmed, cored, cut into julienne
12 ounces bottled marinated artichoke hearts, drained and halved
½ pound Gruyère cheese, cut into julienne
¼ pound thinly sliced prosciutto, cut into julienne
¼ pound thinly sliced hard salami, cut into julienne
½ pound thinly sliced boiled or baked ham, cut into julienne
3 whole cooked chicken breasts, boned and shredded
 (3 to 4 cups)
½ cup Niçoise or other imported black olives (garnish)
3 hard-cooked eggs, shelled and cut into quarters (garnish)
2 cups Our Favorite Vinaigrette (see page 247)

1. Line a large salad bowl with whole red-leaf lettuce leaves.
2. Tear romaine lettuce into medium-size pieces and layer in the lettuce-lined bowl with the watercress, half of the cucumber slices, tomato wedges, pepper julienne, artichokes and cheese, and two thirds of the meat and chicken.
3. Arrange remaining vegetables and meats in a decorative spoke fashion around the top of the salad.
4. Garnish with Niçoise olives and hard-cooked eggs. Cover the salad and refrigerate for 1 hour.
5. To serve, pour vinaigrette over salad and toss.
6 to 8 portions

PERFECT JULIENNE

Preparing a julienne of vegetables can be an exacting exercise. In great chefs' kitchens, "prep" help is expected to spend as much time as necessary at this task so that the chef will have perfect matchstick strips of carrots, leeks, mushrooms, beets, cucumbers, and anything else his heart desires, at his fingertips. While working with some chefs in France we observed a young boy being hit on the hand because the shreds of leek were not of uniform length. The chef was concerned that his clients would return their meals and his reputation would be ruined. For you it needn't be that difficult. These little strips of color serve as a beautiful garnish for many dishes, or combined they make a wonderful vegetable presentation.

MARINATED BEEF SALAD

This salad originated as a way to utilize leftover London Broil, but soon evolved into a salad so special that we found ourselves making extra London Broil so that we could have Marinated Beef Salad. It is a cool solution to the problem of finding salads to please your carnivores. The following recipe is only a suggestion; feel free to improvise with any ingredients you have on hand.

In testing this recipe we marinated a boneless 2-pound sirloin about 2 inches thick in ¼ cup olive oil, ½ cup red wine vinegar and ¼ cup soy sauce for 3 hours before draining it, patting it dry, and panfrying it over the highest possible heat for about 10 minutes on a side.

3 large boiling potatoes
3 to 4 cups cooked beefsteak (preferably medium rare), cut into
  thick julienne
⅔ cup diced sweet pepper, half green and half red
⅓ cup chopped purple onion
1 scallion (green onion), thinly sliced
⅔ cup Garlic Dressing (see page 373)
⅓ cup chopped Italian parsley
lettuce leaves, washed and patted dry
grated rind of 1 orange (garnish)

1. Peel the potatoes. Using a melon-baller, scoop the potatoes into small balls; you should have about 2 cups.
2. Transfer potatoes to a pan of salted cold water and bring to a boil. Reduce heat and cook until balls are tender but not mushy. Drain.
3. Combine potatoes, beef, green and red peppers, onion and scallion in a mixing bowl.
4. Pour on the garlic dressing and toss thoroughly. Add parsley and toss again.
5. Arrange salad on lettuce leaves and garnish with orange rind. Serve immediately. Or refrigerate, covered. Let salad return to room temperature before serving.
   4 portions

MEDITERRANEAN CHICKEN SALAD

Not for dieters only, this tart and tasty Riviera-inspired combination is the most popular lunch with the getting-ready-to-fit-into-the-summer-wardrobe crowd. Since its creation, it has become a real Silver Palate favorite.

1 medium-size yellow onion, peeled and quartered
2 carrots, peeled and chopped
1 leek, white part only, cleaned and sliced
1 teaspoon dried thyme
1 bay leaf
6 parsley sprigs
12 black peppercorns
4 cloves
salt, to taste
3 whole chicken breasts, about 3 pounds
⅓ cup best-quality olive oil
1½ teaspoons dried oregano
juice of 1 lemon
¾ cup imported black olives, Niçoise preferred
2 tablespoons capers, drained
8 cherry tomatoes, halved, or 2 medium-size tomatoes, cut into wedges
¼ pound green beans, cooked
salt and freshly ground black pepper, to taste

1. Measure 4 quarts of water into a large kettle. Add the onion, carrots, leek, thyme, bay leaf, parsley, peppercorns, cloves and salt to taste. Bring to a boil, reduce heat, and simmer uncovered for 15 minutes.

2. Add the chicken breasts, return to the boil, reduce heat, and simmer partially covered until the chicken is done, about 20 minutes. Remove kettle from heat and let chicken cool in the broth.

3. Remove chicken (saving broth for soup), discard skin, and pull the meat from the bones. Tear meat into large pieces and combine in a bowl with the olive oil and oregano. Cover and let stand at room temperature for 1 hour.

4. Add remaining ingredients, toss, and season to taste with salt and pepper. Correct seasoning and serve immediately.

4 to 6 portions

Note: The salad will keep for several days refrigerated. Reserve the green beans and add them just before serving to prevent discoloration.

✢ FROM THE SILVER PALATE NOTEBOOK

Flowers have been considered food by many cultures for centuries. In this age of doing what comes naturally, we think flowers make a most appropriate and beautiful garnish. Use your own good sense: some flowers may tend to be too scented and overpowering. We love them when used with a delicate touch: garnishing plates, floating in a glass of Champagne or scattered in salads.

Some of our favorite flowers include rose petals in salads, tea roses in white wine, and garnishing sprays of pinks, forget-me-nots, wildflowers, chive blossoms, wild thyme and dill flowers, Johnny-jump-ups, yellow bok choy, purple nasturtiums and borage.

Nasturtiums have a pleasant peppery flavor. They bloom in shades of creamy white to deep crimson, and are great in salads or chopped on a sandwich. Pickled nasturtium seed pods can be prepared for eating by marinating them in equal amounts of vinegar and sugar, along with your favorite herbs. These are very special when sprinkled in salads and sauces, used as you would capers.

TARRAGON CHICKEN SALAD

After making this salad fresh every day for four years and never tiring of the taste, we think it's safe to say that this one really wears well. It is dressy enough to serve as a main course; delicious enough to have in a sandwich; and so simple to assemble that you will make it often. For a different taste, substitute black walnuts.

boneless whole chicken breasts, about 3 pounds
1 cup Crème Fraîche (see page 582) or heavy cream
½ cup dairy sour cream
½ cup Hellmann's mayonnaise
2 celery ribs, cut into 1-inch-long pencil strips
½ cup shelled walnuts
1 tablespoon crumbled dried tarragon
salt and freshly ground black pepper, to taste

1. Arrange chicken breasts in a single layer in a large jelly-roll pan. Spread evenly with *crème fraîche* and bake in a preheated 350°F. oven for 20 to 25 minutes, or until done to your taste. Remove from oven and cool.

2. Shred meat into bite-size pieces and transfer to a bowl.

3. Whisk sour cream and mayonnaise together in a small bowl and pour over chicken mixture.

4. Add celery, walnuts, tarragon, salt and pepper to taste, and toss well.

5. Refrigerate, covered, for at least 4 hours. Taste and correct seasoning before serving.

4 to 6 portions

Note: Use accumulated juices from jelly-roll pan to enrich soups or sauces.

MARINATED ITALIAN VEGETABLE SALAD

3 or 4 garlic cloves, peeled and chopped
2 small dried hot red chilies
1 bay leaf
1½ cups peeled carrots, sliced into coins
¾ cup imported white wine vinegar
4 cups cauliflowerets
¾ cup celery cut into ½-inch pieces
2 tablespoons capers, well drained
1 cup assorted imported olives (Sicilian, Alfonso, Kalamata)
1 cup best-quality olive oil

1. Place garlic, chilies and bay leaf in a large bowl.
2. Bring about 3 quarts of salted water to a boil in a pot, drop in carrot coins, and cook until tender but still crisp. Lift carrots from water with a slotted spoon, drain briefly, and drop into the bowl with the garlic mixture. (Keep the water boiling.) Pour the vinegar over the hot carrots and stir.
3. Repeat blanching procedure with cauliflower and then the celery, stirring each vegetable into the vinegar, garlic and herb mixture while hot.
4. Add capers, olives and olive oil and let cool to room temperature before covering. Refrigerate for at least 24 hours. Before serving as part of an antipasto, let return to room temperature and adjust seasoning if necessary.

6 to 10 portions

DUCK AND PEAR SALAD WITH MANGO CHUTNEY DRESSING

Use wild rice if you can — it makes a spectacular salad — or mix wild and brown rice. In any case, this is a perfect salad for an important luncheon or a cool main course on a hot summer night.

2 ducklings, each 4½ to 5 pounds, cooked and cooled (see Step 1)
3 cups cooked rice, cooled
1 cup chopped celery
4 scallions (green onions), cleaned and cut diagonally into ½-inch pieces
grated zest of 1 orange
salt and freshly ground black pepper, to taste
3 ripe but firm eating pears
1 cup lemon juice
Mango Chutney Dressing (recipe follows)

1. We prefer medium-rare duck, roasted at 450°F. for 15 minutes and at 375°F. for another 20 to 30 minutes. If you prefer duck well done, cook longer, until tender, to your taste. Cool. Skin the ducks, remove all flesh from bones, and cut meat into 1-inch cubes.

2. Toss duck meat and cooked rice together in a mixing bowl. Add celery, scallions and orange zest, and season with salt and pepper to taste. Toss again and arrange the salad on a large serving platter.

3. If the skin of the pears seems too thick or spotty, peel them. Otherwise quarter, core, and slice them thinly, and drop the slices into a bowl containing the bottled lemon juice. Toss the slices to coat them thoroughly and let them remain in the juice until you have finished slicing all 3 pears.

4. Arrange pear slices in a decorative fan across the top of the duck salad and serve immediately. Serve Mango Chutney Dressing and offer the peppermill to your guests.

4 to 6 portions

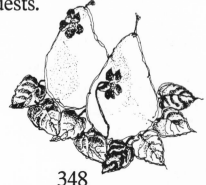

```
┌─────────────────────────────────────┐
│                                       │
│         VERNAL EQUINOX                │
│            SUPPER                     │
│                                       │
│      Chilled Shrimp and               │
│        Cucumber Soup                  │
│                                       │
│     Duck and Pear Salad with          │
│      Mango Chutney Dressing           │
│           ─────────                   │
│                                       │
│      French peasant bread             │
│      Brie Wrapped in Phyllo           │
│           ─────────                   │
│                                       │
│          Lime Mousse                  │
│                                       │
└─────────────────────────────────────┘
```

MIDDLE OF THE NIGHT SANDWICHES

Raiding the refrigerator is to some a habit, to others an event. Shared or taken alone, the midnight snack quells the demons of hunger and allows us to relax, the better to sleep. With planning you can insure that there's a little something that, coupled with inspiration, will get you through the night. Even the Silver Palate doesn't deliver at 3 A.M. (Recipes for italicized ingredients can be found in Index.)

♥ Mix *Chili* with dairy sour cream and chopped onion.

♥ Fill pita bread with *Tarragon Chicken Salad* sprinkled with dried currants and sprouts.

♥ Put shrimp, cooked peas, and sliced scallions tossed with Chutney Mayonnaise on sliced Brioche. Add red-leaf lettuce for color and crunch.

♥ Cut off the top and hollow a French roll. Spread with *Hummus bi Tahini*, add sliced chicken white meat, diced tomato, and pitted black olives. Sprinkle with lemon juice and toasted sesame seeds, and garnish with shredded raw spinach.

♥ Toss cooked bulgur (processed cracked wheat)

349

with olive oil, sliced scallions, grated orange zest and dried currants. Stuff into pita bread and dress with a watercress mayonnaise.

♥ Alternate the thinnest slices of rare roast lamb and charcoal-roasted slices of eggplant on black bread. Dress with lemony *Mint and Yogurt Mayonnaise.*

♥ Try Romaine lettuce on *Raisin Pumpernickel Bread* with avocado slices, tomato, watercress, sliced scallions, a vinaigrette dressing, and cottage cheese.

MANGO CHUTNEY DRESSING

1 whole egg
2 egg yolks
1 tablespoon prepared Dijon-style mustard
¼ cup blueberry vinegar
⅓ cup mango chutney
1 tablespoon soy sauce
salt and freshly ground black pepper, to taste
1 cup peanut oil
1 cup corn oil

1. Combine whole egg, egg yolks, mustard, vinegar, chutney and soy sauce in the bowl of a food processor fitted with a steel blade. Season to taste with salt and pepper and process for 1 minute.

2. With the motor running, dribble in the oil in a slow steady stream. When all oil has been incorporated, shut off motor, scrape down sides of processor bowl, taste, and correct seasoning.

3. Transfer dressing to storage container, cover, and refrigerate until ready to use.

3 cups

SMOKED TURKEY SALAD

This meat-cheese-and-fruit salad, with its nutty, sherry-flavored dressing, is a complete meal. Arrange individual servings on lettuce-lined plates, accompanied by black or whole-wheat bread and a glass of white wine or beer.

1½ pounds smoked turkey (or cooked, lightly smoked ham or
    chicken), skinned and cut into 2-inch julienne
¾ pound Jarlsberg cheese, cut into similar julienne
2 cups seedless green or red grapes, washed and patted dry
1 cup chopped celery
1½ cups Sherry Mayonnaise (recipe follows)
salt and freshly ground black pepper, to taste
1 to 2 tablespoons water-packed green peppercorns, drained

1. Combine the turkey, Jarlsberg cheese, grapes and celery in a mixing bowl.
2. Add the Sherry Mayonnaise and toss gently but well. Season to taste with salt and pepper and toss again. Cover and refrigerate until serving time.
3. Arrange the salad in serving portions and sprinkle with the green peppercorns to taste.
6 portions

"It's *hot!*
I can't get cool,
I've drunk a quart of lemonade.
I think I'll take my shoes off
And sit around in the shade."
— Shel Silverstein
A Light in the Attic

SHERRY MAYONNAISE

This richly flavored mayonnaise complements combinations like the Smoked Turkey Salad, but it is also delicious on such simple fare as a chicken sandwich on white bread. We have also served it as a dip for *crudités* or cold seafood with great success.

1 whole egg
2 egg yolks
1 tablespoon prepared Dijon-style mustard
¼ cup sherry vinegar
salt and freshly ground black pepper, to taste
2 cups corn oil

1. Combine whole egg, egg yolks, mustard and vinegar in the bowl of a food processor fitted with a steel blade, and season to taste with salt and pepper. Process for 1 minute.
2. With the motor still running, dribble in the oil in a slow steady stream.
3. When oil is completely incorporated, shut off machine, scrape down sides of bowl, taste mayonnaise and correct seasoning. Transfer to storage container, cover, and refrigerate until ready to use.

2½ cups

GREEK LAMB AND EGGPLANT SALAD

Another main-course salad, offering wonderful flavors of Greece. Of course you can make this with leftover lamb, but it's so good we often roast half a leg of lamb just for this salad.

5 cups 1-inch cubes of peeled eggplant, about 1 large eggplant
salt for draining eggplant
¼ cup olive oil
¾ pound fresh spinach, washed, dried, with stems removed
4 cups cooked lamb, cut into thick julienne
1 cup imported black olives (Kalamata or Alfonso)
2 to 3 tablespoons toasted pine nuts (see page 279)
Lemon-Garlic Mayonnaise (recipe follows)

1. Layer the eggplant in a colander, salting it generously as you go, and set the colander in the sink or over a plate. Let stand for at least 30 minutes.

2. Rinse eggplant, pat cubes dry with paper towels and arrange in a single layer in a baking dish. Drizzle eggplant with the olive oil and bake at 400°F., turning occasionally, for 20 to 30 minutes, or until tender but not mushy. Remove from oven and cool to room temperature. Taste; add salt if needed.

3. Arrange the spinach leaves around the edge of a serving platter.

4. Combine eggplant and lamb and mound in the center of the platter.

5. Distribute olives over lamb and eggplant and sprinkle pine nuts over all.

6. Serve at room temperature with Lemon-Garlic Mayonnaise and offer the peppermill to your guests.

4 portions

REAL LEMONADE

Mix the juice of 12 lemons with ½ cup sugar in a pitcher, stirring until the sugar dissolves. Add the lemon rinds — cut into strips — and fill the pitcher with ice. Let the ice melt for about 30 minutes. Presto! Serve the lemonade with crushed ice and garnish with a lemon slice and a sprig of fresh mint.

LEMON-GARLIC MAYONNAISE

1 whole egg
2 egg yolks
½ cup fresh lemon juice
salt and freshly ground black pepper, to taste
6 to 8 large garlic cloves, peeled and chopped
2¼ cups best-quality olive oil

1. Combine the whole egg, egg yolks and ¼ cup of the lemon juice in the bowl of a food processor fitted with a steel blade. Season to taste with salt and pepper and process for 1 minute.

2. Drop the garlic through the feed tube and then begin to pour in the olive oil in a slow steady stream. When all of the oil has been incorporated, shut off motor, scrape down sides of processor bowl, taste, and correct seasoning. You may want to add additional lemon juice.

3. Transfer mayonnaise to a storage container, cover, and refrigerate until ready to use.

About 3 cups

WHITE BEAN AND HAM SALAD

Serve this *charcuterie* salad with tart *cornichons* and whole-wheat or black bread. A wonderful autumn or winter lunch, perfect on a picnic. A good dark beer would be especially appropriate here.

1 pound Great Northern or other dried white beans
salt, to taste
1 to 2 cups Garlic-Mustard Dressing (see page 391)
1 medium-size purple onion, peeled and sliced paper-thin
1 cup chopped Italian parsley
1 pound cooked ham, trimmed and cut into 1-inch cubes
salt and freshly ground black pepper, to taste
1 cup best-quality imported black olives (Kalamata or Alfonso)
   (garnish)

1. Rinse and sort through the beans, discarding any pebbles, and soak them overnight in water that covers them by at least 3 inches.

2. Drain beans and transfer them to a kettle. Add cold water to cover the beans by at least 1 inch. Set over moderate heat. Bring to a boil, skimming any scum that may form, and cook beans until tender, about 40 minutes, salting to taste after 30 minutes. Cooking times will vary. It is important not to overcook the beans.

3. Drain beans, transfer them immediately to a mixing bowl, and pour 1 cup of garlic-mustard dressing over the still-hot beans.

4. Add the onion, parsley and ham, season to taste with salt and pepper, and toss again. Cover and refrigerate.

5. To serve, allow salad to return to room temperature. Toss again, correct seasoning (add more dressing if you like), and garnish with the black olives.

6 to 8 portions

ARUGULA AND SWEET RED PEPPER SALAD

This colorful salad is perfectly complemented by a dark and sweetly spicy Balsamic Vinaigrette. Quantities suggested are approximate; adjust proportions to your own taste. You can even eliminate the lettuce altogether and increase the amount of arugula, especially if you like this green as much as we do!

2 large heads of leafy green lettuce (romaine, etc.)
2 bunches of arugula
1 pound fresh mushrooms
3 large sweet red peppers
Balsamic Vinaigrette (recipe follows)

1. Discard outer leaves of lettuce; separate and rinse (if necessary) the inner leaves and dry thoroughly. Wrap and refrigerate.
2. Remove arugula leaves from their stems, rinse, and dry thoroughly. Wrap and refrigerate.
3. Remove stems from the mushrooms and reserve for another use. Wipe each mushroom cap with a damp paper towel or cloth, wrap and refrigerate.
4. Cut away the stems and ribs of the red peppers; discard the seeds. Slice peppers into fine julienne, wrap and refrigerate.
5. To assemble, tear the lettuce leaves into bite-size pieces and combine with the arugula. Divide among 6 chilled salad plates. Slice mushrooms and sprinkle evenly over greens. Arrange red pepper julienne over mushrooms. Drizzle each plate with Balsamic Vinaigrette and serve immediately. (For a more informal presentation, combine all ingredients in a large salad bowl and toss with vinaigrette just before serving.)

6 portions

ARUGULA

Arugula travels under a variety of names — rugula, roquette, rocket cress, rocket or garden rocket — but no matter what you call it, the leaf always makes a distinct impression. Arugula is a European green which is becoming better known in America. First tasted by many in Italian restaurants in New York, arugula, with its pungent, peppery taste, was soon craved by all who savored it. To begin, you might add arugula as a flavoring to other mixed greens. Some mix it with endive, but we serve it pure, tossed with a garlicky vinaigrette. It is also wonderful lightly sautéed with butter to accompany seafood, potatoes or pasta. We cross our fingers that arugula will be available in your area soon. If there's no hope, do grow it yourself; you won't be sorry. When buying or picking, choose the young leaves — the older ones may be too strong.

BALSAMIC VINEGAR

This extraordinary, wine-based vinegar is still made in the northern part of Italy just as it has been for centuries. It is a mellow, sweet-and-sour vinegar with a heady fragrance. It must, by law, be aged for a decade in a variety of kegs made of particular kinds of wood; some batches are aged much longer. The vinegar is transferred from red oak kegs to chestnut, mulberry and juniper in turn, mellowing at each stage. Eventually, a warm, red-brown color and incredible fragrance are achieved. As a result, the taste is very special. The vinegar can be used in salads, sprinkled on cold meats or over hot vegetables, or to deglaze a pan. We even use it to douse our dessert fruits — an intoxicating habit.

BALSAMIC VINAIGRETTE

1 garlic clove, unpeeled
1 tablespoon prepared Dijon-style mustard
3 tablespoons balsamic vinegar*
salt and freshly ground black pepper, to taste
1 cup best-quality olive oil

1. Cut garlic clove into halves and rub the cut sides over the inner surface of a small bowl. Reserve the garlic.

2. Whisk mustard and vinegar together in the bowl. Season with salt and pepper to taste.

3. Dribble oil into the bowl in a slow steady stream, whisking constantly, until dressing is creamy and thickened and all the oil has been incorporated.

4. Taste and correct seasoning. Add reserved pieces of garlic; cover the bowl and let the dressing stand at room temperature until you need it. Remove garlic and rewhisk the dressing if necessary before using.

About 1¼ cups

*available at specialty food shops

AN ALL-ARUGULA SALAD

A salad for arugula lovers. Allow a bunch per person.

bunches of arugula
Garlic-Anchovy Vinaigrette Dressing (recipe follows)

1. Remove arugula leaves from stems, rinse and dry thoroughly. Wrap and refrigerate until ready to dress the salad.

2. Toss arugula in a large bowl with Garlic-Anchovy Dressing to taste. Arrange on plates and serve immediately.

GARLIC-ANCHOVY DRESSING

3 or 4 anchovy fillets
1 to 2 garlic cloves
1 tablespoon prepared Dijon-style mustard
1 egg yolk
¼ cup red wine vinegar
salt and freshly ground black pepper, to taste
1 cup best-quality olive oil

1. Coarsely chop the anchovy fillets, then with a fork mash them in the bottom of a small bowl.

2. Peel and mince the garlic cloves until they are puréed, mashing them against the work surface with the flat of the chopping knife. Add to the anchovies.

3. Whisk in the mustard, then the egg yolk and red wine vinegar, and season with salt and pepper.

4. Dribble the oil into the bowl in a slow, steady stream, whisking constantly, until the dressing is creamy and thickened and all the oil has been incorporated.

5. Transfer dressing to a storage container, cover, and refrigerate until ready to use.

About 1½ cups

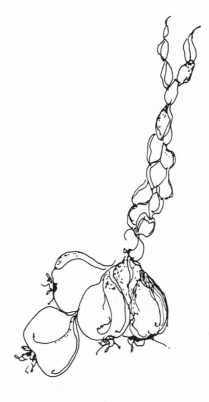

SALADE NICOISE

A salad that never fails to bring the Mediterranean to the table. It's crunchy and fresh-tasting, making a terrific meal in itself. The Silver Palate's version of this classic is in demand all summer long.

8 new potatoes, about 1 pound, well scrubbed
2 pounds green beans, cooked
10 very ripe Italian plum tomatoes, washed and quartered
1 small purple onion, peeled and thinly sliced
½ cup Niçoise olives
¼ cup chopped Italian parsley
pinch of salt
1 teaspoon freshly ground black pepper
¾ cup Our Favorite Vinaigrette (see page 247)
6 hard-cooked eggs, shelled and quartered
12 ounces canned oil-packed white tuna, well drained
2 ounces anchovy fillets (optional)

1. Cook potatoes in boiling salted water until tender but not mushy, about 10 minutes. When cool enough to handle, quarter the potatoes and transfer them to a large bowl.
2. Add green beans, tomatoes, onion, olives, parsley, a pinch of salt and the pepper. Pour ½ cup of the vinaigrette over vegetables and toss gently but well.
3. Transfer mixture to a large serving platter. Arrange the hard-cooked egg quarters around the edge of the platter. Flake the tuna over the salad and arrange the anchovy fillets, if you use them, in a lattice pattern over the tuna. Drizzle with additional vinaigrette and serve at room temperature.

6 to 8 portions

"Give me books, fruit, French wine and fine weather, and a little music out of doors, played by someone I do not know."
— John Keats, 1819

SUMMER SALADS

Summer salads are the best salads of all. Now vegetables and fruits are at their freshest, often imported from no farther than your own garden. Such perfect produce needs only a splash of vinaigrette and a sprinkle of herbs to delight the palate and excite the eye. Tomatoes, potatoes, corn — the most ordinary of foods — become works of art. Most summer salads require little or no cooking, and when served at room temperature reveal more of their subtle flavors.

TOMATO, MONTRACHET
AND BASIL SALAD

Our most popular summer salad.

6 large ripe tomatoes
1 medium purple onion
¼ cup Basil Purée (see page 51)
¼ cup Niçoise or other imported black olives
1 tablespoon chopped Italian parsley
¼ cup best-quality olive oil
dash of red wine vinegar
salt and freshly ground black pepper, to taste
½ Montrachet cheese, or 6 ounces of other mild creamy chèvre

1. Core tomatoes, cut into thick slices, then cut slices into halves. Transfer to a mixing bowl.

2. Peel onion, slice into thin rings, add to bowl, and turn gently with a spoon.

3. Add remaining ingredients except cheese and again turn gently. Cover and refrigerate for 1 hour.

4. Just before serving transfer salad to a serving dish and crumble the Montrachet cheese over all.

6 to 8 portions

RICE AND VEGETABLE SALAD

8 cups hot cooked rice
1½ to 2 cups Our Favorite Vinaigrette (see page 247)
1 sweet red pepper, stemmed, cored, and cut into thin julienne
1 green pepper, stemmed, cored, and cut into thin julienne
1 medium-size purple onion, peeled and diced
6 scallions (green onions), cleaned and finely sliced
1 cup dried currants
2 shallots, peeled and finely diced
*1 package (10 ounces) frozen peas, thawed and blanched in
  boiling salted water for 3 minutes*
½ cup pitted black olives (preferably imported), finely chopped
¼ cup chopped Italian parsley
½ cup chopped fresh dill
salt and freshly ground black pepper, to taste

1. Transfer rice to a mixing bowl and pour 1½ cups vinaigrette into rice. Toss thoroughly. Cool to room temperature.

2. Add remaining ingredients and toss thoroughly. Taste, correct seasoning, and add additional vinaigrette if you like.

3. Serve immediately, or cover and refrigerate up to 4 hours. Return to room temperature before serving.

8 to 10 portions

BACK-PACKING
PICNIC

*Chicken Liver Pâté with
Green Peppercorns*

*Assorted sausages and
mustards*

---

*Brie cheese
Tomato, Montrachet and
Basil Salad*

*French bread with Basil-
Mustard Butter*

---

*Green grapes and
strawberries*

Shortbread Hearts

COOKING WITH ZEST

The zest or outer rind — the colored part of the peel of the citrus fruits — is full of flavorful oils. Lime zest is essential in Lime Mousse; we love orange zest in Blueberry Chicken, Cracked Wheat Salad and Marinated Beef Salad (see Index for recipes). Garnish veal scallops with strips of lemon zest or grate it into homemade sherbets.

Use a vegetable peeler to remove only the thinnest layer of rind (the white inner layer or "pith" is bitter), and julienne with a sharp knife. Or, use the appropriately named "zester," an indispensable little tool that removes long, even, elegant strings of citrus peel in one easy swoop. We couldn't live without ours.

ORANGE AND ONION SALAD

This unusual salad is as good to eat as it is beautiful to look at, and it's often the answer when you are looking for an offbeat salad that will complement Italian or other Mediterranean menus. It should be chilled briefly but should not sit around, since the oranges soon begin tasting like onions and the charm of the whole thing is lost.

6 large, firm, juicy oranges
3 tablespoons red wine vinegar
6 tablespoons best-quality olive oil
1 teaspoon dried oregano
1 medium-size purple onion, peeled and sliced paper-thin
1 cup imported black olives (ideally, tiny black Niçoise olives,
   but Kalamata or Alfonso olives will do)
¼ cup fresh chives, snipped (garnish)
freshly ground black pepper, to taste

1. Peel the oranges and cut each one into 4 or 5 crosswise slices. Transfer the oranges to a shallow serving dish and sprinkle them with the vinegar, olive oil and oregano. Toss gently, cover, and refrigerate for 30 minutes.

2. Toss the oranges again, arrange the sliced onion and black olives over them decoratively, sprinkle with chives, and grind on the pepper.

6 to 8 portions

CRACKED WHEAT SALAD

4 cups water
2 cups bulgur (processed cracked wheat)
1 cup chopped pecans
1 cup dried currants
4 tablespoons chopped Italian parsley
1 tablespoon best-quality olive oil
grated zest of 1 medium-size orange
salt and freshly ground black pepper, to taste

1. In a large saucepan combine water and bulgur. Bring to a boil, reduce heat and simmer, covered, for 35 to 40 minutes, or until water is absorbed and wheat is tender but not mushy.

2. Transfer to a bowl and refrigerate, uncovered, until cool.

3. Add pecans, currants, parsley, olive oil, orange zest, salt and pepper to taste. Toss thoroughly. Serve cool or at room temperature.

8 portions

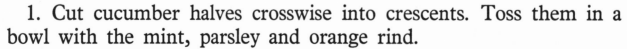

MINTY CUCUMBER SALAD

This cool salad is good year-round but seems most appropriate during the summer. A favorite menu: butterflied leg of lamb, Cracked Wheat Salad and Minty Cucumber Salad, accompanied by hot pita bread.

3 large cucumbers, peeled, halved and seeded
½ cup chopped fresh mint leaves
¼ cup chopped fresh parsley
grated rind of 1 orange
½ cup olive oil
1 cup red wine vinegar
¼ cup granulated sugar

1. Cut cucumber halves crosswise into crescents. Toss them in a bowl with the mint, parsley and orange rind.

2. Whisk oil, vinegar and sugar together in a small bowl and pour over salad. Cover salad and refrigerate for at least 4 hours.

3. Toss again before serving very cold.

6 to 8 portions

MARINATED GARBANZO SALAD

This slightly Middle Eastern concoction makes a good first course arranged on lettuce leaves, or a good accompaniment to simple grilled lamb, chicken or pork.

½ cup best-quality olive oil
1 cup finely minced yellow onions
1 tablespoon dried thyme
½ cup coarsely chopped red pepper
½ cup dark raisins
2 cans (1 pound each) garbanzos (chick-peas), drained and
    rinsed, about 3½ cups
½ teaspoon salt
½ cup white wine vinegar

1. Heat the olive oil in a saucepan. Add the onions and thyme and cook over low heat, covered, until onions are tender and lightly colored, about 25 minutes.

2. Add chopped red pepper and cook for another 5 minutes.

3. Add raisins and garbanzos and cook for another 5 minutes, stirring occasionally. Do not overcook the garbanzos or they will become mushy.

4. Season with salt, transfer to a bowl, and pour the vinegar over the hot mixture.

5. Let vegetables cool to room temperature, then cover and refrigerate for at least 24 hours before serving. Allow to return to room temperature before serving.

6 to 8 portions

SIMPLE SUMMER PLEASURES

Make photo scrapbooks
Watch the clouds
Make lemonade from scratch
Spend the whole day in a hammock

Plant an herb garden
Press flowers
Wear only white for a week
Read romantic Russian novels
Skinny dip in the moonlight
Play all of your old records
Spend a silent day
Fast on fruit juices and water
Write a letter and many postcards
Read poetry
Polish the silver
Visit the library
Wander in the museum
Do crossword puzzles
Go clamming
Go antiquing
Ride horseback around a lake
Make a kite
Go to a country fair
Fill the house with flowers
Make ice cream
Sleep outdoors
Put flowers on a floppy hat
Walk barefoot
Pick the morning glories
Toast marshmallows on the beach
Ride a roller coaster
Have lunch in your bathing suit
Ride in a convertible
Watch shooting stars
Listen to classical music
Hum
Play cribbage
Smell fresh mint
Meander among wildflowers
Ride a roller coaster
Give someone a rub with coconut oil
Snooze in the sun

"Now is the heyday of summer,
The full, warm robust middle age of the year;
The earth, ripe with products as well as promise."
— Daniel Grayson

BASQUE SALAD

A hearty main-course salad of rice, meats and seafood.

¼ cup olive oil
12 scallions, green tops included, thinly sliced
1 scant teaspoon whole saffron
2 cups converted rice
1½ teaspoon salt
4 cups Chicken Stock (see page 587)
1 pound medium-size raw shrimp, shelled and deveined
¼ pound hard sausage (salami, pepperoni, or other), cut into julienne
½ pound prosciutto, thinly sliced
1 green pepper, stemmed, cored and cut into thin julienne
1 red pepper, stemmed, cored and cut into thin julienne
½ cup chopped parsley
salt, to taste
¾ teaspoon freshly ground black pepper

1. Heat oil in a heavy pot. Add scallions and sauté over medium heat, stirring, for 5 minutes or until wilted. Add saffron and cook for 2 minutes longer.

2. Add the rice and stir, coating grains well with oil. Season with 1½ teaspoons salt, pour in chicken stock, and stir. Bring to a simmer, cover, and cook over low heat for 20 minutes, or until rice is just done and all liquid has been absorbed. Fluff with a fork and let cool somewhat.

3. Meanwhile, bring 2 quarts water to a boil, then add shrimp. Immediately remove from heat, cover, and let stand for 2 minutes. Drain shrimp and reserve.

4. Transfer cooked rice to a large bowl. Add shrimp, sausage and prosciutto, red and green peppers, parsley, salt to taste and black pepper. Toss thoroughly. Arrange on a large platter and serve at room temperature.

8 portions

ALL-AMERICAN SALADS

Some salads seem particularly all-American to us. These are the kind that turn up at church suppers, on the menus of rustic inns and restaurants off the beaten track, and in our grandmothers' handwritten "receipt" books. They are simple and good, and deserve, in these sophisticated times, not to be forgotten.

BEET AND ROQUEFORT SALAD WITH WALNUTS

This hearty salad is especially welcome in winter. It goes perfectly with a ham, grilled sausages or the like, and the color combination is striking on a buffet table.

As a variation you may omit the Roquefort and sprinkle the salad generously with chopped fresh dill.

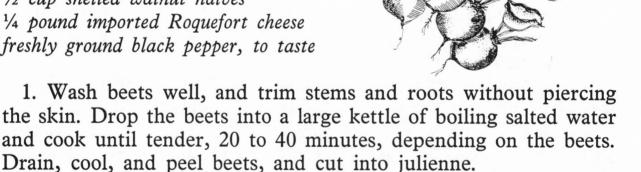

8 to 10 medium-size beets
3 tablespoons red wine vinegar
3 tablespoons walnut oil
½ cup shelled walnut halves
¼ pound imported Roquefort cheese
freshly ground black pepper, to taste

1. Wash beets well, and trim stems and roots without piercing the skin. Drop the beets into a large kettle of boiling salted water and cook until tender, 20 to 40 minutes, depending on the beets. Drain, cool, and peel beets, and cut into julienne.

2. In a mixing bowl toss the beets gently with the vinegar and walnut oil. Taste and add more of either if you like; there should be just enough to coat the beets. Cover and chill until serving time.

3. To serve, toss the walnuts with the chilled beets and arrange in a shallow serving bowl. Allow to return to room temperature. Crumble the Roquefort evenly over the top and grind on black pepper to taste. Serve immediately.

6 to 8 portions

CREAMY COLESLAW

Sheila's version of the delicatessen regular. A fresh taste, perfect with your favorite sandwich.

1 small head of green cabbage, cleaned, cored and cut into slivers
1 large carrot, trimmed, peeled and grated
1 medium-size green pepper, stemmed, seeded and grated
1 cup Hellmann's mayonnaise
½ cup corn oil
½ cup dairy sour cream
2 tablespoons heavy cream
1 teaspoon caraway seeds
salt and freshly ground black pepper, to taste

1. Put cabbage slivers and grated carrot and pepper together in a large bowl.
2. Combine remaining ingredients, with salt and pepper to taste, in a small bowl and whisk together well. Pour over cabbage mixture, stir, cover, and chill for at least 4 hours before serving.
3. Allow slaw to return to room temperature before serving.
6 to 8 portions

AUTUMN APPLE AND WALNUT SALAD

This crisp, nutty salad is rich with autumn colors and the special taste of sherry vinegar.

2 Granny Smith apples, chilled
2 Red Delicious apples, chilled
½ cup sherry vinegar, or more if needed
1 cup chopped celery
3 scallions (green onions), cleaned and cut diagonally into
  ½-inch pieces
½ cup shelled walnut halves
4 to 5 tablespoons walnut oil

1. Wash the apples and dry them well. Core and chop, but do not peel them, and toss them in a bowl with the sherry vinegar.
2. Add celery, scallions and walnut halves, and drizzle with 4 tablespoons of the walnut oil. Toss again.
3. Taste and correct seasoning, adding more vinegar and up to 1 tablespoon more oil as necessary, and serve immediately.
4 to 6 portions

TECHNICOLOR BEAN SALAD

Three-bean salad always seems so limiting, so we've gone a bit further.

1 can (about 1 pound) each of garbanzos (chick-peas), white kidney
  beans, red kidney beans, baby lima beans and black-eyed peas
1 pound fresh green beans, or half green and half yellow wax beans
Garlic Dressing (recipe follows)
1 cup chopped scallions (green onions)
½ cup chopped Italian parsley (garnish)

1. Drain canned beans, rinse thoroughly with water, and drain again.
2. Trim, cook and cool beans according to "Cooking Fresh Green Beans" (see page 256). Drain, pat dry, and cut into 2-inch lengths.
3. Toss canned and fresh beans together in a large bowl. Pour in the dressing, sprinkle on the scallions, and toss again.
4. Cover and refrigerate overnight before serving. Garnish with chopped parsley. Serve at room temperature.
10 to 12 portions

GARLIC DRESSING

1 egg yolk
⅓ cup red wine vinegar
1 tablespoon granulated sugar
1 tablespoon chopped garlic
salt and freshly ground black pepper, to taste
1 cup best-quality olive oil

1. Combine egg yolk, vinegar, sugar, garlic, and salt and pepper to taste in the bowl of a food processor fitted with a steel blade. Process briefly.
2. With the motor running, slowly dribble in the olive oil.
3. Taste, correct seasoning if necessary, and transfer to storage container.
About 1½ cups

BEACH PICNIC

Gazpacho
Assorted quiches
_____

Technicolor Bean Salad
Brioche Bread
_____

Chocolate Mousse
Strawberries

A PICNIC CHECKLIST:

One of the most important elements for successful pic-nicking is complete planning. Love your menu; leave nothing out! Once you're done watching the sun set into the lagoon, it's rough to have forgotten the cork-screw. Make lists of essentials and accessories, and bear in mind that people tend to eat more when they're outdoors. Also, picnics tend to last a long time, and your group may grow in number quite spontaneously along the way.

- ❑ tablecloth
- ❑ flatware, plates and glasses
- ❑ corkscrew and bottle opener
- ❑ thermos or ice for cold drinks
- ❑ thermos for hot drinks
- ❑ good sharp knife
- ❑ light cutting board/serving platter
- ❑ napkins, paper towels
- ❑ matches
- ❑ charcoal, if necessary
- ❑ extra leakproof containers
- ❑ garbage bag
- ❑ Swiss army knife (with corkscrew)
- ❑ spatula
- ❑ candles or flashlight
- ❑ small first-aid kit
- ❑ insect repellant, suntan cream, zinc oxide

EGG SALAD WITH DILL

There is nothing revolutionary about this recipe, but when we reflected on all the bad egg salads we have tasted, it seemed a good idea to include this version. It makes a zesty sandwich, especially when served on black bread. Although the dill is optional, it makes the salad special.

8 hard-cooked eggs
½ cup finely chopped purple onion
⅓ cup chopped fresh dill
½ cup Hellmann's mayonnaise
¼ cup dairy sour cream
¼ cup prepared Dijon-style mustard
salt and freshly ground black pepper, to taste

1. Peel the eggs and quarter them. Place in a mixing bowl with the onion and dill.

2. In another bowl whisk together the mayonnaise, sour cream and mustard and pour over the eggs, onion and dill.

3. Toss gently, season to taste with salt and pepper, and toss again. Cover and refrigerate if you must, but the salad is at its best eaten immediately.

6 portions

MARDI-GRAS SLAW

2 cups shredded red cabbage
2 cups shredded white cabbage
2 cups grated peeled carrots
½ cup finely minced yellow onion
⅓ cup red wine vinegar
¼ cup granulated sugar
1 tablespoon prepared Dijon-style mustard
salt and freshly ground black pepper, to taste
⅔ cup best-quality olive oil
1 tablespoon caraway seeds

1. Toss both kinds of cabbage, the grated carrots and minced onion together in a large bowl. Reserve.

2. In a small bowl whisk together the vinegar, sugar and mustard; season to taste with salt and pepper. Slowly whisk in the oil to form a fairly thick and creamy dressing. Taste and correct seasoning as necessary.

3. Pour half of the dressing over the vegetables in the bowl. Sprinkle on the caraway seeds and toss well. Taste; add additional dressing as you like. Cover and refrigerate for up to 4 hours. Allow to return to room temperature before serving.

6 to 8 portions

"The French approach to food is characteristic; they bring to their consideration of the table the same appreciation, respect, intelligence and lively interest that they have for the other arts, for painting, for literature, and for the theatre. We foreigners living in France respect and appreciate this point of view but deplore their too strict observance of a tradition which will not admit the slightest deviation in a seasoning or the suppression of a single ingredient. Restrictions aroused our American ingenuity, we found combinations and replacements which pointed in new directions and created a fresh and absorbing interest in everything pertaining to the kitchen."
— Alice B. Toklas, 1954

FRENCH DRESSING

From an American family cookbook comes this alternative to the orange horror available on your grocer's shelf today. We've reduced the sugar, and the result is a sweet-tart golden beauty of a dressing that is perfect on a chef's salad or a Reuben sandwich.

2 eggs
½ cup red wine vinegar
⅓ cup granulated sugar
1 tablespoon prepared Dijon-style mustard
½ teaspoon salt
1 teaspoon imported sweet paprika
1 cup vegetable oil

1. Combine eggs, vinegar, sugar, mustard, salt and paprika in the bowl of a food processor fitted with a steel blade. Process for 2 minutes, or until sugar is dissolved.

2. With the motor running, dribble in the oil in a slow steady stream. When all the oil is incorporated, shut off motor, scrape down sides of processor bowl, taste, and correct seasoning if necessary.

3. Transfer to a storage container, cover, and refrigerate.
About 2 cups

POPPY-SEED DRESSING

Tart dressings are more stylish now, but this one still seems good to us, particularly on a spinach salad with rings of purple onion, sliced hard-cooked egg, crumbled crisp bacon and home-made croutons, sautéed in butter with garlic (see page 101).

1 egg
¼ cup granulated sugar
1 tablespoon prepared Dijon-style mustard
⅔ cup red wine vinegar
½ teaspoon salt
3 tablespoons grated fresh yellow onion, plus any juice from
  the grating
2 cups corn oil
3 tablespoons poppy seeds

1. Combine egg, sugar, mustard, vinegar, salt, grated onion and juice in the bowl of a food processor fitted with a steel blade. Process for 1 minute.

2. With the motor running, pour in the oil in a slow, steady stream. When all the oil is incorporated, shut off the motor, taste and correct seasoning.

3. Transfer mixture to a bowl, stir in poppy seeds and refrigerate, covered, until ready to use.

About 1 quart

SALADS OF THE SEA

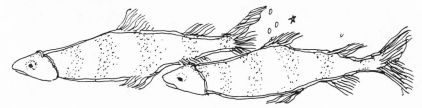

A combination of seafood and vegetables in a main-course salad is light eating at its best, with no lack of flavor or simple enjoyment. Such dining is one of the best ways we know to remain cool, healthy and trim.

SEAFOOD SALAD WITH CREAMY TARRAGON-MUSTARD DRESSING

This salad can be made with any combination of seafood you like — lump crab meat, octopus, squid or conch are all appropriate, although using more than three kinds results in a bit of a jumble. In any case, try to make the salad and serve it immediately, without refrigeration. If you must chill it, be sure to let it return to room temperature before serving.

1 pound medium-size raw shrimp, shelled and deveined
1 pound fresh bay scallops, rinsed thoroughly
½ pound lobster meat (about 1½ cups meat, the equivalent of a
  3¼- to 4-pound lobster), or a similar amount of frozen lobster
  meat, defrosted overnight in the refrigerator
1 cup uncooked tiny peas, fresh or frozen
2 scallions (green onions), trimmed, cleaned and cut diagonally
  into ½-inch pieces
salt and freshly ground black pepper, to taste
1 cup Creamy Tarragon-Mustard Dressing (recipe follows)
2 cups coarsely shredded raw spinach leaves, thoroughly cleaned
  and dried

1. Bring 4 quarts salted water to a boil in a pot. Drop in the shrimp, wait 1 minute, and drop in the scallops. Just before the water returns to a full boil, pour the contents of the pot through a strainer set in the sink. Cool seafood to room temperature.

2. Drain the lobster (if frozen) and sort through it carefully to remove any bits of shell. Reserve several large pieces of lobster meat (particularly claw meat) for garnish and cut the rest into chunks.

3. Reserve 3 or 4 shrimp and scallops for garnish and combine the rest with the lobster meat in a mixing bowl.

4. Add peas and scallions, season lightly with salt and pepper to taste, and pour in the tarragon-mustard dressing. Toss salad gently and add more dressing if you like.

5. Arrange spinach in a border around a shallow serving bowl. Spoon the seafood salad into the center of the bowl and arrange the reserved seafood garnish on top.

6. Serve immediately, offering additional dressing on the side if you like.

6 portions as a first course, 4 portions as a main course

CREAMY TARRAGON-MUSTARD DRESSING

1 whole egg
2 egg yolks
⅓ cup prepared tarragon mustard, or Dijon-style mustard
¼ cup tarragon vinegar
1 teaspoon crumbled dried tarragon
salt and freshly ground black pepper, to taste
1 cup best-quality olive oil
1 cup corn or other light vegetable oil

1. In a blender, or in the bowl of a food processor fitted with a steel blade, combine whole egg, egg yolks, mustard, vinegar and tarragon. Season to taste with salt and pepper and process for 1 minute.

2. Measure out the oil and with the motor still running, dribble the oil into the processor or blender in a slow, steady stream. Shut off the motor, scrape down sides, taste, and correct seasoning.

3. Transfer to a storage container, cover, and refrigerate until ready to use.

About 3 cups

SHRIMP AND GRAPE SALAD
WITH DILL

2 pounds medium-size raw shrimp, shelled and deveined
1 cup dairy sour cream
1 cup Hellmann's mayonnaise
2 cups seedless green grapes, washed and patted dry
½ cup chopped fresh dill, or more to taste
salt and freshly ground black pepper, to taste
lettuce leaves

1. Bring 4 quarts salted water to a boil and drop in the shrimp. Wait 1 minute; empty the pot into a colander set in the sink. Let the shrimp cool in the colander.

2. Transfer the cooled shrimp to a bowl.

3. In a separate small bowl, whisk sour cream and mayonnaise together well.

4. Pour dressing over the shrimp and toss gently. Add the grapes and toss again. Finally, sprinkle on the chopped dill, add salt and pepper to taste, and toss once more and refrigerate, covered, for at least 4 hours.

5. Just before serving, taste, correct seasoning and toss again. Arrange on lettuce leaves and serve immediately.

6 portions as a main course, 8 portions as a first course

```
┌─────────────────────────────────────┐
│                                     │
│         A SEASIDE LUNCH             │
│                                     │
│        Fresh raspberries and        │
│       strawberries with sugar       │
│          and crème fraîche          │
│             ─────────               │
│                                     │
│          Seafood Salad with         │
│        Creamy Tarragon Dressing     │
│                                     │
│          Fresh oysters with         │
│             Shallot Sauce           │
│                                     │
│         Cracked Wheat Salad         │
│             ─────────               │
│                                     │
│          Chocolate Mousse           │
│                                     │
│         Black Walnut Cookies        │
│                                     │
└─────────────────────────────────────┘
```

SALAD SPLENDOR

Salads delight the palate and excite the eye. Suddenly the most ordinary foods, combined to complement each other in color, texture and shape, become works of art.

Foods served at room temperature or raw reveal their subtle flavors. Salad recipes are casual and open to experimentation. Take advantage of the ingredients at hand and let your imagination and taste be your guide. Most of the salads we offer here can be prepared at your leisure and allowed to mellow or marinate until serving time. The pressure is off; all you must do is carefully select and balance the best of all possible ingredients; then enjoy.

SHRIMP AND ARTICHOKE SALAD

2 pounds medium-size raw shrimp, shelled and deveined
2 cups broccoli florets
2 cans (8 ounces each) water-packed artichoke hearts, drained
8 scallions (green onions), cleaned, trimmed and cut diagonally
   into ½-inch pieces
2 cups Sherry Mayonnaise (see page 352)
salt and freshly ground black pepper, to taste

1. Bring 4 quarts salted water to a boil and drop in the shrimp. Wait 1 minute; empty the pot into a colander set in the sink. Let the shrimp cool in the colander.

2. Bring a second pot of salted water to a boil and drop in the broccoli florets. Cook for 3 to 5 minutes, or until stems are just tender; do not overcook. Remove florets from water with a slotted spoon or skimmer and drop into a bowl of ice water. This will stop the cooking process and set the brilliant green color. When broccoli is cool, drain well and reserve.

3. Cut the artichokes into halves or quarters, depending on their size, and combine in a mixing bowl with the shrimp, broccoli and scallions.

4. Add sherry mayonnaise, toss, season with salt and pepper to taste, and toss again. Cover and refrigerate until ready to serve.
   6 portions

SALADS ON THE GREEN

The salads that come after the main course are most often green salads, and while they are called the relief of the dinner, they should by no means be boring.

Need we say that iceberg lettuce from the salad bar, laden with this garnish and that, is not our idea of a "tossed green salad"? It should instead consist of everything cool, green and crisp, gently tossed at the last moment with a superb vinaigrette.

Be adventurous but wise in combining the glorious greens available to you from market and garden. Use a judiciously light dressing, made by hand from fresh, good-quality ingredients. Always serve salads as soon as they are tossed.

Treated thus with imagination and respect, the simple green salad can become one of the glories of your table. Our favorite green combinations and dressings follow.

A GREEN SAMPLER

Salad greens vary dramatically in taste, texture and color. When combined with other summer foods and endless vinaigrettes they can match every mood and occasion.

Be certain to rinse the greens carefully and dry them thoroughly. Keep them crisp in the refrigerator, wrapped in a towel, or stored in a covered bowl until serving time.

ARUGULA: Intense in color and pungent in flavor, it is an ideal companion to softer and sweeter leaves and wonderful on its own. Toss with a strong vinaigrette and sprinkle with sieved, hard-cooked egg.

BELGIAN ENDIVE: Crisp and opalescent, it is so special it makes a great first course combined with thinly sliced prosciutto and red wine basil vinaigrette.

BIBB LETTUCE: Delectably small, tight leaves with a crunchy sweetness. Bibb leaves are best on their own with a light vinaigrette.

BOSTON LETTUCE: Pale green, loosely packed and tender, this fragile green has a pleasing hearty flavor.

CHICORY: Tart and crunchy, it combines well with other vegetables for a salad or entrée course.

CRESS ALBISEOIS: The most delicate of cresses, it deserves a delicate vinaigrette. Watch for it in the market.

DANDELION GREENS: Wild or cultivated, they have a refreshing tart taste alone or in a combination with other greens. Be certain they're young and fresh.

ESCAROLE: Yellow-white leaves with a pleasantly tart flavor that can take stronger dressings than other leaves.

FENNEL GREENS: Snip the feathery tips of anise-flavored fennel into mixed green salads as a seasoning.

FIELD LETTUCE or **LAMB'S TONGUE (MACHE):** A lovely fall and winter green that comes in small bunches. Combine with other greens.

ICEBERG LETTUCE: As a last resort, we think.

LEAF LETTUCE: Curly, green- or red-tipped, the tasty, tender leaves of the various leaf lettuces are rather soft in texture. Especially delicious when young.

NASTURTIUM LEAVES: Use sparingly with milder greens. They give a surprising peppery flavor.

PURSLANE: Vinegary flavor, crisp texture that complements milder greens.

RADICCHIO: A ruby-red miniature leaf with a slightly bitter flavor. This mixes color and flavor with other greens and can stand a hearty vinaigrette.

RED LEAF LETTUCE: Purple-red, it is a soft crinkly lettuce that is good to eat as well as aesthetically pleasing. Use it combined with other sturdier greens.

ROMAINE: Firm tight leaves with a robust nutty flavor. This green can be dressed with a strong vinaigrette.

SORREL: The taste of lemons and light vinegar. This bright green leaf is tart, and should be mixed sparingly with milder leaves.

SPINACH: Dense, small, rounded leaves, and the crinkliest. Don't limit its complements to bacon bits and hard-cooked eggs; its flavor blends well in many combinations.

WATERCRESS: Dark green and spicy with cloverlike leaves, it is becoming a staple. Alone or mixed with others, cress has a beautiful color and is a good taste balancer.

We have some very favorite green salad combinations. Tossed with complementary vinaigrettes (see Index for recipes), the possibilities are endless.

Allow ⅓ to ½ cup of vinaigrette for every 6 servings. The dressing should gently coat the greens, not smother them.

♥ Watercress, Belgian endive cut into julienne, and walnut halves. Serve with Walnut Oil Vinaigrette.

♥ Fresh dark green arugula and delicate Bibb lettuce leaves. Serve with Garlic Dressing.

♥ Romaine lettuce (outer leaves removed), watercress and chicory. Serve with a red wine vinaigrette.

♥ Whole baby Bibb lettuce. Serve with Blueberry Vinaigrette.

♥ Tender young fresh spinach leaves, ruby-red lettuce and seeded sliced cucumbers. Serve with Sesame Mayonnaise.

♥ Belgian endive (separated whole leaves) and slivered white mushrooms. Serve with Champagne Vinaigrette and garnish with freshly snipped chives.

♥ Boston lettuce and baby nasturtium leaves. Serve with Green Peppercorn Vinaigrette.

THE OIL OF THE OLIVE

We adore olive oil. It is the only oil of culinary importance pressed from the flesh of a ripe fruit (not a seed or a nut), and we think that's why it's one of the most delicious and versatile food products in creation. We're not alone in our enthusiasm; more and more cooks are telling us they can't live without it.

Today, olive oil is made anywhere olive trees grow (of course!) and that list stretches to include Spain, Italy, France, Portugal, Greece, Australia, Africa, California, New Zealand, South America, Syria, Turkey and Israel. Olives, like wine grapes, require a warm climate and particularly sandy soil. The best come from Italy and the south of France. Like most good things, olive trees improve with age; interestingly, an olive tree must be 35 years old before it bears fruit.

Italian olive oil has a more pronounced olive flavor, giving it a vaguely nutty or leafy taste. French oil is fruitier with just a hint of peppery spiciness. Spanish oil has a more intense flavor and not much subtlety, while Greek oil has a lighter olive taste but is rich and rather thick in consistency. As we've said elsewhere, we prefer French olive oil to Italian, Spanish or Greek. Too often, these last are made from olives which are not at their peak in order to obtain two harvests. The best oil is made from perfectly ripe fruit. The more an olive matures, the less is its water content and the better the oil will be.

There are a number of qualities of oil on the market today, though we don't think the variety needs to be confusing.

• *Extra Extra* or *Extra Virgin Olive Oil* is the oil made from the very first pressing of the olives. It is usually green, sometimes bordering on greenish black, depending on the filtering the oil has undergone. Its intense flavor and aroma is that of green olives. Extra virgin oil is best for use in salads or marinades, or tossed with just-cooked vegetables.

• *Virgin Olive Oil* is also a direct product of the olive fruit, though it may be the result of a second pressing. It should have a sweetish, nutty flavor.

• *Pure Olive Oil* is made up of oils extracted by treating the previously pressed olive pulp with solvents.

• *Fine Olive Oil* is oil which has also been extracted from olive pulp, to which water has been added. It is perfect for cooking or frying.

There's no reason to feel intimidated when buying olive oil. The basic rule remains; you get the quality you pay for. The better the taste of the ingredient, the better the taste of the prepared dish.

As important as your choice of oil is the care you take of it. Even good oil can go stale or turn rancid if not stored carefully. After 2 weeks opened oil should be stored in a refrigerator, especially in summer. It may become cloudy, but it will clear rapidly upon returning to room temperature.

OTHER OILS

A host of seeds and nuts also produce flavorful oils suitable for cooking.
ALMOND OIL, HAZELNUT OIL: These are sweet, light, delicate oils that are indeed nutty in taste. they are splendid in salads, or tossed with hot vegetables as a change from butter.
PEPPER OILS: The best of these delicately flavored oils balance the richness of grapeseed oil and the spiciness of the pepper.
WALNUT OIL: A very light and delicate oil. It must be used quickly after opening, as its fresh flavor is short-lived. Refrigerate.
HERB-FLAVORED OILS: These are usually olive or grapeseed oils that have been flavored with any number of herbs or spices. We couldn't do without them for our favorite vinaigrettes and marinades. Basil, tarragon, bay leaf, garlic and peppercorns, alone or mixed, are among the flavorings used.

388

VINEGAR

We think of vinegar as a very practical natural product. Basically it is simply fermented fruit juice that has become acidic, though there's a bit of poetry involved as well.

The Chinese made vinegar from rice wine over 3,000 years ago, while the Romans refreshed themselves with a mixture of vinegar and water flavored with mint leaves.

The same soldiers of Caesar's army who filled the hills of Dijon, France, with mustard seeds also helped name vinegar — quite by accident. The conquered French peasants called the Roman wine that had fermented *"vinaigre,"* or sour wine. It was in the Middle Ages that vinegar, seasoned with spices and herbs, first made its appearance in French cuisine.

The bases for vinegar are countless: wine, including sherry and Champagne; malted grain; apples, pears, other fruits and berries, and even sugar and honey.

Americans have become interested in lighter eating habits and in the subtleties of wonderful oils and vinegars. Vinegars have never been more in demand as a creative cooking ingredient.

DISTILLED VINEGARS: These are made by distilling alcohol from grain such as corn, rye, malt or barley. They are the most acidic and lend themselves best to pickling.

WINE VINEGARS: These are made by fermenting wine until it becomes sufficiently acidic. Red and white wine, sherry and even Champagne create mild vinegars. These flavors enhance marinades, salads and sauces in a special manner. Herbs may also be added for additional flavor.

FRUIT VINEGARS: These are being used by modern cooks in any number of dishes; their light fresh flavor is the reason why. Their flavorings include raspberries, blueberries, blackberries, and peaches — the list can grow as long as the list of your local fruit stand's offerings. The flavor these vinegars lend to recipes is inimitable. (We even know one woman who splashes fruit vinegar in her Daiquiris.)

HERB VINEGARS: These are prepared by infusing herbs in a broad range of traditional vinegars. Flavorings include red or green basil, tarragon, oregano, wild thyme, peppercorns, mint, rosemary, dill, chervil, chive blossoms and savory, or combinations of several of these and others. Herb vinegars offer any number of possibilities for the creative cook.

CIDER VINEGAR: This is a mild vinegar tasting of the apples from which it is made.

MALT VINEGAR: This is a strong vinegar mostly appreciated in England.

RASPBERRY VINAIGRETTE

½ *cup olive oil*
½ *cup raspberry vinegar*
½ *teaspoon salt*
freshly ground black pepper
1 tablespoon Crème Fraîche (see page 582)

Combine all ingredients and shake well.
   About 1 cup

GREEN PEPPERCORN VINAIGRETTE

1 tablespoon Homemade Mayonnaise (see page 582)
¼ *cup white wine herb vinegar*
½ *teaspoon crushed green peppercorns*
¾ *cup green peppercorn oil*
2 tablespoons chopped parsley

Combine all ingredients and shake well.
   1 cup

GARLIC-MUSTARD DRESSING

1 egg
⅓ cup prepared Dijon-style mustard
⅔ cup red wine vinegar
salt and freshly ground black pepper, to taste
6 garlic cloves, peeled and chopped
2 cups best-quality imported olive oil

1. Combine the egg, mustard and vinegar in the bowl of a food processor fitted with a steel blade. Season to taste with the salt and pepper and process for 1 minute.

2. With the motor still running, drop the garlic cloves through the feed tube. Then begin dribbling in the olive oil in a slow, steady stream.

3. When all the oil is incorporated, shut off motor, taste, and correct seasoning (the dressing should be very garlicky).

4. Transfer to a storage container and refrigerate until ready to use.

3 cups

THE MUSTARD MAZE

Mustards have been prepared through the centuries. The Chinese cultivated the pods over 3,000 years ago, Hippocrates praised mustard for its alleged medicinal value, Caesar's conquering troops sowed mustard seeds in the hills of Dijon, France, and Thomas Jefferson introduced the mustard plant to Monticello in 1780.

In recent years, poetic license has been taken and the interesting mustard flavors that have been developed have made mustard one of the world's most popular condiments. Over 700 million pounds of mustard are consumed worldwide each year. Interestingly, most of the mustard seeds used in Dijon today are actually grown in the Dakotas, Canada, California, Oregon and Washington State.

Prepared mustard is made from the seeds of several species of the mustard plant, dried, ground, and then mixed with a liquid — from Champagne to milk to vinegar — and often with salt, spices or herbs, until the desired flavor and consistency are reached. Traditional mustards are available in a wide variety, and innovative versions have recently become hotter, spicier, sweeter and more colorful than ever before.

GRAINY MUSTARDS are blends made with whole or coarsely chopped mustard seeds. Use these with ham or corned beef, smoked meats, cold cuts, or as a coating for meats.

DIJON MUSTARD and Dijon-style mustard is made from husked and ground mustard seeds, white wine, vinegar and spice. Many versions are made, some with added flavorings. It has a smooth texture and is easily the most versatile mustard for cooking and eating. ("Dijon" is a general term for this style of mustard produced in Dijon, France, and only mustard made there may label itself as such. An exception to this is the Grey Poupon mustard which has been licensed and is produced in the United States.)

HOT MUSTARD is usually an English or German condiment. These are great with roast beef, sausages or Chinese food. Easily made at home, by mixing ground mustard with enough water, gin, vodka, dry wine, beer or milk to make a smooth paste. Set aside for 1 hour before using and watch out!

SWEET MUSTARD is especially appealing to Americans. There are many kinds on the market today; they are great on ham, pork or chicken. You can make one easily yourself by mixing together 4 ounces ground mustard and 4 cups cider vinegar, letting them sit for 2 to 8 hours (the longer the better), then adding in 2 beaten eggs and one cup sugar and cooking in a double boiler, stirring frequently, until thick. Keep refrigerated between uses. Substitute sherry or red wine vinegar for variations.

PEPPERCORN MUSTARD, made with red or green peppercorns, is wonderful used in a vinaigrette or as a bond in beef and chicken sauces.

HERB MUSTARDS include tarragon, dill, basil, or multicolored mixtures of herbs, a natural combination with mustard. They often include a touch of garlic as well, and are delicious in vinaigrettes and on fruit and poultry.

FRUIT MUSTARDS can be made with orange, lemon, lime and tomato. Other possibilities might include raspberry and strawberry.

WINE MUSTARDS are flavored with sherry, red wine and Champagne. Taste and experiment; let your creativity wander.

CHAMPAGNE DRESSING

The best and most versatile dressing in our repertoire. There is hardly a salad that it will not enhance, and we also use it as an all-purpose dip for *crudités*. Make it with the best French or American Champagne vinegar you can find.

3 egg yolks
1 tablespoon prepared Dijon-style mustard
½ cup Champagne vinegar
salt and freshly ground black pepper, to taste
2 cups corn oil

1. Combine egg yolks, mustard and vinegar in the bowl of a food processor fitted with a steel blade and season to taste with salt and pepper. Process for 1 minute.
2. With the motor still running, dribble in the oil in a slow, steady stream.
3. When all the oil has been incorporated, shut off processor, scrape down sides of bowl, and taste. Correct seasoning if necessary (the dressing should be quite tart), and re-process to blend.
4. Transfer to storage container and refrigerate, covered, until ready to use.

About 3 cups

SHERRY VINAIGRETTE

1 tablespoon prepared Dijon-style mustard
¼ cup sherry wine vinegar
¼ teaspoon salt
freshly ground black pepper, to taste
1½ cups olive oil

1. Whisk the mustard and the sherry vinegar together in a small bowl.
2. Stir in the salt and black pepper to taste.
3. Whisking constantly, dribble the olive oil into the vinegar mixture in a slow, steady stream.
4. Taste, correct seasoning, and reserve, covered, until ready to use.

1¾ cup

WALNUT OIL VINAIGRETTE

2 tablespoons prepared Dijon-style mustard
3 tablespoons red wine vinegar
7 tablespoons walnut oil
½ tablespoon minced parsley
salt and freshly ground black pepper, to taste

Whisk together the mustard and vinegar. Gradually add the oil in a slow, steady stream. Whisk in parsley, and season to taste with salt and pepper.

¾ cup

BASIL-WALNUT VINAIGRETTE

This is a perfect summer vinaigrette — tart, slightly crunchy and full of fresh basil flavor. Try it on sliced, vine-ripened tomatoes; thinly sliced zucchini and chopped purple onion; or our favorite — a cool plateful of crisp-cooked garden-fresh green beans, garnished generously with walnut halves.

1 tablespoon prepared Dijon-style mustard
⅓ cup red wine vinegar
¾ cup coarsely chopped fresh basil leaves
salt and freshly ground black pepper, to taste
1 cup best-quality olive oil
½ cup shelled walnut pieces

1. Combine the mustard, vinegar and basil in the bowl of a food processor fitted with a steel blade, and season to taste with salt and pepper. Process for 1 minute, shut off motor, scrape down sides of bowl, and process for 30 seconds longer.

2. Leave the motor running and dribble in the oil in a slow, steady stream. When the oil is incorporated, drop the walnuts through the feed tube and shut machine off immediately. Check texture of walnuts, they should be chopped evenly and fairly finely, but should still be discernible in the dressing. Process with short bursts of power until you achieve the desired texture. Do not overprocess.

3. Cover and refrigerate until ready to use.

About 1½ cups

HOW TO DRESS A SALAD

Dressings are not to be feared although we hear from many cooking school instructors that this is an area in which otherwise good cooks lack confidence. There is no mystery. A development of your own personal taste will determine which combinations you prefer.

Never drown your salad! Place the dressing in the base of the bowl with layers of greens on top. Toss at the table before serving.

We no longer use the old rule of 2 parts oil to 1 part vinegar for all dressings of the vinaigrette type. With so many new tastes in oils and vinegars available we often use a mix of 4 to 1 to properly balance the flavors and acidity.

HERB VINEGARS

Herb vinegars are beautiful and useful in cooking and in salad-making. Pour good-quality white or red wine vinegar over a generous handful of fresh herbs in a jar and let stand, covered, for 2 weeks. To speed the process, heat the vinegar slightly first. Strain the vinegar or not, as you like. Particularly good are: tarragon in cider vinegar, green and red basil in red wine vinegar; dill flowers, chive blossoms, lemon peel, garlic, oregano, mint, rosemary or wild thyme in white wine vinegar. A great treat for giving and getting.

CHEESES
AND BREADS

BREADS and CHEESES SOLD

274

THE CHEESE BOARD

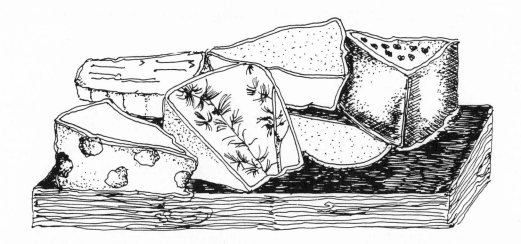

We love cheese (we think most people do) and from the hundreds of cheeses available today, we offer the following selection in our shop. We wish we had room for more.

FRESH CHEESES

Fresh cheeses are those which have not been aged. They are soft, white and creamy, many of them with an uncomplicated taste calling to mind milk or butter. Others may be pungent with herbs or garlic. Fresh cheeses are highly perishable and have only just begun to be imported in any variety. They are rushed here by air from the rural farmhouses where they are made with freshness still intact.

ROBBIOLA DEL BEK is a fresh Italian cow's-milk cheese with a mild raw-milk tang and a delicate, spreadable texture. Try it for breakfast with bagels and cherry jam; or stuff it into a crêpe, warm briefly, and drizzle with your favorite honey.

PETIT-SUISSE, French despite its name, is a sour, delectable fresh cheese. Sprinkle it with sugar and serve with freshly picked blackberries for the ultimate picnic dessert.

FLEUR DE MAQUIS, sometimes called *Brin d'Amour*, is a lusty Corsican farm cheese, made from sheep's milk and sprinkled with savory, rosemary, coriander, and juniper berries.

MASCARPONE is an Italian fresh cheese, ravishingly rich, bland and buttery. **GORGONZOLA DOLCE** is the younger, creamier but still pungent version of Italy's famed blue-veined cheese. In the exquisite **BASIL TORTA**, imported from Milan, the two are alternated with fresh basil for a cheese of such complexity and lightness we like to serve it alone, as a first course.

CHEDDAR CHEESES

What would life be like without Cheddar? Surely these are the most familiar and comfortable of cheeses, appropriate on any cheese board, indispensable for cooking, the quintessential snack, at home with fine wines or a frosty glass of milk.

Crumbly **CHESHIRE** is England's oldest cheese. It is tangy and salty due to the sea marshes where the cattle graze and makes a perfect partner to crunchy raw vegetables. It also melts magnificently; we always have some Cheshire on hand for late-night grilled cheese sandwiches.

Firm, sharp **VERMONT CHEDDAR**, made from raw milk and aged, is a great table cheese; serve it with pears, crackers and sweet butter. We like it as well in an omelet with sautéed apples or in a bracing Cheddar soup.

Not as sharp, but fuller flavored, is **NEW YORK STATE CHEDDAR**, also made from raw milk and aged as long as two years. Our favorite autumn lunch is a slice of this golden beauty, a chunk of Boston brown bread and an icy glass of new cider.

CHEVRES (GOAT CHEESES)

It is ironic that the "poor man's cow" produces some of the world's rarest and most sought-after cheeses. Since goats are temperamental and often withhold their milk, supplies of these tiny, often pungent cheeses are uneven. Until recently they were not much appreciated or exported. Currently undergoing a vogue in this country, goat cheeses are suddenly available in a staggering and mysterious variety. Chèvres range from soft, mild and fresh to hard, shrunken and very strong. Fresh or young goat cheeses have a distinctive sour flavor with a hot pepperlike sting. The hard, dark and shriveled goat cheeses one also finds are these same youngsters, transmuted by age into something altogether more powerful and, except to the true connoisseur, more difficult to appreciate.

BANON is French goat and sheep's- or cow's-milk cheese, dipped into brandy before being wrapped in chestnut leaves and tied with straw.

BOUCHERON is a large log-shaped French goat cheese with a snow-white, chalky texture and a characteristic goat flavor. It is a typical chèvre, and a good introduction for the hesitant beginner.

MONTRACHET is a fresh chèvre, taking its name from the celebrated white Burgundy produced in the same region of France. It is soft, moist and pure white, one of the best of the mild fresh chèvres.

The flat-topped **PYRAMIDE** is a classic shape for a variety of chèvres. This particular cheese is mild and typically goaty when young, increasingly hard and pungent as it ages. It is often rolled in wood ashes (remove before eating if you like, but ashes are harmless); it makes a visually interesting addition to a balanced cheese board.

Chèvres often strike Americans as bizarre. **SAINT-CHRISTOPHE** is such a cheese — a soft and flavorful log, constructed around a small stick for structural support.

CARRÉ D'ALZOU is unusual in that it is a soft-ripening chèvre, developing a soft gooey core, like a Brie, as it ages. Rare, and fabulous.

CAPRICORN is an amazing goat Cheddar coming to us from a small dairy in Iowa. It is a firm white block of cheese with a typical Cheddar texture and a tangy goat flavor with Cheddar undertones. A unique cheese; serve as part of a selection, or alone with a salad course.

BLUE-VEINED CHEESES

Among the blue-veined cheeses are three of the acknowledged great cheeses of the world — Roquefort, Stilton and Gorgonzola.

GORGONZOLA, Italy's famed blue cheese, actually has greenish veins in a golden curd. The sweet Gorgonzola is creamy and spreadable; the aged version, as much as a year old, is dry and crumbly. Both varieties are strong and rich, among the most pungent of the blue cheeses.

STILTON from England is often called the "King of Cheeses," and it is certainly among the top cheeses in the world. A semifirm blue-veined cheese made from milk and (at least in more generous times) cream, it is piquant and mellow, with an obvious Cheddar flavor.

ROQUEFORT from France is to many the best blue-veined cheese. Pliny the Elder, Charlemagne and Casanova have extolled its virtues. Unlike other blue-veined cheeses, Roquefort is made from unskimmed sheep's milk and aged in vast limestone caves. It is firm and creamy-white, and can be strong and salty (a condition necessary if it is to survive export), although brands vary widely.

PIPO CREM' is a delicate French blue-veined cheese with high butterfat and a soft creamy texture. Its mild taste makes it extremely popular, especially to anyone who does not want his blue to have the bite of a Roquefort or the pungency of a Gorgonzola.

BLEU DE BRESSE is one of the softest blue-veined cheeses, and one of the best. It is rich and mild and comes in a tiny 2-ounce size that is perfect for picnicking.

Serve Roquefort after dinner with your best Bordeaux or Cabernet Sauvignon. End a grand meal with Stilton, freshly shelled walnuts and vintage Port. Try the aged Gorgonzola with lots of sweet butter on crusty semolina bread; lavish the younger, softer version in a creamy pasta sauce. Fill a quiche with creamy Pipo Crem', and spread piquant Bleu de Bresse on a hot grilled steak.

FRENCH CHEESES

Soft-ripening **BRIE** is called the "Queen of Cheeses," and is considered by many to be the greatest cheese of all. It is a surface-ripened cheese of cow's milk with a downy white crust. A properly ripened Brie is luxurious, rich and running; it will delight almost every cheese lover.

LOU PERALOU is a new French sheep's-milk cheese, one we like a lot. Made in the Brie style, it is a fuzzy white hexagon; when properly ripened, it is the match for any Brie we have had. Not yet widely available, and usually expensive, but worth it.

FLEUR D'HERMITAGE is a full-flavored, soft-ripened table cheese from the Lorraine region of France. Like the other cheeses in this category, it is a disappointment when served underripe, which it often is. Find a responsible cheese dealer who ripens his cheeses and sells them at their prime, or invest in an entire cheese, and let it develop at home.

TRIPLE CREME CHEESES

Triple crème cheeses are the Marilyn Monroes of the cheese world — uncomplicated but voluptuous. They are astonishingly rich — 75 percent butterfat by weight — and what they lack in complex flavor they more than make up for in sheer lusciousness. Serve them before dessert, or as dessert, or just treat yourself when you're feeling a little blue. Distinctions between the triple crèmes are minor, indeed, but the three we sell the most of are **BRILLAT-SAVARIN, SAINT-ANDRÉ,** and **L'EXPLORATEUR** — all equally delicious, and widely available.

MOUNTAIN CHEESES

The monastery or mountain cheeses are a legacy from monks who had the time, patience and instinct for preserving knowledge. The results of their experiments comprise a group of similar cheeses that are soft and buttery with a pungency that comes from fullness rather than strength.

TOMME DE BEAUMONT is a French cheese from the Savoie. It has a yellow to pinkish orange rind and an ivory interior. It is earthy and can become pungent with age, although it seldom offends.

TOMME DE BREBIS, another cheese from the Savoie, is a tough-rinded sheep's-milk cheese with a firm and softly granular texture — mild, but with character. It is suitable as a table cheese but grateable as well; it makes an admirable substitute for Romano or Gruyère in a recipe where a less aggressive flavor is wanted.

DOUX DE MONTAGNE is from the Pyrenees — a semisoft, firm but tender cheese that is rich but mild, with tiny irregular holes inside a dark brown, waxy rind. It is pleasantly uncomplicated and useful in balancing cheese boards, and in lunch or brunch dishes.

VIRGINIA FARM GOUDA is a delightful symbol of American pioneer spirit. This firm but tender, full-flavored cheese is handmade, in the European tradition, from raw milk, and aged for at least 90 days.

"SWISS" CHEESES

There are three popular Swiss-type alternatives to Emmenthaler: one authentically from Switzerland, one Norwegian, and the third an American-made invention.

GRUYERE, next to Emmenthaler, is Switzerland's most respected cheese. It is firm and tender with small holes, and has a sweet and nutty taste. Splendid as a table cheese, it is also one of the world's great cooking cheeses.

JARLSBERG, from Norway, is a modern descendant of a traditional Norwegian cheese — or so they say. It is very pleasant, with a firm, slightly waxy texture and a sweet but subtle flavor. Good for cooking and for eating.

AG ALUMNI SWISS, now made commercially, originated as a project of agriculture students at Purdue University. It is developing a regional reputation as a sweetly nutty and mild "Swiss" cheese, and we find its tender, supple texture very pleasant. A fat round basketball-shaped cheese, Ag Alumni Swiss melts superbly and makes an appropriately all-American addition to a cheeseburger.

BRIE PINWHEEL

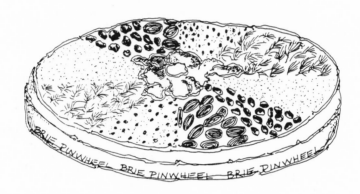

Here is a spectacular treatment when a simple wheel of Brie doesn't seem festive enough.

1 whole ripe Brie, about 5 pounds
1 cup dried currants
1 cup finely chopped walnuts
1 cup chopped fresh dill
½ cup poppy seeds
1 cup slivered blanched almonds

1. Carefully cut away the rind from the top of the Brie. Using the back of the knife, lightly mark the top of the Brie into 10 equal wedge-shaped areas.

2. Sprinkle half of the currants onto one of the wedge-shaped areas and press gently into the surface of the Brie. Repeat procedure with half of the walnuts, dill, poppy seeds and almonds, patting each garnish into a wedge-shaped area as you proceed around the top of the Brie. Use the remaining garnishes on the remaining wedges.

3. Wrap and refrigerate for no more than 4 hours. Allow to stand at room temperature for 30 minutes before serving.

At least 20 portions

AFTER THE
THEATER BUFFET

Blanched fresh asparagus

*Sesame Mayonnaise in a
hollowed purple cabbage*

———————

*Smoked salmon with Dill
Mustard Sauce*

Brie Wrapped in Phyllo

———————

*Garden salad of snow peas,
romaine lettuce, shelled
peas, asparagus tips and
watercress, with
Lemon Vinaigrette*

*Fresh herb butter
Assorted breads and
biscuits*

———————

Fresh strawberries

*Profiteroles
Vanilla ice cream
Hot fudge sauce and
whipped cream*

PORT

On the first crisp day of fall we inevitably know that we'll stop by the kitchen for a glass of Port, some Stilton, and crusty bread with sweet butter — our Autumn tradition.

Port is not as well known in America as it is in Europe, where it is known as an Englishman's drink. The French drink it too, and we wish more people would investigate the rich, heady taste of a good vintage Port.

Port is made by adding a bit of brandy to wine during the fermentation. This stops the process before all the natural sugar has been converted into alcohol. The result is a fruity, slightly sweet wine, with the additional alcoholic boost of the brandy. Vintage Ports lose this sweetness as they age and become drier.

The British make a ritual of after-dinner Port. The host must always pass the decanter to his left, and even today women are often excluded from the company while the men linger over Port and cigars.

Because Port is too often thought of as a dessert wine, many hesitate to serve it. We urge you to taste, experiment and come to your own conclusions. This is an enjoyment that you may have been missing.

We are often asked if the crust of Brie cheese is edible. It is, but remove it after serving if you wish; many do.

BRIE SOUFFLE

A most luxurious brunch dish, served with Champagne and fresh fruit.

8 tablespoons sweet butter, at room temperature
6 slices of good-quality white sandwich bread, crusts removed
1½ cups milk
1 teaspoon salt
dash of Tabasco
3 eggs
1 pound slightly underripe Brie, rind removed

1. Preheat oven to 350°F. Butter a 1½-quart soufflé dish.
2. Butter one side of bread slices and cut each slice into thirds. Whisk together milk, salt, Tabasco and eggs. Coarsely grate the Brie.
3. Arrange half of the bread, buttered side up, on the bottom of the dish. Sprinkle evenly with half of the Brie and then repeat, using remaining bread and Brie. Carefully pour the egg mixture over the bread. Let stand at room temperature for 30 minutes.
4. Bake for 25 to 30 minutes, or until bubbling and golden.
4 to 6 portions

BRIE WRAPPED IN PHYLLO

12 sheets of phyllo pastry (see Working with Phyllo, page 11)
1 pound sweet butter (4 sticks), melted
1 whole Brie, not fully ripe, about 5 pounds

1. Butter a baking sheet large enough to hold the Brie.
2. Lay 5 sheets of phyllo on the baking sheet, brushing melted butter on each layer. Set Brie on top of the phyllo and fold the edges of the phyllo up around the cheese.
3. Cover top of cheese with 6 sheets of phyllo, brushing melted butter on each layer. Tuck ends of pastry under the cheese. Brush top and sides with butter. Preheat oven to 350°F.

4. Fold last sheet of phyllo in a 1-inch-wide strip. Brush it with butter and form a flower shape. Center the flower on top of the Brie and again brush with butter.

5. Bake for 20 to 30 minutes, or until golden brown. Let stand for at least 30 minutes before serving.

20 portions

BAKED BANON

Icy cold salad greens and hot and tangy goat cheese combined on the same plate are a perfect ending to a rustic French meal.

6 tablespoons sweet butter
6 Banon cheeses, leaves removed, or 6 slices, 2 inches thick,
   of Montrachet, about ¾ pound
½ cup mixed dried peppercorns (equal amounts, more or less,
   of black, white, and green)

1. Preheat oven to 350°F.

2. Butter a baking sheet with 3 tablespoons of the butter and arrange the Banons on the sheet.

3. Crush the peppercorns with a rolling pin, or load them into a peppermill, and sprinkle or grind the mixture onto the Banons to taste. Top each cheese with ½ tablespoon butter.

4. Bake the cheeses for 10 to 12 minutes, or until heated through. Serve immediately.

6 portions

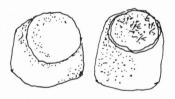

"Cheese: Milk's leap towards immortality."
— **Clifton Fadiman**

MARINATED CHEVRES

1 cup best-quality olive oil
2 bay leaves
6 black peppercorns, slightly crushed
1 tablespoon thyme
4 Crottin or other small hard goat cheeses
1 cup coarsely chopped fresh basil leaves
4 garlic cloves, peeled and halved

1. Combine olive oil, bay leaves, peppercorns and thyme in a small heavy saucepan. Set over moderate heat and cook, stirring occasionally until oil is very hot, about 5 minutes.

2. Arrange cheeses in a single layer in a small heatproof bowl or pan. Sprinkle the chopped basil and garlic over the cheeses and then pour the hot oil and seasonings over them.

3. Let cheeses cool to room temperature, cover, and refrigerate for at least 4 hours before serving. (Cheeses can be stored in their oil marinade for up to 1 week, if kept refrigerated.)

4. To serve, arrange the cheeses on lettuce leaves on individual plates and drizzle with a few spoonfuls of marinade. Or broil the cheeses, basting with marinade, until brown and bubbling.

4 portions

BEST BREADS

The wonderful smell of baking bread cannot be adequately described. When you're driving past a bakery, the aroma can make you think of all the meaningful things in life, and if you're walking past your own kitchen and catch a whiff, you're thankful that you'll be the first to enjoy the warm bread when it is fresh from the oven.

When we travel the U.S. we often hear that "there are no really good bakeries in our town." All we can offer to that complaint is to be patient; good bread is becoming more and more available, following the trend of other recent food phenomena. In the meantime, freshly baked bread is a pleasure well worth the effort involved in making your own.

410

RAISIN PUMPERNICKEL

This uniquely New York bread, reputedly invented in a venerable Manhattan bakery, is now widely copied and available throughout the city. "Black Russian," as it is called, is delicious and more versatile than you might imagine. Try it with a ripe piece of Brie, turn it into a tuna sandwich, or transform it into fabulous French toast. We offer this recipe for those who have never tasted "raisin pump" and for those transplanted New Yorkers who have despaired of ever tasting it again.

1½ cups lukewarm water (105° to 115°F.)
½ cup molasses
1 package active dry yeast
1 tablespoon instant coffee granules
1 tablespoon salt
2 cups medium rye flour
1½ tablespoons unsweetened powdered cocoa
2 cups whole-wheat flour
2 cups bread flour or unbleached, all-purpose flour
2 tablespoons vegetable oil
1 cup raisins
3 to 4 tablespoons cornmeal
1 tablespoon cold water
1 egg white

1. Stir together the lukewarm water and molasses in a large mixing bowl. Sprinkle in the yeast and stir to dissolve. Let stand for 10 minutes, or until slightly foamy.

2. Stir in instant coffee, salt and rye flour. Sprinkle in the cocoa and stir well to combine. Add whole-wheat flour and 1 cup of the bread flour, or enough to make a sticky dough.

3. Turn the bread out onto a lightly floured work surface and let it rest. Wash and dry the bowl.

4. Sprinkle additional flour over the dough and begin to knead. Continue until most or all of the remaining bread flour is incorporated and you have a smooth elastic ball. (Breads with rye flour will always be slightly sticky.)

5. Pour the vegetable oil into the mixing bowl, turn the ball of dough to coat well, cover bowl with a towel, and set aside to rise until dough is tripled in bulk, 3 to 4 hours.

6. Lightly flour the work surface and turn the dough out onto it. Flatten it into a large rectangle and sprinkle with the raisins. Roll up the dough and knead it, to distribute the raisins evenly, for about 5 minutes. Return dough to the bowl, cover, and let rise until doubled.

7. Sprinkle a large baking sheet with 3 to 4 tablespoons cornmeal. Turn the dough out, cut it into 3 pieces, and shape each piece into a small round loaf. Set loaves on the baking sheet, leaving as much room as possible between them, cover, and let rise until doubled.

8. Preheat oven to 375°F.

9. Beat egg white together with 1 tablespoon cold water in a small bowl. When the loaves have risen sufficiently, brush the tops with the egg-white mixture.

10. Bake loaves on the middle rack of the oven for 25 to 35 minutes, or until they are dark brown and sound hollow when bottoms are rapped. Cool completely on racks before cutting or wrapping.

3 loaves

"Without bread, without wine, love is nothing."

— French proverb

White flour was used only in baking for nobility until the last two centuries; isn't it ironic how much we now prefer the dark?

For our shop we buy the best breads we can find from the many excellent bakeries in New York. Most of them are family-run and still use the techniques and equipment the founders brought with them from Europe.

Several varieties are unique to Manhattan, and we offer our versions of these breads, allowing you to re-create the New York bread experience wherever you live.

PATIO PICNIC MENU

Chicken Marbella

Cracked Wheat Salad

Brie cheese
Semolina Bread

Lemon Mousse

Fresh strawberries

SEMOLINA BREAD

Because of its high gluten content and golden color, this makes a spectacular loaf that, while delicious any way you serve it, seems best when dunked into the tomato sauce at the end of an Italian meal. Semolina (or durum or hard winter wheat flour) is available in health-food stores and Italian groceries, and at least one brand is actually labeled pasta flour.

We have found that while a 100-percent semolina loaf is too heavy, a mixture of half semolina and half bread flour (or unbleached all-purpose flour) perfectly duplicates the crisp, light and flavorful loaves available in Manhattan. Since this bread always seems to come sprinkled with sesame seeds we have included them in the recipe, but you can substitute poppy or other seeds, or eliminate them altogether.

2 cups lukewarm water (105° to 115°F.)
1 package active dry yeast
3 cups semolina flour
1 tablespoon salt
2 to 3 cups bread flour or unbleached, all-purpose flour
2 tablespoons olive oil
3 to 4 tablespoons cornmeal
1 egg
sesame seeds (optional)

1. Pour the water into a mixing bowl, stir in the yeast, and let stand for 10 minutes. Stir again to be certain all the yeast is dissolved.

2. Add semolina flour and salt and stir well.

3. Add 2 cups of the bread flour and stir to make a sticky dough. Turn dough out onto a work surface and let rest while you wash and dry the bowl.

4. Begin kneading the dough, sprinkling it with the remaining cup of bread flour as necessary to keep it from sticking to your hands. After about 10 minutes the dough will be smooth and elastic and will have absorbed more or less the last cup of flour.

5. Shape dough into a ball and place it in the bowl. Pour the olive oil over the dough and turn it several times to coat with the oil. Cover bowl with a towel and set aside until dough has tripled in bulk. (The

increase in volume is more important than the time it takes; depending on room temperatures this may be 2 or more hours. Do not try to force the dough to rise more rapidly by setting it on radiators, etc. This can sour the bread. Patience is a virtue.)

6. Punch down the dough, turn it out onto a lightly floured work surface, knead briefly (5 minutes or less), and return it to the bowl. Cover and let rise again until doubled.

7. Punch down the dough, cut it into thirds, and shape each third into a thin loaf about 24 inches long. Sprinkle a baking sheet with 3 to 4 tablespoons cornmeal and arrange the loaves on the sheet, leaving as much room between loaves as possible. Cover and let rise until not quite doubled, about 30 minutes.

8. Preheat oven to 425°F.

9. Beat together the egg and 1 tablespoon water. When the loaves have risen, brush them well with this egg wash. Sprinkle sesame seeds to taste, and slash loaves decoratively on top with a sharp knife, making diagonal cuts.

10. Slide the baking sheet onto the middle rack of the oven and reduce heat to 375°F. Bake for 30 to 40 minutes, or until loaves are brown and sound hollow when the bottoms are thumped. (For a crisper bottom crust, remove loaves from the baking sheet and place them directly on the oven rack for the last 5 to 10 minutes of baking time.)

11. Remove loaves from oven and cool on a rack. Wrap when cool.

3 loaves, about 18 inches long

"Bread deals with living things, with giving life, with growth, with the seed, the grain that nurtures. It is not coincidence that we say bread is the staff of life."

— Lionel Poilâne

BRIOCHE

This recipe is slightly less complex than the traditional French brioche method, but it produces a rich, firm and buttery bread that is completely satisfying. It can be baked in regular loaf pans, yielding a spectacular sandwich and toasting bread. It is perfect for enclosing roasts and other meat to be baked *en brioche*, and of course you can form it into the traditional round brioche shape, delicious served warm from the oven with butter and preserves.

2 cups milk
½ pound (2 sticks) sweet butter
¼ cup granulated sugar
2 packages active dry yeast
4 teaspoons salt
3 eggs, at room temperature
8 cups unbleached, all-purpose flour
2 to 3 tablespoons vegetable oil

1. Combine milk, butter and sugar in a medium-size saucepan and bring to a boil. Remove from heat and pour into a large mixing bowl. Cool to lukewarm (105° to 115°F.).

2. Stir in the yeast and let stand for 10 minutes. Stir in the salt. Beat the eggs thoroughly in a small bowl and add to the milk mixture. Stir in 7 cups of the flour, 1 cup at a time, until you achieve a sticky dough. Flour a work surface and turn the dough out onto it. Wash and dry the bowl.

3. Sprinkle additional flour over the dough and begin to knead it, adding more flour as necessary until you achieve a smooth, elastic dough, about 10 minutes.

4. Pour 2 to 3 tablespoons vegetable oil into the bowl. Turn the ball of dough in the oil to coat well. Set dough aside, covered with a towel, to rise until tripled in bulk, about 2 hours.

5. Punch the dough down, turn out onto a lightly floured work surface, and knead for about 2 minutes. Return dough to the bowl, cover, and let rise again until doubled.

6. Preheat oven to 375°F.

7. Dough is now ready to be formed. If you are baking it in loaf

pans, use 2 pans 9 x 5 x 3 inches, lightly buttered. For traditional brioche, use muffin tins or imported brioche molds, available in varying sizes from cookware shops. If you are enclosing a roast or other food in brioche, proceed according to that recipe. Let formed loaves rise until nearly doubled.

8. Bake for 30 to 40 minutes (slightly less for small brioches) or until golden brown. Loaves will sound hollow when thumped on the bottom. Cool slightly before unmolding; cool completely before wrapping.

2 loaves, or about 2 dozen 3-inch brioches

BREAD FLOUR

Major millers are now marketing a flour especially formulated to duplicate professional bakers' flour. While not always available in all markets, this bread flour is worth seeking out. It makes bread with superior flavor and texture. If you do not find it in your supermarket, ask the manager to begin stocking it.

Challah represents the ceremonial show bread that was placed on the table by the priest in the ancient Temple of Jerusalem. There were twelve such breads, each representing one of the Israelite tribes. Challah was always braided to invest it with special beauty. Each family traditionally places two Challahs on the table for the Sabbath meal, representing double portions of manna from heaven that fell on the sixth day so that the Israelites would not have to collect manna on the seventh day, the day of rest.

CHALLAH

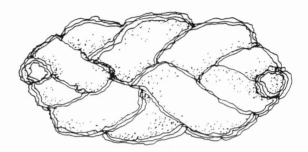

This splendid loaf makes wonderful eating straight from the oven and spread with butter and honey. We love French toast made with it. If any of this bread manages to last long enough to become stale, it makes excellent bread crumbs.

2 cups milk
8 tablespoons (1 stick) sweet butter
⅓ cup granulated sugar
2 packages active dry yeast
4 eggs, at room temperature
2 teaspoons salt
6 cups unbleached, all-purpose flour
⅓ cup cornmeal
1 tablespoon cold water
poppy seeds

1. Bring milk, 6 tablespoons of the butter, and the sugar to a boil together in a medium-size saucepan. Remove from heat, pour into a large mixing bowl, and let cool to lukewarm (105° to 115°F.).

2. Stir yeast into the milk mixture and let stand for 10 minutes.

3. Beat 3 of the eggs well in a small bowl, and stir them and the salt into the milk-and-yeast mixture.

4. Stir in 5 cups of the flour, 1 cup at a time, until you achieve a sticky dough. Flour a work surface lightly and turn the dough out onto it. Wash and dry the bowl.

5. Sprinkle additional flour over the dough and begin kneading, adding more flour as necessary, until you have a smooth elastic dough.

6. Smear the reserved 2 tablespoons butter around the inside of the bowl and add the ball of dough into the bowl, turning to coat it lightly with butter. Cover bowl with a towel and set aside to let dough rise until tripled in bulk, 1½ to 2 hours.

7. Turn dough out onto a lightly floured work surface and cut into halves. Cut each half into 3 pieces. Roll the pieces out into long "snakes" about 18 inches long. Braid three of the snakes together into a loaf and tuck the ends under. Repeat with remaining snakes.

8. Sprinkle a large baking sheet with the cornmeal, and transfer the loaves to the sheet. Leave room between the loaves for them to rise. Cover loaves with the towel and let rise until nearly doubled, about 1 hour.

9. Preheat oven to 350°F.

10. Beat the remaining egg and 1 tablespoon cold water together well in a small bowl. Brush this egg wash evenly over the loaves. Sprinkle immediately with poppy seeds to taste.

11. Set baking sheet on the middle rack of the oven. Bake for 30 to 35 minutes, or until loaves are golden brown and sound hollow when their bottoms are thumped. Cool completely on racks before wrapping.

2 large loaves

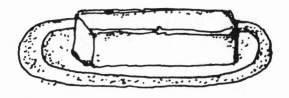

"I do like a little bit of butter to my bread."
— *When We Were Very Young,*
A. A. Milne

GRANDMA CLARK'S SODA BREAD

An authentic gift from the Irish, baked in and served hot from the skillet.

6 tablespoons sweet butter
3 cups unbleached all-purpose flour
1½ teaspoons salt
1 tablespoon baking powder
1 teaspoon baking soda
¾ cup granulated sugar
1½ cups dried currants
1¾ cups buttermilk
2 eggs, well beaten
1 tablespoon caraway seeds (optional)

1. Smear 2 tablespoons of the butter evenly in a 10-inch cast-iron skillet. Line the buttered skillet with a circle of waxed paper. Melt 2 more tablespoons butter in a separate pan and set aside.
2. Preheat oven to 350°F.
3. Sift dry ingredients together. Add currants to dry ingredients and toss well to coat.
4. Whisk together buttermilk, eggs and melted butter. Add to the dry ingredients, along with the caraway seeds if desired, and mix just until blended. Do not overmix.
5. Spoon batter into the prepared skillet and smooth top gently with a spatula. Dot the top with remaining 2 tablespoons butter.
6. Bake until golden brown and puffed, about 60 minutes. Cool slightly, remove from skillet, and cool completely on a rack. Or serve warm directly from the skillet. Cut into wedges.
1 loaf, 6 portions

SILVER PALATE
GENESIS BRUNCH

Champagne

Figs and Prosciutto

Raspberry Mousse

Blackberry Mousse

Lemon Mousse

---

*Croissants with
Strawberry Butter*

---

*Fresh oysters with
Shallot Sauce*

---

*Grandma Clark's Soda
Bread with sweet butter*

Assorted cheeses

Cappuccino

CRACKLING CORNBREAD

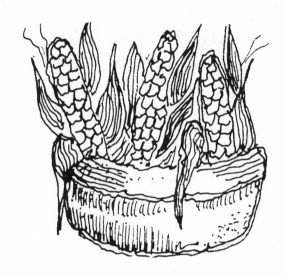

Southern-style goodness. Serve warm with lots of butter and honey.

1 cup stone-ground cornmeal
1 cup unbleached all-purpose flour
⅓ cup granulated sugar
2½ teaspoons baking powder
¼ teaspoon salt
1 cup buttermilk
1 cup diced, crisp-cooked bacon
6 tablespoons sweet butter, melted
1 egg, slightly beaten

1. Preheat oven to 400°F. Grease a 9-inch-square baking pan.
2. Stir dry ingredients together in a bowl. Then stir in buttermilk, bacon, butter and egg and mix gently.
3. Pour batter into the prepared pan, set on the middle rack of the oven, and bake for 25 minutes. Cornbread is done when edges are lightly browned and a knife inserted in the center comes out clean. Cut into 3-inch squares to serve.

9 squares

Variation: Spoon batter into 10 greased muffin cups and bake for about 20 minutes.

BANANA BREAD

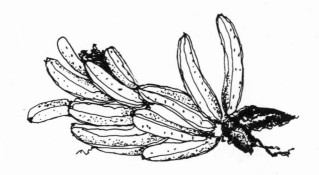

8 tablespoons (1 stick) sweet butter, at room temperature
¾ cup granulated sugar
2 eggs
1 cup unbleached, all-purpose flour
1 teaspoon baking soda
½ teaspoon salt
1 cup whole-wheat flour
3 large, ripe bananas, mashed
1 teaspoon vanilla extract
½ cup shelled walnuts, coarsely chopped

1. Preheat oven to 350°F. Grease a 9 x 5 x 3 inch bread pan.
2. Cream butter and sugar until light and fluffy. Add eggs, one at a time, beating well after each addition.
3. Sift all-purpose flour, baking soda and salt together, stir in whole-wheat flour and add to creamed mixture, mixing well.
4. Fold in mashed bananas, vanilla and walnuts.
5. Pour mixture into the prepared pan. Bake for 50 to 60 minutes, or until a cake tester inserted in the center comes out clean. Cool in pan for 10 minutes, then on rack.

1 loaf

"And the best bread was of my mother's own making — the best in all the land!"

— *Old Memories,* Sir Henry James

423

DATE-NUT BREAD

4 tablespoons sweet butter, cut into 6 chunks
1 cup pitted dates, coarsely chopped
¼ cup brown sugar
¼ cup granulated sugar
¾ cup boiling water
1 egg, beaten
2 cups unbleached, all-purpose flour, sifted
2 teaspoons baking powder
½ teaspoon salt
½ cup shelled black walnuts, coarsely chopped
½ teaspoon vanilla extract
1½ tablespoons rum

1. Preheat oven to 350°F. Grease a 9 x 5 x 3 inch bread pan.
2. Place butter in a large mixing bowl, place dates on top, and pour both sugars over. Pour boiling water over ingredients in the bowl. Let sit for 7 minutes. Stir well.
3. When mixture is cool, add the egg and mix well.
4. Sift flour, baking powder and salt together. Add to date mixture, beating for 30 seconds. Stir in walnuts, vanilla and rum.
5. Pour mixture into prepared pan. Bake for 45 to 50 minutes.
1 loaf

FRUIT BUTTERS

Fruit butters are an especially delicious way to sweeten tea breads. We like Orange Butter on Orange, Banana or Apricot-Raisin Breads. Strawberry Butter is a wonderful addition to Orange Bread, croissants, brioches or crisp waffles. Cream the ingredients together, transfer to a small crock and chill. The butters keep several days in the refrigerator or many weeks in the freezer. Let the butter return to room temperature before serving. Even morning toast seems like a treat with a pat of fruit butter melting on it.

♥ **ORANGE BUTTER:** 8 tablespoons (1 stick) sweet

butter, ⅓ cup orange marmalade, ½ teaspoon confectioners' sugar, grated zest of 1 orange.

♥ **STRAWBERRY BUTTER:** 8 tablespoons (1 stick) sweet butter, ⅓ cup strawberry jam, ½ teaspoon fresh lemon juice and ½ teaspoon confectioners' sugar.

ORANGE PECAN BREAD

8 tablespoons (1 stick) sweet butter, softened
¾ cup granulated sugar
2 eggs, separated
grated rind of 1 large or 2 small oranges
1½ cups unbleached all-purpose flour
1½ teaspoons baking powder
¼ teaspoon baking soda
pinch of salt
½ cup fresh orange juice
1 cup shelled pecans, chopped
Orange Glaze (see page 503)

1. Preheat oven to 350°F. Grease an 8½ x 4½ inch loaf pan.

2. Cream the butter. Add ¾ cup sugar gradually, beating with an electric mixer until light. Beat in the egg yolks, one at a time, and the grated orange rind.

3. Sift the flour with baking powder, baking soda and salt, and add dry mixture to the batter alternately with ½ cup orange juice, beginning and ending with flour. Gently mix in the pecans.

4. Beat the egg whites until stiff and fold them carefully into the batter.

5. Pour batter into the prepared loaf pan, set on the middle rack of the oven, and bake for 50 to 60 minutes.

6. Meanwhile, make the glaze. Spoon the hot syrup over the bread as soon as the bread is removed from the oven. Cool in the pan on a wire rack.

1 loaf

ZUCCHINI BREAD

For best flavor, wrap the breads when cool and let stand overnight before serving. With its sugar, spices and nuts, this is a tea bread, almost cakelike.

1 tablespoon sweet butter
3 eggs
1¼ cups oil
1½ cups granulated sugar
1 teaspoon vanilla extract
2 cups grated unpeeled raw zucchini
2 cups unbleached, all-purpose flour
2 teaspoons baking soda
1 teaspoon baking powder
1 teaspoon salt
1 teaspoon ground cinnamon
1 teaspoon ground cloves
1 cup shelled walnuts, chopped

1. Preheat oven to 350°F. Butter a 9 x 5 loaf pan.
2. Beat eggs, oil, sugar and vanilla until light and thick. Fold grated zucchini into oil mixture.
3. Sift dry ingredients together. Stir into zucchini mixture until just blended. Fold in the walnuts.
4. Pour batter into the buttered loaf pan. Bake on the middle rack of the oven for 1 hour and 15 minutes, or until a cake tester inserted in the center comes out clean.
5. Cool slightly, remove from pan, and cool completely on a rack.
1 loaf

"Sweet" loaves can be enjoyed at teatime or as a snack or simple dessert.

CRANBERRY BREAD

This bread is especially good toasted and buttered.

2 cups unbleached all-purpose flour
½ cup granulated sugar
1 tablespoon baking powder
½ teaspoon salt
⅔ cup fresh orange juice
2 eggs, beaten slightly
3 tablespoons sweet butter, melted
½ cup shelled walnuts, coarsely chopped
1¼ cups cranberries
2 teaspoons grated orange rind

1. Preheat oven to 350°F. Grease an 8 x 4½ x 3 inch bread pan.
2. Sift flour, sugar, baking powder and salt into a mixing bowl.
3. Make a well in the middle of the sifted mixture and pour in orange juice, eggs and melted butter. Mix well without overmixing. Fold in walnuts, cranberries and orange rind.
4. Pour batter into the prepared pan and set on the middle rack of the oven. Bake for 45 to 50 minutes, or until a knife inserted in the center comes out clean.
5. Remove bread from the oven and cool in the pan for 10 minutes. After 10 minutes, remove bread from pan and allow to cool completely on rack. Wrap and put away for 1 to 2 days before serving.

1 loaf

" 'Take some more tea,' the March Hare said to Alice very earnestly.

'I've had nothing yet,' Alice replied in an offended tone, 'so I can't take more.'

'You mean you can't take less,' said the Hatter, 'it's very easy to take more than nothing.' "

— *Alice in Wonderland*, Lewis Carroll

APRICOT-RAISIN BREAD

1 cup boiling water, approximately
¾ cup coarsely chopped dried apricots
½ cup raisins
3 tablespoons plus ½ cup granulated sugar
⅓ cup oil
2 eggs, beaten
2¼ cups unbleached, all-purpose flour
1 tablespoon baking powder
½ teaspoon salt
⅔ cup milk
¾ cup unprocessed bran

raisins

1. Preheat oven to 350°F. Grease a 9 x 5 x 3 inch bread pan.

2. Pour boiling water over apricots and raisins just to cover. Let sit for 10 minutes. Drain well and add 3 tablespoons sugar. Mix well.

3. While fruit is soaking, add the remaining ½ cup sugar to the oil and beat well. Add eggs, one at a time, beating until well mixed.

4. Sift flour, baking powder and salt together and add alternately with milk and bran to oil mixture. Fold in fruits.

5. Pour mixture into prepared pan. Bake for 1 hour, or until a cake tester inserted in the center comes out clean.

6. Remove from oven and cool for 10 minutes. Remove from pan and cool on a cake rack.

1 loaf

LEMON BLACK-WALNUT BREAD

Our favorite loaf for tea; serve with lots of sweet butter.

½ pound (2 sticks) sweet butter
1½ cups granulated sugar
4 eggs, separated
⅔ cup lemon juice
2 tablespoons grated lemon rind
3 cups cake flour
4 teaspoons baking powder
1 cup milk
pinch of salt
1 cup shelled black walnuts, chopped
¼ cup water

1. Preheat oven to 350°F. Butter 2 loaf pans 9 x 5 x 3 inches with 3 tablespoons of the butter.

2. In a mixing bowl cream together remaining butter and 1 cup of the sugar. Beat in the egg yolks, one at a time, then stir in ⅓ cup of the lemon juice, and the grated lemon rind.

3. Combine cake flour with baking powder. Add one third of the flour mixture to the creamed butter and sugar. Then add half of the milk, another third of the flour, remaining milk and remaining flour. Do not overmix.

4. In another bowl beat the egg whites and pinch of salt together until stiff but not dry. Fold beaten egg whites and black walnuts gently into the batter.

5. Pour batter into the prepared pans. Bake on the middle rack of the oven for 45 to 50 minutes, or until a cake tester inserted in the center of a loaf comes out clean.

6. Cool bread slightly, remove from pans, and cool completely on a rack.

7. Boil the remaining ⅓ cup of the lemon juice, water and the remaining ½ cup sugar together in a small saucepan for 2 minutes.

8. Drizzle the lemon syrup over the tops of the cooled loaves and let them set until completely cool before wrapping.

2 loaves

BLACK WALNUTS

Different species of black walnuts are found throughout the U.S. The tree or shrub has dark brown furrowed bark and wide-spreading leaves. It grows fifteen to thirty-five feet in height, with leaves that alternate tapered points and serrated edges. The nut is round, thick-shelled and found inside a greenish-brown husk. It is indeed "a hard nut to crack."

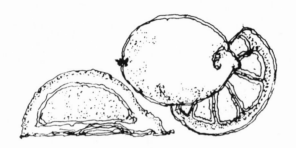

SWEETS

THE COOKIE BASKET

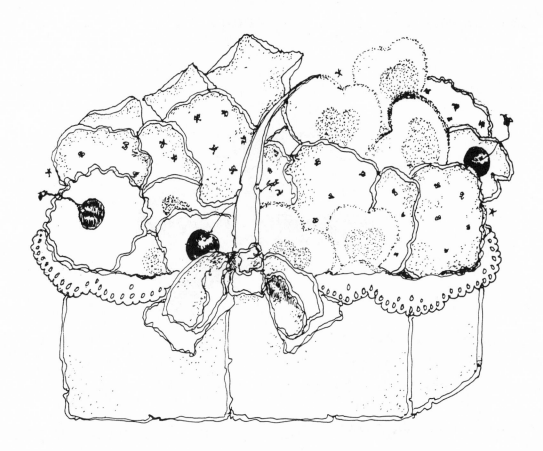

Everyone has a special fondness for cookies, whatever the time of day or occasion. Our philosophy is, the more the merrier, and our Cookie Basket is one of our most popular gift and holiday items. A ribbon-trimmed basket, filled with all kinds of cookies, is a happy invitation for anyone to partake. On a buffet table, at an office party, or just on the sideboard when guests come to call, it's the nicest way we know to present a gift of cookies.

If you are making a batch of different kinds of cookies for a Cookie Basket, remember that the best visual effect is achieved by clustering the same kinds of cookies together. This gives the basket a sense of movement, and a nonconfusing texture. But you don't have to wait to make all of these cookies at once — any one of the following recipes by itself will satisfy even the most discerning sweet tooth and bring smiles all around.

PECAN SQUARES

These are like tiny pecan pies — chewy, gooey and thick with pecans. Try them slightly warmed as an accompaniment to good ice cream.

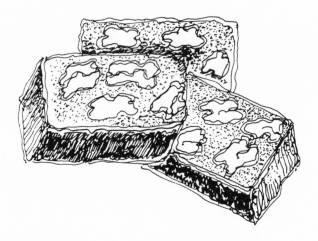

CRUST:

⅔ cup confectioners' sugar
2 cups unbleached all-purpose flour
½ pound (2 sticks) sweet butter, softened

1. Preheat oven to 350°F. Grease a 9 x 12 inch baking pan.
2. Sift sugar and flour together. Cut in butter, using two knives or a pastry blender, until fine crumbs form. Pat crust into the prepared baking pan. Bake for 20 minutes; remove from oven.

TOPPING:

⅔ cup (approximately 11 tablespoons) melted sweet butter
½ cup honey
3 tablespoons heavy cream
½ cup brown sugar
3½ cups shelled pecans, coarsely chopped

1. Mix melted butter, honey, cream and brown sugar together. Stir in pecans, coating them thoroughly. Spread over crust.
2. Return to oven and bake for 25 minutes more. Cool completely before cutting into squares.

36 squares

COCONUT MACAROONS

⅓ cup unbleached all-purpose flour
2½ cups shredded coconut
⅛ teaspoon salt
⅔ cup sweetened condensed milk
1 teaspoon vanilla extract

1. Preheat oven to 350°F. Grease a cookie sheet well.
2. Mix flour, coconut and salt together in a bowl. Pour in condensed milk and vanilla and stir well to make a thick batter.
3. Drop batter by quarter-cupfuls onto the well-greased cookie sheet, allowing an inch of space between cookies. Bake for 20 minutes, or until golden brown. Remove from pan at once, and cool on racks.

About 1½ dozen macaroons

"*Epicure:* One who gets nothing better than the cream of everything, but cheerfully makes the best of it."
— Oliver Hereford

TOFFEE BARS

Light, crisp, and chocolaty.

½ pound (2 sticks) sweet butter
1 cup light brown sugar
1 egg yolk
2 cups unbleached all-purpose flour
1 teaspoon vanilla extract
12 ounces semisweet chocolate chips
1 cup shelled walnuts or pecans, coarsely chopped

1. Preheat oven to 350°F. Grease a 9 x 12 inch baking pan.
2. Cream butter and sugar. Add egg yolk; beat well.

3. Sift in flour, mixing well, then stir in vanilla. Spread butter in the prepared pan. Bake for 25 minutes.

4. Cover cake layer with chocolate chips and return to oven for 3 to 4 minutes.

5. Remove pan from oven and spread melted chocolate evenly. Sprinkle with nuts. Cool completely in pan before cutting.

About 30 bars

ACADEMY AWARD BUFFET

Brie in Phyllo Triangles

Caviar Eclairs

Salmon Mousse with toasts

Carpaccio with Anchovy Mayonnaise

Chicken Liver Pâté with Green Peppercorns

Champagne

A Cookie Basket

BUTTERBALLS

While there are many versions of this cookie, this one has long been a Rosso Christmas tradition and is the best we know.

8 tablespoons (1 stick) sweet butter, softened
3 tablespoons honey
1 cup unbleached all-purpose flour
½ teaspoon salt
1 tablespoon vanilla extract
1 cup shelled pecans, chopped moderately fine
¾ cup confectioners' sugar

1. Preheat oven to 300°F. Grease one or two cookie sheets.
2. Cream butter. Beat in honey; gradually mix in flour and salt, then vanilla. Add pecans. Wrap dough in plastic wrap and chill for 1 hour.
3. Form balls by hand, the size of quarters. Place 2 inches apart on the prepared cookie sheets. Bake for 35 to 40 minutes.
4. Remove from oven; as soon as cool enough to touch, roll in confectioners' sugar. Allow to cool and roll again in sugar.

About 36 cookies

"You have to eat oatmeal or you'll dry up. Anybody knows that."

— *Eloise*, **Kay Thompson**

OATMEAL RAISIN COOKIES

Use the Giant Cookie method for these crisp cookies.

12 tablespoons (1½ sticks) sweet butter
½ cup granulated sugar
1 cup brown sugar
1 egg
2 tablespoons water
1 teaspoon vanilla extract
⅔ cup unbleached all-purpose flour
1 teaspoon ground cinnamon
½ teaspoon salt
½ teaspoon baking soda
3 cups quick-cooking oats
1 cup raisins

1. Preheat oven to 350°F. Grease two cookie sheets.
2. Cream butter and both sugars until fluffy. Add egg and beat thoroughly. Mix in water and vanilla.
3. Sift together flour, cinnamon, salt and baking soda; add to the egg mixture and mix well. Add oats and raisins, and mix.
4. Form cookies on prepared cookie sheets, following the method for giant cookies (see page 443). Bake for 15 to 17 minutes, until edges are done but centers are still soft. Remove to a rack and cool.

25 to 30 large cookies

BLACK WALNUT COOKIES

A butter cookie with a special difference; we think you'll agree that the black walnuts are worth their price.

¾ *pound (3 sticks) sweet butter, softened*
⅔ *cup granulated sugar*
3 eggs
3 cups unbleached all-purpose flour
¼ *teaspoon salt*
½ *teaspoon vanilla extract*
⅔ *cup shelled black walnuts, finely chopped*

1. Cream butter and sugar until light and fluffy. Mix in eggs, one at a time, beating well after each addition; add vanilla.

2. Sift flour with salt and add to creamed mixture. Mix well.

3. Wrap dough in wax paper and refrigerate for 4 to 6 hours. When thoroughly chilled, roll out to ⅜-inch thickness, and cut with a 1-inch-diameter cookie cutter. Place 1½ inches apart on ungreased cookie sheets. Sprinkle cookies with black walnuts and chill again for 45 minutes.

4. Preheat oven to 325°F.

5. Bake for 15 minutes, or until cookies are evenly and lightly browned. Remove from sheets and cool on a rack.

5 dozen cookies

"The rule is jam tomorrow and jam yesterday, but never jam today."

— *Alice in Wonderland,* Lewis Carroll

439

LINZER HEARTS

These tiny hearts melt in your mouth.

¾ pound (3 sticks) sweet butter, softened
1¾ cups confectioners' sugar
1 egg
2 cups unbleached all-purpose flour, sifted
1 cup cornstarch
2 cups shelled walnuts, finely grated
½ cup red raspberry preserves

1. Cream butter and 1 cup of the sugar until light and fluffy. Add egg and mix well.

2. Sift together the flour and cornstarch; add to creamed mixture and blend well. Mix walnuts in thoroughly.

3. Gather dough into a ball, wrap in wax paper, and chill for 4 to 6 hours.

4. Roll dough out to ¼-inch thickness. Using a small heart-shaped cookie cutter about 1½ inches long, cut out cookies and place on an ungreased cookie sheet. Chill cookies for 45 minutes.

5. Preheat oven to 325°F.

6. Bake cookies for 10 to 15 minutes, or until they are evenly and lightly browned. Remove and cool on a rack.

7. While they are still warm, spread half of the cookies with raspberry preserves, using ¼ teaspoon of jam for each. Top each with one of the remaining cookies.

8. Sift the remaining ¾ cup confectioners' sugar into a bowl and press tops and bottoms of the cookies into the sugar to coat.

4 dozen cookies

BROWNIES

Traditional American brownies — what could be better?

½ pound (2 sticks) sweet butter
4 ounces unsweetened chocolate
4 eggs
2 cups granulated sugar
½ cup unbleached all-purpose flour
1 teaspoon vanilla extract
⅔ cup shelled walnuts, coarsely chopped

1. Preheat oven to 350°F. Grease and flour a 9 x 12 inch baking pan.

2. Melt butter and chocolate in the top part of a double boiler over boiling water. When melted, set aside to cool to room temperature.

3. Meanwhile, beat eggs and sugar until thick and lemon-colored; add vanilla. Fold chocolate mixture into eggs and sugar. Mix thoroughly.

4. Sift flour and fold gently into batter, mixing just until blended. Fold in walnuts.

5. Pour into the prepared pan. Bake for 25 minutes, or until center is just set. Do not overbake.

6. Allow brownies to cool in pan for 30 minutes before cutting into bars.

28 large brownies

GIFT OF FOOD

One tradition we love and keep is the gift of food. This is something special that comes from the heart. A gift will remind the recipient of the giver as it is enjoyed. An especially nice gift is a tiny loaf of bread or a fruit tart, wrapped in a pretty ribbon and accompanied by a copy of the recipe. Or you might fill an antique basket with homemade cookies, candies, or a jam, chutney, or other preserve put up in your own kitchen.

SWEETMEATS

These are rich little treasures, great with coffee.

CRUST:

½ pound (2 sticks) sweet butter, at room temperature
1⅔ cups brown sugar
1⅔ cups unbleached all-purpose flour

1. Preheat oven to 350°F. Grease a 9 x 12 inch baking pan.
2. Cream butter and brown sugar together. Add flour and mix well. Pat mixture into the prepared baking pan. Bake for 15 to 20 minutes. Remove from oven.

TOPPING:

1 cup brown sugar
4 eggs, slightly beaten
2 tablespoons unbleached all-purpose flour
2 cups shelled walnuts, coarsely chopped
1 cup shredded coconut

1. Mix sugar and eggs. Add flour; stir well. Fold in walnuts and coconut. Pour topping onto crust.
2. Bake for 20 to 25 minutes longer, until topping is set. Cool in pan and cut into squares.

30 squares

"Cooking is like love — it should be entered into with abandon or not at all."

— Kitchen graffiti

SHORTBREAD HEARTS

Another Silver Palate favorite, good year-round, but essential on Valentine's Day.

¾ pound (3 sticks) sweet butter, softened
1 cup confectioners' sugar
3 cups unbleached all-purpose flour, sifted
½ teaspoon salt
½ teaspoon vanilla extract
¼ cup granulated sugar

1. Cream butter and confectioners' sugar together until light.
2. Sift flour and salt together and add to creamed mixture. Add vanilla and blend thoroughly.
3. Gather dough into a ball, wrap in wax paper, and chill for 4 to 6 hours.
4. Roll out chilled dough to ⅝-inch thickness. Using a 3-inch-long heart-shaped cookie cutter, cut out cookies. Sprinkle tops with granulated sugar. Place cut-out cookies on ungreased cookie sheets and refrigerate for 45 minutes before baking.
5. Preheat oven to 325°F.
6. Bake for 20 minutes, or until just starting to color lightly; cookies should not brown at all. Cool on a rack.

20 cookies

GIANT COOKIES

Chocolate-chip cookies have always been one of The Silver Palate's passions. We even sponsored a contest before our first day of business to pick the best cookie-maker, and were the first on our block to sell giant chocolate-chip cookies. Today they're still a best seller, and the technique couldn't be simpler. Apply it to your own favorite recipe, or use our prize-winner that follows.

After you've made the basic batter, use an average-size ice-cream scoop for portioning the dough. Drop the ball onto a greased cookie sheet, wet your hand with water, and SPLAT the dough ball out into a 5-inch round. Repeat with remaining dough and bake according to directions.

The resulting cookie is spectacular — a real handful!

MOLASSES COOKIES

These soft, chewy, spicy cookies are one of the store's most popular. Don't expect them to be crisp; they are not ginger-snaps. They stay moist, in an airtight tin, for at least a week.

12 tablespoons (1½ sticks) sweet butter
1 cup granulated sugar
¼ cup molasses
1 egg
1¾ cups unbleached all-purpose flour
½ teaspoon ground cloves
½ teaspoon ground ginger
1 teaspoon ground cinnamon
½ teaspoon salt
½ teaspoon baking soda

1. Preheat oven to 350°F.
2. Melt butter, add sugar and molasses, and mix thoroughly. Lightly beat egg and add to butter mixture; blend well.
3. Sift flour with spices, salt and baking soda, and add to first mixture; mix. Batter will be wet.
4. Lay a sheet of foil on a cookie sheet. Drop tablespoons of cookie batter on foil, leaving 3 inches between the cookies. These will spread during the baking.
5. Bake until cookies start to darken, 8 to 10 minutes. Remove from oven while still soft. Let cool on foil.
24 very large flat cookies

CHOCOLATE-CHIP COOKIES

The basic chocolate-chip cookie.

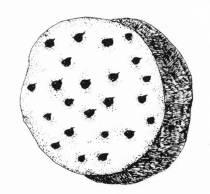

½ pound (2 sticks) sweet butter, softened
1 cup brown sugar
¾ cup granulated sugar
2 eggs
1 teaspoon vanilla extract
2 cups unbleached all-purpose flour
1 teaspoon baking soda
1 teaspoon salt
1½ cups semisweet chocolate chips

1. Preheat oven to 325°F. for giant cookies; 350°F. for regular cookies. Grease a cookie sheet.

2. Cream butter and both sugars together until light and fluffy. Add eggs and vanilla and mix well.

3. Sift dry ingredients together and stir in, mixing thoroughly. Add chocolate chips to batter, and form cookies according to method for giant cookies.

4. Bake on the prepared cookie sheet, on the middle rack, for 15 to 17 minutes for giant cookies; 8 to 10 minutes for regular cookies. Remove from oven while centers are slightly soft. Cool on the baking sheet for 5 minutes before transferring cookies to a rack to cool completely.

25 cookies, 5 inches across, or about 80 regular cookies

♥ VARIATIONS:

♥ Add 1 cup chopped walnuts
♥ Add 1 cup unsalted peanuts
♥ Add 1 cup shredded coconut
♥ Substitute 1 teaspoon mint extract for the vanilla extract

AMERICAN AS APPLE . . .

"**A**s American as apple pie" has become a familiar phrase, probably because we produce more apples than any other nation. We owe much, according to legend, to John Chapman — otherwise known as Johnny Appleseed — who spent half a century planting apple orchards in the newly settled American colonies. Later, orchards spread from coast to coast, and the apple, its lore and the good things made from it, became a part of American life.

In spring, apple blossoms sweeten the air. In summer the wide, friendly branches make tree houses a joy. As autumn nips in, the apple harvest begins, and the cycle starts again. Is an apple a day enough?

At the turn of the century over 1000 named varieties of apples were known in America. Commercialization of growing has reduced that number, but a comfortable assortment is still to be found. On the next page is a guide to their seasons, characteristics, and uses.

APPLE CHART

NAME	SEASON	COLOR	FLAVOR/ TEXTURE	EATING	PIE
Astrachan	July–Aug	Yellow/Greenish Red	Sweet	Good	Good
Baldwin	Oct–Jan	Red/Yellowish	Mellow	Fair	Fair
Cortland	Oct–Jan	Green/Purple	Mild, Tender	Excel.	Excel.
Delicious, Red	Sept–June	Scarlet	Sweet, crunchy	Excel.	Good
Delicious, Golden	Sept–May	Yellow	Sweet, semifirm	Excel.	Excel.
Empire	Sept–Nov	Red	Sweet, crisp	Excel.	Good
Fameuse	Sept–Nov	Red	Mild, crisp	Excel.	Fair
Granny Smith	Apr–July	Green	Tart, crisp	V. Good	V. Good
Gravenstein	July–Sept	Green w/red stripes	Tart, crisp	Good	Good
Ida Red	Oct	Red	Rich	Good	Good
Jonathan	Sept–Jan	Brilliant red	Tart, tender, crisp	V. Good	V. Good
Macoun	Oct–Nov	Dark red	Tart, juicy, crisp	Excel.	Good
McIntosh	Sept–June	Green to red	Slightly tart, tender, juicy	Excel.	Excel.
Newtown Pippin	Sept–June	Green to red	Slightly tart, firm	V. Good	Excel.

Variety	Season	Color	Texture/Flavor		
Northern Spy	Oct	Red	Crisp, tart	V. Good	V. Good
Rhode Island Greening	Sept–Nov	Green	Very tart, firm	Poor	Excel.
Rome Beauty	Oct–June	Red	Tart, firm, slightly dry	Good	V. Good
Stayman–Winesap	Oct–Mar	Red	Semifirm, sweet, spicy	V. Good	Good
Winesap	Oct–June	Red	Slightly tart, firm, spicy	Excel.	Good
Yellow Transparent	July–Aug	Yellow	Tart, soft	Poor	Excel.
York Imperial	Oct–Apr	Greenish Yellow	Mild, firm	Fair	Good

We've made a tradition of Medieval Apple Tart, taught to us by a Frenchwoman, Madame Bouchard of Villeneuve-sur-Lot. Whenever we bake it, we are always reminded of that afternoon in Madame Bouchard's country kitchen. She stretched and rolled her fresh strudel dough by hand while her husband peeled the apples. Later, while the tart baked, we shared an Armagnac. We've substituted phyllo pastry for the strudel, but the result is just as delicious.

MEDIEVAL APPLE TART

This light, tender and flaky version of a regional French *croustade* is made with thinly sliced apples and Grand Marnier. Serve it warm with a dollop of *crème fraîche*.

12 phyllo leaves, fresh or thoroughly defrosted
1 pound (4 sticks) sweet butter
1 cup granulated sugar
6 tablespoons Grand Marnier or Calvados, approximately
6 medium-size tart apples, peeled, cored and thinly sliced

1. Unwrap the phyllo leaves and cover them with a damp towel for 10 minutes. Melt the butter. Preheat oven to 425°F.

2. Using a pastry brush, lightly butter a 14-inch baking pan. Lay a phyllo leaf on the pan. Remember to re-cover the unused phyllo with the damp towel each time. Brush the phyllo with some of the melted butter, and sprinkle with 1 tablespoon of the sugar and 1 teaspoon of Grand Marnier. Repeat, using 5 more phyllo leaves.

3. Arrange the apples in the center of the top sheet of phyllo in a circular mound about 6 inches in diameter. Brush them with butter and sprinkle with sugar and Grand Marnier.

4. Stack 6 more leaves of phyllo on top of the apples, repeating the buttering and sprinkling with sugar and Grand Marnier. The top (twelfth) sheet of phyllo should only be buttered.

5. Trim off the corners of the phyllo sheets so you have a large round, about 8 inches in diameter. Turn the edges of the phyllo up and pinch lightly to seal. Be tidy, but don't work too long on this; the tart should look rustic.

6. Set the tart on the middle rack of the oven and bake for 30 to

40 minutes, or until golden. If pastry becomes too brown before this time, cover it loosely with foil.

7. Serve the tart immediately, or reheat gently before serving.

4 to 6 portions

JOHNNY APPLE SAUCE

This fresh and chunky apple compote is named in honor of the man who became a legend. It is delicious hot or cold, and is equally at home as dessert or a tart accompaniment to pork and game entrées.

2½ cups water
4 tablespoons strained fresh lemon juice
7 medium-size Granny Smith or other firm, tart apples
½ cup granulated sugar
⅔ cup good French Sauternes
6 tablespoons red currant jelly
2 cinnamon sticks
grated zest of 2 lemons
½ cup shelled walnuts, coarsely chopped (optional)
⅓ cup raisins (optional)

1. Mix half of the water and half of the lemon juice together in a bowl.

2. Peel and core the apples and cut them into 1½-inch irregular chunks. As you cut each apple, drop the pieces into the water to prevent discoloration.

3. In a medium-size saucepan with a heavy bottom, combine remaining water and lemon juice, the sugar and the Sauternes. Bring to a boil, reduce to a simmer, and add the apple chunks. Partially cover and cook gently until apples are just tender; apple chunks should remain whole.

4. With a slotted spoon, transfer apples to a bowl. Add the currant jelly and cinnamon sticks to the syrup remaining in the pan. Set over medium heat, bring to a boil, reduce to a simmer, and cook until syrup is reduced by one third. Stir in the lemon zest.

5. Pour the syrup over the apples. Stir in the walnuts and raisins if you use them. Serve warm; or cool, cover and refrigerate.

6 portions

> "No mean woman can cook well, for it calls for a light head, a generous spirit, and a large heart."
>
> — Paul Gauguin

CINNAMONY BAKED APPLES

2 cups water
2¼ cups brown sugar
1½ tablespoons ground cinnamon
1½ tablespoons fresh lemon juice
6 medium-large tart baking apples, washed (do not peel)
¾ cup raisins
½ cup shelled pecans, chopped
1 tablespoon grated lemon zest
3 tablespoons Calvados or applejack
3 tablespoons sweet butter

1. Preheat oven to 375°F.
2. Mix water, ¾ cup of the brown sugar, ½ tablespoon of the cinnamon and the lemon juice in a saucepan. Bring to a boil and cook for 3 minutes. Remove syrup from heat and reserve.
3. Remove the apple cores, but do not cut all the way through the bottoms.
4. In a bowl, mix remaining 1½ cups brown sugar, the raisins, pecans, lemon zest and remaining 1 tablespoon cinnamon. Fill each apple to within ¼ inch of the top. Pour 1 teaspoon of applejack over the filling in each apple and top with ½ tablespoon butter.
5. Transfer apples to a baking dish 9 x 13 inches and pour syrup over apples. Pour remaining tablespoon of the applejack into the syrup.
6. Bake apples for 40 minutes, or until tender, basting them occasionally with syrup in pan.
7. When apples are done, transfer them with a slotted spoon to a serving dish. Pour syrup from pan into a small saucepan, bring to a boil, and cook until slightly reduced, about 5 minutes. Cool slightly, pour a tablespoon of syrup over each apple, and serve remaining syrup on the side.
6 portions

452

PRESERVING

The art of preserving food by sealing it hermetically in containers was devised only in the early 19th century, unlike some of the more familiar methods of food preservation (i.e., salting, freezing, curing, drying, smoking and pickling) that have been with mankind almost since the days of the caveman.

The credit for first developing the process goes to Nicolas-Francois Appert, a Parisian confectioner and distiller who won a 12,000-franc prize from the French government in 1810. His discovery allowed the French army to carry more varied supplies for greater distances without risking spoilage. He used his prize money to found the House of Appert, the first commercial business venture in canning and preserving.

PRESERVES are made from perfect fruits, either whole or in large pieces, cooked with sugar (often a smaller portion of sugar than jams) only long enough for the syrup to thicken while the fruit still holds its shape.

JAMS are made from fruit, usually a single kind, that has been chopped or crushed, then cooked with sugar (or, less usually, honey) until the mixture is thick.

JELLY is sweetened and jellied fruit juice. It contains no pieces of fruit, but is sparkling, clear and tender and can be unmolded from the jar in which it is preserved.

MARMALADES are halfway between jelly and jam; small pieces of fruit, usually citrus, and peel are suspended in a transparent jelly.

CONSERVES are jamlike combinations of fruits, nuts and sugar, cooked until thick.

CHUTNEYS are relishes made by combining fruits and vegetables with such tart or sweet ingredients as honey, sugar, spices and vinegar. They capture the best of the sweet and the sour.

FRUIT SPREADS are made from sieved or long-cooked fruit pulp, cooked with "sweetening" and, usually, spices, to a spreadable (but not jelled) consistency.

SAUTEED APPLES WITH CALVADOS

Serve these apple-brandy spiked apples as an accompaniment to pork or ham. They are also delicious folded into omelets or crêpes.

6 cooking apples (Golden Delicious are a good choice)
8 tablespoons (1 stick) sweet butter
½ cup firmly packed brown sugar
⅔ cup Calvados

1. Core the apples, and peel them if you like. (We prefer the added texture of the peels, but peeled apples look more sophisticated.) Cut the apples crosswise into ¼-inch-thick slices.
2. Melt about 2 tablespoons of the butter in a skillet and add a single layer of apple slices. Raise the heat and sauté the slices, turning occasionally, until browned, about 5 minutes. With a slotted spoon, transfer apples to a bowl. Repeat with more butter and another batch of apples until all have been cooked.
3. Add brown sugar to the butter remaining in the skillet and stir over heat until it dissolves. Add the Calvados and bring to a boil. Boil for 5 minutes, stirring constantly.
4. Return apples to the skillet, reduce heat, and simmer for another 5 minutes, or until apples are heated through. Do not overcook. Transfer apples to a heated dish and serve immediately.
   6 to 8 portions

ELLEN'S APPLE TART

Ravishingly caramelized apples on a circle of flaky puff pastry; the best apple tart we have ever eaten.

4 medium-to-large tart cooking apples, peeled, cored and halved
¾ cup granulated sugar
3 tablespoons water
2 tablespoons sweet butter
1 tablespoon fresh lemon juice
1 teaspoon freshly grated nutmeg
2 tablespoons Calvados or applejack
1 pound Puff Pastry (see page 575)

1. Poach apples according to the method described in Poached Fruit (see page 527), removing them from the syrup while they are still slightly firm; omit the cooling period in the syrup. Transfer apples to a strainer set over a bowl and allow them to cool completely.

2. Meanwhile, pour sugar and water into a 10-inch cast-iron frying pan. Set over medium heat and cook, watching carefully, until sugar syrup reaches a golden brown. Remove immediately from heat and set the pan on a cool surface. The caramelized sugar will harden.

3. Place 1 apple half, rounded side down, on the caramelized sugar in the center of the pan. Surround with 6 of the remaining halves, placing them close together. Slice the last half into 6 slices and place them in the spaces between the apples in the ring, with their rounded edges outwards.

4. Melt the butter in a saucepan. Whisk in lemon juice, nutmeg and applejack, and drizzle over apples.

5. Preheat oven to 425°F.

6. Roll out puff pastry to ¼-inch thickness, and cut out a round 12 inches in diameter. Place over apples and roll edges of pastry back 1 inch all around to give edges a finished look.

7. Place the tart in the preheated oven; preheating is very important to ensure puff pastry rising. Bake for 30 to 35 minutes, or until pastry is a deep golden brown and syrup is bubbling around edges. If pastry browns too quickly, cover it with a piece of foil.

8. When tart is done, remove from oven and let it set for 15 minutes. Invert onto a serving platter. Serve warm or at room temperature.

8 to 10 portions

SUNDAY
LUNCH MENU

*Chicken Liver Pâté with
Green Peppercorns*

*Pâté de Campagne with
Walnuts*

Layered Vegetable Terrine

*Cornichons and pickled
wild cherries*

———

Bouillabaisse

*An All-Arugula Salad with
Balsamic Vinaigrette*

———

Ellen's Apple Tart

CALVADOS

Normandy, on the northern coast of France, has long been famous for its apples and for Calvados, the fiery apple brandy that has been made there since the sixteenth century. It is traditionally served much younger than other brandies, although the best is that which has aged in oak for 12 years and is a potent drink indeed. In cooking it imparts a special fruity tang and complexity. Although the taste of Calvados is unique, you can substitute American apple brandy (applejack) in most recipes.

APPLE MOUSSE WITH
APPLE BRANDY SAUCE

A light, rich and sophisticated ending to an important autumn dinner. We serve it with one of our favorite French Sauternes — Château Filhot, Château Climens, or the fabulous Château d'Yquem.

4 medium-size tart apples, peeled and cored
1 teaspoon ground cinnamon
⅛ teaspoon freshly grated nutmeg
2 tablespoons fresh lemon juice
⅓ cup Calvados or applejack
5 egg yolks
⅔ cup granulated sugar
1⅔ cups milk
1 tablespoon unflavored gelatin
1 cup heavy cream, chilled
1½ teaspoons vanilla extract
Apple Brandy Sauce (recipe follows)

1. Chop apples and combine in a heavy saucepan with cinnamon, nutmeg, lemon juice and half of the Calvados. Set over medium heat and cook, stirring constantly, until apples are tender enough to mash, about 30 minutes.

2. Transfer apples to the bowl of a food processor fitted with a steel blade, or use a food mill fitted with the medium disc, and process until smooth. Transfer to a bowl, cover, and refrigerate.

3. Meanwhile, beat egg yolks and sugar together, off heat, in the top pan of a double boiler until they are light yellow and glossy. In a saucepan, heat milk to not quite scalding.

4. Set eggs and sugar over simmering water in lower pan of the double boiler and whisk in the warm milk. Cook, stirring constantly, until custard coats the back of a spoon, about 10 minutes. Remove from heat.

5. Sprinkle gelatin over remaining Calvados in a small saucepan and heat until gelatin is completely dissolved. Whisk gelatin mixture into the custard and transfer custard to a cool bowl. Refrigerate for 1 to

2 hours, or until mixture is just beginning to set.

6. Whip the cream until soft peaks form; whip in vanilla. Mix chilled custard and applesauce together well, gently fold in the whipped cream, and divide the mousse equally among 6 dessert dishes, or pour it into a large serving bowl.

7. Chill, for 4 hours, or until completely set. Serve accompanied by Apple Brandy Sauce (recipe follows).

6 portions

APPLE BRANDY SAUCE

¼ cup Calvados or applejack
¼ cup honey
2½ tablespoons sweet butter
3 tablespoons fresh lemon juice
¼ teaspoon freshly grated nutmeg
pinch of salt
grated rind of 1 lemon

1. Warm Calvados in a skillet over medium heat. Remove liqueur from heat, ignite it, and let it burn until flames die out.

2. Stir in honey, butter, lemon juice, nutmeg, salt and lemon rind. Cool to room temperature.

3. Drizzle sparingly over Apple Mousse.

Sauce for 6 servings of mousse

"Don't sit under the apple tree with anyone else but me."
— The Andrews Sisters, 1940

APPLESAUCE RAISIN CAKE

½ pound (2 sticks) sweet butter
2 cups granulated sugar
2 eggs
2 cups chunk-style applesauce*
3 cups unbleached all-purpose flour
1 teaspoon ground cinnamon
1 teaspoon freshly grated nutmeg
2 teaspoons baking soda
1 teaspoon vanilla extract
1 cup raisins
Lemon-Orange Icing (recipe follows)

1. Preheat oven to 325°F. Butter and flour a 10-inch tube pan.
2. In a mixing bowl, cream together butter and sugar until light and fluffy. Add the eggs, one at a time, beating well after each addition. Stir in puréed applesauce and vanilla.
3. Sift flour, cinnamon, nutmeg, and baking soda together; then sift dry ingredients over applesauce mixture, sprinkle in raisins, and blend gently but thoroughly.
4. Pour batter into tube pan and set on the middle rack of the oven. Bake for 1 hour and 10 to 15 minutes, or until a cake tester inserted into the cake comes out clean.
5. Cool in the pan for 15 minutes. Turn out onto a cake rack and cool completely.
6. When cool, drizzle with Lemon-Orange Icing.
8 to 10 portions.

*Or make Johnny Applesauce (see page 451), omitting walnuts and raisins. Purée until smooth, and use 2 cups.

LEMON-ORANGE ICING

1 cup confectioners' sugar
½ teaspoon ground cinnamon
1½ tablespoons fresh lemon juice
1½ tablespoons fresh orange juice

1. Sift confectioners' sugar and cinnamon into a small bowl.
2. Dribble in juices, stirring constantly until icing is smooth. Drizzle over cooled cake.

Enough icing for 1 Applesauce Raisin Cake

CHUNKY APPLE WALNUT CAKE

Dark, moist and chunky, with a dream of a glaze.

1½ cups vegetable oil
2 cups granulated sugar
3 eggs
2 cups unbleached, all-purpose flour, sifted
⅛ teaspoon ground cloves
1¼ teaspoons ground cinnamon
¼ teaspoon ground mace
1 teaspoon baking soda
¾ teaspoon salt
1 cup whole-wheat flour, sifted
1¼ cups shelled walnuts, coarsely chopped
3¼ cups coarse chunks of peeled and cored Rome Beauty apples
3 tablespoons Calvados or applejack
Apple Cider Glaze (recipe follows)

1. Preheat oven to 325°F.
2. In a large bowl, beat vegetable oil and sugar until thick and opaque. Add eggs, one at a time, beating well after each addition.
3. Sift together all-purpose flour, cloves, cinnamon, mace, baking soda and salt, then stir in whole-wheat flour. Add to oil and egg mixture and mix until well blended.
4. Add walnuts, apple chunks and Calvados all at once and stir batter until pieces are evenly distributed.

460

5. Pour batter into a greased 10-inch round cake pan. Bake for 1 hour and 15 minutes, or until a cake tester inserted in the center comes out clean.

6. Let cake rest for 10 minutes, then unmold and pour glaze over warm cake, or cut cake and pour glaze over slices.

One 10-inch cake, 10 to 12 portions

APPLE CIDER GLAZE

4 tablespoons sweet butter
2 tablespoons brown sugar
6 tablespoons granulated sugar
3 tablespoons Calvados or applejack
4 tablespoons sweet cider
2 tablespoons fresh orange juice
2 tablespoons heavy cream

1. Melt butter in a small saucepan and stir in both sugars.

2. Add remaining ingredients, stir, and bring to a boil. Reduce heat slightly and cook for 4 minutes.

3. Remove from heat and cool slightly. Pour while still warm over warm cake.

1½ cups glaze

"Nothing is really work unless you'd rather be doing something else."

— *Peter Pan*, James Barrie

SOUR-CREAM APPLE PIE

A little slice goes a long way.

CRUST:

2½ cups unbleached all-purpose flour
5 tablespoons granulated sugar
¾ teaspoon salt
¾ teaspoon ground cinnamon
6 tablespoons sweet butter, chilled
6 tablespoons shortening, chilled
4 to 6 tablespoons apple cider or juice, chilled

1. Sift flour, sugar, salt and cinnamon into a bowl. Cut in butter and shortening with a fork or pastry cutter until mixture resembles rolled oats.

2. Moisten with just enough cider, tossing ingredients lightly with a fork, to permit the dough to be formed into a ball. Wrap and refrigerate for 2 hours.

3. Cut off one third of the dough and return it to the refrigerator. Roll out the other two thirds between 2 sheets of wax paper. Line a greased 9-inch pie pan with the dough. Trim overhang and crimp decoratively.

4. Preheat oven to 350°F.

FILLING:

5 to 7 tart apples
⅔ cup dairy sour cream
⅓ cup granulated sugar
1 egg, lightly beaten
¼ teaspoon salt
1 teaspoon vanilla extract
3 tablespoons unbleached all-purpose flour

1. Peel, core and thinly slice apples; drop slices into a mixing bowl.

2. Whisk together sour cream, sugar, egg, salt, vanilla and flour in a small bowl. Pour mixture over apples and toss well to coat. Spoon apples into pastry-lined pie pan.

TOPPING:

3 tablespoons brown sugar
3 tablespoons granulated sugar
1 teaspoon ground cinnamon
1 cup shelled walnuts, chopped

1. Mix sugars, cinnamon and walnuts together and sprinkle evenly over apple filling.

2. Roll out remaining pastry between sheets of wax paper to form a 10-inch circle. Cut into ½-inch strips, and arrange these lattice-fashion over apples; trim ends of strips and crimp edge of crust decoratively.

3. Set pie on the middle rack of the oven and bake for 55 to 65 minutes. If crust browns too quickly, cover loosely with foil. Pie is done when juices are bubbling and apples are tender.

4. Serve warm or cool, topped, if you like, with whipped cream or vanilla ice cream.

6 portions

IT'S THE BERRIES

The berry season is one that comes and goes all too fast. As soon as they appear in the market, they vanish into the baskets of modern berry-pickers. Of our favorites, strawberries, raspberries and blackberries are delicate and must be treated with care; blueberries are sturdier and keep longer. All should be stored in a dark but cool and airy place, preferably not the refrigerator, since it encourages mold. If you must refrigerate them, don't wash them first. It's best to eat berries as quickly as possible after picking or purchasing them.

Berries are wonderful to eat as they are, or with just a little *crème fraîche* or whipped cream flavored with a fruit liqueur. Eat one kind alone or combined with others in dozens of ways. Make the most of them this season. It's the Berries!

ZABAGLIONE

This dessert is wonderfully versatile, since it can be served hot or cold, is good by itself, and is even better as a topping for a combination of berries. We like equal parts of blueberries, raspberries and strawberries.

8 egg yolks
¾ cup granulated sugar
⅓ cup Marsala wine

1. Mix ingredients together in the top part of a double boiler and cook over rapidly boiling water, whisking constantly until mixture doubles in bulk and thickens.
2. Remove from heat and whisk for another minute.
3. Pour mixture warm over fresh berries, serve it in a tall glass by itself, or chill it and serve as a sauce for berries.
   6 portions

You can't go wrong with the beloved strawberry. The French discovered an ancestor of the large, lush berry we know in Chile in the eighteenth century, and eventually produced, by crossing it with the tiny wild berries of North America, the forerunners of today's varieties. Today wild berries are scarce, but the cultivated version grows in all but the hottest desert. Americans have made it their national berry.

CHAMPAGNE SABAYON

A simple and elegant cousin of zabaglione. Spoon it over fresh berries in stemmed glasses.

4 egg yolks
⅓ cup granulated sugar
¾ cup Champagne
2 tablespoons Kirsch

1. Whisk the egg yolks and the sugar together in the top part of a double boiler over boiling water until foamy.
2. Add the Champagne and whisk constantly until thick and creamy, about 10 minutes.
3. Remove from heat, add the Kirsch, and serve immediately.
2½ cups, sauce for about 4 cups berries, 4 to 6 portions

AUTUMN DINNER PARTY

Zucchini-Watercress Soup

Fruit-Stuffed Cornish Hens

Ginger Candied Carrots

Nutted Wild Rice

Pavlova

465

PAVLOVA

Created in honor of the great ballerina.

4 egg whites, at room temperature
¼ teaspoon salt
¼ teaspoon cream of tartar
1 cup fine granulated sugar
4 teaspoons cornstarch
2 teaspoons white wine vinegar
1 teaspoon vanilla extract
1 cup heavy cream, chilled
2 to 3 cups strawberries, sliced and sprinkled with sugar and
Grand Marnier

1. Preheat oven to 275°F.
2. Beat egg whites, salt and cream of tartar together in a bowl until the whites hold a stiff peak. Add the sugar, a few tablespoons at a time, beating until mixture is stiff and glossy. Beat in the cornstarch, then the vinegar and the vanilla.
3. Butter and lightly flour a loose-bottomed 8-inch cake pan and fill gently with the meringue mixture, spreading it higher around the edges than in the center of the pan to form a depression.
4. Bake cake for 1 to 1¼ hours, or until meringue is firm and lightly browned. Pavlova will remain moist inside. Cool slightly, unmold, slide onto a serving plate, and cool completely.
5. Lightly whip cream. Just before serving, spread the Pavlova with whipped cream and then with the strawberries. Serve immediately.
4 to 6 portions

STRAWBERRY ICE CREAM

Churning homemade ice cream is traditionally one of the great American pastimes. It's even better when the ice cream being churned is the all-American strawberry.

1⅓ cups milk
2⅔ cups heavy cream
½ vanilla bean, split
8 egg yolks
1¼ cups granulated sugar
1 pint ripe strawberries

1. Combine milk and heavy cream in a large, heavy saucepan. Add vanilla bean and bring almost to a boil. Reduce heat and simmer for 5 minutes.

2. Whisk the egg yolks together with 1 cup of the sugar until smooth and all sugar is dissolved. Remove milk mixture from heat, remove vanilla bean, and whisk 1 cup of the hot milk thoroughly into the eggs. Stir well, then whisk the egg mixture back into the milk.

3. Return saucepan to the stove and cook over low heat, whisking constantly, just until the custard thickens; do not let it boil. Strain the custard, cool, and chill well.

4. Meanwhile, rinse, drain and stem the strawberries. Crush them and stir in the remaining sugar. Let stand for 30 minutes.

5. Combine strawberries with chilled custard. Transfer to ice cream maker and freeze according to manufacturer's instructions.

1½ quarts

"Doubtless God could have made a better berry, but doubtless God never did."

— Dr. William Butler, 1535–1618

Strawberries are so called from the old English word straw — meaning to cover the ground with scattered things. It is a fruit of full summer.

STRAWBERRY SHORTCAKE

One of our mothers long ago showed her spirit by announcing a dinner of only strawberry shortcake. Though we promised to keep it secret, we were typical elementary school students and couldn't wait for "Show and Tell" the next day. The memory of that dinner made the family laugh together for years.

2 cups unbleached all-purpose flour
2 tablespoons granulated sugar
¾ teaspoon salt
1 tablespoon baking powder
4 tablespoons sweet butter, chilled
½ cup light cream
sweet butter, softened, for topping
6 cups strawberries, sliced and sugared to taste
1½ cups heavy cream, chilled
12 perfect strawberries (garnish)

1. Preheat oven to 450°F.
2. Sift flour, sugar, salt and baking powder together into a mixing bowl.
3. Cut in the 4 tablespoons butter until mixture resembles oats. Pour in cream and mix gently until just blended.
4. Roll dough out on a floured work surface to a thickness of ⅝ inch. Cut into 3-inch circles with a cookie cutter. Gather scraps, roll again and cut more rounds; you should have 6 rounds.
5. Bake shortcakes on a greased baking sheet for about 10 minutes, or until puffed and lightly browned.
6. Cool the biscuits slightly, split them, and spread softened butter lightly over the cut surfaces. Set the bottoms on dessert plates; spoon on sliced strawberries, and crown with the tops of the biscuits. Whip chilled cream, and spoon a dollop onto each shortcake, then garnish with a single perfect strawberry. Serve immediately.

6 shortcakes

Note: To make drop biscuits, use an additional ¼ cup cream and drop the dough by large spoonfuls onto the baking sheet. Bake as directed.

STRAWBERRY CHOCOLATE TART

A pretty way to serve strawberries.

9-inch prebaked Sweet Buttery Tart Crust (see page 580)
Chocolate Filling (recipe follows)
1½ pints strawberries, washed, stemmed and dried
½ cup Red Currant Glaze (see page 595)
sprig of fresh mint (garnish)

1. While chocolate filling is still warm, spread it in the tart shell. Filling should be about ⅛ inch thick.
2. Place berries, tips up, over the warm chocolate filling in a circular pattern, working from the outside in until the surface is covered.
3. Warm the glaze until thin enough to brush easily, then coat berries evenly.
4. Refrigerate tart for 2 hours; remove from refrigerator 45 minutes before serving. Garnish with a mint sprig.
8 portions

CHOCOLATE FILLING

1 cup semisweet chocolate pieces
2 tablespoons sweet butter, melted
3 tablespoons Kirsch
¼ cup confectioners' sugar, sifted
1 tablespoon water

1. Melt chocolate in a bowl placed over simmering water. This will take about 20 minutes. When chocolate has reached 110°F., add melted butter and Kirsch. Whisk quickly and thoroughly until smooth.
2. Add confectioners' sugar and water, continuing to whisk until smooth.
3. While the mixture is still warm, pour it into the tart shell.

STRAWBERRY WAYS

♥ Top *Crème Brulée* (see page 521) with crushed fresh strawberries.

♥ Steep strawberries in a goblet of red wine; add a bit of honey if you like. Serve with a spoon.

♥ Toss strawberries with sugar and Grand Marnier to taste; leave at room temperature for a few hours. Serve in small bowls, or spoon over vanilla ice cream.

♥ Sweeten ripe berries with fresh orange juice to taste. A sprinkle of dark rum is nice too.

If we had to choose just one favorite berry, it would be the raspberry, the most elegant of all. Raspberries have been cherished for centuries, and they never seem to be abundant or affordable enough to be taken for granted. When the season is at its peak, eat them plain or with a bit of cream. Pure pleasure!

"One third of a tumbler filled with raspberry vinegar — add ice, a teaspoon of sugar and top with carbonated water. Garnish with fresh berries and a mint leaf."

— *The Virginia Housewife,*
Mary Randolph, 1824

RED RASPBERRY PIE

4 cups raspberries, picked over
1 cup granulated sugar
⅓ cup Crème de Cassis (black currant liqueur)
4 tablespoons cornstarch
1 tablespoon fresh lemon juice
pinch of salt
1 recipe Piecrust (see page 578)
2 tablespoons sweet butter
3 paper-thin slices of lemon

1. Preheat oven to 425°F.
2. Toss raspberries and sugar together in a mixing bowl. Whisk Cassis and cornstarch together in a small bowl until smooth. Stir Cassis mixture, lemon juice, and salt gently into berries.
3. Roll out two thirds of the pastry and line the pie pan; leave edges untrimmed. Spoon in the berries, dot with butter, and arrange lemon slices overlapping slightly in the center of the berries.
4. Roll out remaining pastry into a 10-inch round and cut into ½-inch strips. Arrange over berries in a lattice pattern. Trim overhanging pastry; bring edge of lower crust over lattice and crimp edge decoratively.
5. Set on the middle rack of the oven and bake at 425°F. for 15 minutes. Lower heat to 350°F. and bake for another 30 to 40 minutes, or until crust is golden brown and filling is bubbling.

6 to 8 portions

FIG AND RASPBERRY TART

12 figs, green or purple
½ cup Kirsch
9-inch prebaked Sweet Buttery Tart Crust (see page 580)
1 cup Pastry Cream (see page 578)
½ pint basket raspberries, picked over
Red Currant Glaze (see page 595)

1. If using green figs, carefully peel them and leave whole. If using purple figs, cut them lengthwise into halves but do not peel. Pour Kirsch over figs in a bowl, cover, and refrigerate for 12 hours, stirring occasionally.

2. To assemble the tart, spread pastry cream in the baked tart shell. Remove the figs from Kirsch and drain them. If using green figs, cut them into quarters, but do not cut completely through the base. Fan the quarters out like flower petals, and arrange close together over the surface of pastry cream. If using purple figs, arrange the halves cut side down. Fill in spaces between figs with raspberries.

3. Warm the currant glaze and brush over the tart to glaze all the fruit. Serve within 3 hours of assembling.

6 to 8 portions

RASPBERRY-SAUTERNES
DESSERT SOUP

On the hottest day of the hottest summer we can remember, we found ourselves expecting some Very Important People for dinner. When all was ready except a dessert, we had time for an elaborate finale or a run to the beach, but not both. Inspiration, in the form of a well-iced bottle of Sauternes in the back of the refrigerator, led to this creation — quick, easy and elegant. (Our tan looked great at dinner, too!)

1 bottle of good, but not great, French Sauternes, chilled
3 cups fresh raspberries
½ cup Crème Fraîche (see page 582)
fresh mint leaves (garnish)

1. Pour the Sauternes into a mixing bowl.
2. Sort through the raspberries, discarding any less-than-perfect berries. Crush about half of the berries with the back of a spoon and stir all of them into the Sauternes. Cover and refrigerate at least 4 hours.
3. Just before serving, measure the *crème fraîche* into a small bowl. Ladle out 2 cups of the chilled Sauternes and whisk it gradually into the *crème fraîche*. Now whisk this mixture back into the remaining Sauternes in the mixing bowl. Ladle into chilled soup bowls or Champagne tulips, apportioning the raspberries fairly, and garnish each serving with a sprig of fresh mint. Serve immediately.

4 to 6 portions

DAMSON PLUM BRANDY

Follow the recipe for Raspberry Cordial substituting damson plums at their peak. Pierce the skin of each plum several times with a fork. Stir each week, letting brandy mature for at least 4 months. If you time it right, the brandy will be ready by Christmas Eve. Serve the fruit over ice cream and serve the brandy around the fire afterwards.

RASPBERRY CORDIAL

For the fullest flavor let this steep until Christmas time; then give as a gift or enjoy it yourself.

2 cups granulated sugar
2 pints ripe raspberries, picked over
1 quart vodka

1. Place the sugar in a 3-quart glass jar with a lid. Add the raspberries and the vodka, and cover.
2. Place in a dark cool place. Each week for about 2 months open the jar and stir the cordial.
3. Strain the finished cordial through a very fine sieve into a lovely decanter. Its color is vibrant.

1½ quarts

Robert Frost called these dewy bunches of blue "a vision of thieves," though they needn't be stolen to be enjoyed. These are blueberries, and we're thankful that cultivators have made them readily available. Today's blues are generously grand and as popular as Fats Domino when he sang "Blueberry Hill."

The scarcest of all American berries is the blackberry. Count yourself lucky if you happen to have a thicket on your property or in your neighborhood. The wild blackberry is very tart; the cultivated varieties tend to be less so. All members of the blackberry tribe lend themselves to superb jams and pies. Some people dislike the large seeds the berries hide; that means more blackberries are left for us!

BLUEBERRY-LEMON TART

Other fruits can be used in place of the blueberries. Try combining green and red seedless grapes, blueberries and thinly sliced peaches, or lightly sautéed apple slices sprinkled with plumped raisins. Use your imagination and enjoy!

1 cup lemon juice (about 6 lemons)
5 tablespoons grated lemon zest
½ cup (1 stick) melted sweet butter
6 eggs, slightly beaten
1 cup granulated sugar
9-inch partially baked Sweet Buttery Tart Crust, 1 inch deep
  (see page 580)
1½ cups blueberries, rinsed, sorted and dried
confectioners' sugar

1. Preheat oven to 400°F.
2. Whisk lemon juice, grated zest and melted butter in a medium-size bowl. Beat in eggs and sugar; mix well.
3. Pour into the partially baked tart shell and bake about 20 minutes or until golden brown.
4. Arrange blueberries (or other fresh fruit) over the warm filling, pressing lightly. When cool, dust with confectioners' sugar.
8 portions

BLACKBERRY ICE

This ice makes the most of the blackberry's tart, intense flavor. Delicious on a summer's day, especially if you've spent the afternoon picking the berries in a hot thicket.

6 cups ripe blackberries
½ cup granulated sugar
juice of 2 lemons
¾ cup Crème de Cassis (black currant liqueur)

1. Combine all ingredients in a heavy saucepan and set over medium heat. Cook, stirring frequently, for 20 minutes, or until all berries have burst.

2. Cool mixture slightly and force through a sieve or through the fine disc of a food mill. Cool the resulting purée completely.

3. Pour cooled mixture into a shallow metal pan (a cake tin is ideal), and set it in your freezer.

4. When the mixture is about half frozen, in 2 to 3 hours, remove the pan from the freezer, scrape the blackberry ice out of the pan into a bowl, and beat with a wire whisk until soft and icy parts are completely mixed. Return the ice to the pan, set it back in the freezer, and freeze completely.

5. The ice will be very solid. To serve, temper in refrigerator for 15 to 30 minutes before attempting to dish up.

6 portions

Blackberries are found throughout the U.S. In the west, the berries grow in mountainous country, mostly at higher altitudes. The blackberry is a shrub with thorns. The stems are flowering and clustered; the flower is white and five-petaled. The leaflets are 3 to 5 in number and the fruit is black or dark purple. The blackberry is sometimes called bramblebush.

BLACKBERRY MOUSSE

Search field or market for these black wonders; they're worth it. The flavor and color of the mousse are gorgeous.

1 tablespoon unflavored gelatin
2 tablespoons cold water
juice and grated zest of 1 orange
2 pint baskets blackberries, or 2 bags (10 ounces each) frozen berries
    without sugar; reserve several for garnish
2 egg yolks
½ cup granulated sugar
2 tablespoons Cointreau
2 cups heavy cream
2 kiwis, peeled and sliced (optional garnish)

1. Soak gelatin in the cold water in a saucepan for 5 minutes. Add orange juice, grated orange zest and berries, and bring just to a boil, stirring. Cool to room temperature.

2. Beat egg yolks and sugar in a bowl until pale yellow. Add Cointreau and beat for another minute.

3. Put egg yolk mixture in the top pan of a double boiler over simmering water. Stir until slightly thickened and hot to the touch. Cool to room temperature.

4. Add egg yolk mixture to blackberry mixture and stir until well blended. Whip heavy cream to soft peaks and fold gently into blackberry and egg yolk mixture. Divide among serving dishes and chill until ready to serve.

5. Garnish with sliced kiwis, each topped with a whole berry, or with berries alone.

8 to 10 portions

MOUSSE MAGIC

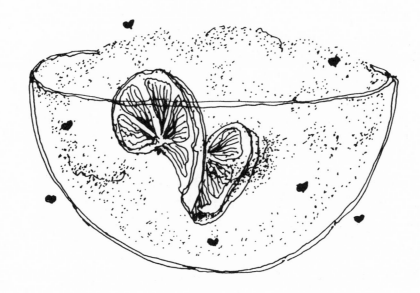

After a heavy meal, when guilt pangs are running high, a smooth mousse is a perfect dessert. Our shop is never without a row of these treats already put up in individual cups to take home. You can present your dessert mousses the same way — spooned into stemmed glasses, chilled and appropriately garnished — or, more simply, chilled in a large bowl and then spooned onto dessert plates at the table. Either way, your guests will love them, and appreciate an elegant finale.

Our tart and buttery Lime Mousse has been one of the store's most popular desserts for years. Team it with a chocolate brownie for a sensational dessert. As a variation, substitute fresh lemon juice and grated zest for the lime to make lemon mousse.

LIME MOUSSE

8 tablespoons (1 stick) sweet butter
5 eggs
1 cup granulated sugar
¾ cup fresh lime juice (6 or 7 limes)
grated zest of 5 limes
2 cups heavy cream, chilled

1. Melt butter in the top part of a double boiler over simmering water.

2. Beat eggs and sugar in a bowl until light and foamy. Add mixture to melted butter. Cook gently, stirring constantly, until mixture becomes a custard, about 8 minutes. Do not overcook or eggs will scramble.

3. Remove custard from heat and stir in lime juice and grated zest. Cool to room temperature.

4. This step is unorthodox but crucial. Using an electric mixer, whip chilled cream until very stiff — almost, but not quite, to the point where it would become butter.

5. Stir lime custard into whipped cream until just incorporated. Pour into 8 individual serving glasses or a serving bowl. Chill for at least 4 hours.

8 portions

PEACH MELBA MOUSSE

3 ripe peaches, peeled, pitted and quartered
⅔ cup raspberries, picked over
3 tablespoons peach brandy, plus a little more for garnish
1 tablespoon unflavored gelatin
3 tablespoons fresh lemon juice
⅓ cup granulated sugar
⅛ teaspoon almond extract
pinch of salt
½ cup heavy cream, chilled
2 egg whites

1. Purée peaches, raspberries, and brandy in a blender or a food processor fitted with a steel blade.

2. In a saucepan soak gelatin in lemon juice for 5 minutes. Add puréed fruits, sugar, almond extract, and salt. Bring just to a boil, stirring. Remove from heat, transfer to a bowl, and cool to room temperature.

3. Whip cream to soft peaks and gently fold into fruit mixture. Refrigerate until mixture just begins to set, 1 hour.

4. Beat egg whites until stiff. Gently fold half the egg whites into mousse. Fold in remaining egg whites making sure there are no lumps.

5. Spoon into dessert glasses or a serving bowl. Chill for 4 hours. To serve, drizzle a few drops of peach brandy over each portion.

4 portions

MOCHA MOUSSE

Rich and delicious.

⅓ *cup granulated sugar*
6 tablespoons prepared espresso or strong coffee
6 ounces semisweet chocolate
4 tablespoons light cream
3 egg whites
1½ cups heavy cream, chilled

1. In a heavy saucepan, dissolve sugar in coffee over medium heat. Set aside.

2. In the top part of a double boiler set over simmering water slowly melt chocolate. When melted, whisk in light cream and the coffee mixture, stirring until smooth. Cool.

3. Beat egg whites to soft peaks. Gently fold in ½ cup of the chocolate mixture. Pour this mixture back into chocolate mixture, folding gently. Beat chilled cream to soft peaks and fold in gently until totally mixed.

4. Pour into 8 individual dessert glasses or a large serving dish, and chill for 4 hours.

8 portions

EUROPEAN
SEND-OFF
BUFFET

*Salmon Mousse with dabs
of black caviar and
sprigs of fresh dill*

Black bread rounds

Pâté Maison

----

*Chicken Marbella, cut
into bite-sized pieces*

*Rice and Vegetable Salad
with Creamy Tarragon
Dressing*

*Cold blanched asparagus
Red wine vinaigrette*

Sliced hard-cooked eggs

----

*L'Explorateur,
Montrachet and Basil
Torta cheeses*

----

*Blackberry Mousse
Lime Mousse*

A Cookie Basket

STRAWBERRY MOUSSE

2½ pint baskets strawberries, stemmed, washed and drained
2 tablespoons fresh lemon juice
1 tablespoon unflavored gelatin
6 tablespoons boiling water
2 egg yolks
⅔ cup granulated sugar
2 tablespoons Cointreau
2 cups heavy cream, chilled
additional whole strawberries (garnish)

1. Combine strawberries, lemon juice and gelatin in the bowl of a food processor fitted with a steel blade. Purée until smooth. Pour in boiling water and process again, briefly. Let mixture cool to room temperature.

2. Beat egg yolks and sugar together until pale yellow and thick. Whisk in Cointreau and beat for another minute. Pour egg mixture into the top part of a double boiler set over simmering water and stir until slightly thickened and hot to the touch. Cool to room temperature.

3. Combine strawberry and egg mixtures and chill until just beginning to set.

4. Whip cream to soft peaks and fold gently into chilled mousse mixture. Spoon into 8 to 10 individual dessert glasses or a serving bowl. Chill for at least 4 hours. Garnish with whole strawberries before serving.

8 to 10 portions

AMARETTO MOUSSE

4 tablespoons sweet butter
5 eggs
1 cup granulated sugar
1½ teaspoons unflavored gelatin
¾ cup amaretti (tiny macaroons), crushed
1½ tablespoons Amaretto liqueur
1½ cups heavy cream, chilled

1. Melt butter in top part of a double boiler over simmering water.
2. In a bowl, beat eggs with sugar and add gelatin. Add to melted butter and cook, stirring constantly, until thickened, 6 to 8 minutes. Remove from heat.
3. Add ½ cup of the crushed *amaretti* and the Amaretto. Blend well. Cool, then refrigerate until mixture just begins to set.
4. Whip cream to soft peaks. Gently fold into Amaretto mixture. Spoon into 8 to 10 individual serving glasses or a serving bowl. Chill until set, about 4 hours.
5. Just before serving, sprinkle with reserved crushed *amaretti*.
8 to 10 portions

GINGER PUMPKIN MOUSSE

4 eggs
7 tablespoons granulated sugar
1 tablespoon unflavored gelatin
1½ cups pumpkin purée (or canned pumpkin)
¾ teaspoon ground cinnamon
½ teaspoon freshly grated ginger
¼ teaspoon grated nutmeg
1 cup heavy cream
minced crystallized ginger (garnish)

1. Beat eggs with sugar until mixture is light colored and thick. Add gelatin and beat to blend well. Mix in pumpkin purée and spices and chill mixture until it begins to set.
2. Whip cream into soft peaks; fold into pumpkin mixture. Pour into 4 to 6 dessert dishes or a large serving bowl.
3. Chill for 4 hours. Before serving decorate with crystallized ginger.
4 to 6 portions

FLOWER CUPS

Crisp cookie cups to fill at the last minute with your favorite mousse or sorbet.

1⅓ cups unbleached all-purpose flour
¾ cup confectioners' sugar
3 egg whites, lightly beaten
2 egg yolks, lightly beaten
1 teaspoon grated orange zest
1 tablespoon Cointreau
1 large orange

1. Preheat oven to 350°F.
2. Sift flour and sugar together. Add egg white, egg yolks, orange zest and Cointreau. Mix well. Let batter sit for 20 minutes.
3. Grease a baking sheet and mark 5-inch circles on the surface (use a saucer as a guide), placing them well apart. Using a tablespoon, drop 1 spoonful of batter in the center of each circle, spreading batter to cover area evenly and neatly.
4. Bake cookies for 5 to 6 minutes, until edges are browning but center is still soft. Working quickly, remove cookies with a spatula and form cupped shapes, using the orange as a mold. Set shaped cookies on a rack to cool.
5. Let sheet cool, wipe clean, grease again, and make, bake, and cool another batch of cups; repeat until all batter has been used.

15 to 20 cookie cups

✦ FROM THE SILVER
PALATE NOTEBOOK

Catch the first violets when the snow is melting and add their mild flavor to spring greens. Surprise your guests by floating violets in great goblets of white wine, or topping a mousse with violet leaves and blossoms. For an elegant garnish for ice cream, sorbet or chocolate cake, dip violets into superfine sugar and let them dry until they are brittle, usually about 2 days.

ESSENTIALLY CHOCOLATE

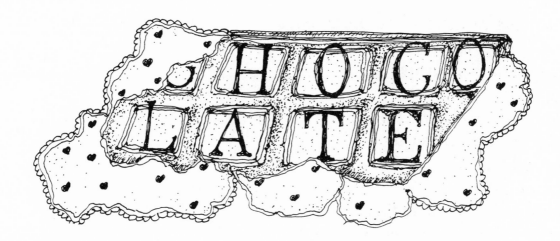

Chocolate is smooth, sweet and rich. For those who love it as we do, here is a collection of the most delicious chocolate desserts we could gather together.

**SUMMER
SATURDAY
LUNCHEON**

*Consommé with
Asparagus and Dill*

---

*Seafood Salad with Creamy
Tarragon Dressing*

Cracked Wheat Salad

Chocolate Mousse

Fresh raspberries

CHOCOLATE MOUSSE

A fabulous experience for anyone who adores chocolate.

1½ pounds semisweet chocolate chips
½ cup prepared espresso coffee
½ cup Grand Marnier
4 egg yolks
2 cups heavy cream, chilled
¼ cup granulated sugar
8 egg whites
pinch of salt
½ teaspoon vanilla extract
candied rosebuds (optional garnish)

1. Melt chocolate chips in a heavy saucepan over very low heat, stirring; add espresso coffee, then stir in Grand Marnier. Let cool to room temperature.

2. Add egg yolks, one at a time, beating thoroughly after each addition.

3. Whip 1 cup of the cream until thickened, then gradually beat in sugar, beating until stiff. Beat egg whites with salt until stiff. Gently fold egg whites into cream.

4. Stir about one third of cream and egg mixture thoroughly into chocolate mixture. Then scrape remaining cream and egg mixture over lightened chocolate base and fold together gently. Pour into 8 individual dessert cups or a serving bowl. Refrigerate for 2 hours, or until set.

5. At serving time, whip remaining cup of cream until thickened, add vanilla and whip to soft peaks. Top each portion of the mousse with a share of the cream and the optional rosebuds.

8 portions

TYPES OF CHOCOLATE

For cooking, unsweetened dark chocolate, also called baking chocolate, is most often used, although powdered cocoa (powdered chocolate with most of the cocoa butter, or fat, removed) and semisweet and dark sweet chocolate have many uses.

White chocolate is not chocolate at all, but cocoa butter, sugar and milk, plus additional flavorings.

Sad to say, the world is full of artificial chocolate these days. Chocolate gluttons may not mind, but those with more sensitive palates will always be able to distinguish the bland and waxy artificial product from the genuine article. To protect yourself before the fact, read labels. Chocolate grades and ingredients are clearly marked, and if you are wary you need never taste the phony stuff.

CHOCOLATE HAZELNUT CAKE

The best chocolate cake in the universe.

4 eggs, separated
1 cup granulated sugar
4 ounces unsweetened chocolate
12 tablespoons (1½ sticks) sweet butter
1 cup plus 1 tablespoon cake flour
¼ teaspoon salt
3 tablespoons very finely ground skinned hazelnuts
Hazelnut Buttercream (recipe follows)
Chocolate Icing (recipe follows)
8 whole hazelnuts (garnish)

1. Beat egg yolks and sugar together until mixture is thick and pale yellow.

2. Meanwhile, in the top part of a double boiler set over simmering water, melt the chocolate with the butter, whisking constantly until smooth; cool slightly.

3. Preheat oven to 350°F. Grease an 8-inch springform pan. Line the bottom with a circle of wax paper. Grease the paper and lightly flour lining and sides of pan.

4. Pour chocolate-butter mixture into egg mixture and stir just to blend. Fold in flour, salt and ground hazelnuts.

5. Whip egg whites until stiff and fold gently into batter.

6. Pour the cake batter into prepared pan and rap the pan lightly

489

on a work surface to eliminate any air bubbles.

7. Set on the middle rack of the oven and bake for 35 to 40 minutes, or until edges are firm and inside is set but still somewhat soft. Do not worry if top cracks slightly. Cool in the pan, set on a rack, for 1 hour. Remove sides of pan and cool cake to room temperature.

8. When cake is cool, invert it onto a serving plate and spread top and sides with hazelnut buttercream. Refrigerate cake for 30 minutes.

9. Remove cake from refrigerator and spread top and sides with warm chocolate icing. Work quickly, as icing sets.

10. Decorate the top of the cake with 8 whole hazelnuts. Refrigerate the cake for at least 1 hour before cutting and serving.

1 cake, 8 portions

HAZELNUT BUTTERCREAM

1¼ cups shelled hazelnuts
5 tablespoons corn syrup
2 tablespoons brandy
1 cup confectioners' sugar, sifted
4 tablespoons sweet butter, softened

1. Roast hazelnuts on a baking sheet in a 350°F. oven for 10 to 15 minutes, or until their skins have loosened. Remove from oven and rub between towels to remove skins.

2. Transfer to the bowl of a food processor fitted with a steel blade, and run machine until nuts begin to form a paste, like peanut butter in texture.

3. Scrape paste into a bowl and stir in corn syrup and brandy. Let set for 20 minutes. (Can be prepared in advance and refrigerated. Let return to room temperature before proceeding with recipe.)

4. Cream confectioners' sugar and butter together until light and fluffy. Add hazelnut paste and mix thoroughly.

Enough for top and sides of one 8-inch layer

CHOCOLATE ICING

4 tablespoons sweet butter
4 ounces semisweet chocolate
3 tablespoons cream
⅔ cup sifted confectioners' sugar, approximately
1 teaspoon vanilla extract

1. Melt butter and chocolate together in the top part of a double boiler over simmering water, whisking constantly.

2. Remove pan from heat and beat in cream. Sift in confectioners' sugar and vanilla. Icing should be very smooth. Spread while warm.

Enough for top and sides of one 8-inch cake layer.

HAZELNUTS

Hazelnuts (also called filberts — the terms are used interchangeably) have long been regarded by European pastry makers as one of the supreme dessert nuts. Their delicious flavor appears alone and in combination, especially with chocolate, in dozens of desserts. They are usually expensive and quite perishable — two reasons that have deterred Americans from appreciating hazelnuts as fully as they might. This is especially unfortunate since hazelnuts are grown in the northwest United States and thus are quite available.

Buy hazelnuts from a reputable dealer with a good turnover to ensure freshness. Store them in the freezer, well-wrapped, if you must keep them for any length of time. Their skins can be tough and are often removed before cooking with the nuts. Spread the hazelnuts in a single layer on a baking sheet and toast at 350°F. for ten to fifteen minutes. Cool slightly, and rub them between your fingers or in a kitchen towel. Their skins will flake off easily.

DECADENT CHOCOLATE CAKE

The name says it all.

1 cup boiling water
3 ounces unsweetened chocolate
8 tablespoons (1 stick) sweet butter
1 teaspoon vanilla extract
2 cups granulated sugar
2 eggs, separated
1 teaspoon baking soda
½ cup dairy sour cream
2 cups less 2 tablespoons unbleached, all-purpose flour, sifted
1 teaspoon baking powder
Chocolate Frosting (recipe follows)

1. Preheat oven to 350°F. Grease and flour a 10-inch tube pan. Knock out excess.

2. Pour boiling water over chocolate and butter; let stand until melted. Stir in vanilla and sugar, then whisk in egg yolks, one at a time, blending well after each addition.

3. Mix baking soda and sour cream and whisk into chocolate mixture.

4. Sift flour and baking powder together and add to batter, mixing thoroughly.

5. Beat egg whites until stiff but not dry. Stir a quarter of the egg whites thoroughly into the batter. Scoop remaining egg whites on top of the batter and gently fold together.

6. Pour batter into the prepared pan. Set on the middle rack of the oven and bake for 40 to 50 minutes, or until the edges have pulled away from the sides of the pan and a cake tester inserted into the center comes out clean. Cool in pan for 10 minutes; unmold and cool completely before frosting.

12 portions

CHOCOLATE FROSTING

2 tablespoons sweet butter
¾ cup semisweet chocolate chips
6 tablespoons heavy cream
1¼ cups sifted confectioners' sugar, or as needed
1 teaspoon vanilla extract

Place all ingredients in a heavy saucepan over low heat and whisk until smooth. Cool slightly; add more sugar if necessary to achieve a spreading consistency. Spread on cake while frosting is still warm.

COCKTAIL BUFFET MENU

Brie, Brillat-Savarin and Boucheron cheeses with red, green and purple grape clusters

---

Walnuts in bowls

Linzertorte

Decadent Chocolate Cake with whipped cream

Coffee spiced with cinnamon sticks

"Give me the luxuries of life and I will willingly do without the necessities."

— Frank Lloyd Wright

CHOCOLATE FRUITS

Strawberries, raspberries, cherries, grapes, tangerine and orange sections, bananas, and apple and pear slices are our favorite fruits for coating with chocolate.

Melt your favorite semisweet or sweet bar chocolate, cut up, over very low heat in a small deep pan; remove from heat. Whenever possible, leave the stems and leaves on whole fruits; be sure the surface of fruit is as dry as possible. Using a toothpick to hold the fruit, dip the fruit into the chocolate, then wipe the excess off against the edge of the pan. If you can, place the other end of the toothpick in a piece of styrofoam, allowing the fruit to dry upside down. Work quickly so that the chocolate doesn't become too thick. If it does, simply set it over low heat for a moment or two. Chocolate-covered fruits should be eaten within 24 hours.

BITTERSWEET CHOCOLATE CAKE

14 ounces semisweet chocolate (the darkest you can find)
3 tablespoons cold water
12 eggs, separated
2 cups granulated sugar
¾ pound plus 4 tablespoons (3½ sticks) sweet butter, softened
1 cup unbleached all-purpose flour, sifted
confectioners' sugar

1. Preheat oven to 325°F. Butter and sugar a 10-inch springform pan and tap out any extra sugar.

2. Grate or break chocolate into small pieces. Place in top part of a double boiler with the cold water. Melt over simmering water, whisking until smooth. Let chocolate cool slightly.

3. Beat egg yolks with the granulated sugar until they are thick and pale yellow and form a ribbon when they fall from the beater. Fold in warm chocolate. Stir in the very soft butter and then fold in the sifted flour. Mix thoroughly but gently.

4. Beat egg whites until stiff. Stir a large spoonful of the chocolate mixture into the beaten egg whites. Mix well. Pour this mixture into chocolate mixture; fold together gently, incorporating whites completely. Be very careful at this stage not to overmix.

5. Turn batter into the springform pan. It will come close to the top of the pan. Set on the middle rack of the oven and bake for 1 hour and 20 minutes, or until cake tester inserted in center comes out clean. Cool on rack for 15 minutes, then remove outer rim. Allow cake to cool completely before removing bottom of pan. Refrigerate.

6. When ready to serve, using a paper doily as a stencil, sprinkle with confectioners' sugar to make a design. Serve cold.

20 small but sweet portions

CHOCOLATE-GLAZED PEARS

A perfectly elegant dessert.

Fruit Poaching Syrup (see page 527)
6 large pears
⅓ cup dried apricots, coarsely chopped
⅓ cup raisins
⅓ cup shelled black walnuts
Chocolate Glaze (recipe follows)
6 candied violets (garnish)

1. Prepare poaching syrup and simmer for 10 minutes.

2. Peel pears and core them from the bottom, leaving stems in place. Reserve cores.

3. Poach the pears in the syrup, standing them upright, for about 12 minutes, or until tender but not mushy. Let pears cool in the poaching syrup.

4. Meanwhile, combine apricots and raisins in a small bowl. Measure out 1 cup of hot syrup from the pot of pears, pour over fruit and let stand for 1 hour.

5. Drain pears and gently pat very dry. Drain soaked dried fruits and combine with black walnuts. Stuff some of the mixture into each pear, leaving ½ inch of space at the bottom. Trim a piece ½-inch thick from the end of each reserved pear core and plug the pear cavities. Arrange pears well apart on a baking sheet.

6. Using a large spoon, gently and slowly pour the chocolate glaze over each pear. Be careful to coat completely without being overly generous. Set a candied violet next to each stem and let the chocolate set completely, about 45 minutes.

7. To serve, gently transfer pears to individual serving plates.

6 portions

CHOCOLATE GLAZE

10 ounces semisweet chocolate, in pieces
3 tablespoons solid vegetable shortening

Melt chocolate and shortening in a stainless-steel bowl over simmering water, whisking until smooth. Cool slightly before using.
  Enough glaze for 6 pears

PROFITEROLES

These tender puffs filled with ice cream and drizzled with chocolate fudge sauce are one of the easiest and most delicious desserts we know.

⅔ cup water
4 tablespoons sweet butter
1 tablespoon granulated sugar
½ teaspoon salt
1 cup unbleached all-purpose flour, sifted
4 eggs, at room temperature
1 pint vanilla or coffee ice cream, approximately
Chocolate Fudge Sauce (recipe follows)
1 cup heavy cream, chilled

1. Preheat oven to 450°F. Grease a cookie sheet.
2. In a heavy saucepan, combine water, butter, sugar and salt. Bring to a boil. Remove from heat and add flour all at once. Stir hard until mixture forms a ball in the middle of the saucepan. Cool slightly.
3. Add eggs, one at a time, beating after each addition until dough shines.
4. Drop rounded teaspoons of dough onto cookie sheet. Set on the middle rack of the oven and bake for 5 minutes, then reduce heat to 350°F. Continue baking until sides of puffs are completely firm and color is golden, about fifteen minutes. Cool puffs on a cake rack.
5. At serving time, cut off tops of puffs and set lids aside. Whip cream until stiff. Fill puffs with vanilla or coffee ice cream. Replace tops and arrange puffs in a large bowl.
6. Cover with hot fudge sauce and lots of whipped cream, and serve at once.
  4 to 6 portions

Note: Puffs can be filled with ice cream and frozen 1 to 2 hours in advance of serving time.

A RUSSIAN BRUNCH

Lemon Vodka

———

*Blini with sour cream
and caviar*

*Scotch salmon
Russian Pumpernickel*

———

*Chocolate-dipped
strawberries*

CHOCOLATE FUDGE SAUCE

This is a deep, dark, fudgy sauce that hardens on ice cream to a thick, delicious glaze.

4 ounces unsweetened chocolate
3 tablespoons sweet butter
⅔ cup water
1⅔ cups granulated sugar
6 tablespoons corn syrup
1 tablespoon rum

1. Melt chocolate and butter very slowly in a heavy saucepan. Meanwhile, heat the water to boiling. When chocolate and butter have melted, add water and stir well.

2. Add the sugar and corn syrup and mix until smooth. Turn the heat up and stir until mixture starts to boil; adjust the heat so that sauce is just maintained at the boiling point. Allow the sauce to boil, without stirring, for 9 minutes.

3. Remove sauce from heat and cool for 15 minutes. Stir in the rum. Serve sauce warm over ice cream or profiteroles.

2½ cups

" 'How long does getting thin take?' Pooh asked anxiously."
— *Winnie the Pooh,*
A. A. Milne

CHOCOLATE PEANUT BUTTER BITES

¾ *cup brown sugar*
1 pound confectioners' sugar
8 tablespoons (1 stick) sweet butter
2 cups peanut butter
1 cup unsalted peanuts
12 ounces semisweet chocolate chips
1 tablespoon sweet butter

1. Mix first 5 ingredients together. Pat into an ungreased jelly-roll pan, about 15 x 10 inches and 1 inch deep. Flatten top with a rolling pin.
2. Melt chocolate chips and butter in the top part of a double boiler over simmering water. Spread chocolate on peanut butter mixture.
3. Cut into bite-size squares. Chill for 15 to 20 minutes. Remove from pan. Serve chilled.
50 or more bites

✤ FROM THE SILVER
PALATE NOTEBOOK

Plan your party to follow one of three natural progressions:
• Serve from one table, beginning the evening with finger food which is then refreshed with a spread of more substantial food; later clear the table to serve dessert and coffee.
• Have waiters serve finger food from trays while entrées and salads are served buffet style. Coffee and dessert may be served either way or not at all.
• Serve different courses in various rooms to create the element of surprise and encourage people to circulate.

CHOCOLATE TRUFFLES

The most direct chocolate experience we know. Offer these confections to guests with coffee, or give them at holiday time.

¼ cup heavy cream
2 tablespoons Grand Marnier
6 ounces German's sweet chocolate, broken up
4 tablespoons sweet butter, softened
powdered unsweetened cocoa

    1. Boil cream in a small heavy pan until reduced to 2 tablespoons. Remove from heat, stir in Grand Marnier and chocolate, and return to low heat; stir until chocolate melts.
    2. Whisk in softened butter. When mixture is smooth, pour into a shallow bowl and refrigerate until firm, about 40 minutes.
    3. Scoop chocolate up with a teaspoon and shape into rough 1-inch balls. Roll the truffle balls in the unsweetened cocoa.
    4. Store truffles, covered, in the refrigerator. Let truffles stand at room temperature for 30 minutes before serving.
24 truffles

Variations: Substitute dark rum, Cognac, or another liqueur for the Grand Marnier. Try Kahlúa, Framboise, Crème de Menthe, or Amaretto.

HOT FROM THE OVEN

We all have memories of cakes, tarts or pies cooling on the windowsill. The American tradition of freshly baked pastry is one we carry on at The Silver Palate. Favorites in this category change continually, but standards remain constant — cakes should be moist, pies fruit-filled and flaky, and tarts as beautiful as can be.

BISHOP'S CAKE

Our search for a truly moist poundcake ended here. Delicious, especially when served with a scoop of tart sorbet.

½ pound (2 sticks) sweet butter
2 cups granulated sugar
2 cups unbleached all-purpose flour
1 tablespoon fresh lemon juice
1 teaspoon vanilla extract
5 eggs

1. Preheat oven to 350°F. Grease and flour a 10-inch bundt pan.
2. Cream butter and sugar gradually; beat until fluffy.
3. Sift flour and add to butter mixture. Stir just enough to blend.
4. Add lemon juice and vanilla; stir well. Add eggs, one at a time, mixing well after each addition.

5. Pour batter into the prepared bundt pan. Bake for 1 hour and 15 minutes, or until a cake tester inserted into the center of the cake comes out clean. (After 30 minutes, cover cake closely with aluminum foil.)

6. When cake is done, cool in its pan on a cake rack for 10 minutes. Remove from pan and cool completely.

8 to 10 portions

CARROT CAKE

In the beginning, Sheila's mother drove her famous carrot cakes down to Manhattan daily from her Connecticut kitchen. The cake became a Silver Palate classic; it may now become yours as well.

3 cups unbleached all-purpose flour
3 cups granulated sugar
1 teaspoon salt
1 tablespoon baking soda
1 tablespoon ground cinnamon
1½ cups corn oil
4 large eggs, lightly beaten
1 tablespoon vanilla extract
1½ cups shelled walnuts, chopped
1½ cups shredded coconut
1⅓ cups puréed cooked carrots
¾ cup drained crushed pineapple
Cream-Cheese Frosting (recipe follows)
confectioners' sugar for dusting top

1. Preheat oven to 350°F. Grease two 9-inch springform pans.

2. Sift dry ingredients into a bowl. Add oil, eggs and vanilla. Beat well. Fold in walnuts, coconut, carrots and pineapple.

3. Pour batter into the prepared pans. Set on the middle rack of the oven and bake for 50 minutes, until edges have pulled away from sides and a cake tester inserted in center comes out clean.

4. Cool on a cake rack for 3 hours. Fill cake and frost sides with cream-cheese frosting. Dust top with confectioners' sugar.

10 to 12 portions

CREAM-CHEESE FROSTING

8 ounces cream cheese, at room temperature
6 tablespoons sweet butter, at room temperature
3 cups confectioners' sugar
1 teaspoon vanilla extract
juice of ½ lemon (optional)

1. Cream together cream cheese and butter in a mixing bowl.
2. Slowly sift in confectioners' sugar and continue beating until fully incorporated. Mixture should be free of lumps.
3. Stir in vanilla, and lemon juice if you use it.
Frosting for a 2-layer cake

A DANISH BRUNCH

Gravlax with lemon wedges
Dill Mustard Sauce

Pickled herring in
sour cream with
chopped fresh dill

Red Beet Salad

Minty Cucumber Salad

———

Pâté Maison
Crackers and Rye Bread
with sweet butter

———

Orange Cake

———

Danish Blue and Havarti
cheeses

ORANGE CAKE

8 tablespoons (1 stick) sweet butter, softened
¾ cup granulated sugar
2 eggs, separated
grated zest of 2 oranges
1½ cups unbleached all-purpose flour
1½ teaspoons baking powder
¼ teaspoon baking soda
¼ teaspoon salt
½ cup fresh orange juice
Orange Glaze (recipe follows)

1. Preheat oven to 350°F. Grease a 10-inch bundt pan.
2. Cream the butter and gradually add the sugar, beating until light. Beat in egg yolks, one at a time, and the orange zest.
3. Sift the flour with baking powder, baking soda and salt. Add dry ingredients alternately with the orange juice to the batter.
4. Beat the egg whites until stiff and fold them into the batter.
5. Pour batter into the prepared bundt pan. Bake for 30 to 35 minutes, or until sides of cake shrink away from edges of pan and a cake tester inserted in the center comes out clean.
6. Cool for 10 minutes in pan, unmold onto a rack, and drizzle with Orange Glaze while warm. Cool before serving.

8 to 10 portions

ORANGE GLAZE

¼ cup fresh orange juice
¼ cup granulated sugar

Combine orange juice and sugar in a small saucepan and simmer gently for 5 minutes, stirring occasionally, until a light syrup forms.

ORANGE POPPY-SEED BUNDT CAKE

8 tablespoons (1 stick) sweet butter, at room temperature
1½ cups granulated sugar
4 eggs
2 cups unbleached all-purpose flour
2½ teaspoons baking powder
½ teaspoon salt
¾ cup milk
½ cup poppy seeds
1 teaspoon vanilla extract
grated zest of 2 oranges
double recipe Orange Glaze

1. Preheat oven to 325°F. Grease a 10-inch bundt pan.
2. Cream butter and sugar together in a mixing bowl until light and fluffy. Add eggs, one at a time, beating well after each addition.
3. Sift flour, baking powder and salt together. Add to creamed mixture alternately with milk. Mix well after each addition.
4. Fold in poppy seeds, vanilla and grated orange zest. Pour batter into the prepared bundt pan.
5. Set on the middle rack of the oven and bake for 50 to 60 minutes, or until edges shrink away slightly from sides of pan and a cake tester inserted into the center comes out clean. Let cake cool in the pan for 30 minutes before turning it out onto a cake rack.
6. When cake has cooled, prick holes in it 1½ inches apart with a long toothpick, and pour the Orange Glaze evenly over top. Serve warm with ice cream on side.

12 portions

GLAZED LEMON CAKE

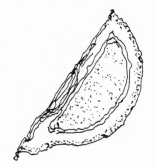

½ pound (2 sticks) sweet butter, softened
2 cups granulated sugar
3 eggs
3 cups unbleached, all-purpose flour, sifted
½ teaspoon baking soda
½ teaspoon salt
1 cup buttermilk
2 tightly packed tablespoons grated lemon zest
2 tablespoons fresh lemon juice
Lemon Icing (recipe follows)

1. Preheat oven to 325°F. Grease a 10-inch tube pan.
2. Cream butter and sugar until light and fluffy. Beat in eggs, one at a time, blending well after each addition.
3. Sift together flour, baking soda and salt. Stir dry ingredients into egg mixture alternately with buttermilk, beginning and ending with dry ingredients. Add lemon zest and juice.
4. Pour batter into prepared tube pan. Set on the middle rack of the oven and bake for 1 hour and 5 minutes, or until cake pulls away from sides of pan and a tester inserted in the center comes out clean.
5. Cool cake in the pan, set on a rack for 10 minutes. Remove cake from pan and spread on icing at once, while cake is still hot.

8 to 10 portions

LEMON ICING

1 pound confectioners' sugar
8 tablespoons (1 stick) sweet butter, softened
3 tightly packed tablespoons grated lemon zest
½ cup fresh lemon juice

Cream sugar and butter thoroughly. Mix in lemon zest and juice; spread on warm cake.

Have dinner in an unlikely place — the living room, in front of the fireplace; the kitchen, with all hands helping final assembly; the library; outdoors anytime it's comfortable. Transform a basement, a garage or a poolroom into another world with fabrics, plants, flowers or candlelight.

If you're lucky enough to have a pretty kitchen, use it as much as possible for entertaining. Involve your guests; serve from it at informal parties.

"Looks can be deceiving — it's eating that's believing."
— James Thurber

CHESTNUT CAKE

Light and moist, our favorite yellow cake.

2 cups granulated sugar
4 eggs
1 cup vegetable oil
1 cup dry white wine
2½ cups unbleached all-purpose flour
½ teaspoon salt
2¼ teaspoons baking powder
1 teaspoon vanilla extract
Chocolate Icing (see page 491), warm
¾ cup sweetened chestnut purée*
whole chestnuts preserved in syrup* (optional garnish)

1. Preheat oven to 350°F. Grease and flour two 9-inch round layer cake pans.

2. Beat sugar and eggs together, using an electric mixer, for 30 seconds on medium speed. Add oil, wine, flour, salt, baking powder and vanilla; beat for 1 minute.

3. Pour batter into the prepared pans. Set on the middle rack of the oven and bake for 30 minutes, or until cake has pulled away from sides of pan and a knife inserted in the center comes out clean.

4. Let cakes cool in pans for 5 minutes. Turn them out on rack and let cool for at least 2 hours before frosting.

5. Arrange 1 cake layer on a serving plate. Spread with warm chocolate icing. Set second layer on top of first and spread with chestnut purée. Cover sides of cake with remaining icing. Decorate top with well-drained whole preserved chestnuts if desired. Chill cake for 45 minutes before serving.

8 or more portions

*available at specialty food shops

BANANA CAKE

Lush and delicious.

½ pound (2 sticks) sweet butter
1 cup granulated sugar
2 eggs
1 cup mashed ripe bananas
1¾ cups unbleached all-purpose flour
½ teaspoon salt
⅔ teaspoon baking soda
5 tablespoons buttermilk
1 teaspoon vanilla extract
Cream-Cheese Frosting (see page 502)
1½ to 2 medium-size, firm but ripe, bananas, sliced
1½ cups shelled chopped walnuts

1. Preheat oven to 350°F. Grease and flour two 9-inch layer cake pans.

2. Cream butter and sugar together until light and fluffy. Add eggs, one at a time, beating well after each addition. Add mashed bananas, mixing thoroughly.

3. Sift dry ingredients and add to butter and egg mixture. Stir until flour has been incorporated completely. Add buttermilk and vanilla. Mix for 1 minute.

4. Pour batter into the prepared pans. Set on the middle rack of the oven and bake for 25 to 30 minutes or until a cake tester inserted into the center comes out clean.

5. Cool in pans on a rack for 10 minutes. Unmold and cool on rack for 2 hours.

6. When cooled, place one layer on a serving plate and frost with

Cream-Cheese Frosting. Arrange slices of banana over frosting; cover with second layer and frost top and sides of cake.

7. Cover sides of cake with chopped nuts, holding nuts in palm and pressing firmly to sides of cake. Dust top of cake with confectioners' sugar.

10 to 12 portions

PEACH CAKE

CAKE:

4 tablespoons sweet butter
¼ cup granulated sugar
1 egg
1 cup unbleached all-purpose flour
1½ teaspoons baking powder
½ teaspoon salt
¼ cup milk
3 ripe peaches, peeled and sliced

1. Preheat oven to 350°F. Grease well a heavy 9-inch skillet.
2. Cream butter and sugar until light. Beat in egg.
3. Sift dry ingredients together. Beat half into creamed mixture; beat in half of the milk. Repeat, beating well.
4. Pour batter into prepared skillet. Arrange peach slices on top of batter. Bake for 25 minutes.

TOPPING:

½ cup granulated sugar
½ teaspoon ground cinnamon
¼ teaspoon grated nutmeg
4 tablespoons sweet butter

1. Meanwhile, cut ingredients for topping together in a small bowl with a fork. After cake has baked for 25 minutes, open oven and quickly crumble topping over peaches.
2. Close oven and bake for another 8 minutes, or until cake is firm and has pulled away from edges of the skillet. Serve warm, accompanied by a pitcher of heavy cream.

8 portions

MAY DAY PICNIC

*Assorted crudités with
Tapenade Dip and
Pesto Mayonnaise*

Cold Roast Veal

Beet and Roquefort Salad

French bread and butter

---

*Peach Cake
vanilla ice cream*

Iced espresso

COCONUT CAKE

A simple cake, for coconut lovers.

*2 layers of yellow cake, baked and cooled (see Chestnut Cake,
    page 506)*
2 cups dairy sour cream
1 teaspoon vanilla extract
5 cups shredded coconut
1 cup sifted confectioners' sugar

1. Mix sour cream, vanilla and coconut in a mixing bowl. Blend well. Add sugar to coconut mixture and mix thoroughly.

2. Place 1 cake layer on a cake platter and spread top with half of coconut mixture. Place second layer on top of first and spread with remaining coconut mixture, leaving sides of cake unfrosted.

8 or more portions

LINZERTORTE

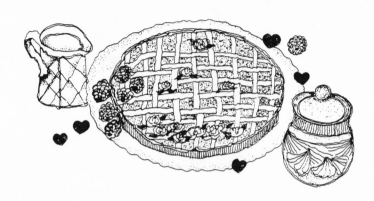

½ pound plus 4 tablespoons (2½ sticks) sweet butter, at room temperature
1 cup granulated sugar
1½ teaspoons grated lemon zest
2 eggs
1¼ cups unbleached all-purpose flour
½ teaspoon ground cinnamon
¼ teaspoon ground cloves
¼ teaspoon salt
1¼ cups blanched almonds, finely ground
⅔ cup raspberry preserves
confectioners' sugar for dusting top

1. Preheat oven to 325°F.
2. Cream butter and sugar together until light. Add grated zest and eggs and mix well.
3. Sift flour, spices and salt together. Add flour mixture and almonds to butter mixture and blend thoroughly.
4. Pat half of this mixture evenly into the bottom of a 9-inch false-bottom tart pan. Spread preserves to within ½ inch of the sides.
5. Transfer remaining dough to a pastry bag and form a ring around the edge, then squeeze out a lattice crust on top.
6. Set on the middle rack of the oven and bake for 50 minutes, or until the lattice is evenly browned and the preserves are bubbling. Sprinkle top lightly with confectioners' sugar. Serve warm or cold.

6 to 8 portions

PECAN PIE

Golden and lush, but not too sweet; a taste of the Old South.

4 eggs
1 cup dark brown sugar
¾ cup light corn syrup
½ teaspoon salt
¼ cup melted sweet butter (½ stick)
1 teaspoon vanilla extract
2 cups shelled pecans, chopped
9-inch unbaked Piecrust (see page 578)
⅓ cup shelled pecan halves

1. Preheat oven to 400°F. Line a 9-inch pie pan with the pastry.
2. Beat eggs well in a large bowl. Add brown sugar, corn syrup, salt, melted butter and vanilla to the eggs, and mix thoroughly.
3. Sprinkle chopped pecans in pastry-lined pan. Pour egg mixture over pecans. Arrange pecan halves around edge of filling next to crust for decoration.
4. Set on the middle rack of the oven and bake for 10 minutes. Reduce heat to 325°F. and bake for 25 to 30 minutes longer, or until set.
5. Remove from oven and let cool to room temperature before serving.

8 portions

OLD-FASHIONED LEMON PIE

This one is even better than the one you remember your grandmother making.

1¼ cups milk
1⅛ cups granulated sugar
3 tablespoons cornstarch
3 egg yolks, slightly beaten
juice of 3 lemons
grated zest of 2 lemons
1 teaspoon vanilla extract
9-inch unbaked Piecrust (see page 578)
1 cup lemon marmalade
3 kiwis, peeled and thinly sliced

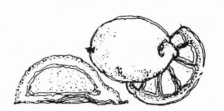

1. Preheat oven to 325°F. Line a 9-inch pie pan with the pastry.
2. Heat the milk in top pan of a double boiler over simmering water. Mix sugar with the cornstarch and whisk into the milk. Add the beaten egg yolks. Stir well and cook for 3 minutes. Pour in lemon juice and zest and vanilla. Blend thoroughly.
3. Pour filling into the pastry-lined pan. Set on the middle rack of the oven and bake for 25 minutes, or until set.
4. Cool pie 10 minutes. Melt lemon marmalade over low heat and brush a thin layer of it over the surface of the pie. Arrange the sliced kiwis in an overlapping layer to cover top of pie completely. Brush again, generously, with remaining marmalade. Cool completely before cutting.

6 to 8 portions

KITE-FLYING PICNIC

Pâté de Campagne with Walnuts

Salad Niçoise

Marinated Chèvres

French bread and Ravigote Butter

Old Fashioned Lemon Pie

Fresh strawberries

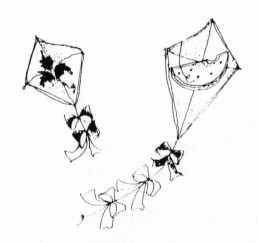

"I prefer the errors of enthusiasm to the indifference of wisdom."

— Anatole France

PUMPKIN PIE

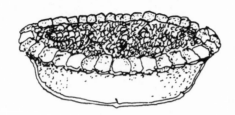

Save room for a piece of this one.

3 eggs
⅓ cup granulated sugar
⅓ cup brown sugar
2 cups canned puréed pumpkin
1 teaspoon ground ginger
1½ teaspoons ground cinnamon
½ teaspoon ground cloves
½ teaspoon ground allspice
¼ teaspoon ground cardamom
pinch of salt
¾ cup heavy cream
¾ cup half-and-half
½ recipe Piecrust (see page 578)
pecan halves (garnish)

1. Preheat oven to 450°F.
2. Beat eggs and both sugars together until light. Stir in pumpkin purée, spices and salt and mix thoroughly. Stir in cream and half-and-half.
3. Roll out pastry on a lightly floured work surface, and line a 9-inch pie pan with it; trim and crimp edges. Pour in the filling.
4. Bake the pie at 450°F. for 8 minutes, then reduce heat to 325°F. and bake for another 40 to 45 minutes, or until filling is set (a knife inserted in the center will come out clean).
5. Arrange pecan halves decoratively around the edge, pressing them lightly into the warm filling. Arrange another 5 pecans in a flower pattern in the center of the pie. Cool completely before cutting.

6 portions

PINWHEEL FRUIT TART

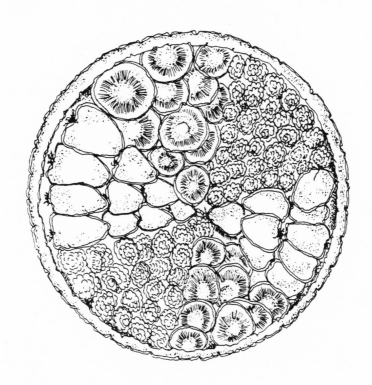

4 kiwi fruits
1½ cups Pastry Cream (see page 578)
9-inch prebaked Sweet Buttery Tart Crust (see page 580)
1 pint basket raspberries, picked over
1 pint basket strawberries, rinsed, stemmed, patted dry, halved
*   lengthwise*
Red Currant Glaze (see page 595), warmed

1. Peel kiwis and slice thin.
2. Spread pastry cream in cooled tart shell.
3. Make a pinwheel design over cream, arranging each fruit in a whorl pattern, first using raspberries, then strawberries (cut sides down), then layered slices of kiwis. Repeat with remaining fruit.
4. Brush the fruit with the Red Currant Glaze. Serve within 2 to 3 hours.
8 to 10 portions

HARVEST TART

1 cup pitted prunes
1 cup dried apricots
1 cup chopped peeled apples
½ cup golden raisins
⅓ cup granulated sugar
½ cup shelled walnut halves
¼ cup melted sweet butter
⅔ cup Grand Marnier
double recipe of Sweet Buttery Tart Crust (see page 580)
1 egg, beaten

1. Preheat oven to 350°F.
2. Combine prunes, apricots, apples and raisins in a heavy saucepan. Add water just to cover, set over moderate heat, and simmer until fruit is tender, about 20 minutes. Drain fruit thoroughly and chop.
3. Return fruit to saucepan, add sugar, walnuts, melted butter and Grand Marnier, and simmer for 5 minutes, stirring occasionally. Cool to room temperature.
4. Roll out half of the pastry dough on a lightly floured board and use it to line a 9-inch pie pan. Spoon filling into pastry-lined pan, mounding it slightly. Trim excess crust, leaving about 1 inch all around.
5. Roll out remaining dough to a 10½-inch round and cut into ½-inch strips. Arrange strips lattice-fashion over the filling, trim ends, and turn up the edge of the bottom crust over the ends of the strips; crimp decoratively. Brush lattice top lightly with beaten egg.
6. Bake tart for 30 to 35 minutes, or until top is golden brown and filling is bubbling. Serve warm or cool.

1 tart, 6 to 8 portions

ALMOND TART

CRUST:

¾ cup unbleached all-purpose flour, sifted
1 tablespoon granulated sugar
5 tablespoons sweet butter, cold
½ teaspoon vanilla extract
2 to 3 teaspoons water, or as needed

1. Mix flour and sugar together. Working quickly, cut in cold butter with 2 knives or a pastry blender until mixture resembles oatmeal. Add vanilla and 2 teaspoons of the water and toss with a fork until dough just holds together. (Add more water, a few drops at a time, if necessary.) Do not overwork.

2. Press dough evenly into an 8-inch false-bottom tart pan. Chill in refrigerator for 45 minutes.

3. Preheat oven to 400°F.

4. Line the chilled dough with aluminum foil and fill with dried beans. Bake in the lower part of oven for 8 minutes. Remove foil and beans and bake for 5 minutes longer. Remove from oven.

FILLING:

½ cup granulated sugar
3 tablespoons apricot preserves
¾ cup sliced blanched almonds
½ cup heavy cream
2 tablespoons Amaretto liqueur
¼ teaspoon salt

1. Stir sugar and apricot preserves together in a bowl, mixing well. Add remaining ingredients, blending thoroughly. Pour into partially baked shell.

2. Set on the middle rack of the oven and bake for 25 to 30 minutes, until filling top is golden brown. Cool and serve.

10 to 12 portions

AFTER-DINNER COFFEES

Try these delicious combinations after special dinners, when something more festive than regular coffee is called for.

♥ **KAHLUA COFFEE:** Add 1 ounce of Kahlúa to a cup of rich coffee; top with whipped cream and sprinkle with grated orange zest.

♥ **ALMOND COFFEE:** Add 1 ounce of Amaretto liqueur to a cup of hot coffee, and top with a dollop of whipped cream and toasted almond slivers.

♥ **BRANDY COFFEE:** Combine 2 tablespoons sugar and 1 ounce of brandy with a cup of hot coffee; stir in 1 teaspoon sweet butter and garnish with a cinnamon stick.

COMFORTING CONCLUSIONS

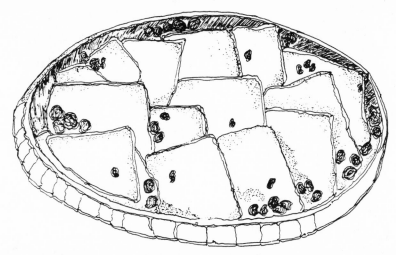

These are the sweets that soothe, that we first readily appreciated when we had our tonsils out or were home on a rainy Saturday afternoon. We enjoy them now especially when the grown-up world seems to be too much to bear, and each brings back memories of favorite times gone by.

BREAD PUDDING

A childhood favorite, with a very adult sauce. This is an adaptation of a recipe given to us by Alzina Pierce of the Bon Ton Restaurant in New Orleans, another proof that a recipe is certainly a living thing.

1 loaf of stale French bread
1 quart milk
10 tablespoons (1¼ sticks) sweet butter, softened to room temperature
4 eggs
1½ cups granulated sugar
2 tablespoons vanilla extract
1 cup raisins
1 cup confectioners' sugar
4 tablespoons whiskey

1. Crumble the bread into a bowl. Pour the milk over it and let stand for 1 hour.
2. Preheat oven to 325°F. Grease a 9 x 13 x 2 inch baking dish

519

with 1 to 2 tablespoons of the butter.

3. In another bowl beat together 3 eggs, the granulated sugar and the vanilla extract. Stir this mixture into the bread mixture. Stir in the raisins.

4. Pour into the prepared baking dish, place on the middle rack of the oven, and bake until browned and set, about 1 hour and 10 minutes. Cool to room temperature.

5. To make sauce, stir 8 tablespoons butter and confectioners' sugar together in the top of a double boiler over simmering water until sugar is dissolved and mixture is very hot. Remove from the heat. Beat the remaining egg well and whisk it into the sugar mixture. Remove pan from base and continue beating until sauce has cooled to room temperature. Add whiskey to taste.

6. To serve, preheat broiler. Cut pudding into squares and transfer each square to a heatproof serving dish. Spoon whiskey sauce over pudding and run under broiler until bubbling.

8 to 10 portions

TODAY'S TIMES

When we reflect on life in the city, we're often reminded of Russell Baker's column in the May 30, 1980, issue of *The New York Times*. Entitled "Elephant's Eye High," the article asks, "Do you ever wish you had it to do over again, folks? Do you wish you'd have taken up the kind of work where you could call people 'folks', instead of 'Sir' and 'Deadbeat' and 'Big Shot' and 'Meathead'? The kind of life where you say 'By golly!' and 'There's a heap of goodness in this old world of ours'? Remember where your granddaddy was sitting when he was advising you not to go off to the city? In a rocking chair. Remember where the rocking chair was situated? On the front porch. You don't have a rocking chair, do you? Don't have a porch either, I bet."

Well, for all the things we've lost — sitting on the porch swing at sunset, smelling the honeysuckle — think of all the things we've gained. The trick is in holding on to a little of each.

CREME BRULEE

Long a favorite at The Silver Palate, this is a dessert that, while comforting, can also end a dinner party elegantly.

2⅓ cups heavy cream
⅔ cup milk
¼ cup granulated sugar
3 whole eggs
3 egg yolks
1 teaspoon vanilla extract
¾ cup light brown sugar

1. Preheat oven to 300°F.
2. Heat cream, milk and sugar in a heavy saucepan to almost boiling. In a separate bowl beat whole eggs and extra egg yolks together well.
3. Gradually whisk the heated mixture into the eggs, then return mixture to the saucepan. Cook over moderate heat, stirring constantly with a wooden spoon, until the custard coats the back of the spoon (3 to 4 minutes); remove from heat. Stir in vanilla.
4. Pour custard into 6 individual custard dishes or into 1 shallow baking dish about 9 inches across. Set dish or dishes in a large pan and place on the middle rack of the oven. Pour hot water into the outer pan to come level with custard.
5. Bake for 35 to 45 minutes, until center of custard is set. When done, remove custard from water bath and cool. Cover and chill.
6. A few hours before serving, preheat broiler. Sift brown sugar evenly over top of custard, spreading to the edges. Set custard under broiler as close to heat as possible. Broil until browned but not burned, about 1½ minutes. Watch closely. Remove and chill.
   6 portions

PEACH COBBLER

A dessert that brings memories of summer.

4 cups peeled and sliced ripe peaches
⅔ cup plus 3 tablespoons granulated sugar
1 teaspoon grated lemon zest
1 tablespoon fresh lemon juice
¼ teaspoon almond extract
1½ cups unbleached all-purpose flour
1 tablespoon baking powder
½ teaspoon salt
⅓ cup vegetable shortening
1 egg, lightly beaten
¼ cup milk
1 cup heavy cream, chilled
3 to 4 tablespoons peach brandy or peach cordial

1. Preheat oven to 400°F. Butter a 2-quart baking dish.
2. Arrange peaches in baking dish. Sprinkle with ⅔ cup sugar, the lemon zest and juice, and almond extract.
3. Bake for 20 minutes.
4. While peaches are baking, sift flour, 1 tablespoon of the remaining sugar, the baking powder and salt together into a bowl. Cut in shortening until mixture resembles cornmeal. Combine beaten egg and milk and mix into dry ingredients until just combined.
5. Remove peaches from oven and quickly drop dough by large spoonfuls over surface. Sprinkle with remaining 2 tablespoons sugar. Return to the oven for 15 to 20 minutes, until top is firm and golden brown.
6. Whip cream to soft peaks. Flavor with peach brandy to taste.
7. Serve cobbler warm, accompanied by whipped cream.
4 to 6 portions

> "Had I but one penny in the world, thou shouldst have it for gingerbread."
>
> — *Love's Labor's Lost,*
> **William Shakespeare**

GINGERBREAD

1⅔ cups unbleached all-purpose flour
1¼ teaspoons baking soda
1½ teaspoons ground ginger
¾ teaspoon ground cinnamon
¾ teaspoon salt
1 egg, lightly beaten
½ cup granulated sugar
½ cup molasses
½ cup boiling water
½ cup vegetable oil
Lemon Glaze (recipe follows)

1. Preheat oven to 350°F. Grease and flour a 9-inch square baking pan.

2. Sift dry ingredients together into a mixing bowl. Add egg, sugar and molasses. Mix well.

3. Pour boiling water and the oil over mixture. Stir thoroughly until smooth.

4. Pour batter into the prepared pan. Set on the middle rack of the oven and bake for 35 to 40 minutes, or until top springs back when touched and the edges have pulled away slightly from the sides of the pan.

5. While the gingerbread is still hot, pour glaze over top and cool in the pan, set on a rack.

12 portions

LEMON GLAZE

⅔ cup confectioners' sugar
3 tablespoons fresh lemon juice

Sift sugar into a bowl; add lemon juice and mix well.

CAPPUCCINO ICE

A mellower variation on the classic Italian espresso ice.

*3 cups prepared strong coffee, made at least partially with
 dark-roast "espresso" coffee
1 cup half-and-half
1 cup granulated sugar*

1. Combine ingredients in a saucepan and set over medium heat. Stir constantly until the mixture is about to boil and all the sugar is dissolved.

2. Cool to room temperature, pour into a shallow pan (an 8-inch square cake tin is ideal), and freeze.

3. The mixture will take from 3 to 6 hours to freeze and, because of its relatively low sugar content, will be very solid. To serve, set in refrigerator for 30 minutes to temper the texture slightly.

1 quart, at least 6 portions

CAMPARI-ORANGE ICE

Another afternoon cooler, this one with the special taste of Campari, Italy's bright red, bitter apéritif.

*3 cups strained fresh orange juice
1 cup Campari
juice of 1 lemon
1 cup granulated sugar*

1. Combine all ingredients in a heavy saucepan and set over moderate heat. Stir constantly until the mixture is about to boil and all the sugar is dissolved.

2. Cool to room temperature. Pour into a shallow pan (an 8-inch square cake tin is ideal), and set in the freezer.

3. The mixture will take from 3 to 6 hours to freeze and because of its relatively low sugar content, well be very solid. To serve, set in refrigerator for 30 minutes to temper the texture slightly.

1 quart, at least 6 portions

LEMON ICE

2 cups strained fresh lemon juice
2 cups water
2 cups granulated sugar

1. Combine lemon juice with water in a small saucepan. Stir in the sugar.

2. Set saucepan over moderate heat. Bring to a boil, stirring constantly, then remove from heat and cool to room temperature.

3. Pour the lemon mixture into a shallow pan (an 8-inch square cake tin is ideal) and set it in your freezer.

4. The ice will be ready in 3 to 6 hours, depending on the efficiency of your freezer. Because of the high sugar content, this ice will usually be soft enough to serve, so you may as well make it in advance of the day you'll be needing it.

1 quart of very intense ice, 6 or more portions

**SUMMER SUPPER
BY THE POOL**

*Asparagus spears with
Sesame Mayonnaise,
Green Herb Dipping Sauce
and Aïoli Sauce*

---

*Greek Lamb and
Eggplant Salad*

*Linguine with Tomatoes
and Basil*

---

*Arugula salad with
red wine vinaigrette*

Black bread

---

*Lemon, Cappuccino and
Campari-Orange Ices*

DATE-NUT PUDDING

Traditionally served at our family's winter holiday dinners, this pudding will warm your heart.

8 tablespoons (1 stick) sweet butter
1 cup granulated sugar
2 eggs, beaten
1 cup milk
1½ tablespoons unbleached all-purpose flour
1½ teaspoons baking powder
1 cup pitted dates, coarsely chopped
1 cup shelled walnuts, coarsely chopped
1 cup heavy cream, chilled

1. Preheat oven to 325°F. Grease well a glass or ceramic baking dish, 9 x 13 x 2 inches.
2. Cream butter, gradually adding sugar and cream until light.
3. Add eggs, milk, flour and baking powder; mix well. Fold in dates and walnuts.
4. Turn into the prepared baking dish and place on the middle rack of the oven. Bake for 50 to 60 minutes, or until set.
5. Serve slightly warm or at room temperature with a spoonful of the cream, whipped to soft peaks.

8 portions

"He may do it with a better grace but I do it more natural."
— *Twelfth Night,*
William Shakespeare

POACHED FRUIT

Fruits poached in a syrup gain flavor and sophistication, as well as easing the pressure on a busy cook. Light and beautiful, they may wait in your refrigerator for 3 to 4 days until you are ready to serve them.

1½ cups granulated sugar
piece of a cinnamon stick
6 whole cloves
half a vanilla bean
zest of 1 lemon, cut into fine julienne
1 pound fruit of your choice

1. Combine sugar, cinnamon stick, cloves, vanilla bean and the lemon zest in 1 quart water.
2. Simmer for 10 minutes.
3. Add 1 pound fruit of your choice (apples and pears should be peeled, cored and quartered; peaches and apricots should be poached whole and peeled only after they are cool). Bring syrup back to the simmer and cook fruit gently for about 12 minutes, or until fruit is tender but not mushy. Do not overcook!
4. Remove pan from heat and let fruit cool in the syrup.
5. The fruit is now ready to be served, but can be stored in the poaching liquid in the refrigerator.

VARIATIONS:

♥ Substitute a fruity red wine such as Beaujolais or Zinfandel for half of the water when poaching pears. Serve in small bowls with a spoonful or two of chilled syrup, and sprinkle with crumbled *amaretti*.

♥ Substitute dry white wine for half of the water when poaching apricots or peaches. Top with chilled raspberry sauce and garnish with whole raspberries and fresh mint.

♥ Prepare syrup using apple cider instead of water. Soak a handful of raisins in dark rum for 1 hour. Poach apples in the syrup, add the raisins to the syrup while it is still warm, and spoon over warm apples. Sprinkle with pecans to taste.

♥ A secret of many French chefs is to add 6 to 10 whole black peppercorns to the poaching syrup for extra flavor and spiciness.

THE GRAND FINALE

After-dinner drinks have always been popular in America. Now, with our new desire to end a meal less heavily, Cognac, Armagnac, fruit brandies, or *eaux-de-vie* brandies made from grape pomace such as *marc* and *grappa* are replacing fruit liqueurs in popularity.

A true fruit brandy, or *eau-de-vie,* must be distilled entirely from the fruit itself; the result is a dry, often colorless liquid whose aroma bursts forth from the uncorked bottle. It's almost as if you've been transported to an orchard or a berry field.

Some prefer these "brandies" served ice cold. We like them at room temperature, but in any case, offer them in your finest tiny glasses. They are expensive, since they are the pure essence of the fruit, but worth experiencing.

ESSENCE	FRUIT	ORIGIN	NOTES
Armagnac	Saint-Emilion, Meslier and Picpoule grapes	Gers and Landes, France	Armagnac is amber to brown in color, depending on age. The smoother and more richly flavored are aged five years or longer in beach oak.
Applejack	Apples	United States	An American favorite, but without the rich body of Calvados.
California Brandy	Thompson Seedless grapes	California	These pale gold brandies are not yet the equal of the European, but are pleasant to sip and excellent for cooking.
Calvados	Apples	Normandy, France	Rich in color and crisp apple flavor, it reflects the sophistication of aging.
Cognac	Saint-Emilion, Folle Blanche and Colombard grapes	France	Cognacs are brandies; not all brandies are cognacs. A true Cognac is made only in the Cognac region, with a lengthy aging process. The resulting amber liquid is worth the price.
Grappa	Grape pomace	Piedmont and Friuli, Italy	A by-product of the wine-making pricess. It has a fiery and biting flavor.
Fraise	Strawberries	France	An *eau-de-vie* which is not sweet, but fully fruit-flavored.
Framboise	Raspberries	France	Made from the essence of 40 pounds of fruit per bottle, it fairly explodes with the smell and flavor of raspberries.

Marc de Bourgogne	Grape pomace	Burgundy, France	Another by-product of the wine-making process; it is often considered harsh and "plebeian," but in France it is the favorite of the rural gentry.
Mirabelle	Yellow plums	Lorraine and Alsace, France	Clear and delicate — this is a spectacular sipping brandy.
Pear Brandy	Williams pears	France, Switzerland, Germany	An *eau-de-vie* with the full, elegant flavor of pears. An experience.

THE BRUNCH BUNCH

RISE AND SHINE

Brunch has become many Americans' favorite way to fill a weekend day with special people. Whether you're a late sleeper or an avid early morning jogger, whether you've traveled to church or just out to get the great thick Sunday paper, whether you're in the mood for a football game or chamber music, brunch is just the thing for that unstructured day called Sunday. (And we think Saturdays are deserving of some special treatment too.) Brunch can be for any number, but make it light, informal and pretty. A buffet allows people to come and go comfortably as they please, indoors or out. For two or twenty, brunch should be light and lingering, allowing the day to drift where it may. Make sure you have enough copies of the papers to keep everyone happy!

HOW TO MAKE AN OMELET

While it's true that the simplest dishes are often the most difficult to make, we think there is an unnecessary amount of fuss made concerning omelet-making. At the bottom line, an omelet is nothing more than eggs, butter and body English. Fillings, toppings and garnishes can enhance the finished product, but won't disguise an overbeaten, overcooked or poorly formed disaster. In other words, it all begins with the egg and ends with technique. Once you have managed to turn out a perfectly cooked, golden-brown oval of an omelet, the rest will take care of itself.

There are as many omelet techniques as there are cooks; after a failure or two, you will arrive at your own. Our advice is to make an omelet a day for a week; like getting to Carnegie Hall, omelet-making requires practice. Sooner or later the particular combination of timing, wrist action and intuition that works for you will produce a perfect omelet. Here, as a guideline, is our no-nonsense approach to omelet-making.

THE PAN

A lot of mystique is attached to the omelet pan. Many cooks require a certain kind or weight of pan, some swearing that it must be steel, or cast iron, or aluminum, or coated with a nonstick surface. And more than one professional we know insists that the pan used for omelets must never be washed.

In our experience, however, the size of the pan is the only critical factor. For a 2- or 3-egg omelet, sufficient for 1 portion, we recommend a 5- to 6-inch skillet. Small pans give a thick and often under-cooked omelet, while too large a pan gives a thin omelet that is easily over-cooked.

As far as the actual construction of the pan is concerned, some of the best omelets we ever made were cooked in a heavy, black, straight-sided cast-iron skillet over an open fire. Other favorites include a #24 iron French chef's crêpe pan and an inexpensive nonstick department-store skillet. We wash them when they need it, we try not to scratch their cooking surfaces, and we oil the chef's pan occasionally to keep it from rusting. The rest is hoopla.

THE EGGS

Use the freshest eggs possible. If you have access to new-laid eggs, by all means use them. City dwellers, however, will usually have to rely on the nearest high-volume supermarket, where a steady turnover of dated eggs is some assurance of freshness.

Crack the eggs into a small bowl. Cold eggs are harder to overcook; room-temperature eggs make a slightly fluffier omelet — take your choice. Sprinkle in a pinch of salt and beat the eggs briefly with a fork. Do not overbeat: your goal here is to mingle the whites and yolks so lightly that the finished omelet will have striations of both. Homogenizing the texture of the eggs produces a tougher omelet. Grind in a little black pepper and set the eggs aside.

THE OMELET TECHNIQUE

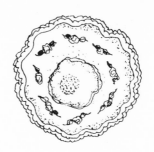

1. Set the pan on the burner. Have at hand a tablespoon of softened butter, a fork, the prepared eggs, and the plate you plan to serve the omelet on.

2. Turn the heat under the skillet to medium-high and drop in the butter. As the butter begins to melt, it's worth noting that from here on out it will probably take you longer to read the rest of this recipe than to make the omelet. The butter will melt, begin to foam, and then the foam will subside. The pan is ready for the eggs.

3. Pour eggs in all at once, take the skillet handle with one hand and the fork with the other, and begin gently stirring the eggs with the flat of the fork as if you were scrambling them. Raise and lower the skillet from the burner to control the heat.

4. As the bottom of the omelet begins to set, lift it with the fork to allow the uncooked egg to run underneath. When the eggs are almost done to your liking, return the skillet to the burner, shut off the heat and arrange any filling you like across the center of the omelet at a right angle to the handle of the pan.

5. Now grip the skillet handle with your palm upward, raise the handle and bring the far edge of the skillet over the edge of the serving plate. With the fork, start the upper edge of the omelet rolling at the same time you bring the handle of the skillet further over the plate. You have just tipped and rolled the omelet out of the pan at the same time.

Wet omelet fillings and sauces are better added after the omelet has been rolled. Cut a short, deep slit in the top of the omelet, spread it open slightly, and spoon in the filling or sauce; pour a share over the top of the omelet.

6. Don't worry if the omelet is untidy — it will still taste good and you'll gain control as you practice. One professional chef's trick we like is to place a paper towel over the rolled omelet and use the palms of both hands gently to shape the omelet into the classic oval. This also blots up excess butter. Garnish the omelet and serve immediately.

FILLING THE PERFECT OMELET

The possibilities are endless, and improvisation is the name of the game. An omelet should be generously filled but not grossly overstuffed; about ¼ to ⅓ cup of filling is ample for each 3-egg omelet. Here are some of our favorites to get you started.

♥ *Apple & Cheddar Omelet:* Dice unpeeled tart apples, sauté in butter until golden, fold into omelet together with diced Vermont or other sharp Cheddar cheese.

♥ *Creamed Mushroom Omelet:* Prepare and roll omelet; cut a short deep slit in the top and spoon in hot Creamed Mushrooms (see page 295).

♥ *Ratatouille Omelet:* Roll hot Ratatouille (see page 281) into the omelet.

♥ *Omelet Grandmère:* Fill omelet with crisp-cooked bacon, sautéed diced potatoes and sweet onion. Lavish with chopped parsley.

♥ *Ricotta-Tomato Omelet:* Flavor fresh ricotta cheese to taste with basil, minced garlic and grated Parmesan; fold into omelet and top with hot Tomato Coulis (see page 324).

♥ *Sausage Ragoût Omelet:* For a hearty suppertime omelet, fold hot Sausage Ragoût (see page 222) into omelet. Sprinkle with grated Parmesan cheese before serving.

♥ *Omelet Normandy:* Fold hot Sautéed Apples with Calvados (see page 454) into omelet; top with a dollop of *Crème Fraîche* (page 582).

♥ *Watercress Omelet:* Wilt fresh watercress briefly in hot butter. Lift with a slotted spoon and roll into omelet.

♥ *SoHo Omelet:* Combine crisp-cooked bacon, grated sharp Cheddar cheese and tender leaves of raw spinach and roll into omelet. The heat of the eggs will gently cook the spinach while leaving its fresh taste intact.

DANISH MARY ICE

This icy sorbet with its kick of aquavit is a perfect way to start a summer brunch.

2 cups tomato juice
6 ounces aquavit
½ cup fresh lemon juice, more or less
2 egg whites
1 teaspoon salt
freshly ground black pepper, to taste
fresh dill (garnish)

1. Process all ingredients except fresh dill together in the bowl of a food processor fitted with a steel blade. Taste and correct seasonings.
2. Pour into an ice-cube tray or freezer container and freeze at least overnight.
3. If time allows, let the ice freeze completely, then remove from container, process briefly to break up ice crystals, and refreeze. Ice will be slushy.
4. Spoon into stemmed wineglasses and garnish with fresh dill.
4 portions

Variation: This ice can also be made with vodka. Garnish with a fresh basil leaf.

AQUAVIT

Aquavit is distilled from grain or potatoes. Like gin, it is a flavored alcohol; herbs, spices and seeds, most commonly caraway, fennel or dill, contribute flavor. It is best ice-cold from the freezer and traditionally is served in small glasses alongside large glasses of cold beer.

BISMARCKS

A light and wonderful way to begin a Sunday any time of the year.

8 tablespoons (1 stick) sweet butter
½ cup milk
½ cup unbleached all-purpose flour
2 eggs
fresh lemon juice to taste
confectioners' sugar for dusting

1. Put butter in a heavy frying pan or a shallow casserole. Place in an oven set at 475°F.

2. Meanwhile, mix milk, flour and eggs lightly to make a batter.

3. When the butter has melted, add batter to the pan and bake for 12 minutes. Remove from oven and place bismarck on a plate.

4. Pour a little of the melted butter on the pancake, and squeeze on a little lemon juice to taste. Roll it up like a loose jelly roll and sprinkle with confectioners' sugar.

VARIATIONS:

♥ Sprinkle with brown sugar
♥ Forget the sugar and use a fruit- or maple-flavored syrup
♥ Spread with a favorite fruit preserve or fresh berries
♥ Lightly sprinkle with Grand Marnier
♥ Fill with chestnut cream
♥ Top with cooked link sausages after 4 minutes of cooking time

"Oysters are the usual opening to a winter breakfast . . . Indeed, they are almost indispensable."
— Almanach des Gourmandes, 1803

BUCKWHEAT CREPES

2½ cups milk
4 tablespoons sweet butter, cut up
1 cup buckwheat flour, sifted*
1 cup unbleached all-purpose flour, sifted*
¼ teaspoon salt
4 eggs
vegetable oil for frying

1. Warm the milk in a small saucepan with the butter. When the butter has melted, set aside to cool slightly.

2. Pour both flours into the bowl of a food processor fitted with a steel blade. Add the salt and process for an instant to blend.

3. With the motor running, pour in the milk and butter mixture and then drop in the eggs; process just until blended. Let batter stand for 30 minutes.

4. Brush a 7-inch crêpe pan with a paper towel dipped into vegetable oil. Set over medium heat and heat until smoking. Pour ¼ cup batter into the pan and immediately tilt and turn the pan so that batter will cover the surface evenly. The crêpe may have a few holes; this is fine. Turn the crêpe when under side is well browned, 3 or 4 minutes, and cook the other side for 2 or 3 minutes. Slide crêpe out onto a kitchen towel to cool. Repeat with remaining batter, stacking finished crêpes; add additional milk if batter seems too thick, and re-oil skillet after each crêpe.

5. When crêpes are cool, use immediately, or layer with wax paper and refrigerate or freeze.

16 crêpes, 7-inch size

*Sift flours into dry-measure cups and sweep level with a knife.

CREPE FILLINGS:

♥ Apples, walnuts, and raisins sautéed in butter and sprinkled with cinnamon, sugar and lemon juice.

♥ Ratatouille (see page 281) and sausage.

♥ Curried mushrooms: Sauté sliced mushrooms and onions in butter, season to taste with curry powder, and simmer with heavy cream until thickened.

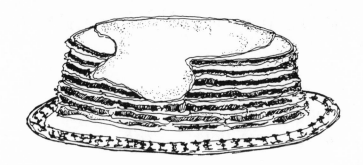

♥ Goat cheese and honey: Spread fresh mild goat cheese on a crêpe; sprinkle with walnuts if you like, roll up, and warm briefly. Drizzle with honey.

♥ Jam crêpes: Roll your favorite jam or preserve into a crêpe, and sprinkle it with confectioners' sugar.

♥ Santa Fe: Spread hot Chili for a Crowd (see page 220) on a crêpe, sprinkle with grated Cheddar cheese, chopped scallion and black olives, roll, and bake until bubbling.

**A SUNDAY
IN NEW YORK
BRUNCH**

Iced Pepper Vodka

---

*Smoked salmon,
Cream cheese,
Bagels or English muffins*

---

*Orange juice
Coffee*

Fresh berries with sugar

---

*Saint-André,
Robbiola Del Bek,
Lou Peralou cheeses*

> " 'But wait a bit,' the Oysters cried,
> 'Before we have our chat.
> For some of us are out of breath,
> And all of us are fat!' "
> — *Through the Looking Glass,*
>   Lewis Carroll

BLACK FOREST CREPE TORTE

This is a wonderfully comforting brunch dish that also manages to look elegant and complex. If you have the tricky components prepared in advance and refrigerated, the torte will go together in a matter of minutes. Pass the *crème fraîche* and let guests help themselves.

2 cups Béchamel Sauce (see page 585)
1½ cups Gruyère cheese, grated
16 Buckwheat Crêpes (see page 541)
32 very thin slices of Black Forest ham (look for the round shape)
8 tablespoons (1 stick) sweet butter
freshly ground black pepper, to taste
8 ounces Crème Fraîche (see page 582)

1. Preheat oven to 400°F.
2. Warm béchamel sauce in a heavy saucepan over low heat until just hot. Add the cheese and whisk until smooth. Season with black pepper.
3. On a round heatproof platter spread 4 tablespoons of the béchamel and cheese in a crêpe-size circle. Place a crêpe on sauce and cover with 2 slices of ham. Dot with bits of butter. Continue this sequence of layers (crêpe, ham, butter) until all crêpes and ham are used, ending with crêpe.
4. Pour remaining béchamel sauce over the torte. Bake for 20 minutes, or until browned and bubbling. To serve, cut into 6 wedges. Accompany with *crème fraîche*.

6 portions

"My wife and I tried to breakfast together, but we had to stop or our marriage would have been wrecked."
—Winston Churchill

SAUTEED CHICKEN LIVERS WITH BLUEBERRY VINEGAR

The tart fruity sauce is a perfect complement to rich chicken livers. Serve them at brunch with fried potatoes; at dinner with wild rice.

4 tablespoons sweet butter
4 scallions (green onions), including green tops, chopped
1 cup unbleached all-purpose flour
generous pinch each of ground ginger, mace, allspice, nutmeg, and cloves
salt and freshly ground black pepper, to taste
1 pound chicken livers halved, trimmed, and patted dry
⅓ cup blueberry vinegar
⅓ cup Crème Fraîche (see page 582) or heavy cream
½ cup fresh blueberries (optional garnish)

1. Melt the butter in a large heavy skillet and gently sauté the scallions for 5 minutes. Set aside.

2. Shake the flour in a plastic bag with the spices, salt and pepper. Drop the livers into the bag with the flour, shake them to coat well, and empty bag into a strainer set over a bowl. Shake the strainer to remove excess flour.

3. Return the skillet with the scallions to the stove, raise the heat, and when hot add the livers and cook, turning occasionally, for about 5 minutes, or until livers are browned and slightly stiffened. Remove them with a spoon and keep warm.

4. Add the vinegar to the skillet and deglaze over high heat, scraping up any browned bits and reducing the vinegar to a few syrupy spoonfuls.

5. Whisk in the *crème fraîche* and boil for 1 minute. If you are using fresh blueberries, add them to the sauce and simmer gently for another 2 or 3 minutes, just long enough to heat the berries through without overcooking them.

6. Arrange the livers on serving plates and spoon the sauce over them. Serve immediately.

4 portions as an appetizer, 2 or 3 portions as a main course

AN ENGLISH GRILL BREAKFAST

Fresh apricot nectar

Biscuits, breads with preserves, marmalade and sweet butter

Smoked trout with Apple Horseradish Mayonnaise

———

Baked Ham

Sautéed Chicken Livers with Blueberry Vinegar

Danish bacon

Boiled, poached, fried, scrambled or shirred eggs

———

American coffee, English tea, hot chocolate

A SUREFIRE WAY TO COOK BACON

Place thick slices of bacon on a foil-covered baking sheet (foil makes cleaning up easier). Bake in a 350°F. oven for about 6 minutes. Turn and bake for another 2 or 3 minutes. No spatters, and the bacon is flat and perfect every time.

SOUR-CREAM COFFEECAKE

This classic is worth timing so that you can serve it 30 minutes out of the oven.

16 tablespoons (2 sticks) sweet butter
2¾ cups granulated sugar
2 eggs, beaten
2 cups unbleached all-purpose flour
1 tablespoon baking powder
¼ teaspoon salt
1 cup dairy sour cream
1 tablespoon vanilla extract
2 cups shelled pecans, chopped
1 tablespoon ground cinnamon

1. Preheat oven to 350°F. Grease a 10-inch bundt pan and lightly dust the inside with flour.
2. Cream together the butter and 2 cups of the sugar. Add eggs, blending well, then the sour cream and vanilla.
3. Sift together the flour, baking powder and salt.
4. Fold the dry ingredients into the creamed mixture, and beat until just blended. Do not overbeat.
5. In a separate bowl, mix remaining ¾ cup sugar with pecans and cinnamon.
6. Pour half of the batter into the bundt pan. Sprinkle with half of the pecan and sugar mixture. Add remaining batter and top with the rest of the pecan mixture.
7. Set on the middle rack of the oven and bake for about 60 minutes, or until a cake tester inserted in the center comes out clean. Serve warm.

10 portions

ANGIE'S COFFEECAKE

1 package active dry yeast
1 cup lukewarm milk (105° to 115°F.)
3 tabelspoons granulated sugar
4 cups unbleached all-purpose flour
1 teaspoon salt
1¼ cups vegetable shortening
2 whole eggs
1 egg, separated
1 pound (4 sticks) sweet butter, softened to room temperature
2 cups brown sugar
2 cups shelled pecans, coarsely chopped
3 cups coarsely chopped dates
1 tablespoon ground cinnamon
2¼ cups confectioners' sugar
2 tablespoons warm honey
½ cup fresh lemon juice (2 or 3 lemons)

1. Dissolve the yeast in the lukewarm milk in a small bowl. Stir in granulated sugar and let stand for 10 minutes.

2. Sift flour and salt together. Cut in vegetable shortening until mixture resembles rolled oats. Stir in milk and yeast mixture. Beat the whole eggs and the egg yolk together and stir gently but thoroughly into the dough. Cover with a towel and set aside to rise until tripled, about 3 hours.

3. Grease 3 jelly-roll pans, 9 x 13 inches. Divide risen dough into thirds, and roll out 1 piece of dough thinly into a rectangle about 3 times the size of a jelly-roll pan. Slide a pan under the center third of the dough.

4. Set aside one third of the softened butter. Divide remaining butter into thirds and spread half of one portion over the center portion of the dough on the pan. Sprinkle ⅓ cup of the brown sugar, ⅓ cup of the chopped pecans and ½ cup of the chopped dates evenly over the buttered center section of dough. Sprinkle with ½ teaspoon of the cinnamon. Fold one side of the dough over the center section. Again spread with softened butter and sprinkle with the same amounts of brown sugar, pecans and dates. Fold the final third of the dough

over the center section and set aside for 2½ to 3 hours. Repeat with remaining dough and ingredients.

5. Preheat oven to 400°F.

6. Mix together the reserved butter, 1 cup of the confectioners' sugar, the reserved egg white and the warmed honey. Cut 3 deep decorative slits in the risen coffeecakes, being careful not to cut through to the bottom layer. Spread the honey mixture evenly over the tops of the cakes.

7. Set on the middle rack of the oven and bake for 25 to 30 minutes, or until puffed, brown and firm. Cool slightly.

8. Mix together remaining confectioners' sugar and the lemon juice and drizzle over warm coffeecakes. To serve, cut into narrow strips and serve warm.

9. Coffeecake can be wrapped in foil and frozen. Defrost and rewarm slightly in the foil before serving.

3 coffee cakes, each 9 x 13 inches

Angie's Coffeecake was a gift to us from a good neighbor in Kalamazoo; we pass it along to you. While it appears to be an all-day project (it is not), you'll find it is well worth the effort.

HOUSEGUESTS

It has been said that there are two kinds of people in the world: hosts and guests. Happily, most people get the chance to be a little of both. When those people who don't usually live together gather under one roof to spend a week or weekend, it's not really fair for either group to have to be as literally categorized as one or the other. The great host is one who treats his guests as he treats his family. Great guests are those who know instinctively that they have been invited to amuse themselves by day and their host by night.

548

FRUIT SALADS

It's not really necessary to have a recipe for a fruit salad; almost any combination of fresh seasonal fruits can begin or end a meal on a satisfactory note. You may add a light touch of sugar or honey, some lemon juice, finely chopped mint or liqueur, according to the sweetness of the fruit and your own taste.

Add such sweetening just before serving, as sugars tend to draw the natural juices out of fruit. We have also learned that melon combined with other fruits becomes soft unless added at the very last moment.

♥ Combine peeled and sliced kiwis with strawberries. Steep in red wine, and serve a glass of the same wine with the fruit.

♥ Mix 3 kinds of melon with orange and lemon juice. Sprinkle with lots of chopped fresh mint.

♥ Combine seedless green grapes, blueberries and honeydew balls. Sprinkle with dark rum and grated fresh orange zest.

♥ Toss chilled grapefruit sections with honey, lime juice and fresh mint leaves.

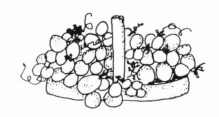

MINTED FRUIT SALAD

Substitute other seasonal fresh fruits as you please.

1 pint basket strawberries
3 kiwi fruits
1 medium-size ripe cantaloupe
1 medium-size ripe honeydew melon
handful of fresh mint leaves
½ cup fresh orange juice
¼ cup fresh lemon juice
3 tablespoons granulated sugar

1. Wash, drain and hull strawberries.
2. Peel kiwis and slice thin, reserving 1 sliced kiwi for garnish.
3. With a melon-baller, cut balls from cantaloupe and honeydew melons.
4. Mix all fruits together except for reserved kiwi.
5. Chop mint leaves and tender stems very fine and sprinkle on fruits.
6. Mix orange and lemon juice with sugar and pour over all. Toss salad gently and thoroughly.
7. Arrange reserved kiwi slices on top and garnish with a fresh mint leaf. Chill for 2 to 3 hours and serve cold.

12 portions

BLACK FRUIT SALAD

1 cup black cherries, pitted
1 cup black grapes
½ cup blueberries or black currants
⅓ cup light brown sugar
juice of 1 lemon
1 cup dairy sour cream
fresh mint sprigs

1. Combine fruits and sprinkle with brown sugar and lemon juice. Let stand for 2 hours, tossing several times.
2. Lift out fruit with slotted spoon and divide equally among 4 balloon wine glasses.
3. Stir sour cream into collected juices in bowl.
4. Serve fruits topped with a dollop of the sour cream sauce and a sprig of fresh mint.
4 portions

Variation: We also like a combination of green grapes, kiwis and green apples. You can also use a mixture of just grapes.

THE BIG BREAD SANDWICH

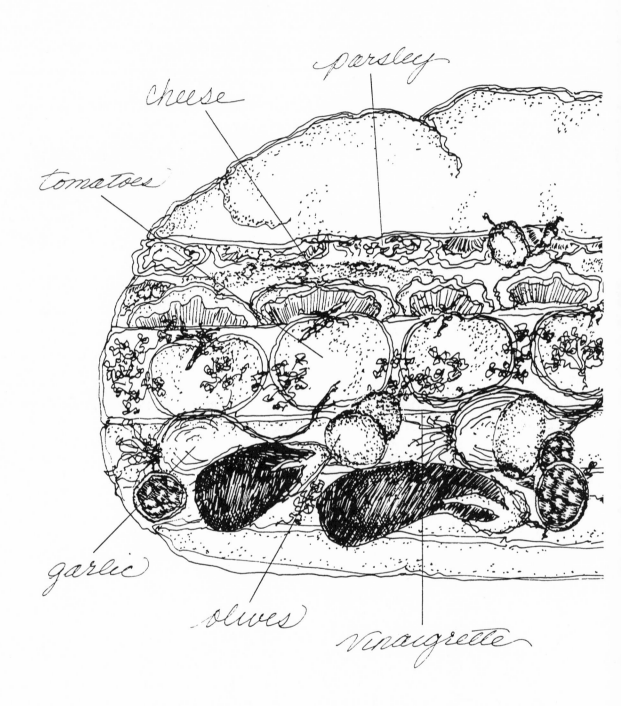

This special sandwich seems, more and more often, to be the answer for almost every entertaining occasion — from brunch to picnics to late-night suppers. The Big Bread can easily serve any number of people, and makes a spectacular-looking, edible centerpiece for a buffet. It is self-contained, portable, and may be served indoors or out.

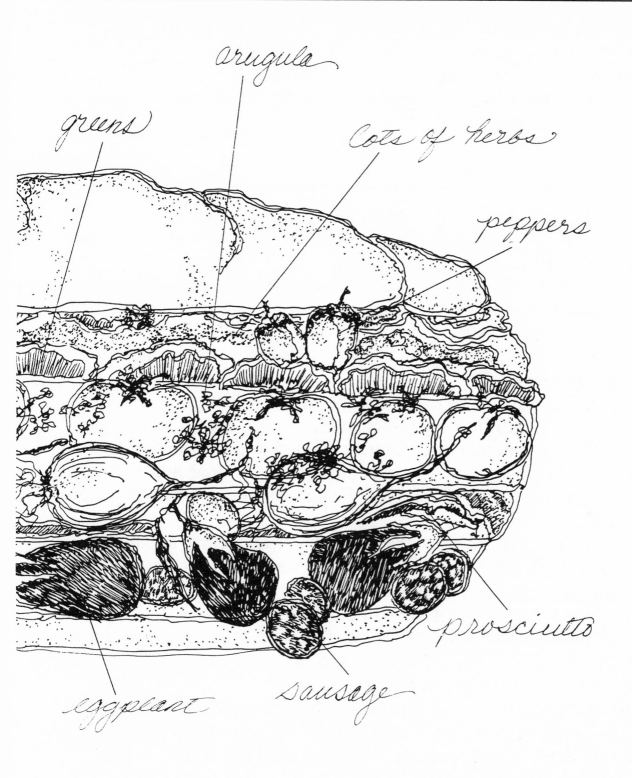

greens

arugula

lots of herbs

peppers

prosciutto

eggplant

sausage

You can make your own bread or buy good bakery bread if time is short. The loaf should be 12 to 14 inches wide, about the same in length, and at least 4 inches high, either round or rectangular. Any type of bread will make perfectly delicious Big Bread Sandwiches, (Recipes on next page.)

THE BIG BREAD

4 cups lukewarm water (105° to 115°F.)
2 tablespoons molasses
2 packages active dry yeast
11 to 12 cups unbleached all-purpose flour, more if needed
2½ tablespoons salt
3 tablespoons olive oil
cornmeal, to cover baking sheet

1. Stir the lukewarm water and the molasses together in a very large bowl. Sprinkle in the yeast, stirring to dissolve all the particles, and let stand for 10 minutes.

2. Begin adding the flour, 1 cup at a time, stirring as you go. Add the salt and beat well after 5 cups of flour have been incorporated, then stir in 5 more cups of flour.

3. Turn the dough out onto a heavily floured work surface. Wash and dry the bowl.

4. Sprinkle 1 cup of remaining flour over the dough and begin to knead it; dough will be very sticky at this point. Keep kneading and adding more of the remaining flour as needed to keep the dough from sticking to your hands or to the board. It's a big loaf and will need a lot of kneading, about 15 minutes. Dough is ready when it is smooth and elastic.

5. Pour the olive oil into the dried bowl and turn the dough in it to coat it with oil. Cover dough with a towel and let it stand until tripled in bulk; this may take 1½ hours or it may take 3. The volume is what to watch here, not the time it takes.

6. Turn the risen dough out onto the floured work surface and knead again, for about 5 minutes. Shape into a ball, turn again in the bowl, cover, and let rise until doubled in volume.

7. Sprinkle a large baking sheet evenly with cornmeal. Turn dough out onto work surface and shape it into a large oval loaf. Transfer to baking sheet, cover, and let rise until doubled, about 1 hour.

8. Preheat oven to 450°F.

9. Rub the risen loaf generously with flour. Slash it shallowly across the top with a sharp knife. Set on the middle rack of the oven and bake for 15 minutes. Reduce heat to 375°F. and bake for another 30 minutes, or until loaf is well browned and sounds hollow when tapped on the bottom crust. Let cool.

MARINATED EGGPLANT LIVIA

1 eggplant (about 1 pound)
salt for draining eggplant, plus additional to taste
1½ cups fruity green olive oil
2 small dried red chilies
3 whole garlic cloves, slightly crushed
3 tablespoons red wine vinegar
2 tablespoons dried oregano
1 tablespoon dried basil
1 tablespoon coarsely crushed black peppercorns

1. Cut the unpeeled eggplant into ⅛-inch crosswise slices. Arrange them in layers in a colander, salting heavily as you do so. Weight with a heavy plate or bowl and let stand for 1 hour.

2. Whisk together remaining ingredients. Rinse eggplant slices well, pat them dry with paper towels, and arrange in layers in bowl, pouring the marinade over each layer as you go.

3. Cover the eggplant and let it marinate, refrigerated, for 3 days, stirring it once a day.

4. Drain the eggplant, fish out chilies and garlic, and use eggplant in sandwiches, in salads, or as part of an antipasto. Save marinade for another use.

4 portions or enough for 1 Big Bread Sandwich

A BREAD BOX

A giant brioche or loaf of bread, hollowed and filled with miniature sandwiches decoratively shaped and imaginatively filled, makes a splendid centerpiece for any kind of buffet.

Cut off the top of the loaf with a serrated knife and reserve the top. Pull out the soft interior crumb of the bread, being careful to leave the crust intact, and save crumb for another use or discard.

With a rolling pin, flatten slices of thin sandwich bread and then cut into shapes using cookie cutters. Make sandwiches with your choice of fillings, spreads or flavored butters, and arrange inside the hollow loaf. Set the top back on, wrap, and refrigerate until serving.

BUFFET SANDWICHES

The best brunches are the laziest, stretching into the afternoon and beyond, with guests that come and go. They call for casual but substantial food, and we love to offer an array of interestingly shaped and flavored sandwiches, arranged in a gingham-lined basket. They look and taste marvelous, and revive appetities without slowing the day's activities. Best of all, they are easy on the cook. Add a pitcher of Lemonade (see page 354), chill bottles of wine or beer, and toss a salad. The rest of the day will take care of itself. (Recipes for italicized ingredients can be found in Index.)

♥ Put thinly sliced roast veal spread with *Anchovy Mayonnaise* on black bread. Sprinkle with capers.

♥ Try smoked *Filet of Beef,* equal parts of Roquefort and cream cheese, and sprigs of watercress on pumpernickel rolls.

♥ Spread country pâté on a green apple slice with Brie cheese on a French roll.

♥ Butter black bread with *Anchovy Butter;* pile high with thinly sliced radishes and watercress.

♥ Stack *Steak Tartare* and thinly sliced red onion on black bread roll. Grind on lots of black pepper.

♥ Mix lump crab meat, diced green pepper and cream cheese to a spreadable consistency, and spread on a bagel.

♥ Layer carpaccio with *Ravigote Butter* on black bread. Sprinkle with chopped parsley.

♥ Purée equal parts of cooked shrimp and softened butter; season to taste with salt, pepper and lemon juice; spread on whole-wheat bread and top with a slice of cherry tomato.

♥ Make *Egg Salad,* top with asparagus tips, and sprinkle with chopped fresh dill.

♥ Combine smoked red caviar, onions, lemon juice, cream cheese and dill.

♥ Put prosciutto on a pear slice with a spread of Gorgonzola cheese.

556

♥ Arrange thinly sliced chicken breast, tarragon mayonnaise, walnuts and watercress on black bread.
♥ Try lobster with *Tomato-Basil Mayonnaise* and arugula on white bread.
♥ Put paper-thin roast beef and sweet butter on white bread.
♥ Spread *Pecan Cream Cheese* on *Banana Bread.*

THE BIG BREAD SANDWICH

1 loaf of Big Bread
1 cup ricotta cheese
½ cup grated imported Romano cheese
1 egg yolk
5 tablespoons chopped Italian parsley, approximately
½ teaspoon ground black pepper, plus additional to taste
¼ teaspoon salt, plus additional to taste
Marinated Eggplant Livia
1 cup Garlic Anchovy Dressing (see page 359)
16 very thin slices of prosciutto
10 plum tomatoes, cut horizontally into 1-inch slices
8 thin slices of Fontina cheese
2 bunches of arugula (about 2 cups), rinsed, dried, de-stemmed
dried oregano, to taste
3 green bell peppers, seeded and cut into thin strips
4 sweet red peppers, seeded and cut into thin strips
2 tablespoons olive oil, approximately
6 sweet Italian sausages, cut lengthwise into halves
6 hot Italian sausages, cut lengthwise into halves
1 cup sliced pitted black olives

1. Slice the bread horizontally into 4 slices 1 inch thick.

2. Combine ricotta cheese, Romano cheese, egg yolk, 2 tablespoons chopped parsley, ½ teaspoon ground black pepper and ¼ teaspoon salt in a small bowl. Spread the cheese mixture on the bottom bread layer. Arrange the Eggplant Livia over the cheese and pour on a bit of the marinade from the eggplant. Top with the next slice of bread.

3. Pour some of Garlic Anchovy Dressing over the bread. Cover with layers of prosciutto, tomatoes, Fontina cheese, arugula, salt, pep-

per, and oregano to taste, more parsley and more vinaigrette. Cover with the third slice of bread.

4. Sauté the red and green peppers in about 2 tablespoons olive oil, together with the sweet and hot sausages, until peppers and sausages are browned. Add salt and pepper to taste. With a slotted spoon transfer sausages and peppers to the third layer of bread, topping with sliced black olives and lots more parsley and oregano. Drizzle the cooking oil over the cut side of the top layer and set the layer in place.

5. Wrap the sandwich in clear plastic wrap. Place between 2 cookie sheets, put something heavy on top to weight the sandwich, and refrigerate for 3 hours.

6. To serve: Place on a large cutting board and cut into wedges with a serrated knife.

10 to 12 portions

BRUNCH DRINKS

Brunch drinks fall into several categories; the strength you choose is up to you and may have something to do with your whereabouts and temperance of the previous evening. They range from morning wake-up potions, for medicinal purposes only, to mellow sipping drinks that pace you through the afternoon.

A GOOD SPICY BLOODY MARY

The Bloody Mary has become an American weekend wake-up call, with variations substituting aquavit for the vodka, or adding consommé (for a Bull Shot). Garnish with fresh basil, dill, oregano or black peppercorns. While delicious chilled, in the traditional way, it is also good hot, served in a mug on the top of a mountain anywhere.

1 quart tomato juice
½ cup fresh lemon juice
2 tablespoons prepared horseradish
freshly ground black pepper, to taste
several hefty dashes of Worcestershire sauce, to taste
several hefty dashes of Tabasco, to taste
1½ cups vodka
chopped basil leaves (garnish)

1. Combine all ingredients except vodka and basil in a large saucepan. Heat to simmering for 5 or 6 minutes. Let cool.
2. Pour a jigger of vodka into an ice-filled red-wine goblet or tall thin glass. Add the Bloody Mary mixture and top with chopped basil and a basil leaf. Let chill.

6 to 8 portions

VARIATIONS:

♥ Mexican: substitute tequila for vodka
♥ Texas Style: add 2 tablespoons barbecue sauce
♥ Oriental: add soy sauce and grated fresh ginger root
♥ Sea Style: use canned mixed clam-and-tomato (Clamato) juice instead of tomato juice

---

A VIRGINIA HUNT BREAKFAST

Bloody Marys

Baked Ham with Glazed Apricots

Barbecued beans

Mixed green salad with Champagne Vinaigrette

Biscuits and honey

Fresh Lady apples with Virginia Gouda cheese and Brillat-Savarin cheese, garnished with fresh black cherries

Crackling Cornbread

BEER

Beer, once the drink of the working class, is now making its appearance in white-wine and Champagne circles and is said to be the beverage of the eighties. Are we ever glad! Even if you haven't sipped a beer since your last college football game, you owe it to yourself to try again with gusto. Who among us doesn't crave a frosty mug of brew from time to time?

Serious beer drinkers always order by brand, and though the array of available ales, stouts, lights, imports, etc., grows daily, a good host can be content with offering at most two or three beers — a domestic light, a domestic premium and one of the imports with a national reputation. We have been to beer-tasting parties, however, where a dozen or more varieties were presented, along with the appropriate fare. In some circles, they've replaced wine tastings. Whatever beer you serve, be sure it is properly chilled and that you offer a tall, well-designed beer glass, also chilled. It does not take much effort to make a beer drinker happy.

SPARKLING WATERS

The trend toward light drinks reaches its ultimate in sparkling waters. No host is safe these days without a stock of at least one sparkling water and appropriate lemon twists and lime wedges. Buy domestics or imports as you see fit, chill them in advance, and offer other garnishes (such as fresh mint, a strawberry, or a twist of orange peel) as well.

561

BLACK SANGRIA

Use your most elegant glass pitcher.

cherries, blackberries and black grapes
1 strip of peel from a whole lemon
½ cup strongly brewed black tea
1 bottle dry red wine
chilled club soda, to taste

1. Place fruits and lemon peel in a 2½-quart pitcher.
2. Add the tea and enough wine to cover. Chill remaining wine.
3. Before serving, pour remaining wine in pitcher. Stir, and add ice and club soda to taste.

4 to 6 portions

WHITE SANGRIA

A favorite summer cooler.

1 bottle of dry white wine
2 kiwis, peeled and sliced
1 large pear, sliced very thin
1 cup seedless green grapes
2 tablespoons superfine sugar
2 tablespoons Calvados or Armagnac
3 tablespoons Cointreau
1½ cups bottled sparkling water
sprigs of mint or fresh flowers (garnish)

1. Pour wine into a large glass pitcher. Add kiwis, pear, grapes, sugar, Calvados and Cointreau to the pitcher. Cover and refrigerate for 4 to 5 hours.
2. To serve, stir well, add sparkling water, and pour over ice in tall glasses. Garnish with a flower or a sprig of mint.

6 glasses

FRESH FRUIT DAIQUIRI

White Caribbean rum has made its way north to become a year-round favorite. Fresh fruit and rum combined bring an island mood to a cold winter day, and are also perfect all summer long.

ice cream, vanilla or fruit-flavored
white rum
fresh strawberries, peaches, raspberries, blueberries, or any
  combination thereof
sprigs of fresh mint (garnish)

The proportions are flexible. Whip in a blender until smooth and serve over ice; garnish with fruit and a sprig of mint.

CHAMPAGNE

Champagne is one thing we can never get enough of. Every bottle is the memory of a party, an indulgence after a Sunday morning jogging workout, or the accompaniment to a soliloquy delivered under the midnight stars. Do serve it in a tulip or Champagne flute; the bubbles last longer and it's so pretty.

VARIATIONS:

♥ Add an extra large ripe strawberry with the stem left on
♥ Try a dash of raspberry syrup and 1 large teaspoon of fresh raspberries
♥ Float blueberries and blackberries
♥ Stir in a spoonful each of orange juice and lemon juice and a sprig of mint
♥ Slice and peel a kiwi and a pair of strawberries and pour Champagne over them

CHAMPAGNE COCKTAIL

The best of all worlds.

1 ounce Cognac
½ ounce Grand Marnier
6 ounces Champagne, chilled
3 raspberries

Mix together Cognac and Grand Marnier in a goblet, fill with Champagne, and garnish with raspberries.

CHAMPAGNE IN THE MORNING

To begin the day effervescently, there is nothing like Champagne. With fresh violets floating, or garnished with a mimosa blossom, Champagne makes any gathering an occasion. The drier the Champagne the better here: We like *Brut*. While vintage Champagnes are wonderful, we've found some very affordable, and delightful, nonvintages from California, and most recently a Spanish Champagne that comes in a black bottle. Our advice is to find one you like and can afford so that you can drink it whenever the mood strikes.

KINDS OF CHAMPAGNE

NONVINTAGE: Wine from a year's harvest blended with reserve wines to produce the Champagne characteristic of each house.
VINTAGE: Wine made in exceptional years only; vintage Champagnes usually aren't produced more than once or twice a decade.
TÊTE DE CUVÉE: A superior blend made especially for the connoisseur.

564

BLANC DE BLANCS: A Champagne made from exclusively white (Pinot Blanc) grapes rather than a mixture of black (Pinot Noir) and white grapes.

ROSÉ: Champagne tinted by leaving the skin of black grapes in for longer than the normal period.

"I never drink anything stronger than gin before breakfast."
— W. C. Fields

BRUNCH FOR TWO

Brunch for two can be a joint kitchen affair, shared in front of a fire, on the terrace or in the garden. You can also take it, and yourselves, back to bed. However you celebrate the late-morning meal, here are some ideas to increase your pleasure:

• For a special breakfast treat, scramble eggs slowly in butter to desired doneness, season with freshly ground black pepper and top the eggs with black caviar.

• Celebrate morning with Champagne, fresh raspberries and cream, croissants with butter and Brie cheese, eggs any way you like them, and café au lait.

• Stock a small bedside refrigerator with fresh orange juice, vodka, Scotch salmon, cream cheese with chives, fresh lemon and bagels. If you want hot coffee, you'll have to get out of bed. Sorry!

KIR ROYALE

A royal version of the cocktail classic.

2 ounces Framboise
1 bottle of the best Crème de Cassis (black currant liqueur)
Champagne

Add Framboise to Crème de Cassis and keep on hand as a mixer.
Put 1 demitasse spoonful of the mixture into a glass of Champagne
so that the wine becomes lightly pink, and serve as an apéritif.

MIMOSA

A splendid way to begin the day.

Champagne
fresh orange juice
fresh mint leaves (garnish)

Fill each glass two-thirds full with Champagne. Top each off with
fresh orange juice and garnish with a mint leaf.

COFFEES

So many millions of pounds of various kinds of coffee are shipped
to the United States every year that choosing among them can be
difficult. We don't roast our own, or claim to be experts on the subject,
but we'd like to share with you the way we like to brew and serve
it.

MAKING COFFEE

Our choice of coffee makers for years has been the Melitta pot. To use it, bring cold tap water to a boil and pour it over the freshly ground beans in the pot's filter cone. Having the water pass through the coffee only once is believed to make the best brew by most coffee lovers, and that has to include us.

The proportion of coffee to water is a matter of preference; we go by the following measures:

Regular-strength coffee:
1 coffee measure or 2 tablespoons to 6 ounces water.
Extra-strength coffee:
1 coffee measure or 2 tablespoons to 4 ounces water.
Double-strength coffee:
2 coffee measures or 4 tablespoons to 6 ounces water.

A second method is to use a glass "plunger" pot which allows the water and coffee to steep together for 4 or 5 minutes, then separates them by means of a plunger disc. Some of these pots hold 10 to 12 cups and so are easier to deal with than a smaller filter-cone pot when we have guests.

Espresso, ideally, should be brewed properly in an espresso maker, and served with a twist of lemon and a sugar cube.

TYPES OF COFFEE

For the best coffee, always buy freshly roasted beans. Grind them at home as you need them, and keep the rest in the freezer. They will keep for up to 2 months that way. Select the roast best suited to your intended use. The following list may help.

COLOMBIAN: A South American bean with rich, all-round flavor. Good by itself or blended with other beans.

COSTA RICAN: A Central American bean; excellent flavor.

FRENCH ROAST or **ITALIAN ROAST:** Full espresso; beans roasted to a glossy near-black.

HAWAIIAN KONA COFFEE: Mild, sweet, full-flavored and full-bodied.

HOUSE BLEND: Try it once and judge for yourself.

JAMAICAN BLUE MOUNTAIN AND HIGH MOUNTAIN SUPREME: Two superb, mellow rare coffees: Blue Mountain is extremely rare; High Mountain only slightly less so; both are sweet-tasting with fine flavor and full body. If you ever see either, buy it, no matter what the price.

MOCHA JAVA: Genuine Java coffee blended with Mocha coffee.

PUERTO RICAN: An excellent coffee; very little shipped here.
VIENNA ROAST: Mild espresso; lighter than French or Italian roast.

EUROPEAN VARIATIONS

CAFÉ AU LAIT: Equal amounts of hot, freshly brewed, strong French roast and warm milk poured into a cup simultaneously.
CAPPUCCINO: A taste of Italy that is easily made without a cappuccino machine by whipping warm milk in a blender for 1 minute to produce a bit of foam. Combine equal quantities of very strong, freshly brewed Italian-roast coffee with the frothy milk; dust with chocolate shavings and ground cinnamon and serve with sugar.

"Nanny likes her coffee hot hot hot."
— *Eloise*, Kay Thompson

BASICS

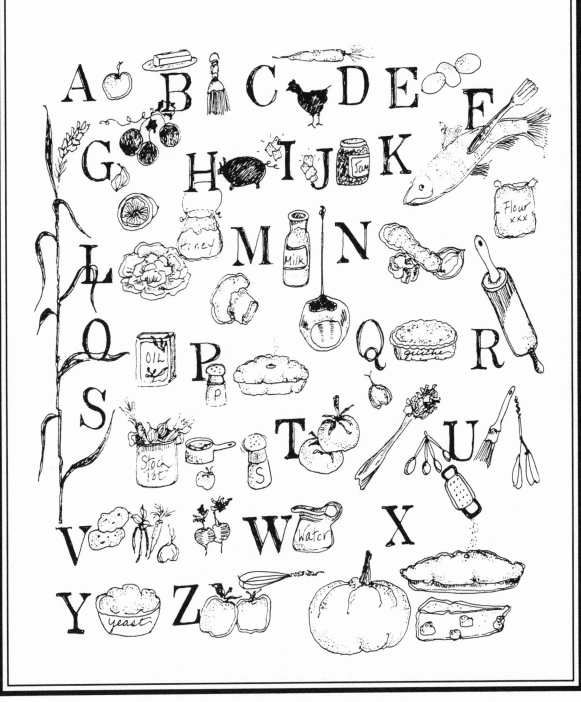

METRIC CONVERSION CHARTS

TABLESPOONS AND OUNCES
(U.S. Customary System)

GRAMS
(Metric System)

1 pinch = less than ⅛ teaspoon (dry)	0.5 gram
1 dash = 3 drops to ¼ teaspoon (liquid)	1.25 grams
1 teaspoon (liquid)	5.0 grams
3 teaspoons = 1 tablespoon = ½ ounce	14.3 grams
2 tablespoons = 1 ounce	28.35 grams
4 tablespoons = 2 ounces = ¼ cup	56.7 grams
8 tablespoons = 4 ounces = ½ cup (1 stick of butter)	113.4 grams
8 tablespoons (flour) = about 2 ounces	72.0 grams
16 tablespoons = 8 ounces = 1 cup = ½ pound	226.8 grams
32 tablespoons = 16 ounces = 2 cups = 1 pound	453.6 grams or 0.4536 kilogram
64 tablespoons = 32 ounces = 1 quart = 2 pounds	907.0 grams or 0.907 kilogram
1 quart = (roughly 1 liter)	

TEMPERATURES: °FAHRENHEIT (F.) TO °CELSIUS (C.)

−10°F.	=	−23.3°C. (freezer storage)
0°F.	=	−17.7°C.
32°F.	=	0°C. (water freezes)
50°F.	=	10°C.
68°F.	=	20°C. (room temperature)
100°F.	=	37.7°C.
150°F.	=	65.5°C.
205°F.	=	96.1°C. (water simmers)
212°F.	=	100°C. (water boils)

300°F.	=	148.8°C.
325°F.	=	162.8°C.
350°F.	=	177°C. (baking)
375°F.	=	190.5°C.
400°F.	=	204.4°C. (hot oven)
425°F.	=	218.3°C.
450°F.	=	232°C. (very hot oven)
475°F.	=	246.1°C.
500°F.	=	260°C. (broiling)

CONVERSION FACTORS

ounces to grams: multiply ounce figure by 28.3 to get number of grams

grams to ounces: multiply gram figure by .0353 to get number of ounces

pounds to grams: multiply pound figure by 453.59 to get number of grams

pounds to kilograms: multiply pound figure by 0.45 to get number of kilograms

ounces to milliliters: multiply ounce figure by 30 to get number of milliliters

cups to liters: multiply cup figure by 0.24 to get number of liters

Fahrenheit to Celsius: subtract 32 from the Fahrenheit figure, multiply by 5, then divide by 9 to get Celsius figure

Celsius to Fahrenheit: multiply Celsius figure by 9, divide by 5, then add 32 to get Fahrenheit figure

inches to centimeters: multiply inch figure by 2.54 to get number of centimeters

centimeters to inches: multiply centimeter figure by .39 to get number of inches

QUICHES

Nothing is quite so quick and satisfying to assemble as a quiche. Provided you have a bit of *Pâté Brisée* in your freezer (and since it freezes beautifully you should), some eggs and heavy cream or half-and-half on hand, you can leave the rest up to the improvisations of the moment. A handful of mushrooms sautéed with a shallot and finished with a little sherry or Port to taste can join grated Swiss cheese in an elegant quiche. Onions and salami or pepperoni, left over from last night's pizza, can be hearty and delicious. Combine cold crab meat with a bit of sautéed green pepper; team cooked chicken with black olives and Cheddar; try scallions sautéed in butter — add grated cheese as you like, or not at all. A bit of ham or bacon, fresh herbs, even some cooked Italian sausage — all can enliven a meal by flavoring a quiche. The possibilities are endless and always fascinating.

For a 10-inch quiche crust (and we think this is the best size) you will need 2 to 3 cups of filling and 3 eggs beaten with 1½ cups of cream, heavy or light. Season the egg mixture generously with salt, nutmeg and fresh black pepper to taste. Top the assembled quiche with cheese if it seems appropriate.

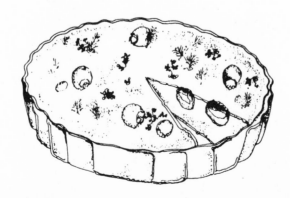

PATE BRISEE

1½ cups unbleached all-purpose flour
½ teaspoon salt
pinch of granulated sugar
5½ tablespoons (⅔ stick) sweet butter, chilled
3 tablespoons vegetable shortening, chilled
¼ cup ice water

1. Sift the flour, salt and sugar together into a bowl; add butter and shortening and cut them into dry ingredients with a pastry blender or 2 knives until mixture is like coarse meal.

2. Sprinkle on and blend in enough of the ice water to make a workable dough, mixing water in lightly with a fork.

3. Turn dough out onto your work surface and, using the heel of your hand, smear the dough away from you, about ¼ cup at a time. Scrape up the smeared dough into a ball, wrap, and refrigerate for at least 2 hours.

4. Unwrap dough, place on floured work surface, and pound it a few times with your rolling pin to soften it. Roll it out ⅛ inch thick, or to desired thickness.

5. Drape dough over quiche pan or tart pan, ease it into the pan without stretching, pat into place, trim off excess, and crimp edge if desired. Refrigerate for 30 minutes.

6. Preheat oven to 400°F.

7. Remove chilled dough from refrigerator and prick the bottom and sides well with a fork. Line the pan with foil or wax paper; fill with beans or rice to weight the crust. Bake for 10 minutes, until dough is just beginning to color.

8. Remove from oven, remove weights and lining, and cool slightly. You now have a partially baked shell which can be filled and rebaked for a quiche or tart.

9. For a fully baked shell, for a fresh fruit tart, for example, remove weights and lining from shell after 10 minutes and continue to bake until it is golden brown and crisply flaky, about 25 minutes total. Cool completely before filling.

One 11-inch shell or 5 to 6 small tart shells

PATE A CHOUX

½ cup water
4 tablespoons sweet butter
½ teaspoon salt
½ cup sifted unbleached all-purpose flour
3 eggs

1. Combine water, butter and salt in a small saucepan and bring to a boil.

2. Remove pan from heat and pour in the flour all at once. Stir well to combine and return to medium heat. Cook, stirring constantly, until the mixture becomes sticky and pulls away in a ball from the sides of the pan.

3. Remove pan from heat, cool for a moment or two, and stir in 2 of the eggs, one at a time, making certain the first egg is completely incorporated before adding the second, and beating vigorously at the end.

4. Preheat oven to 400°F.

5. Lightly grease a baking sheet. Drop the batter onto the sheet by spoonfuls of the size required by the recipe, or pipe out of a pastry bag into desired shapes.

6. Beat remaining egg in a small bowl. Brush the tops only of the puffs, éclairs, etc., with beaten egg. Set the baking sheet on the middle rack of the oven. Reduce heat to 375°F. and bake puffs for 20 minutes, or until they have puffed and are firm and golden brown.

7. Remove puffs from oven. Using a small knife, cut a slit in the side of each puff or éclair; this will let out steam that would otherwise make the puffs soggy. Cool puffs completely on a rack before proceeding with filling and serving.

About 25 cocktail-size puffs or cocktail éclairs

PUFF PASTRY

4 cups unbleached all-purpose flour
2 teaspoons salt
1 to 1¼ cups ice water, as needed
¾ pound (3 sticks) sweet butter, well chilled

1. Measure the flour by scooping a dry-measure cup into the container and sweeping off the excess with a knife. Place 3½ cups of the flour in a mixing bowl. Refrigerate remaining ½ cup.

2. Dissolve the salt in 1 cup of the ice water, and then gradually stir ice water into the flour. When all the flour is moistened and is just beginning to hang together in a ragged dough, stop adding water. Turn the dough out onto your work surface and gather it into a ball. Dough may be crumbly; it will certainly look awful; this is as it should be. Wrap the dough in clear plastic wrap or bag, and refrigerate for 1 hour or longer.

3. Remove dough from the refrigerator, lightly flour your work surface, and roll out the dough very evenly into a square about 12 x 12 inches.

4. Remove the butter from the refrigerator and unwrap it. Beat it with a rolling pin a few times to soften it, and then sprinkle on it the chilled ½ cup flour. Mash and knead the butter further, using the rolling pin and the heel of your hand, until it is smooth and creamy and all the flour is incorporated. This should not go on so long that the butter begins to melt. (Hands can be dipped in cold water for about 1 minute, then dried, before kneading in flour, to keep butter from becoming too warm.) Your goal is to get the butter and the dough to as nearly the same texture as possible. Form the butter into a rectangle.

5. Fold square of dough in half. Center the rectangle of butter on the folded dough and fold the long sides of the dough over it, enclosing it completely. Pinch to seal. Gather dough around ends and pinch to seal. Sprinkle it very lightly with flour and turn it over, seam side down. Roll it out gently into a rectangle and fold it one third of the way over itself. Fold the other end over this, as if folding a letter.

6. Rotate the dough 90 degrees and roll it out again into a rectangle 20 x 24 inches. Again fold one end one third of the way in, and then fold the other end over that. You now have the "letter" of dough again. Gently press ends of 2 fingers into the dough; you have made 2 of the

575

6 turns, and this will mark it so you don't forget. Rewrap and refrigerate it for at least 1 hour.

7. Remove dough from refrigerator once more and unwrap it. If it is very cold, let it sit for 10 minutes or so before rolling, otherwise the hardened butter may tear its way out of the package. Lightly flour the work surface and again roll out the dough into a rectangle 20 x 24 inches. Form the "letter," roll out again, and again fold in thirds. Mark the dough with 4 depressions; you have completed 4 of the 6 turns. Rewrap and refrigerate the dough for at least 1 hour.

8. Repeat step 7. The dough has now been turned 6 times and is ready to be shaped and baked. It can also be refrigerated for a few days or frozen for up to several weeks at this point.

About 2 pounds puff pastry

ABOUT PUFF PASTRY

Puff pastry is one of the glorious foundations of French baking. It is nothing more than hundreds of layers of butter and hundreds of layers of flour and water dough, but such is its magic that it rises to amazing heights, as much as 5 to 10 times the height of the original dough. The result is light, crisp, and ravishingly buttery.

The classic uses of this pastry are many. It can be formed into pastry shells, large, small, or smaller, and filled with savory appetizer mixtures, or it can be used for extravagant entrées and magnificent desserts. It is the basis for Napoleons. Cut into decorative shapes, it becomes *fleurons* — the haute-cuisine garniture *par excellence*. The *nouvelle cuisine* has embraced its crisp delicacy and adapted it to newer uses. In short, it's wonderful stuff.

Unfortunately, this pastry has the reputation of being difficult to make. While it's true there are a few tricks involved, and the method at first seems unnecessarily complicated, puff pastry is really no more difficult to make than a good piecrust, and much more impressive. The careful steps outlined in the recipe reveal that for much of the time the puff pastry is relaxing in the refrigerator, while you are out playing tennis. Less than an hour of work, total, is needed and this can be stretched out over a day or even two. The result then waits in your refrigerator or freezer until you are ready for it.

In these modern times, it is also possible to buy frozen prepared puff pastry. We feel that it's good to know how to make your own, but once you have gotten the hang of making it, this frozen pastry can be a time saver, *if* you can find a reliable brand. Read the list of ingredients; if it includes anything but flour, butter, salt and water, you will probably be disappointed. (We have even seen some brands that contain no butter at all.) After you have located a reputable brand, defrost and prepare it according to the directions on the package.

Before beginning, it will help if you try to visualize what is going to happen. First, you will prepare a simple dough of flour and water. After a short rest, this will be rolled out and used to wrap up a square of kneaded, softened butter. This "package" will again be rolled out, folded triple, and then rolled and tripled 5 more times. These 6 "turns" create the hundreds of alternating butter and flour layers. The pastry rises so spectacularly because moisture and handling activate the gluten, the elastic web of protein that makes bread dough stretchy, but makes pastry dough tough if it isn't outwitted. The puff pastry dough is refrigerated after every turn in order to allow the gluten to relax. The chilling also keeps the butter from melting — an occurrence that would ruin the pastry. The refrigerated resting periods should be at least an hour long, but can be much longer, and this is where you gain a measure of flexibility.

PASTRY CREAM

2 cups milk
½ cup granulated sugar
4 tablespoons unbleached all-purpose flour
2 egg yolks
1 tablespoon sweet butter
2 teaspoons vanilla extract

1. Scald milk in a heavy saucepan.

2. While milk is heating, whisk sugar and flour together in a stainless-steel mixing bowl.

3. When milk is scalded, remove skin and slowly pour milk into flour and sugar, whisking constantly. Place bowl over a saucepan of simmering water and cook, stirring, until mixture lightly coats the back of a spoon, about 10 minutes.

4. Add egg yolks and cook, stirring constantly, until mixture heavily coats the back of a spoon, about 10 minutes more. Remove from heat.

5. Add butter and vanilla and mix well. Chill; before chilling cover top with a light coating of butter, or cover surface directly with plastic wrap, to prevent formation of a skin.

2½ cups pastry cream

PIECRUST

2½ cups unbleached all-purpose flour
2 teaspoons granulated sugar
1 teaspoon salt
8 tablespoons (1 stick) sweet butter, chilled
6 tablespoons vegetable shortening, chilled
5 to 6 tablespoons ice water, as needed

1. Sift flour, sugar and salt into a mixing bowl. Add chilled butter and shortening. Working quickly and using your finger-tips or a pastry blender, rub or cut fat into dry ingredients until the mixture resembles coarse meal.

2. Sprinkle on ice water, 2 to 3 tablespoons at a time, and toss

with a fork. Turn dough out onto your work surface and, using the heel of your hand, smear dough away from you, about ¼ cup at a time. Scrape it up into a ball and wrap in wax paper. Chill in refrigerator for 2 hours.

3. Roll dough out to ¼-inch thickness on a floured work surface. Line a 9-inch pie plate with half of the dough. Crimp edges for a single-crust pie.

4. For prebaking, line dough in the pie plate with foil and fill with beans or rice. Bake in a 425°F. oven for 8 minutes, then remove beans and lining. Prick bottom of dough with a fork and return pie plate to oven to 10 to 13 minutes longer, or until crust is golden brown.

One 9-inch double crust, or two 9-inch single crusts

"Simple cooking cannot be trusted to a simple cook."
— Countess Morphe

CREME FRAICHE

This cultured heavy cream thickens and develops a delicate sour taste as it sits. Spoon it over fruit desserts and fresh berries, with which its tart flavor is delicious. Use it to add body and richness to sauces. Since it can be boiled without fear of separation, it is more versatile than dairy sour cream. Stir a few spoonfuls into butter-warmed vegetables for a simple sauce. Whisk a dollop into a salad dressing for extra thickness. Since *crème fraîche* keeps under refrigeration for at least 2 weeks, we are seldom without some in our kitchen.

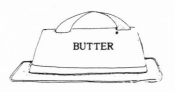

SWEET BUTTERY TART CRUST

1⅔ cups unbleached all-purpose flour
¼ cup very fine granulated sugar
½ teaspoon salt
10 tablespoons (1¼ sticks) sweet butter, chilled
2 egg yolks
1 teaspoon vanilla extract
2 teaspoons cold water

1. Sift flour, sugar and salt into a mixing bowl. Cut chilled butter into pieces into the bowl. Using your fingertips, rapidly rub the butter and dry ingredients together until the mixture resembles coarse meal. Be careful to use only your fingertips, as your palms will warm the dough.

2. Stir egg yolks, vanilla and water together and add to the flour-butter mixture and blend in, using a fork. Shape dough into a ball. This should not take more than 30 to 45 seconds.

3. Place the ball of dough on a pastry board. With the heel of your hand, smear about ¼ cup of dough away from you into a 6- to 8-inch smear; repeat until all dough has been dealt with. Scrape dough together; re-form into a ball, wrap in wax paper, and chill for 2 to 3 hours.

4. Roll out dough between 2 sheets of wax paper, or use a floured pastry cloth and floured stockinette on your rolling pin, into a round large enough to line your pan. Work quickly, as the dough can become sticky.

5. Line either an 8- or 9-inch false-bottom tart pan with the dough, fitting it loosely into pan and pressing to fit sides. Trim edges ¾ inch outside top of pan, and fold this edge over to inside, and press into place with fingers. Chill.

6. Preheat oven to 425°F.

7. Line dough in the tart pan with a piece of aluminum foil or wax paper and weight with rice or beans. Bake for 8 minutes. Remove foil and beans. Prick the bottom of the dough with a fork in several places. For a partially baked shell, return to oven for 3 to 4 minutes longer. For a fully baked shell, return for 8 to 10 minutes longer, or until edges are a light brown.

One 8-inch to 9-inch tart shell

FLAVORED MAYONNAISES

Homemade Mayonnaise, combined with other ingredients and blended in the food processor, yields variations of dressings and spreads limited only by your imagination. Some favorites:

♥ **ANCHOVY MAYONNAISE:** 1 cup Homemade Mayonnaise, 1 tablespoon anchovy paste (or more or less to taste).

♥ **CHUTNEY MAYONNAISE:** 1 cup Homemade Mayonnaise, ¼ cup mango chutney.

♥ **CORIANDER MAYONNAISE:** 1 cup Homemade Mayonnaise, prepared with lime juice instead of lemon, 1 loosely packed cup of fresh coriander (cilantro) leaves, rinsed and patted dry.

♥ **PESTO MAYONNAISE:** 1 cup Homemade Mayonnaise, ½ cup Pesto (see page 132) completed through the addition of the cheeses.

♥ **TOMATO-BASIL MAYONNAISE:** 1 cup Homemade Mayonnaise, 1 tablespoon tomato paste, 3 tablespoons finely chopped fresh basil, dash of Tabasco, salt and freshly ground black pepper to taste.

♥ **MINT AND YOGURT MAYONNAISE:** 1 cup Homemade Mayonnaise, ½ cup plain yogurt, 1 cup fresh mint leaves, rinsed and patted dry, 1 to 2 tablespoons fresh lemon juice (stirred into mixture after processing).

♥ **APPLE HORSERADISH MAYONNAISE:** 1 cup Homemade Mayonnaise, ¾ medium-size tart red apple (unpeeled), cored and sliced thinly (then halve the slices), 1½ tablespoons finely minced yellow onion, ¼ cup drained prepared horseradish, 1 tablespoon fresh lemon juice, pinch of white pepper, and ¼ cup chopped fresh dill (optional).

CREME FRAICHE

1 cup heavy cream (not ultra-pasteurized)
1 cup dairy sour cream

1. Whisk heavy cream and sour cream together in a bowl. Cover loosely with plastic wrap and let stand in the kitchen or other reasonably warm spot overnight, or until thickened. In cold weather this may take as long as 24 hours.

2. Cover and refrigerate for at least 4 hours, after which the *crème fraîche* will be quite thick. The tart flavor will continue to develop as the *crème fraîche* sits in the refrigerator.

2 cups

HOMEMADE MAYONNAISE

Luscious and versatile; and ready in minutes.

2 egg yolks
1 whole egg
1 tablespoon prepared Dijon-style mustard
pinch of salt
freshly ground black pepper, to taste
¼ cup fresh lemon juice
2 cups corn or other vegetable oil, or best-quality olive oil

1. Combine egg yolks, whole egg, mustard, salt and freshly ground black pepper to taste and half of the lemon juice in the bowl of a food processor fitted with a steel blade. Process for 1 minute.

2. With the motor running, dribble in the oil in a slow steady stream. When all the oil is in, shut motor off, and scrape down sides of bowl with a spatula.

3. Taste the mayonnaise. Correct seasoning if necessary; if you are using a vegetable oil, you will probably need the remaining lemon juice. Scrape mayonnaise into a storage container, cover, and refrigerate until ready to use. Mayonnaise will keep safely, if refrigerated, for at least 5 days. Let it return to room temperature before stirring.

3 cups

SAUCE HOLLANDAISE

3 egg yolks
1 to 2 tablespoons fresh lemon juice
pinch of salt
½ pound (2 sticks) sweet butter, melted
white pepper, to taste

1. Whisk the egg yolks and 1 tablespoon of the lemon juice together in a small heavy saucepan or the top pan of a double boiler. Add a pinch of salt and whisk until sauce is thick and creamy.

2. Set the pan over very low heat, or over simmering water in the lower pan of the double boiler, and begin whisking immediately. Continue to whisk until the egg mixture just begins to thicken; the sign of this is that the wires of the whisk will begin to leave "tracks" in which you can see the bottom of the pan.

3. Remove pan from the heat and begin to dribble in the melted butter, whisking constantly. Incorporate all the butter, but leave the milky residue behind.

4. Add white pepper to taste and a spoonful or two of additional lemon juice if you like. The sauce will keep, covered, in a warm (not hot) place for at least 30 minutes.

About 1½ cups

SAUCE BEARNAISE

Sherry vinegar makes this hearty butter-based sauce even better. Try it on beef, lamb or other meat.

½ cup sherry vinegar (or white wine vinegar)
¼ cup dry white vermouth
1 tablespoon finely chopped shallot
½ teaspoon dried tarragon
pinch of salt
3 egg yolks
½ pound (2 sticks) sweet butter, melted

1. Combine the vinegar, vermouth, shallot, tarragon and salt in a small heavy saucepan. Bring to a boil, lower the heat, and simmer until reduced to a few spoonfuls. Cool to room temperature.

2. Strain the cooled mixture into another small heavy saucepan, or the top pan of a double boiler, and whisk in the egg yolks. Beat until thick and creamy.

3. Set the pan over very low heat, or over simmering water in the lower pan of the double boiler, and begin whisking immediately. Continue to whisk until the egg mixture just begins to thicken; the surest sign of this is that the wires of the whisk will begin to leave "tracks" in which you can see the bottom of the pan.

4. Remove pan from the heat and begin to dribble in the melted butter, whisking constantly. Incorporate all the butter, but leave the milky residue behind.

5. Taste, and correct seasoning; add a few more drops of vinegar if you like. Set sauce aside, covered, in a warm (not hot) place. The sauce will keep for at least 30 minutes.

About 1½ cups

"Every morning must start from scratch, with nothing on the stoves — that is cuisine."

— **Fernand Point**

✤ FROM THE SILVER
PALATE NOTEBOOK

Don't ever entertain a larger number than you honestly feel comfortable with, or prepare any dish that you've never done before.

When inviting guests, be specific about arrival time, what kind of an occasion it is, extent of food and drink, and approximate length of the evening. Nothing is more dismaying than arriving in formal dress, expecting a sit-down dinner, and being served cheese and nuts at a casual backyard party.

BECHAMEL SAUCE

4 tablespoons sweet butter
6 tablespoons unbleached all-purpose flour
2 cups milk
salt, freshly ground black pepper, and freshly grated nutmeg, to taste

1. Melt butter in a heavy saucepan. Sprinkle in the flour and cook gently, stirring almost constantly, for 5 minutes. Do not let the flour and butter brown at all.

2. Meanwhile, bring the milk to a boil. When milk reaches a boil, remove butter and flour mixture from heat and pour in the boiling milk all at once. As the mixture boils and bubbles, beat it vigorously with a wire whisk.

3. When the bubbling stops, return the pan to medium heat and bring the béchamel to a boil, stirring constantly for 5 minutes. Season to taste with salt, pepper and nutmeg. Use at once, or scrape into a bowl, cover, and refrigerate until use.

2 cups thick sauce

Note: For 2 cups medium sauce, use 3 tablespoons butter and 4 tablespoons all-purpose flour with the same amount of milk.

BEEF STOCK

4 pounds meaty beef bones (shank, neckbones, etc.)
1 calf's foot, cleaned and split
⅓ cup vegetable oil
4 cups finely chopped yellow onions
2 leeks, white part only, well cleaned and sliced
3 cups chopped peeled carrots
2 small or 1 medium parsnip, peeled and chopped
1½ tablespoons dried thyme
4 bay leaves
6 whole cloves
12 black peppercorns
6 parsley sprigs
1 tablespoon salt
1 can (6 ounces) tomato paste
water, as needed

1. Preheat oven to 400°F.

2. Spread beef bones and calf's foot in a baking pan just large enough to hold the meat in a single layer. Bake for 1½ hours, or until meats are very brown. Turn pieces occasionally and drain rendered fat as necessary.

3. Heat the oil in a large pot. Add the onions, leeks, carrots and parsnips and cook over high heat, stirring often, until well browned, about 25 minutes.

4. Add browned bones and calf's foot to the vegetables, along with the remaining ingredients.

5. Pour 1 cup water into the pan in which the meats were browned and set over high heat. Stir and scrape up any caramelized particles from the bottom and sides. Pour liquid into the pot. Add additional water to cover ingredients well, and set pot over medium heat. When the stock reaches a boil, skim, reduce heat so liquid simmers, partially cover, and simmer for 4 hours. Skim occasionally.

6. Strain out and discard the solids, and refrigerate or chill, then freeze the stock. Before using refrigerated stock or freezing chilled stock, remove any fat that has solidified on top.

About 2 to 3 quarts

CHICKEN STOCK

Homemade chicken stock is an indispensable basis for soups and sauces; its richness and freshness put it head and shoulders above canned. Refrigerate if you're using it within a few days, or stash it in the freezer — frozen assets of the very best kind.

¼ cup vegetable cooking oil
3 pounds (more or less) chicken necks and backs
4 cups chopped yellow onions
2 cups chopped peeled carrots
small handful parsley sprigs
2 cans (1 quart, 14 ounces each) chicken broth
water, as needed
1 tablespoon dried thyme
4 bay leaves

1. Pour the oil into a large heavy pot and heat until almost smoking. Pat the chicken parts dry with paper towels and drop into the hot oil. Toss and turn them until well browned, about 15 minutes.

2. Add chopped onions and carrots and continue to cook, stirring frequently, until vegetables are beginning to brown lightly and are losing their crunch.

3. Add remaining ingredients, using enough water to cover solids by 2 inches, and bring the stock to a boil. Boil vigorously for 15 minutes, skimming off all scum. Reduce heat, cover, and simmer briskly for 2 hours, skimming occasionally if necessary.

4. Cool the stock slightly, then pour it through a strainer set over a bowl, pressing hard on the vegetables and chicken parts with the back of a spoon to extract as much flavor as possible.

5. Cover stock and refrigerate overnight. Skim any congealed fat from the stock before using. Transfer defatted stock to storage containers, label, and freeze.

3 quarts

FISH STOCK

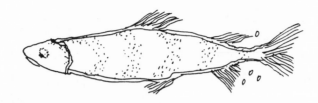

4 tablespoons sweet butter
¾ cup peeled and chopped carrots
2 cups finely chopped yellow onions
1 cup chopped celery
1 cup chopped mushrooms (stems fine to use)
10 cups water, or as needed
2 cups dry white wine
pinch of salt (optional)
12 white peppercorns
6 parsley sprigs
1 bay leaf
1 teaspoon dried thyme
*bones and heads of 6 or 7 white-fleshed non-oily fish (flounder, sole, weakfish, etc.), viscera and gills removed**

1. Melt the butter in a 4-quart soup pot. Add the carrots, onions, celery and mushrooms and cook, covered, over low heat for 25 to 30 minutes, stirring occasionally, until vegetables are tender and lightly colored.

2. Add remaining ingredients, using enough water to cover the solids, and bring slowly to a boil. Reduce heat and simmer, partially covered, for 30 minutes, no longer.

3. Remove stock from heat and cool. Pour through a cheesecloth-lined strainer and discard solids.

4. Taste the stock. If it seems to lack intensity, return it to the pot and boil for another 15 to 20 minutes.

5. Store the stock, covered, in the refrigerator, or chill, remove any solid fat that rises to the surface, and freeze. Remove fat from refrigerated stock before serving.

2 to 3 quarts

*Order the bones from your fish dealer and tell him you are using them for stock. He will do the rest.

BARBECUING

Barbecue now knows no season. Cooking over coals just makes food taste great, and if time is taken for marinating or enhancing the meat, fish or poultry with a sauce or chutney, simplicity becomes sublime.

Barbecuing has been so strongly associated with America because American Indians used the technique extensively. Mastering the age-old technique of barbecuing is not complicated, but it does require some attention to detail. Remember, no rushing allowed. The slower your timing when you cook, the juicier, tenderer and tastier the results will be.

• Layer charcoal wider than the size of the food that you are grilling.

• Coals take 30 to 45 minutes to achieve the gray ash coating and glowing red inside that is ideal for grilling. Smoking should be done during the last 15 to 20 minutes of cooking.

• Fruitwood (peach, apple, cherry, pear, apricot, citrus) and even oak, maple, hickory and sprigs of pine can be used to add an exciting dimension to your grilling. For a wonderful flavor, soak the leaves and branches in water before setting them over the fire so that you will get smoke, not flames. Try this easy smoking technique also with fresh or dried juniper berries, whole sweet spices such as cinnamon, cloves, nutmeg and orange or lemon peel. Placing a bundle of fresh herbs over the coals produces a great flavor, too.

• Make sure that your grill is absolutely clean.

• Marinating adds flavor and breaks down any toughness to make meats tender.

• Olive oil in a marinade insures that the meat won't stick to the grill. If you're not marinating, brush oil lightly over the meat before taking it to the grill.

• We like to precook many foods before grilling. It insures that they will not dry out during a lengthy time over the coals but will still have the wonderful aroma and flavor that only outdoor grilling gives. This is especially true of chicken, spareribs and whole roasts. We always allow at least 30 minutes of cooking time for basting and cooking over the coals.

This sauce is quick, easy and fresh-tasting. Since it's made from canned tomatoes, it can be available year-round. Keep some on hand in the freezer for use in lasagna and eggplant Parmigiana, or for a quick dish of spaghetti. Add fresh seafood, canned tuna, or crisp-cooked vegetables (about 1 cup for each 3 cups of sauce) to improvise your own sauce; the possibilities are endless.

QUICK TOMATO SAUCE

½ cup best-quality olive oil
3 cups finely chopped yellow onions
2 medium-size carrots, peeled and finely chopped
2 cans, 28 ounces each, peeled plum tomatoes in tomato purée
1 tablespoon dried basil
1 teaspoon dried thyme
1 teaspoon salt
⅛ teaspoon cayenne pepper
1 bay leaf
1 cup finely chopped Italian parsley
4 garlic cloves, peeled and finely chopped
1 tablespoon balsamic or other mild vinegar (optional)

1. Heat the oil in a heavy pot. Add the onions and carrots and cook, covered, over low heat until vegetables are tender, about 25 minutes.

2. Add the tomatoes, basil, thyme, salt, cayenne pepper and bay leaf. Cook over medium heat, stirring occasionally, for 30 minutes.

3. Remove the bay leaf and transfer the tomato mixture to the bowl of a food processor fitted with a steel blade, or use a food mill fitted with a medium disc, and purée.

4. Return sauce to the pot and set the pot over medium heat. Add the parsley and garlic and cook for another 5 minutes.

5. Taste and correct seasoning. Add the balsamic vinegar if the sauce seems to lack intensity. Serve immediately, or cool to room temperature, cover, and refrigerate or freeze.

About 2 quarts

SPICY TOMATO SAUCE

Another tomato sauce, this one made with fresh tomatoes and long-simmered to bring out the flavors of the herbs. We use lots of pepper and serve this sauce on gnocchi, or use it when making lasagna or Eggplant Parmigiana (see page 285).

½ cup best-quality olive oil
2 cups finely chopped yellow onions
4 pounds ripe plum or other meaty tomatoes, skinned and seeded
6 ounces (1 can) tomato paste
2 tablespoons minced fresh basil
½ teaspoon dried oregano
1 teaspoon salt
1 tablespoon freshly ground black pepper
4 cups water
5 garlic cloves, peeled and finely minced
½ cup finely chopped Italian parsley

1. Heat olive oil in a large deep pot. Add onions and cook, covered, over low heat until tender and lightly colored, about 25 minutes.

2. Add tomatoes, tomato paste, basil, oregano, salt and pepper. Simmer for 10 minutes, stirring occasionally.

3. Add the water and cook very slowly, uncovered, for 3 hours.

4. Stir in the garlic and parsley and simmer for another 5 minutes.

5. Taste and correct seasoning if necessary. Use immediately, or cool to room temperature before covering. Refrigerate or freeze.

About 3 quarts

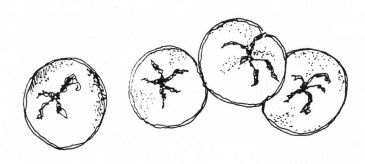

SAFFRON RICE

Follow the method for Parsleyed Rice, adding a few threads of saffron as you bring the water to the boil. Reduce the butter by half, and omit the parsley.

PARSLEYED RICE

We prefer untreated long-grain rice, but you can use converted rice if you like, following package directions.

4 cups water, or Chicken Stock (see page 587)
2 cups uncooked long-grain rice
1 tablespoon salt
8 tablespoons (1 stick) sweet butter, cut into 8 pieces
1½ cups finely chopped Italian parsley

1. Bring the water or stock to a boil in a heavy pan. Stir in the rice and salt, return to a boil, reduce the heat to low, and cover tightly. Let the rice cook, undisturbed, for 25 minutes.

2. Uncover the pan, add the butter and parsley (do not stir), and cover. Remove pan from heat and let stand for 5 minutes.

3. Uncover pan, toss rice with a fork to mix in the butter and parsley, and serve immediately.

6 cups cooked rice, 6 to 8 portions

WILD RICE

Wild rice is one of North America's most distinguished native foods. It grows in the shallow, muddy lakes and lowland waterways of Minnesota and Wisconsin, among other places. The Indians called it *menomin* and gathered it into canoes piloted through still water.

Wild rice has slender ash-brown to blackish grains and a distinctive nutty taste. The best grades are usually those with the longer, darker grains. It has been said that there is nothing wilder than wild rice, and we agree. We like to use this special rice alone, though astronomical prices (and price increases) have challenged us to develop recipes using it with wheat and other kinds of rices.

NUTTED WILD RICE

1 cup (½ pound) raw wild rice
5½ cups defatted Chicken Stock (see page 587) or water
1 cup shelled pecan halves
1 cup yellow raisins
grated rind of 1 large orange
¼ cup chopped fresh mint
4 scallions (green onions), thinly sliced
¼ cup olive oil
⅓ cup fresh orange juice
1½ teaspoons salt
freshly ground black pepper, to taste

1. Put rice in a strainer and run under cold water; rinse thoroughly.
2. Place rice in a medium-size heavy saucepan. Add stock or water and bring to a rapid boil. Adjust heat to a gentle simmer and cook uncovered for 45 minutes. After 30 minutes check for doneness; rice should not be too soft. Place a thin towel inside a colander and turn rice into the colander and drain. Transfer drained rice to a bowl.
3. Add remaining ingredients to rice and toss gently. Adjust seasonings to taste. Let mixture stand for 2 hours to allow flavors to develop. Serve at room temperature.

6 portions

HUMMUS BI TAHINI

Serve this Middle-Eastern chick-pea and sesame spread as a dip with torn pieces of hot pita bread or as a component of a cold lunch or appetizer plate.

4 cups (about 2½ cans) garbanzos (chick-peas), drained
½ cup tahini (sesame paste)★
⅓ cup warm water
⅓ cup best-quality olive oil
juice of 2 or 3 lemons
4 or more garlic cloves
1½ teaspoons salt
2 teaspoons ground cuminseed
freshly ground black pepper, to taste

1. Combine chick-peas, tahini, warm water, olive oil and juice of 1 lemon in the bowl of a food processor fitted with a steel blade. Process until smooth and creamy, pausing once or twice to scrape down sides of the bowl with a spatula.

2. Add garlic, salt, cuminseed and pepper to taste, and process to blend. Taste and correct seasoning if necessary. Add more lemon juice to taste. Scrape into a storage container, cover, and refrigerate until ready to use.

1 quart

★available at specialty food shops

"If you want a golden rule that will fit everybody, this is it: Have nothing in your houses that you do not know to be useful, or believe to be beautiful."

— *Beauty of Life,*
William Morris, 1880

PECAN CREAM CHEESE

½ cup shelled pecans
8 ounces cream cheese, softened

1. Chop pecans coarsely in food processor fitted with a steel blade.
2. Add softened cream cheese and process until smooth. Scrape out with a rubber spatula, cover, and refrigerate until ready to use.
   1 cup

RED CURRANT GLAZE

3 tablespoons red currant jelly
1 tablespoon Kirsch

Whisk jelly and Kirsch together over medium heat until smooth. Use glaze while warm.

VERSATILE VINEGAR

Some interesting uses for vinegars include these:
• Moisten and fluff a chocolate cake by adding 1 tablespoon vinegar to the baking soda.
• If something is too sweet, add 1 tablespoon cider vinegar.
• Marinate and tenderize meats in vinegar.
• Add 1 tablespoon vinegar to poaching eggs to make the whites retain their shape
• Add vinegar to the cooking water of artichokes and red vegetables to keep them from discoloring.
• A touch of vinegar will disguise the fact that you've reduced the salt in a recipe.
• Put vinegar on sunburn to take the sting away.
• Add vinegar to dishwater to make the crystal come out clear.
• Clean glass by rubbing it with vinegar.

THE SILVER PALATE
PRODUCT LIST

The Silver Palate has created, in addition to the prepared dishes sold in the shop, a group of products available also in specialty shops throughout the United States. They include vinegars, oils, mustards, chutneys, preserves, brandied fruits, and sweet sauces.

CHUTNEYS & SAUCES

Onion Chutney
Plum Chutney
Blueberry Chutney
Tomato-Apple Chutney
Jalapeño Chili Chutney
Barbecue Sauce
Apricot Mustard Sauce

MUSTARDS

Dill Mustard Sauce
Green Peppercorn Garlic
    Mustard
Sweet & Rough Mustard
Orange Mustard
Tarragon Shallot Mustard
Tomato Herb Mustard
Basil Mustard
Emerald Herb Mustard
Red Wine Mustard

HERBS

Country Herbs
Sweet & Savory Spices
Four Peppercorns
Peppercorn Bouquet

OILS

Walnut Oil
Basil Oil
Pink Pepperberry Oil
Green Peppercorn Oil

VINEGARS

Blueberry Vinegar
Raspberry Vinegar
Tarragon Vinegar
Wild Thyme Vinegar
Red Wine Basil Vinegar
White Wine Herb Vinegar
Sherry Vinegar
Champagne Vinegar

PICKLED FRUITS & VEGETABLES

Pickled Wild Cherries
Zucchini Pickles
Cornichons
Spiced Onion Mosaic
Vegetable Mosaic

NUTS

Sugar & Spice Nuts
Hot & Spicy Pecans
Pesto Walnuts
Coconut Almonds

SWEET SAUCES

Fudge Sauce
Raspberry Fudge Sauce
Fudge Sauce Grand Marnier
Caramel Pecan Sauce
Caramel Fudge Sauce
It's the Berries

PRESERVES

American Country Berries
   Preserves
American Concord Grape
   Preserves
American Peach Preserves
American Sour Cherry Preserves
American Strawberry Preserves
Apricot Preserves
Black Currant Preserves
Blueberry Preserves
Cherry Preserves
Chestnut Cream Preserves
Fig Preserves
Four Red Fruits Preserves
Lemon Preserves
Orange Marmalade
Peach Preserves
Raspberry Preserves
Strawberry Preserves
Wild Strawberry Preserves

BRANDIED FRUIT

Brandied Winter Fruit
Chestnuts in Grand Marnier
Fruit Mélange in Cognac
Brandied Peaches
Vanilla Clementines
Scarlet Fruits in Port

INDEX

A

Aïoli, 66-69
  sauce, 69
Aïoli platters, 66-67
  vegetables, fish and beef for, 68
Almond tart, 517
Almond coffee, 518
Amaretto mousse, 485
Anchovy butter, 197
Anchovy dressing with garlic, 359
Anchovy mayonnaise, 581
Apéritifs, 54
Appetizers, *see* Hors d'oeuvres
Apple brandy sauce, 458
Apple cider glaze, 461
Apple(s), 446-463
  autumn salad, with walnuts, 372
  bluefish baked with, and
    mustard, 194
  cake, chunky with
    walnuts, 460-461
  cinnamony baked, 452
  cornbread-sausage stuffing
    with, 162
  -horseradish mayonnaise, 581
  mousse, with brandy
    sauce, 457-458
  pie, sour-cream, 462-463
  purée, beet and, 331
  sautéed, with Calvados, 454
  shrimp and snow peas
    with, 191-192
  types of (chart), 448-449
Applesauce:
  Johnny, 451
  raisin cake, 459
Apple tarts:
  Ellen's, 455
  medieval, 450-451

Apricot(s):
  bread, with raisins, 428
  glazed, baked ham with, 167
Aquavit, 539
Artichoke hearts, 67
Artichoke(s), 66, 237-241
  and endive, lamb chops with, 206
  herb mayonnaise for, 238
  one-step, 238
  pasta sauce Raphael, 117
  salad, shrimp and, 383
Artichokes, stuffed, 239
  Fontecchio, 240-241
Arugula, 356, 357
Asparagus, 242-254
  consommé with dill and, 251
  cooking of, 243
  and egg salad, 253
  en croute, 254
  layered vegetable terrine, 50-53
  mayonnaises for, 244-245
  omelet, 253
  -Parmesan soufflé, 252-253
  poached eggs on, 253
  with prosciutto, 248
  sauce, 246
  soft-cooked egg and, 245
  soup, cream of, 250
  strudel, 249
  vinaigrettes for, 247
Avgolemono (Greek lemon soup), 92
Avocado(s):
  dip, 34
  ham salad with, 339-340
  truffles and, 294

B

D

Daiquiri, fresh fruit, 563
Damson plum brandy, 474
Date-nut bread, 424
Date-nut pudding, 526
Dazzlers (hors d'oeuvres), 55–69
   foie gras, 58
   new potatoes with black
     caviar, 61
   shallot sauce, 65
   vegetables, fish and beef for
     aïoli platters, 68
   see also Aïoli; Aïoli platters;
     Caviar; Oysters
Desserts, *see* Sweets
Dijon-style mustard:
   chicken Dijonnaise, 153
   dip, with green peppercorns, 36
   our favorite vinaigrette, 247
   see also Salad dressings; Sauces
Dill, 306
   butter, 197
   consommé with asparagus
    and, 251
   egg salad with, 375
   with new potatoes, 298
   sauce, with mustard, 28
   shrimp and grape salad with, 381
   soup, with tomatoes, 325
Dips:
   avocado, 34
   caviar, 63
   dill mustard, 28
   green herb, 245
   green peppercorn mustard, 36
   Roquefort, 34
   tapenade, 37
Dressings, *see* Salad dressings

Drinks, brunch, 559–566
Duck:
   autumn salad with green
    beans, 258–259
   with forty cloves of
    garlic, 313–314
   and pear salad with mango
    chutney dressing, 348
Duxelles, 291–292

E

Eggplant, 276–285
   cooking with, 277
   with herbs, 282
   marinated, livia, 555
   oil-roasted summer
    vegetables, 283–284
   parmigiana, 285
   peasant caviar, 279
   ratatouille, 281
   salads, 278, 353
Eggs:
   hard boiled, 67
   for omelets, 536
   poached, on asparagus, 253
   salads, 253, 375
Endive:
   and artichokes, lamb chops
    with, 206
   Belgian, scoop, 36
Escabeche, 199–200

F

Figs, 5, 473
Filo, *see* phyllo
Finger food, fancy, 4–22
   barbecued bits, 20–21
   cheese straws, 10

cocktail puffs, 16
gougère, 15
mushrooms stuffed with walnuts and cheese, 18
peppers Provençal, 8
phyllo triangles, 12
sausage-stuffed mushrooms, 17
sesame, ham and cheese bites, 4-5
stuffed grape leaves, 16
Finger food, fancy miniature:
chèvre tarts, 7
lamb kebabs, 19
quiches, 6-7
Fish, 189-202
with beef and vegetables for aïoli platters, 68
bluefish baked with apples and mustard, 194
buying and keeping of, 202
Elvira, 209
escabeche, 199-200
fresh, cooking of, 196
red snapper with butter and shallot sauce, 316
salade Niçoise, 360
salads, 379-383
stock, 588
striped bass, baked, with fennel, 196-197
swordfish steaks, 195
Taramosalata, 25
turbot en bourride, 83
varieties of, 190-191
see also Cod; Salmon
Flour, 412, 417
Flower cups, 486
Flowers, flavoring with, 345
Foie gras, 58
Foil, baking in, 203-210
Food mills, 250

Frosting:
chocolate, 493
cream-cheese, 502
see also Icing
Fruit:
brandied, 474, 596
brandies, chart of, 530-531
butter, 424-425
chocolate, 495-496
daiquiri, fresh, 563
pickled, 596
poached, 527-528
ragoût, and winter pork, 223-224
salad, black, 551
salad minted, 550
salads, 549-551
salads, combinations for, 549
soups, 95-97
spreads, 453
-stuffed loin of pork, 177-178
-stuffed Rock Cornish hens, 158-159
and vegetables, lamb chops with, 205
see also specific fruits

G

Game, 181-187
pheasant with leek and pecan stuffing, 184-185
ragoût of rabbit forestière, 182-183
venison stew, 186-187
Garbanzos, *see* Chick peas
Garlic, 66, 69
baked, 312
dishes seasoned with, 312
duck with forty cloves of, 313-314

608

I, J

Ice(s),
 blackberry, 477
 Campari-orange, 524
 cappuccino, 524
 Danish Mary, 539
 lemon, 525
Ice Cream:
 profiteroles, 496
 strawberry, 467
Icing:
 chocolate, 491
 lemon, 505
 lemon-orange, 460
 see also Frosting *and* Glazes

Jams, 453
Jellies, 453

K

Kahlúa coffee, 518
Kebabs, miniature lamb, 19
Kir royale, 566
Kiwi fruit, 478

L

Lamb:
 Greek salad with eggplant, 353
 kebabs, miniature, 19
 marinade for, 19
 navarin of, 230-231
 roast, with peppercorn crust, 169
Lamb chops:
 with artichokes and endive, 206
 with mushrooms and herbs, 204
 Oriental, 170
 with vegetables and fruits, 205
Lasagna, green, 126-127
Layered vegetable terrine, 50-53

Leeks:
 layered vegetable terrine, 50-53
 Niçoise, 310
 and pecan stuffing, pheasant
  with, 184-185
 purée, with potato, 334
 tarte Saint-Germain, 311
Lemonade, 354
Lemon(s): 157
 butter, 239
 cake, glazed, 505
 chicken, 156
 -garlic mayonnaise, 354
 glaze, 523
 and herbs, chicken with, 210
 ice, 525
 icings, 460, 505
 loaf, with black walnuts, 429
 pie, old-fashioned, 512
 serving ideas for, 157
 and sherry marmalade,
  veal chops with, 172
 soup *(avgolemono)*, Greek, 92
 tart, with blueberries, 476
 variety of uses for, 157
 vinaigrette, 340
Lentil:
 soup, 262
 and walnut salad, 268-269
Lettuce, kinds of, 385-386
Lime mousse, 480
Linguine:
 with tomatoes and basil, 130
 with white clam sauce, 125
Linzer hearts, 440
Linzertorte, 510
Lobster:
 and tarragon, with pasta, 128
 twice-baked potatoes
  with, 301-302

M

616

618

T

V